...crit Mademoiselle Charlotte — ...
...aison — je vous ai oubliée

Eh bien Monsieur dites-moi cela franchemen...
...ur moi un choc — n'importe ce sera toujour...
...ieux que l'incertitude.

Je ne veux pas relire cette lettre — je l'envoie
...l'ai écrite — Pourtant j'ai ~~toujours le conseu~~
...il y a des personnes froides et sensées qui ...
...ant "elle déraisonne" — Pour toute vengean...
...uite ~~ces personnes je~~ un seul jour les tour...
...ai depuis huit mois — on verrait alors
...raison...ent pas le même

On souffre en silence tant qu'on en a la force
...te force manque on parle ~~et~~ ~~toujours~~ sans
...es paroles.

~~Je ne ... les cheveux de ...~~
~~...~~

Je souhaite à Monsieur le bonheur et la pros...

The Brontës: A Life in Letters

———————————

The Brontës: Selected Poems
The Tournament in England c.1100–1400
Tournaments: Jousts, Chivalry and Pageant in the
Middle Ages (with Richard Barber)
The Brontë Yearbook
The Brontës
Charlotte Brontë: Juvenilia 1829–35

Emily Brontë's diary paper, written on 31 July 1845. Her sketch shows Emily sitting on a stool in her bedroom with her writing desk on her knee, inscribing this paper; her dog, Keeper, is at her feet, and Anne's dog, Flossy, lies on her bed.

The Brontës: A Life in Letters

JULIET BARKER

THE OVERLOOK PRESS

WOODSTOCK & NEW YORK

First published in the United States in 1998 by
The Overlook Press, Peter Mayer Publishers, Inc.
Lewis Hollow Road
Woodstock, New York 12498

Library of Congress Cataloging-in-Publications Data

Barker, Juliet R. V.
The Brontës : a life in letters / Juliet Barker.
p. cm.
Includes bibliographical references and index.
1. Brontë family—Biography. 2. Authors, English—19th century—Biography.
3. Brontë family—Correspondence. 4. Authors, English—19th century—
Correspondence. 5. Yorkshire (England)—Biography. I. Title
PR4168.B37 1998 823'.809—dc21 [B] 97-24201

Manufactured in the United States of America

ISBN 0-87951-838-3
First Edition
1 3 5 7 9 8 6 4 2

Contents

List of Illustrations

Illustration Acknowledgements

The author and publishers are grateful to the following for permission to reproduce illustrations: Simon Warner for nos. 1, 3, 34; The Brontë Society, Haworth for the frontispiece and nos. 2, 4–10, 12, 14, 16, 19–28, 31–3; Woodhouse Grove School for no. 11; Leeds City Art Gallery for no. 13; National Portrait Gallery, London for nos. 15, 29; British Library for no. 17; Private Collection for no. 18; Scarborough Library and North Yorkshire County Council for no. 23; *Illustrated London News* of 5 July 1851 for no. 30.

Acknowledgements

All the letters in this collection have, where possible, been located in manuscript and newly transcribed for this edition. I am therefore grateful to the trustees and curators of the following collections for permission to publish transcripts of manuscripts in their possession: The Beinecke Rare Book and Manuscript Library, Yale University; Henry W. and Albert A. Berg Collection, The New York Public Library; The Department of Manuscripts, British Library, London; The Brontë Parsonage Museum, Haworth; The Brotherton Collection, Leeds University Library; The George Dunlop Papers, Rare Book and Manuscript Library, Columbia University; the Syndics of The Fitzwilliam Museum, Cambridge; The Houghton Library, Harvard University; The Charles Roberts Autograph Letters Collection, Haverford College Library, Haverford, Pennsylvania; The Historical Society of Pennsylvania, Philadelphia; The Harry Ransom Humanities Research Center, University of Texas at Austin; The Huntington Library, San Marino, California; The Walpole Collection, The King's School, Canterbury; The Department of Manuscripts, National Library of Scotland, Edinburgh; The Carl H. Pforzheimer Collection of Shelley and His Circle, The New York Public Library Astor, Lenox and Tilden Foundations; The Pierpont Morgan Library, New York; The Morris L. Parrish and Robert H. Taylor Collections, Department of Rare Books and Special Collections, Princeton University Library; The Department of Rare Books and Special Collections, Rush Rhees Library, University of Rochester, New York; The John Rylands University Library of Manchester; The Ella Strong Denison Library, Scripps College, Claremont, California; The Smith, Elder & Co. Archives, John Murray, London; The Master and Fellows of Trinity College, Cambridge; The United Society for the Propagation of the Gospel, London; The West Yorkshire Archive

xi

Service of Calderdale at Halifax and of Kirklees at Huddersfield; The Wordsworth Trust, Dove Cottage, Grasmere.

I am also grateful to Lynda Glading, Barbara Malone, William Self and June Ward-Harrison for permission to quote from manuscripts in their possession, and to Joan Coleridge for permission to quote from Hartley Coleridge's letter to Branwell Brontë.

Additional Brontë letters, for which I have been unable to trace a manuscript source, are taken from *The Brontës: their lives, friendships and correspondence*, edited by T. J. Wise and J. A. Symington (Oxford, Basil Blackwell, 1932–4), though, where applicable, I have preferred readings from the far more accurate *The Letters of Charlotte Brontë: Volume One 1829–1847*, edited by Margaret Smith (Oxford, Clarendon Press, 1995). Emily and Anne's 1841 diary papers have been transcribed from the facsimiles in Clement K. Shorter's *Charlotte Brontë and Her Circle* (London, Hodder & Stoughton, 1896). For reviews of the Brontë novels, I have used *The Brontës: the critical heritage*, edited by Miriam Allott (London, Routledge & Kegan Paul, 1974), and *The Brontë Sisters: selected sources for college research papers*, edited by Ruth H. Blackburn (New York, SUNY at Stony Brook, 1964). Lucy Martineau's letter of 10 December 1849 to her son is reproduced from the transcript in *BST*: 19:1&2:45–7, and Mrs Gaskell's letter of 29 October 1853 to Richard Monckton Milnes from *The Letters of Mrs Gaskell*, edited by J. A. V. Chapple and Arthur Pollard (Manchester, MUP, 1966). Ellen Nussey's *Reminiscences* have been drawn from various manuscript sources and printed extracts in *Brontë Society Transactions*, *The Brontës: their lives, friendships and correspondence* (see above) and T. W. Reid, *Charlotte Brontë: a monograph* (New York, Scribner & Co., 1877).

I have also incurred debts of a wholly different kind, mainly to my husband, James, and my children, Edward and Sophie; my son tells me, often and at length, that they have all suffered from my obsession with the Brontës. For that I apologize (again) and express my gratitude for their forbearance, however reluctantly bestowed. I would also like to thank the rest of my family, particularly my much put-upon parents, Richard and Judith Bateson, my friends and our incomparable nanny, Lisa Goddard, who have, between them, more than made up for my failings. Thanks are also due to my agent, Andrew Lownie, and my publishers, Penguin, for their much-needed support and generously expressed confidence in me.

ACKNOWLEDGEMENTS

Finally, I would like to thank all those readers of *The Brontës* who took the time and trouble to write to me; their letters have been the greatest accolade that any writer could hope or wish for. To one of them, especially, I am indebted. His wonderfully funny letters have entertained and educated me – and left me begging for more. I can think of no one more appropriate to whom this book should be dedicated.

This book is dedicated
with affection, respect and gratitude
to
John Burless of Raffles,
Queensland grazier and kindred spirit.

Introduction

'Men's letters are proverbially uninteresting and uncommunicative,' the newly-married Charlotte Brontë declared to her friend, Ellen Nussey, in 1854. Mindful that her husband was reading over her shoulder as she wrote, she explained that he thought she wrote 'too freely' and was 'incautious' in what she said.

> Arthur says such letters as mine never ought to be kept – they are dangerous as lucifer matches – so be sure to follow a recommendation he has just given 'fire them' – or 'there will be no more' such is his resolve. I can't help laughing – this seems to me so funny. Arthur however says he is quite 'serious' and looks it, I assure you – he is bending over the desk with his eyes full of concern.

If Ellen refused to promise that she would burn all Charlotte's letters in future, Arthur Bell Nicholls threatened to censor his wife's correspondence. The result, as Charlotte laughingly pointed out, would be

> such notes as he writes to Mr Sowden – plain, brief statements of facts without the adornment of a single flourish – with no comment on the character or peculiarities of any human being – and if a phrase of sensibility or affection steals in – it seems to come on tiptoe – looking ashamed of itself – blushing 'pea-green' as he says – and holding both its shy hands before its face.

Faced with such a choice, Ellen capitulated and gave the required promise, freeing the friends to write 'any dangerous stuff we please to each other'. Fortunately for all admirers of the Brontës, Ellen reneged on her promise – with exactly the consequences Arthur Bell Nicholls had foreseen and feared: 'the passing of letters into hands and under eyes for which they were never written'.

Reading these same letters now, it is easy to understand why Ellen simply could not destroy them – and why Charlotte's husband thought it so important that she did. Unlike the letters of so many literary figures, they were not written with an eye to publication, in mannered, measured English, with every phrase carefully turned and polished and every sentiment weighed and calculated. They were dashed off in the heat of the moment, scrawled, sometimes almost illegibly, in pencil during a few minutes' respite from teaching duties or by firelight late in the evening when all the household was in bed. Into them Charlotte poured all her hopes and fears, her frustrations and bitterness, her joys and her deepest griefs. They are, at times, funny and witty, acutely observant and poisonously sarcastic, courageous and unbearably moving. Through them, we see Charlotte growing up before our eyes, watch her develop and mature as a person and as a writer. We see her make mistakes and change her mind, but most of all we live her life with her, as it appeared to her and as she lived it at the time, without the benefit of hindsight and wider knowledge. The earliest letters are stilted and formal, written as school exercises under the watchful eye of Miss Wooler. As a genuine friendship gradually takes hold, they acquire warmth and intimacy; mutual trust encourages the confidences, gossip and indiscretions which Arthur Bell Nicholls so feared. To these letters we are indebted for the daily record of Charlotte's life, her trials and tribulations as a teacher and governess, a daughter and sister.

Yet even to Ellen, her friend for so many years, Charlotte could not tell everything. Indeed, the one great central secret was never fully shared with her. Ellen knew nothing of her friend's literary ambitions, had no idea that Charlotte had been obsessed since childhood with the fictional world of Angria and was unaware that she had ever published anything until presented with copies of the sisters' books after Emily's death. Even then, though Charlotte would tell Ellen about the people and places she had visited in connection with her literary career, she never shared her intellectual interests with her.

Such thoughts were reserved for Mary Taylor, her clever, radical school-friend, who had literary aspirations of her own. Unfortunately, Mary destroyed almost all Charlotte's letters when she emigrated to New

Zealand, leaving us with a gaping hole in our knowledge about this side
of Charlotte's life. The survival of one long and highly dramatic letter,
describing the 'pop visit' of 'Currer and Acton Bell' to London which
resulted in the revelation of their true identity to Charlotte's publishers,
makes us realize the depth of that loss. On the other hand, once *Jane Eyre*
had been accepted for publication, Charlotte acquired a whole range of
new correspondents with whom she could now share her creative ideas
and opinions. William Smith Williams, the reader at the firm who had
first recognized Charlotte's potential, became an especial friend; he and
James Taylor, who also worked at Smith, Elder & Co., were responsible
for sending her boxes of books which she would never otherwise have
had the opportunity or incentive to read. They not only informed and
educated her but, by way of response, she felt obliged to formulate her
own ideas about art and writing. She was also able to discuss freely with
them the development of her next books, seeking their advice and opinions
but, at the same time, being more than capable of standing her ground
when she believed them to be wrong.

After the deaths of her sisters, whose influence had been such an
important part of her own creative process, Charlotte's correspondence
with her friends at Smith, Elder & Co. became doubly precious. At this
traumatic time of her life, as she forced herself to come to terms with the
loneliness of her position, she literally lived through her letters. They were
the only means of communication she had with the world outside Haworth
to which she wished so passionately to belong. 'I have had no letters from
London for a long time –', she wrote to Ellen in 1850, shortly after the
publication of *Shirley*,

> and am very much ashamed of myself to find – now when that
> stimulus is withdrawn – how dependent upon it I had become – I
> cannot help feeling something of the excitement of expectation till
> post-hour comes and when day after day it brings nothing – I get
> low. This is a stupid, disgraceful, unmeaning State of things – I feel
> bitterly enraged at my own dependence and folly – It is so bad for
> the mind to be quite alone – to have none with whom to talk over
> little crosses and disappointments and laugh them away. If I could
> write I daresay I should be better but I cannot write a line. However
> (D.V.) I shall contend against the idiocy.

To George Smith, when sending him the manuscript of *Villette* in 1852, she would also confess, 'I can hardly tell you how much I hunger to have some opinion besides my own, and how I have sometimes desponded and almost despaired because there was no one to whom to read a line – or of whom to ask a counsel.'

The unveiling of Charlotte's relationship with George Smith, the tall, dark, handsome and deliciously young director of the firm, is one of the great pleasures of the correspondence. Personal acquaintance irrevocably altered it from one of rather formal mutual respect to one of teasing affection which frequently spilled over into flirtation. Perhaps the most fascinating aspect of this change is that, the more flirtatious the correspondence, the more firmly Charlotte clung to her persona as 'Currer Bell'. It is as if the male pseudonym freed her from the conventions which would normally attach to an interchange of letters between an unmarried man and a single woman, allowing her to say things she would never have dared to say to his face. The devastation she felt on learning that he was engaged to be married to someone else has never been more eloquently expressed than in what must surely be the most extraordinary letter of congratulation ever sent:

> My dear Sir
>   In great happiness, as in great grief – words of sympathy should be few. Accept my meed of congratulation – and believe me
>   Sincerely yours
>   C.Brontë

Charlotte's letters inevitably form the bulk of any edition of Brontë correspondence because she was the most prolific letter writer in the family and the one with the widest range of correspondents. Only a handful of notes exist from Emily and they are as uncommunicative and enigmatic as the lady herself. One can only concur whole-heartedly with her own self-analysis in telling Ellen that she would get Anne to write her 'a proper letter – a feat that I have never performed'.

Anne's letters too are extremely rare. Like Emily, she seems to have had no friends outside the family with whom to correspond. The very few letters that do exist are all the more precious because, unlike Emily's, they do give considerable insight into the character of the youngest of the Brontës. Her quiet courage and genuine piety are inspirational; once read, who could forget her words to Ellen, particularly knowing that they were written only a few weeks before she died?

> I have no horror of death: if I thought it inevitable I think I could quietly resign myself to the prospect, in the hope that you, dear Miss Nussey, would give as much of your company as you possibly could to Charlotte and be a sister to her in my stead. But I wish it would please God to spare me not only for Papa's and Charlotte's sakes, but because I long to do some good in the world before I leave it. I have many schemes in my head for future practise – humble and limited indeed – but still I should not like them all to come to nothing, and myself to have lived to so little purpose. But God's will be done.

In stark contrast to such simple, unassuming words are the characteristically ebullient letters of Branwell. Whether haranguing the editor of *Blackwood's Magazine* or William Wordsworth on their imperative duty to assess his literary abilities, or affecting, for the benefit of friends, a casualness about his future prospects which he certainly did not feel, Branwell usually wrote as he spoke – impetuously and with considerable bravado. His later letters are therefore all the more moving as he came to the gradual realization that time had passed by and he had achieved nothing; that he had allowed his foolish but undoubtedly genuine love for his employer's wife, Mrs Robinson, to blight any hope of future success; and, bitterest of all, that he had failed to live up to the expectations of his father and sisters. His last letters, barely coherent pleas for money so that he could avoid being sent to jail for debt, are a sordid illustration of the depths to which this once brilliant and much beloved boy had fallen.

The Reverend Patrick Brontë is perhaps the least well represented in this edition. There is a simple reason for this. Though he was forever discharging letters espousing and campaigning for his favourite causes to newspapers, politicians, fellow clergymen and parishioners, most of them require setting in a historical or philosophical context which is inappropriate to the rest of the book. This does not mean that he is totally excluded, only that the resulting selection does not reflect either the number or subject-range of his letters. Those that are included reveal a man of great emotional depth who was devoted to his wife and children; afflicted with the worst of human tragedies, that of outliving all his family, he bore their loss with a grief that still sears the page but was endured with extraordinary faith and courage. It is no accident that his letters begin and end this volume.

The choice of letters throughout the book has been determined by two factors. First and foremost, the sheer power of the writing: I have deliberately not included complete letters but only selected the best, most vivid and most important passages from them. Secondly, their relevance: again deliberately, I have chosen to allow the Brontës to tell their story in their own words with as little editorial interference as possible. Those seeking a more comprehensive and balanced account should turn to my biography, *The Brontës*, which first prompted this edition of letters. Like Mrs Gaskell before me, I could not help but be seduced by the immediacy and eloquence of the Brontës' letters. The discipline of the biographical form and the absolute necessity of including only apposite quotation meant that, reluctantly and, at times, belligerently, I felt obliged to omit passages of quite outstanding lyricism or humour or interest. Thus was born the idea for a volume of letters, in which such extravagance would be indulged and even encouraged.

Many of the letters are published here for the first time, either because the notoriously inaccurate editions of the past omitted or mistranscribed them or because they have only been discovered since the publication of *The Brontës*. Amongst the latter group are a number of important ones: Branwell and Patrick's letter of 16 November 1835 to William Robinson, for instance, which supports my thesis that Branwell never went to the Royal Academy as previous biographies had suggested; Patrick's letter of 23 February 1838 to John Driver of Liverpool, which again confirms that many options other than a career as a portrait painter were still being considered for Branwell's future, including the idea of a situation in a bank; and the fuller version of Branwell's October 1845 letter to Francis Grundy which, with its previously edited-out abuse of his employer and references to Mrs Robinson as 'one whom I must, till death, call my <u>wife</u>', lends further support to my claim that the affair was a sexual one. Even the recent feminist reinterpretation of Charlotte's letter to Robert Southey, which, against all the evidence, decided that she was being sarcastic at the Poet Laureate's expense, has deservedly been dealt a death-blow. The discovery of the unedited version of Southey's letter, quoting Charlotte's original lost letter, and accompanied by one from Charlotte to his son, written on 26 August 1850, confirms that she wrote in good faith. 'When I wrote to your Father I was very young;' she told the Reverend Charles Southey, 'I needed the benevolent yet stern advice he gives me, and fortunately I had just enough sense to feel its value and to resolve on its adoption. At this moment I am grateful to his memory for the well-timed check received in my girlhood at his hand.'

To the letters chosen for inclusion in this volume, I have added certain pieces of autobiographical writing which fill major omissions in the correspondence. I have drawn particularly on Emily and Anne's diary papers and the fragments which form Charlotte's misnamed 'Roe Head Journal'; without them, the reader would have no idea that the Brontës had been writing fiction feverishly and continuously since childhood. Also included are a selection of contemporary accounts of the family which give an outsider's view and, I think, allow the reader to pause and reflect on the impression that these extraordinary people made on others; it is all too easy to get caught up in the Brontës' own writings and lose one's own sense of normality. Finally, I have included a number of contemporary reviews of the Brontës' publications. Their novels have been classics for so long that today we tend to forget what a sensation they created when first published and how their authors were vilified for producing fiction deemed inappropriate to their sex. Placing such reviews side by side with the Brontës' own responses to them gives the latter greater meaning and enables us to appreciate more fully the courageous stand they took in refusing to allow their writing to be judged by any other standard than its own intrinsic merit.

All biography, of necessity, is an intrusion into the private lives of individuals. One cannot help agreeing with Arthur Bell Nicholls that it is morally wrong to make public letters which were intended only to be seen by one or two well-known and trusted recipients. It is not a fate most of us would wish to befall our own correspondence. And yet what a loss to the world of literature that letters as vivid, powerful and eloquent as those of the Brontës should moulder away unseen! There can be no excuse for exposing them once more to public view. All one can say is that the triumphs and tragedies of that remarkable family have never been better told than by the Brontës themselves and that, through the letters which tell their story, they rise, Phoenix-like, and live again for each and every one of us.

Juliet Barker
April 1996

A Brontë Chronology

1812   Marriage of the Reverend Patrick Brontë (b. 17 April 1777 at Emdale, County Down, Ireland) and Maria Branwell (b. 15 April 1783 at Penzance, Cornwall), at Guiseley, near Bradford, Yorkshire (29 December).

1814   Birth of Maria (d.o.b. not known; baptized 23 April).

1815   Birth of Elizabeth (8 February); the family move to Thornton.

1816   Birth of Charlotte (21 April).

1817   Birth of Patrick Branwell (26 June).

1818   Birth of Emily Jane (30 July).

1820   Birth of Anne (17 January); the family move to Haworth where Patrick has been appointed perpetual curate of St Michael and All Angels Church.

1821   Death of Mrs Brontë from ovarian cancer (15 September); Aunt Branwell comes to live with the family.

1824   Maria, Elizabeth, Charlotte and Emily go to the Clergy Daughters' School at Cowan Bridge.

1825   Death of Maria from tuberculosis (6 May); death of Elizabeth from tuberculosis (15 June); Charlotte and Emily permanently removed from the school; all the children are taught at home by their father and aunt.

1826   Patrick brings Branwell a set of toy soldiers from Leeds which inspire the creation of an imaginary world, Glasstown, founded by these 'Twelve'; the children begin to record the adventures of their heroes and heroines in plays, poems, magazines and novelettes written in tiny handmade books.

1831   Charlotte goes to Roe Head School at Mirfield where, for three terms, she wins the school prize for 'Emulation rewarded'; she makes lifelong friends in her fellow pupils Ellen Nussey and Mary Taylor, and in her headmistress, Miss Margaret Wooler.

1832   Charlotte leaves Roe Head and teaches her sisters at home; she goes to stay with Ellen at Birstall for the first time.

1833   Ellen's first visit to Haworth.

1834   Charlotte and Branwell create Angria, a new imaginary kingdom of their own; Emily and Anne break away to form their own, Gondal; Charlotte exhibits two of her pencil drawings at the Leeds Exhibition.

1835   Branwell takes lessons with the portrait painter William Robinson at Leeds, in preparation for entry into the Royal Academy; Charlotte returns to Roe Head as a teacher, taking Emily with her as a pupil; two months later, Anne replaces Emily, who cannot settle at the school.

1837   Branwell writes to *Blackwood's Magazine* and William Wordsworth, Charlotte to Robert Southey, seeking approval of their writings; Anne falls seriously ill at Roe Head, causing Charlotte to quarrel with Miss Wooler and the withdrawal of the sisters from the school; once at home Anne recovers, but does not return.

1838   Charlotte returns to Miss Wooler's school, which moves from Roe Head to Dewsbury Moor; she becomes increasingly depressed, leaves again in the late spring but returns for the winter term, her last at the school; Branwell sets up as a professional portrait painter in Bradford and Emily becomes a school teacher at Law Hill, Halifax.

1839   Charlotte finally leaves Miss Wooler's school; Branwell gives up his artistic career (February) and Emily resigns from Law Hill (March); Anne becomes governess to the Inghams at Blake Hall, Mirfield but is dismissed at Christmas; Charlotte takes a three-month posting as governess to the Sidgwicks at Stonegappe, Lothersdale; William Weightman appointed curate at Haworth; Charlotte and Ellen holiday together at Bridlington.

1840   Branwell becomes tutor to the Postlethwaite boys at Broughton-in-Furness and meets Hartley Coleridge, then becomes clerk on the Manchester & Leeds Railway at Sowerby Bridge; Anne becomes governess to the Robinson family of Thorp Green, near York.

1841   Charlotte becomes governess to the White family of Upperwood

House, Rawdon, resigning in December; Branwell promoted to clerk in charge at Luddenden Foot railway station.

1842   Patrick escorts Charlotte and Emily to the Pensionnat Heger in Brussels where they are to become pupils; Branwell dismissed from the Leeds & Manchester Railway (March); deaths of William Weightman (September) and Martha Taylor and Aunt Elizabeth Branwell (October); Charlotte and Emily return home.

1843   Charlotte returns to Brussels where she becomes increasingly obsessed with her love for Monsieur Heger; Branwell joins Anne at Thorp Green where he is to be tutor to Edmund Robinson but rapidly becomes entangled with Mrs Robinson; Emily remains at Haworth as the family housekeeper.

1844   Charlotte returns from Brussels (January); the sisters plan but fail to establish a school of their own at Haworth Parsonage.

1845   Arthur Bell Nicholls appointed curate of Haworth; Anne resigns just before Branwell is dismissed from Thorp Green following the discovery of his affair with Mrs Robinson; Charlotte discovers a manuscript book of Emily's poems and persuades her sisters to publish a book of their poems; they also begin to write their first novels for publication.

1846   Publication of *Poems* by Currer, Ellis and Acton Bell (May) by Aylott & Jones; Mrs Robinson's husband dies and she tells Branwell that his will effectually prevents their union, driving him to despair and drink; Patrick's sight is restored by an operation for the removal of cataracts and, while nursing him, Charlotte begins to write *Jane Eyre*.

1847   Anne's *Agnes Grey* and Emily's *Wuthering Heights* accepted for publication by T. C. Newby; Charlotte's *The Professor* refused by him and by Smith, Elder & Co., who accept *Jane Eyre* and publish it (October) to instant success; Newby belatedly publishes *Wuthering Heights & Agnes Grey* (December).

1848   Publication by T. C. Newby of Anne's second novel, *The Tenant of Wildfell Hall*; he sells the book in the United States as an early work by Currer Bell; Charlotte and Anne go to London to prove their separate identities to both sets of publishers; Branwell dies of tuberculosis (24 September), as does Emily three months later (19 December).

1849   Anne dies of tuberculosis at Scarborough (28 May) and is buried there; Charlotte's new novel, *Shirley*, is published by Smith, Elder & Co. (October); she visits London (December), staying with her publisher, George Smith, for the first time, and meets Thackeray and Harriet Martineau; her true identity begins to be known.

1850   Charlotte stays again with George Smith in London, sits for her portrait to George Richmond, and accompanies George Smith to Edinburgh; stays with the Kay Shuttleworths at Briery Close, Windermere and meets Mrs Gaskell; publication by Smith, Elder & Co. of *Wuthering Heights & Agnes Grey*, with a biographical notice by Charlotte; stays with Harriet Martineau at Ambleside (December).

1851   Charlotte considers a proposal of marriage, deferred five years, from James Taylor of Smith, Elder & Co., who is about to go to India on behalf of the firm; visits London to attend Thackeray's lectures and the Great Exhibition and Mrs Gaskell in Manchester; begins to write *Villette* but becomes seriously ill through mercury poisoning.

1852   Dogged by ill health and unhappiness, Charlotte finally completes *Villette* (November); Arthur Bell Nicholls unexpectedly proposes marriage to her (December) and is rejected.

1853   Publication of *Villette* (January) during Charlotte's last visit to London; Arthur Bell Nicholls is forced to resign his curacy, taking up a post at Kirk Smeaton, near Pontefract; Mrs Gaskell stays at Haworth Parsonage (September); George Smith gets engaged to be married.

1854   Charlotte demands from her father the right to become better acquainted with Arthur Bell Nicholls and finally secures his consent to their engagement (April); Charlotte visits Mrs Gaskell, Ellen and the Taylors of Gomersal; she marries Arthur Bell Nicholls (29 June) at Haworth and they honeymoon in Ireland, returning to live at Haworth Parsonage with Patrick.

1855   Charlotte dies in the early stages of pregnancy (31 March); Patrick asks Mrs Gaskell to write her *Life of Charlotte Brontë*.

1857   Publication by Smith, Elder & Co. of Mrs Gaskell's *Life of Charlotte Brontë* and Charlotte's first novel, *The Professor*.

1860   Publication by Smith, Elder & Co. of Charlotte's last unfinished novel, *Emma*, with an introduction by Thackeray, in the *Cornhill Magazine.*

1861   Death of Patrick Brontë (7 June); Arthur Bell Nicholls returns to Ireland.

1906   Death of Arthur Bell Nicholls (2 December) at Banagher, Ireland.

A Note to the Text

All the letters in this edition have been newly transcribed from the manuscripts, preserving the erratic spellings, grammar and punctuation of the originals. To avoid repeated and intrusive use of [*sic*], such oddities are not marked, a practice which may occasionally jar the modern reader. In the later letters, however, where they appear much less frequently, I have used [*sic*] on several occasions to confirm that readings such as 'and' for 'an' and 'than' for 'that' are indeed correct transcripts of the original manuscript and not simply printer's errors. I have also preserved the Brontës' own accenting of their unusual name, which varied according to personal whim and the period in which they were writing. For clarity and uniformity, however, I have always used the most famous version in my own text. The only editorial changes which have been made to the text are the omission of repeated words where this is clearly accidental, the removal or closure of quotation marks where these are incomplete, and a standardization to single quotation marks throughout the letters.

Apart from Margaret Smith's exemplary *The Letters of Charlotte Brontë: Volume One 1829–1847* (Oxford, Clarendon Press, 1995), most other editions of Brontë letters and manuscripts are inaccurate and misleading, with bowdlerized or editorially altered texts often misattributed to the wrong date or recipient. To avoid unnecessary intrusion, I have not drawn attention to this in my text, but readers should be aware that most of my transcripts will differ, sometimes considerably, from those in other sources. Where a transcript is significantly different from previous printed versions this is indicated by a single asterisk next to the letter heading. In the nineteen instances where a letter is being published for the first time in book form in this edition, a double asterisk is used.

The following abbreviations of frequently used names have been used:

Anne: Anne Brontë (1820–49), youngest of the Brontë sisters, author of *Agnes Grey* (1847) and *The Tenant of Wildfell Hall* (1848).

Branwell: Patrick Branwell Brontë (1817–48), only brother of the Brontë sisters.

Charlotte: Charlotte Brontë (1816–55), eldest of the four Brontë children who survived into adulthood, author of *Jane Eyre* (1847), *Shirley* (1849), *Villette* (1853), *The Professor* (1846, published posthumously in 1857) and *Emma* (unfinished, published posthumously, 1860).

Ellen: Ellen Nussey (1817–97), life-long friend of Charlotte Brontë.

Emily: Emily Brontë (1818–48), author of *Wuthering Heights* (1847).

Patrick: Reverend Patrick Brontë (1777–1861), perpetual curate of Haworth and father of Charlotte, Branwell, Emily and Anne.

Chapter One

1821–30

Patrick to the Reverend John Buckworth; Haworth, 27 November 1821

My dear wife was taken dangerously ill on the 29th of January last; and in a little more than seven months afterwards she died. During every week and almost every day of this long tedious interval I expected her final removal. For the first three months I was left nearly quite alone, unless you suppose my six little children and the nurse and servants to have been company. Had I been at D[ewsbury] I should not have wanted kind friends; had I been at H[artshead] I should have seen them and others occasionally; or had I been at T[hornton] a family there who were ever truly kind would have soothed my sorrows; but I was at H[aworth], a stranger in a strange land. It was under these circumstances, after every earthly prop was removed, that I was called on to bear the weight of the greatest load of sorrows that ever pressed upon me. One day, I remember it well; it was a gloomy day, a day of clouds and darkness, three of my little children were taken ill of a scarlet fever; and, the day after, the remaining three were in the same condition. Just at that time death seemed to have laid his hand on my dear wife in a manner which threatened her speedy dissolution. She was cold and silent and seemed hardly to notice what was passing around her. This awful season however was not of long duration. My little children had a favourable turn, and at length got well; and the force of my wife's disease somewhat abated. A few weeks afterwards her sister, Miss Branwell, arrived, and afforded great comfort to my mind, which has been the case ever since, by sharing my labours and sorrows, and behaving as an affectionate mother to my children. At the earliest opportunity I called in different medical gentlemen to visit the beloved sufferer; but all their skill was in vain. Death pursued her unrelentingly. Her

I

constitution was enfeebled, and her frame wasted daily; and after above seven months of more agonizing pain than I ever saw anyone endure she fell asleep in Jesus, and her soul took its flight to the mansions of glory. During many years she had walked with God, but the great enemy, envying her life of holiness, often disturbed her mind in the last conflict. Still, in general she had peace and joy in believing, and died, if not triumphantly, at least calmly and with a holy yet humble confidence that Christ was her Saviour and heaven her eternal home.

Do you ask how I felt under all these circumstances? I would answer to this, that tender sorrow was my daily portion; that oppressive grief sometimes lay heavy on me and that there were seasons when an affectionate, agonizing <u>something</u> sickened my whole frame, and which is I think of such a nature as cannot be described, and must be felt in order to be understood. And when my dear wife was dead and buried and gone, and when I missed her at every corner, and when her memory was hourly revived by the innocent yet distressing prattle of my children, I do assure, my dear sir, from what I felt, I was happy at the recollection that to sorrow, not as those without hope, was no sin; that our Lord himself had wept over his departed friend, and that he had promised us grace and strength sufficient for such a day.

When his wife, Maria, died of ovarian cancer at the age of thirty-eight on 15 September 1821, the Reverend Patrick Brontë was faced with the prospect of bringing up six children on his own. The eldest, also called Maria, was only seven, the youngest, Anne, not yet two; the other children, born in quick succession, were Elizabeth, aged six, Charlotte, aged five, Branwell, the only boy, aged four, and Emily, aged three. To add to his problems, it was only eighteen months since the family had moved to Haworth, a small industrial township on the edge of the Yorkshire moors. As perpetual curate of St Michael and All Angels Church Patrick enjoyed security of tenure, the right to live rent-free in the Parsonage and an annual salary of around two hundred pounds, but with all the debts incurred during his wife's illness and six small children to feed, clothe and educate, money was extremely tight. Fortunately, Elizabeth Branwell, who had come from Penzance to nurse her dying sister, temporarily took charge of the children and household arrangements, though she made it clear that she intended to return home to Cornwall as soon as possible. Under her watchful eye and in the care of two young servant girls, Sarah and Nancy Garrs, the young Brontës soon settled into a happy routine of family prayers, lessons and afternoon walks upon the moors. Even at this early age, however, their extraordinary imaginative and intellectual powers were apparent as they enacted plays of their own devising and invented fictional characters based on the historical heroes of their father's lessons.

Sarah Garrs, nurse to the Brontë children, quoted by Marion Harland, in Charlotte Brontë at Home *(New York, G. P. Putnam's Sons, 1899)*

One day in the autumn or winter succeeding Mrs Brontë's death, Charlotte came to her nurse, wild and white with the excitement of having seen 'a fairy' standing by Baby Anne's cradle. When the two ran back to the nursery, Charlotte flying on ahead, treading softly not to frighten the beautiful visitant away, no one was there besides the baby sleeping sweetly in the depths of her forenoon nap. Charlotte stood transfixed; her eyes wandered incredulously round the room.

'But she *was* here, just now!' she insisted. 'I really and truly did see her!' – and no argument or coaxing could shake her from the belief.

Patrick to Mrs Gaskell, his daughter Charlotte's biographer; Haworth, 30 July 1855

When my children were very young, when as far as I can rem[em]ber, the oldest was about ten years of age and the youngest about four – thinking that they knew more, than I had yet discover'd, in order to make them speak with less timidity, I deem'd that if they were put under a sort of cover, I might gain my end – and happen[in]g to have a mask in the house, I told them all to stand, and speak boldly from under cover of the mask – I began with the youngest

3

– I asked what a child like her most wanted – She answer'd, age and experience – I asked the next what I had best do with her brother Branwell, who was sometimes, a naughty boy, She answered, reason with him, and when he won't listen to reason whip him – I asked Branwell, what was the best way of knowing the difference between the intellects, of men and women – he answer'd by considering the difference between them as to their bodies – I then asked Charlotte, what was the best Book in the world, she answered, the Bible – and what was the next best, she answer'd the Book of Nature – I then asked the next, what was the best mode of education for a woman, she answered, that which would make her rule her house well – Lastly I asked the oldest, what was the best mode of spending time she answer'd, by laying it out in preparation for a happy eternity – I may not have given precisely their words, but I have nearly done so as they made a deep and lasting impression on my memory –

With no prospect of remarrying and Aunt Branwell anxious to return to Penzance, Patrick had very little option but to send his children away to school if he wished them to receive an education that would enable them to earn their own livings. This was essential, for at his death they would inherit nothing: even the Parsonage would revert to the church and they would be homeless as well as portionless.

When the Clergy Daughters' School opened at Cowan Bridge, forty-five miles from Haworth on the Leeds–Kendal turnpike road, it seemed the obvious answer. Intended for the daughters of impoverished clergymen of the Evangelical persuasion, it boasted an impressive list of patrons and offered a sound education at half the usual price. Patrick could afford to educate four daughters there instead of two. Maria and Elizabeth were sent there in July 1824, to be joined a few months later by Charlotte and then Emily. Each of them received a damning report on admission – but no more so than the other pupils.

At that time, the curriculum for all middle and upper-class girls was limited to rote learning from set texts in English grammar, history and geography, a little basic arithmetic (known as ciphering) and 'accomplishments' such as French, music and drawing. The girls at the Clergy Daughters' School had to have some knowledge of all these things if they were to be governesses and teachers but their charitable status – and the fact that some of them would end up as servants or keeping house for their families – was also recognized in the fact that they were also expected to know how to 'work'. This was a term which referred to plain sewing, such as hemming sheets and making shirts, nightshirts and underwear, a drudgery that was also frequently imposed on governesses and was greatly resented by the Brontë sisters. For three of his daughters, Patrick paid a premium so that they would receive the more academic education, which included 'the accomplishments', intended as preparation for careers in teaching. Only Elizabeth, the least intellectual, appears to have been submitted for the standard education, suggesting that Patrick had designated her as the future family housekeeper.

School for Clergymen's Daughters, advertisement in the Leeds Intelligencer, *4 December 1824*

The House will be enlarged and altered for the Accommodation of Sixty Pupils: each Girl is to pay £14 a Year (Half in Advance) for Clothing, Lodging, Boarding, and Educating; and £1 Entrance towards the Expense of Books, &c. The Education will be directed according to the Capacities of the Pupils, and the Wishes of their Friends. In all Cases, the great Object in View will be their intellectual and religious Improvement; and to give that plain and useful Education, which may best fit them to return with Respectability and Advantage to their own Homes, or to maintain themselves in the different Stations of Life to which Providence may call them. If a more liberal Education is required for any who may be sent to be educated as Teachers and Governesses, an extra Charge will probably be made.

★ *Admissions register of the Clergy Daughters' School, Cowan Bridge,*
1824–39

No	Girl's name	Age	Parents' name and Residence	When admitted	How supported	Diseases had
17	Maria Bronté	10	Patrick B Haworth near Keighley Yorkshire	1824 July 21st	Parent	Vaccinated Chicken pox Scarlet fever H. Cough

Acquirements on entering	Left School	Where gone	For what educated	General Remarks
Reads tolerably – Writes pretty well – Ciphers a little – Works very badly – Knows a little of Grammar very little of Geography & History. Has made some progress in reading French but knows nothing of the language grammatically	1825 Feby 14th		Governess	Left School in ill health 14 Feby died 6th May 1825. Her Father's account of her is; "She exhibited during her illness many symptoms of a heart under divine influence." – Decline.

No	Girl's name	Age	Parents' names and Residence	When admitted	How supported	Diseases had
18	Elizabeth Bronté	9	As above	do [1824] [July 21st]	Parent	Vaccinated Scarlet fever H. Cough

Acquirements on entering	Left School	Where gone	For what educated	General Remarks
Reads little – Writes pretty well – Ciphers none – Works very badly – Knows nothing of Grammar, Geography, History or Accomplishments	1825 May 31st			Left School in ill health 31st May died 15th June 1825 – died in decline.

No	Girl's Name	Age	Parents' name and Residence	When admitted	How supported	Diseases had
30	Charlotte Brontë	8	Patrick B Haworth near Keighley Yorkshire	1824 Augst 10th	Parent	Vaccinated H. Cough

Acquirements on entering	Left School	Where gone	For what educated	General Remarks
Reads tolerably – Writes indifferently – Ciphers a little and works neatly. Knows nothing of Grammar, Geography, History or Accomplishments	1825 June 1st	Home	Governess	Altogether clever of her age but knows nothing systematically

No	Girl's Name	Age	Parents' name and Residence	When admitted	How supported	Diseases had
44	Emily Brontë	5¾	Patrick B Haworth near Keighley Yorkshire	1824 Novbr 25th	Parent	H. Cough

Acquirements on Entering	Left School	Where gone	For what educating	General Remarks
Reads very prettily & Works a little.	1825 June 1st	Home	Governess	Left School June 1st 1825

Patrick's plans and hopes were soon to be rudely shattered. In February 1825 he was summoned to the school to find Maria dying of tuberculosis; he fetched her home, where she died, aged eleven, just three months later. Less than three weeks after burying his eldest daughter, Elizabeth was sent home, also in the terminal stages of the disease. Belatedly realizing the danger, Patrick rushed to Cowan Bridge the next day to remove Charlotte and Emily; two weeks later, Elizabeth died, aged ten. Though the younger girls escaped the endemic disease of the place, Charlotte, in particular, was mentally scarred for life. Catharsis would come with *Jane Eyre*, but she never forgave the school and its founder, the Reverend William Carus Wilson, always holding them responsible for her elder sisters' deaths.

Pupil at the Clergy Daughters' School (possibly Charlotte herself), quoted by Mrs Gaskell in her Life of Charlotte Brontë *(1857)*

The dormitory in which Maria slept was a long room, holding a row of narrow little beds on each side, occupied by the pupils; and at the end of this dormitory there was a small bed-chamber opening out of it, appropriated to the use of Miss Scatcherd. Maria's bed stood nearest the door of this room. One morning, after she had become so seriously unwell as to have had a blister applied to her side (the sore from which was not perfectly healed), when the getting-up bell was heard, poor Maria moaned out that she was so ill, so very ill, she wished she might stop in bed; and some of the girls urged her to do so, and said they would explain it all to Miss Temple, the superintendent. But Miss Scatcherd was close at hand, and her anger would have to be faced before Miss Temple's kind thoughtfulness could interfere; so the sick child began to dress, shivering with cold, as, without leaving her bed, she slowly put on her black worsted stockings over her thin white legs (my informant spoke as if she saw it yet, and her whole face flashed out undying indignation). Just then Miss Scatcherd issued from her room, and, without asking for a word of explanation from the sick and frightened girl, she took her by the arm, on the side to which the blister had been applied, and by one vigorous movement whirled her out into the middle of the floor, abusing her all the time for dirty and untidy habits. There she left her. My informant says, Maria hardly spoke, except to beg some of the more indignant girls to be calm; but, in slow, trembling movements, with many a pause, she went down stairs at last – and was punished for being late.

Miss Evans, superintendent of the Clergy Daughters' School and the 'Miss Temple' of Jane Eyre, to Mrs Gaskell; c. 1855

The second, Elizabeth, is the only one of the family of whom I have a vivid recollection, from her meeting with a somewhat alarming accident, in consequence of which I had her for some days and nights in my bed-room, not only for the sake of greater quiet, but that I might watch over her myself. Her head was severely cut, but she bore all the consequent suffering with exemplary patience, and by it won much upon my esteem. Of the two younger ones (if two there were) I have very slight recollections, save that one, a darling child, under five years of age, was quite the pet nursling of the school.

Charlotte to William Smith Williams, reader at her publishers, Smith, Elder & Co.; Haworth, 5 November 1849

I wonder who that former schoolfellow of mine was . . . or how she had been enabled to identify Currer Bell with C.Brontë. She could not have been a Cowan Bridge girl, none of them can possibly remember me. They might remember my eldest sister, Maria; her prematurely developed and remarkable intellect, as well as the mildness, wisdom, and fortitude of her character, <u>might</u> have left an indelible impression on some observant mind amongst her companions. My second sister, Elizabeth, too, may perhaps be remembered, but I cannot conceive that I left a trace behind me. My career was a very quiet one. I was plodding and industrious, perhaps I was grave, for I suffered to see my sisters perishing, but I think I was remarkable for nothing.

The crisis caused by the deaths of Maria and Elizabeth and the removal of Charlotte and Emily from the school sealed Aunt Branwell's fate: she felt herself duty bound to remain with her sister's family. A victim of her own sense of duty, she was too old and set in her ways by the time they had eventually outgrown her care to return to her beloved Penzance. For her, living in Haworth was a penance. For the remaining Brontë children, however, their home was a sanctuary to which they would always return with gratitude and pleasure. Though the deaths of their two eldest sisters left their mark on each of them, they quickly settled back into the old routine of morning lessons with their father, followed by sewing for the girls until a Yorkshire dinner reassembled the whole family. In the afternoons, while their father did his parish visiting, they were free to wander over the moors, ranging far and wide over the hills which were to inspire and inform their work. Already, they were deeply absorbed in the imaginary worlds which they had invented and, so deeply did they identify with their creations, that their games would often end in furious quarrels.

Patrick to Mrs Gaskell; Haworth, 24 July 1855

When mere children, as soon as they could read and write, Charlotte and her brother and sisters, used to invent and act little plays of their own, in which the Duke of Wellington my Daughter Charlotte's Hero, was sure to come off, the conquering hero – when a dispute would not infrequently arise amongst them regarding the comparative merits of him, Buonaparte, Hannibal, and Caesar – When the argument got warm, and rose to its height, as their mother was then dead, I had sometimes to come in as arbitrator, and settle the dispute, according to the best of my judgement. Generally in the management of these concerns, I frequently thought, I discovered signs of rising talent, which I had seldom or never before seen, in any of their age. As they had few opportunities, of being in learned, and polished society in their retired country situation they formed a little society amongst themselves – with which they seem'd contented and happy –

Francis Leyland, a friend of Branwell's, from his book The Brontë Family *(London, Hurst & Blackett, 1886)*

In acting their early plays, they performed them with childish glee, and did not fail at times to 'tear a passion to tatters.' They observed that Tabby [Aykroyd, the new servant] did not approve of such extra-ordinary proceedings; but on one occasion, with increased energy of action and voice, they so wrought on her fears that she retreated to her nephew's house, and as soon as she could regain her breath, she exclaimed, 'William! Yah mun gooa up to Mr Brontë's, for aw'm sure yon childer's all gooin mad, and aw darn't stop 'ith hause ony longer wi' 'em; an' aw'll stay here woll yah come back!' When the nephew reached the parsonage, 'the childer set up a great crack o' laughin',' at the wonderful joke they had perpetrated on faithful Tabby.

Patrick's gift of twelve wooden soldiers to Branwell in June 1826 inspired the most important and longest lasting stories, those of the 'Young Men'. At first, these were also acted out, each child 'playing' at being his or her own chief character but as the young Brontës became more literate they began to record the activities of their heroes in tiny books, fashioned from scraps of paper, which mimicked their favourite periodicals, plays, newspapers and novels. Their unconventional upbringing, especially the remarkable latitude of their reading which their father unfashionably refused to censor, was reflected in their work. The young Brontës' apprenticeship in writing had begun.

Charlotte, The History of the Year; 12 March 1829

Once papa lent my Sister Maria A Book it was an old Geography and she wrote on it[s] Blank leaf papa lent me this Book. the Book is an hundred and twenty years old   it is at this moment lying Before me while I write this   I am in the kitchin of the parsonage house Hawarth   Taby the servent is washing up after Breakfast and Anne my youngest Sister (Maria was my eldest) is kneeling on a chair looking at some cakes whiche Tabby has been Baking for us. Emily is in the parlour brushing it   papa and Branwell are gone to Keighly Aunt is up stairs in her Room and I am siting by the table writing this in the kitchin. Keighly is a small twon four miles from here papa and Branwell are gone for the newspaper the Leeds Intelligencer – a most exellent Tory news paper edited by Mr Edward Wood the proprietor [is] Mr Hernaman   we take 2 and see three Newspapers as such   we take the Leeds Inteligencer [par?]ty Tory and the Leeds Mercury Whig Edited by Mr Bains and His Brother Soninlaw and his 2 sons Edward and Talbot – We see the Jhon Bull   it is a High Tory very violent   Mr Driver Lends us it as Likewise Blackwoods Magazine the most able periodical there is   the editor is Mr Christopher North an old man 74 years of age   the 1st of April is his Birthday   his company are Timothy Ticklar Morgan Odoherty

Macrabin Mordecai Mullion Warrell and James Hogg a man of most extraordinary genius a Scottish Sheppherd.

Our plays were established Young Men June 1826 Our fellows July 1827 islanders December 1827. those are our thre[e] great plays that are not kept secret. Emily's and my Bed play's where Established the 1st December 1827 the other March 1828 – Bed plays means secret plays they are very nice ones all our plays are very strange ones there nature I need not write on paper for I think I shall always remember them. the young man play took its rise from some wooden soldier's Branwell had Our fellows from Esops fables and the Islanders from several events whi[c]h happened. I will skecth out the origin of our plays more explicit[l]y if I can

papa bought Branwell some soldiers at Leeds when papa came home it was night and we where in Bed so next morning Branwell came to our Door with a Box of soldiers Emily and I jumped out of Bed and I snat[c]hed up one and exclaimed this is the Duke of Wellington it shall be mine!! when I said this Emily likewise took one and said it should be hers when Anne came down she took one also. Mine was the prettiest of the whole and perfect in every part Emilys was a Grave looking ferllow we called him Gravey Anne's was a queer litle thing very much like herself he was called waiting Boy Branwell chose Bonaparte   March 12 1829

the origin of the Odears was as follows we pretended we had each a large Island inhabited by people 6 miles high the people we took out of Esops fables Hay Man was my cheif Man Boaster Branwells Hunter Annes and Clown Emily's our Cheif Men where 10 miles high except Emilys who was only 4.   March 12 1829.

Charlotte, Tales of the Islanders; 31 July 1829

The play of the Islanders was formed in December 1827 in the following maner. One night about the time when the cold sleet and dreary fogs of November are succeeded by the snow storms & high peircing nightwinds of confirmed winter we where all sitting round the warm blazing kitchen fire having just concluded a quarrel with Taby concerning the propriety of lighting a candle from which she came of[f] victorious no candle having been produced a long pause

suceeded which was at last broken by B[ranwell] saying in a lazy
maner I don't know what to do this was reechoed by E[mily] and
A[nne]

T   wha ya may go t'bed

B   I'd rather do anything [than] that
&C   your so glum tonight

C   well supose we had each an Island

B   if we had I would choose the Island of Man

C   & I would choose Isle of Wight

E   the Isle of Arran for me

A   & mine should be Guernsey

C   the D of Wellington should be my cheif man

B   Herries should be mine

E   Walter Scott should be mine

A   I should have Benti[n]ck

here our conversation was interrupted by [the] to us dismal sound
of the clock striking 7 & we where sumoned of[f] to bed. the next
day we added several others to our list of names till we had got
allmost all the cheif men in the kingdom.

Charlotte, A Strange Occurrence; 22 June 1830

The following strange occurrence happened on the 22 of June 1830.
at that time papa was very ill confined to his bed & so weak that he
could not rise without assistance. Taby & I were alone in the Kitchen,
about half past 9 anti-meridian. suddenly we heard a knock at the
door, Taby rose & opened it, an old man appeared standing without,
who accosted her thus, OM   does the parson live here? T   yes,
OM   I wish to see him,   T   he is poorly in bed OM   indeed I
have [a] message for him. T   who from? OM   from the LORD.

13

T who? OM, the LORD, he desires me to say that the bridegroom is coming & that he must prepare to meet him; that the cords are about to be loosed & the golden Bowl broken, the Pitcher broken at the fountain & the wheel stopped at the cistern. here he concluded his discourse & abruptly went away. as Taby closed the door I asked her if she knew him, her reply was that she had never seen him before nor any one like him. Though I am fully persuaded that he was some fanatical enthusiast, well-meaning perhaps but utterly ignorant of true piety, yet I could not forbear weeping at his words spoken so unexpectedly at that particular period.

Branwell, Introduction to the History of the Young Men;
15 December 1830

It was sometime in the summer of the year AD 1824 when I being desirous to possess a box of soldiers asked papa to buy me one which shor[t]ly afterwards he procured me from Bradford They were 12 in number price 1s 6d and were the best I ever have had soon after this I got from Keighly another set of the same number. These Soldiers I kept for about a year untill either Maimed Lost burnt or destroyed by various casualties they

'departed and left not a wreck behind!'

Now therefore not satisfied with what I had formerly got I purchased at Keighly a band of Turkish musicians whi[c]h I continued to keep till the summer of AD 1825 when Charlotte and Emily returned from school where they had been during the days of my former sets. I remained for 10 months after they had returned without any soldiers when on June the 5th AD 1826 papa procured me from Leeds another set (those were the 12s) w[h]ich I kept for 2 years though 2 or 3 of them are in being at the time of my writing this (Dec 15 AD 1830) Sometime in 1827 I bought another set of Turkish Musi[ci]ans at Halifax and in 1828 I purchased the last Box a band of Indians at Haworth. both these I still keep. here now ends the catalogue of soldiers bought by or for me And I must now conclude this Introduction already to[o] long with saying, that what is contained in this History is a statement of what Myself Charlotte Emily and Ann[e] rea[l]ly pretended did happen among the 'Young Men' (that being the name we gave them) during the period of nearly 6 years . . .

Chapter Two

1829–36

In September 1829, the Brontë children accompanied Aunt Branwell to Cross-Stone, some six miles across the moors from Haworth, to stay with their great-aunt's widower, the Reverend John Fennell. Under her aunt's watchful eye, the thirteen-year-old Charlotte laboriously inscribed the following little letter to her father in her best copperplate hand; Patrick recognized the significance of this short, stiff, but otherwise unremarkable note, writing proudly upon it 'Charlotte's first letter –'.

Charlotte to Patrick; Cross-Stone Parsonage, Todmorden, 23 September 1829

Parsonage House, Crosstone

My Dear Papa,

At Aunts, request I write these lines to inform you that 'if all be well' we shall be at home on Friday by dinner time, when we hope to find you in good health – On account of the bad weather we have not been out much, but notwithstanding we have spent our time very pleasantly, between reading, working, and learning our lessons, which Uncle Fenell has been so kind as to teach us every day, Branwell has taken two sketches from nature, & Emily Anne & myself have likewise each of us drawn a piece from some views of the lakes which Mr Fenell brought with him from Westmoreland, the whole of these he intends keeping – Mr Fenell is sorry he cannot accompany us to Howarth on Friday for want of room, but hopes to have the pleasure of seeing you soon, all unite in sending their kind love with your

Affectionate Daughter, Charlotte Bronte

Apart from the disastrous ten months at Cowan Bridge, Charlotte had never been to school. If she was to equip herself to earn her own living, an absolute necessity given her father's financial situation, she needed a more formal education than that offered by her aunt and father. It was essential that she should return to school and, in January 1831, she travelled the twenty miles from Haworth to Mirfield to take up residence at Roe Head School. After an inauspicious start, she soon made friends and settled happily into the school routine.

Mary Taylor, Charlotte's school-friend, to Mrs Gaskell; 18 January 1856

I first saw her coming out of a covered cart, in very old-fashioned clothes, and looking very cold and miserable. She was coming to school at Miss Wooler's. When she appeared in the schoolroom her dress was changed, but just as old. She looked a little old woman, so short-sighted that she always appeared to be seeking something, and moving her head from side to side to catch a sight of it. She was very shy and nervous, and spoke with a strong Irish accent.

Ellen Nussey, Charlotte's school-friend, Reminiscences; 1871

Arriving at school about a week after the general assembling of the pupils, I was not expected to accompany them when the time came for their daily exercise, but while they were out, I was led into the school-room, and quietly left to make my observations. I had come to the conclusion it was very nice and comfortable for a school-room, though I had little knowledge of school-rooms in general, when, turning to the window to observe the look-out I became aware for the first time that I was not alone; there was a silent, weeping, dark little figure in the large bay-window; she must, I thought, have risen from the floor. As soon as I had recovered from my surprise, I went from the far end of the room, where the book-shelves were, the contents of which I must have contemplated with a little awe in anticipation of coming studies. A crimson cloth covered the long table down the centre of the room, which helped, no doubt to hide the shrinking little figure from my view. I was touched and troubled at once to see her so sad and tearful. I said *shrinking*, because her attitude, when I saw her, was that of one who wished to hide both herself and her grief. She did not shrink, however, when spoken to, but in very few words confessed she was 'home-sick'. After a little of such comfort as could be offered, it was suggested to her that there was a possibility of her too having to comfort the speaker by and by for the same cause. A faint quivering smile then lighted her face; the tear-drops fell; we silently took each other's hands, and at once we felt that genuine sympathy which always consoles, even though it be unexpressed.

Roe Head was different from the Clergy Daughters' School in almost every respect. It was run by the five Miss Wooler sisters in a pleasant house with large grounds in an area where Patrick had held curacies and still had many friends. Usually only about eight girls boarded, though more attended on a daily basis, and most were the daughters of well-to-do local merchants and minor gentry. The regime was kindly and teaching was geared to the abilities and talents of the individual. This was fortunate, given Charlotte's hitherto unconventional education.

Mary Taylor to Mrs Gaskell; 18 January 1856

We thought her very ignorant, for she had never learnt grammar at all, and very little geography . . . She would confound us by knowing things that were out of our range altogether. She was acquainted with most of the short pieces of poetry that we had to learn by heart: would tell us the authors, the poems they were taken from, and sometimes repeat a page or two, and tell us the plot . . . She used to draw much better, and more quickly, than anything we had seen before, and knew much about celebrated pictures and painters. Whenever an opportunity offered of examining a picture or cut of any kind, she went over it piecemeal, with her eyes close to the paper, looking so long that we used to ask her 'what she saw in it.' She could always see plenty, and explained it very well. She made poetry and drawing at least exceedingly interesting to me; and then I got the habit, which I have yet, of referring mentally to her opinion on all matters of that kind . . .

Through sheer hard work, Charlotte mastered the unfamiliar school disciplines and rapidly worked her way to the top of the class where she remained throughout the three half-years of her schooling. Two fellow pupils were to become life-long friends, Ellen Nussey, a quiet, conventional and pious girl from nearby Birstall, and Mary Taylor, a Radical, intellectual and totally unconventional girl from Gomersal. Their contrasting natures prompted different responses from Charlotte. Though glimpses of the stimulating correspondence she shared with Mary can be caught in the more prosaic letters to Ellen, almost all Charlotte's letters to Mary were destroyed. This is an irreparable loss because Mary was Charlotte's confidante for ambitions and frustrations, particularly in the literary field, from which Ellen was deliberately excluded. Reading the letters to Ellen in isolation, one would never get the impression that their author was the creator, with her brother, Branwell, of an imaginary world, Angria, peopled with heroic figures whose lives and adventures were often more real and always more absorbing to Charlotte than what was actually happening around her. Ellen simply had no idea that her friend inhabited an 'infernal world' of her own creation. Nevertheless, the letters to Ellen give us a precious insight into Charlotte's development during these early years. The first stilted letters, so similar in style to the one Charlotte wrote her father from Cross-Stone, were apparently written as school exercises.

Charlotte to Ellen; Roe Head, 11 May 1831

Dear Ellen

I take advantage of the earliest opportunity to thank you for the letter you favoured me with last week and to apologize for having so long neglected to write to you, indeed I believe this will be the first letter or note I have ever addressed to you. I am extremely obliged to your Sister for her kind invitation and I assure you that I should very much have liked to hear Mr Murray's lectures on Galvinism as they would doubtless have been both amusing and instructive. But we are often compelled 'to bend our inclinations to our duty' (as Miss Wooler observed the other day) and since there [are] so many holidays this half-year it would have appeared almost unreasonable to ask for an extra holiday; besides we should perhaps have got behind-hand with our lessons so that, everything considered it is perhaps as well that circumstances have deprived us of this pleasure

Believe me to remain
Your affect. friend
C.Brontë

Roe-Head. – May 11th–31

Charlotte to Ellen; Haworth, 13 January 1832

The receipt of your letter gave me an agreeable surprise, for notwithstanding your faithful promises you must excuse me if I say that I had little confidence in their fulfilment knowing that when School-girls once get home they willingly abandon every recollection which tends to remind them of school & indeed they find such an infinite variety of circumstances to engage their attention and employ their leisure hours that they are easily persuaded that they have no <u>time</u> to fulfil promises made at School   it gave me great pleasure however to find that you and Miss Taylor are exceptions to the general rule ... I was glad to hear Mr Taylor was pleased with Miss Mary's drawings. Tell her I hope she will derive benefit from the perusal of Cobbett's lucubrations but I beg she will on no account burden her memory with passages to be repeated for my edification lest I should not justly appreciate either her kindness or their merit since that worthy personage & his principles whether private or political are no great favourites of mine. Remember me to your Sisters and Mother give my best love to Dear Polly and little Miss Boisterous and accept the same dearest Ellen

From your affectionate friend
Charlotte Brontë

Charlotte to Branwell; Roe Head, 17 May 1832

Dear Branwell,

As usual I address my weekly letter to you – because to you I find the most to say. I feel exceedingly anxious to know how, and in what state you arrived at home after your long, and I should think very fatiguing journey. I could perceive when you arrived at Roe-Head that you were very much tired though you refused to acknowledge it. After you were gone many questions and subjects of conversation recurred to me which I had intended to mention to you but quite forgot them in the agitation which I felt at the totally unexpected pleasure of seeing you. Lately I had begun to think that I had lost all the interest which I used formerly to take in politics but the extreme pleasure I felt at the news of the Reform-bill's being thrown out by the House of Lords and of the expulsion or resignation of Earl Grey, &c. &c. convinced me that I have not as yet lost <u>all</u> my penchant for politics. I am extremely glad that Aunt has consented to take in Frazer's Magazine for though I know from your description of its general contents it will be rather uninteresting when compared with 'Blackwood' still it will be better than remaining the whole year without being able to obtain a sight of any periodical publication whatever, and such would assuredly be our case as in the little wild, moorland village where we reside there would be no possibility of borrowing, or obtaining a work of that description from a circulating library. I hope with you that the present delightful weather may contribute to the perfect restoration of our dear Papa's health and that it may give Aunt pleasant reminiscences of the salubrious climate of her native place. With love to all believe [me] dear Branwell to remain

Your affectionate sister
Charlotte

At the end of June 1832, Charlotte's formal schooling ended and she returned to Haworth to pass on her newly acquired knowledge to her sisters. As a reward for winning the silver medal for achievement during each of her three terms, she was allowed to take it home with her. She also carried with her the good wishes of her school-friends, some of whom, to her surprise, continued to keep in touch with her. One of them, Ellen Nussey, even invited her to stay at her grand family home, The Rydings, at Birstall. Though this made Charlotte uncomfortable because it reinforced her sense of being socially inferior to Ellen, their friendship remained undimmed, and after her return Charlotte immediately reassumed the dominant, rather patronizing tone of their earlier correspondence.

Ellen, Reminiscences; 1871

The last day Charlotte was at school she seemed to realize what a sedate, hard-working season it had been to her. She said, 'I should for once like to feel *out and out* a school-girl; I wish something would happen! Let us run round the fruit garden (running was what she never did); perhaps we shall meet some one, or we may have a fine for trespass.' She evidently was longing for some never-to-be-forgotten incident. Nothing, however, arose from her little enterprise. She had to leave school as calmly and quietly as she had lived there.

Martha Taylor, Mary's younger sister, to Ellen; Roe Head,
17 May 1832

I wonder how we shall go on next half year without you and Miss Brontë. I think the school-room will look strange without Miss Brontë at the head of the class . . . I think I shall feel Miss Brontë's loss very much as she has always been very kind to me.

Charlotte to Ellen; Haworth, 21 July 1832

You ask me to give you a description of the manner in which I have passed every day since I left School: this is soon done as an account of one day is an account of all. In the morning from nine o'clock till half-past twelve – I instruct my Sisters & draw, then we walk till dinner   after dinner I sew till tea time, and after tea I either read, write, do a little fancy-work or draw, as I please. Thus in one delightful, though somewhat monotonous course my life is passed. I have only been out to tea twice since I came home, we are expecting company this afternoon & on Tuesday next we shall have all the Female teachers of the Sunday-school to tea.

Ellen, Reminiscences; 1871

Charlotte's first visit from Haworth was made about three months after she left school. She travelled in a two-wheeled gig, the only conveyance to be had in Haworth except the covered cart which brought her to school. Mr Brontë sent Branwell as an escort; he was *then* a very dear brother, as dear to Charlotte as her own soul; they were in perfect accord of taste and feeling, and it was mutual delight to be together. Branwell probably had never been far from home before! he was in wild ecstasy with everything. He walked about in unrestrained boyish enjoyment, taking views in every direction of the old turret-roofed house, the fine chestnut trees on the lawn (one tree especially interested him because it was 'iron-garthed,' having been split by storms, but still flourishing in great majesty), and a large rookery, which gave to the house a good background – all these he noted and commented upon with perfect enthusiasm. He told his sister he 'was leaving her in Paradise, and if she were not intensely happy she never would be!'

During this visit, the two girls decided that in future they should write to each other in French. Charlotte was undoubtedly the driving force behind the idea. She loved what she called 'the universal language' and was always afraid that, without practice, she would lose the skills in it that she had so painstakingly acquired at Roe Head. On her return to Haworth, Charlotte eagerly penned a hasty thank-you note in remarkably fluent and polished French which only served to reinforce Ellen's doubts about the wisdom of attempting to match her friend. She declined to respond in kind and Charlotte was reluctantly forced to abandon the experiment.

Charlotte to Ellen; Haworth, 18 October 1832

Nous sommes encore partu et il y a entre nous dix sept milles de chemin: le bref quinzaine pendant lequel je fus chez vous c'est envolé et desormais il faut compter ma visite agréable parmi le nombre de choses passées.

J'arrivait à Haworth en parfaite sauveté sans le moindre accident ou malheur. Mes petites soeurs couraient hors de la maison pour me rencontrer aussitôt que la voiture se fit voir, et elles m'embrassaient avec autant d'empressement, et de plaisir comme si j'avais été absente pour plus d'[un] an. Mon Papa, ma Tante, et le monsieur dont mon frére avoit parlé, furent tous assemblés dans le Salon, et en peu de temps je m'y rendis aussi. C'est souvent l'ordre du Ciel que quand on a perdu un plaisir il y en a un autre prêt à prendre sa place. Ainsi je venois de partir de trés chérs amis, mais tout à l'heure je revins à des parens aussi chers et bons.

Charlotte to Ellen; Haworth, 1 January 1833

Accept my congratulations on the arrival of the 'New Year' every succeeding day of which will I trust find you <u>wiser</u> and <u>better</u> in the <u>true</u> sense of those much-used words. The first day of January always presents to my mind a train of very solemn and important reflections and a question more easily asked than answered frequently occurs viz: How have I improved the past year and with [what] good intentions do I view the dawn of its successor? these my dearest Ellen are weighty considerations which (young as we are) neither you nor I can too deeply or too seriously ponder. I am sorry your too great diffidence arising I think from the want of sufficient confidence in your own capabilities prevented you from writing to me in French as I think the attempt would have materially contributed to your improvement in that language.

In July 1833 Ellen paid her first and long-awaited visit to Haworth Parsonage. Her impressions, though recorded many years later and coloured by her later knowledge, are important because they give the first outsider's picture of the Brontë family.

Ellen, Reminiscences; 1871

My first visit to Haworth was full of novelty and freshness . . . Even at this time, Mr Brontë struck me as looking very venerable, with his snow-white hair and powdered coat-collar. His manner and mode of speech always had the tone of high-bred courtesy. He was considered somewhat of an invalid, and always lived in the most abstemious and simple manner . . . Miss Branwell was a very small, antiquated little lady. She wore caps large enough for half a dozen of the present fashion, and a front of light auburn curls over her forehead. She always dressed in silk. She had a horror of the climate so far north, and of the stone floors in the parsonage. She amused us by clicking about in pattens whenever she had to go into the kitchen or look after household operations. She talked a great deal of her younger days; the gayeties of her dear native town, Penzance, in Cornwall; the soft, warm climate, etc. The social life of her younger days she used to recall with regret; she gave one the idea that she had been a belle among her own home acquaintances. She took snuff out of a very pretty gold snuff-box, which she sometimes presented to you with a little laugh, as if she enjoyed the slight shock and astonishment visible in your countenance. In summer she spent part of the afternoon in reading aloud to Mr Brontë. In the winter evenings she must have enjoyed this; for she and Mr Brontë had often to finish their discussions on what she had read when we all met for tea. She would be very lively and intelligent, and tilt arguments against Mr Brontë without fear.

'Tabby', the faithful, trustworthy old servant, was very quaint in appearance – very active, and, in these days, the general servant and factotum. We were all 'childer' and 'bairns,' in her estimation. She still kept to her duty of walking out with the 'childer,' if they went any distance from home, unless Branwell were sent by his father as a protector . . .

Emily Brontë had by this time acquired a lithesome, graceful figure. She was the tallest person in the house, except her father. Her hair, which was naturally as beautiful as Charlotte's, was in the same unbecoming tight curl and frizz, and there was the same want of complexion. She had very beautiful eyes – kind, kindling, liquid eyes; but she did not often look at you; she was too reserved. Their colour might be said to be dark gray, at other times dark blue, they varied so. She talked very little. She and Anne were like twins – inseparable companions, and in the very closest sympathy, which never had any interruption.

Anne – dear, gentle Anne – was quite different in appearance from the others. She was her aunt's favourite. Her hair was a very pretty, light brown, and fell on her neck in graceful curls. She had lovely, violet-blue eyes, fine penciled eyebrows, and clear, almost transparent complexion. She still pursued her studies, and especially her sewing, under the surveillance of her aunt. Emily had now begun to have the disposal of her own time. Branwell studied regularly with his father, and used to paint in oils, which was regarded as study for what might be eventually his profession. All the household entertained the idea of his becoming an artist, and hoped he would be a distinguished one . . .

In fine and suitable weather delightful rambles were made over the moors, and down into the glens and ravines that here and there broke the monotony of the moorland. The rugged bank and rippling brook were treasures of delight. Emily, Anne, and Branwell used to ford the streams, and sometimes placed stepping-stones for the other two; there was always a lingering delight in these spots, − every moss, every flower, every tint and form, were noted and enjoyed. Emily especially had a gleesome delight in these nooks of beauty, − her reserve for the time vanished. One long ramble made in these early days was far away over the moors to a spot familiar to Emily and Anne, which they called 'The Meeting of the Waters.' It was a small oasis of emerald green turf, broken here and there by small clear springs; a few large stones served as resting-places; seated here, we were hidden from all the world, nothing appearing in view but miles and miles of heather, a glorious blue sky, and brightening sun. A fresh breeze wafted on us its exhilarating influence; we laughed and made mirth of each other, and settled we would call ourselves the quartette. Emily, half reclining on a slab of stone, played like a young child with the tadpoles in the water, making them swim about, and then fell to moralizing on the strong and the weak, the brave and the cowardly, as she chased them with her hand. No serious care or sorrow had so far cast its gloom on nature's youth and buoyancy, and nature's simplest offerings were fountains of pleasure and enjoyment.

Charlotte to Ellen; Haworth, 11 September 1833

Since you were here, Emily has been very ill; her ailment was Erysipelas in the arm, accompanied by severe bilious attacks, and great general debility: her arm was obliged to be cut in order to remove the noxious matter which had accumulated in the inflamed parts; it is now I am happy to say nearly healed, her health is in fact almost perfectly re-established: though the sickness still continues to recur at intervals. Were I to tell you of the impression you have made on every one here, you would accuse me of flattery. Papa and Aunt are continually adducing you as an example for me to shape my actions and behaviour by, Emily & Anne say 'they never saw any one they liked so well as Miss Nussey' and Tabby whom you have absolutely fascinated talks a great deal more nonsense about your Ladyship than I choose to report: you must read this letter dear Ellen without thinking of the writing for I have indited it almost all in the twilight. It is now so dark that notwithstanding the singular property of 'seeing in the Night time' – which the young ladies at Roe Head used to attribute to me, I can scribble no longer:

For two years after Ellen's visit to Haworth, the friendship was maintained by a series of letters in which Charlotte often struggled to find something to say, not least because she could not share the consuming passion and fervent activity of her imaginary worlds with her friend. Ellen could know nothing of the hundreds of thousands of words she and Branwell, writing in partnership as they had since childhood, poured out on the adventures of their great heroes, Arthur Wellesley, Duke of Zamorna, and Alexander Percy, Earl of Northangerland. Emily and Anne, too, had their secret world, Gondal, which was equally absorbing, as is self-evident from Emily's diary paper, written in November 1834, when she was sixteen years old.

Charlotte to Ellen; Haworth, 11 February 1834

According to custom I have no news to communicate indeed I do not write either to retail gossip or to impart solid information, my motives for maintaining our mutual correspondence are in the first place to get intelligence from you, and in the second that we may remind each other of our separate existences; without some such medium of reciprocal converse; according to the nature of things you, who are surrounded by society and friends, would soon forget that such an insignificant being as myself, ever lived; I however in the solitude of our wild little hill village, think of my only un-related friend, my dear ci-devant school companion daily, nay almost hourly. Now Ellen, don't you think I have very cleverly contrived to make a letter out of nothing?

Charlotte to Ellen; Haworth, 20 February 1834

I was greatly amused at the tone of nonchalance which you assumed while treating of London, and its wonders, which seem to have excited anything rather than surprise in your mind: did you not feel awed while gazing at St Paul's and Westminster Abbey? had you no feeling of intense, and ardent interest, when in St James' you saw the Palace, where so many of England's Kings, had held their courts, and beheld the representations of their persons on the walls. You should not be too much afraid of appearing country-bred, the magnificence of London has drawn exclamations of astonishment, from travelled men, experienced in the World, its wonders, and its beauties.

Charlotte to Ellen; Haworth, 4 July 1834

You ask me to recommend some books for your perusal; I will do so in as few words as I can. If you like poetry let it be first rate, Milton, Shakespeare, Thomson, Goldsmith, Pope (if you will though I don't admire him) Scott, Byron, Camp[b]ell, Wordsworth and Southey. Now Ellen don't be startled at the names of Shakespeare, and Byron. Both these were great men and their works are like themselves, You will know how to choose the good and avoid the evil, the finest passages are always the purest, the bad are invariably revolting you will never wish to read them over twice; Omit the Comedies of Shak[e]speare and the Don Juan, perhaps the Cain of Byron though the latter is a magnificent Poem and read the rest fearlessly, that must indeed be a depraved mind which can gather evil from Henry the 8th from Richard 3d from Macbeth and Hamlet and Julius Cesar, Scott's sweet, wild, romantic Poetry can do you no harm nor can Wordsworth's nor Campbell's nor Southey's, the greatest part at least of his some is certainly exceptionable, For History read Hume, Rollin, and the Universal History if you can I never did. For Fiction – read Scott alone all novels after his are worthless. For Biography, read Johnson's lives of the Poets, Boswell's life of Johnson, Southey's life of Nelson, Lockhart's life of Burns, Moore's life of Sheridan, Moore's life of Byron, Wolfe's Remains, For Natural History, read Bewick, and Audubon, and Goldsmith and White of Selborne. For Divinity, but your brother Henry will advise you there. I only say adhere to standard authors and don't run after novelty. If you can read this scrawl it will be to the credit of your patience.

Emily and Anne, diary paper; Haworth, 24 November 1834

November the 24 1834 Monday Emily Jane Bronte Anne Brontë I fed Rainbow, Diamond, Snowflake Jasper pheasent alias this morning Branwell went down to Mr Drivers and brought news that Sir Robert peel was going to be invited to stand for Leeds   Anne and I have been peeling Apples for Charlotte to make an apple pudding and for Aunts [illegible] and apple   Charlotte said she made puddings perfectly and she was of a quick but lim[i]ted Intellect   Taby said just now come Anne pillopatate (ie pill a potato)   Aunt has come into the Kitchen just now and said where are your feet Anne   Anne answered on the floor Aunt   papa opened the parlour Door and gave Branwell a Letter saying here Branwell read this and show it to your Aunt and Charlotte – The Gondals are discovering the interior of Gaaldine   Sally mosley is washing in the back-Kitchin

It is past Twelve o'clock   Anne and I have not tid[i]ed ourselv[e]s, done our bed work or done our lessons and we want to go out to play   We are going to have for Dinner Boiled Beef Turnips, potato's and applepudding   the Kitchin is in avery untidy state   Anne and I have not Done our music excercise which consists of b majer Taby said on my putting a pen in her face Ya pitter pottering there instead of pilling a potate   I answered O Dear, O Dear, O Dear I will derictly   with that I get up, take a Knife and begin pilling finished pilling the potatos   papa going to walk Mr Sunderland expected

  Anne and I say I wonder what we shall be like and what we shall be and where we shall be if all goes on well in the year 1874 – in which year I shall be in my 57th year Anne will be going in her 55th year Branwell will be going in his 58th year And Charlotte in her 59th year   hoping we shall all be well at that time we close our paper
Emily and Anne   November the 24 1834

Charlotte to Ellen; Haworth, 13 March 1835

What do you think of the course Politics are taking? I make this inquiry because I now think you have a wholesome interest in the matter; formerly you did not care greatly about it. B[aines] you see is triumphant. Wretch! I am a hearty hater, and if there is any one I thoroughly abhor, it is that man. But the Opposition is divided, red hots, and luke warms; and the Duke (par excellence <u>the</u> Duke) and Sir Robert Peel show no sign of insecurity, though they have already been twice beat; so 'courage, mon amie.' Heaven defend the right: as the old chevaliers used to say, before they joined battle. Now Ellen, laugh heartily at all this rodomontade, but you have brought it on yourself; don't you remember telling me to write such letters to you as I write to Mary Taylor? Here's a specimen; hereafter should follow a long disquisition on books, but I'll spare you that.

Charlotte to Ellen; Haworth, 8 May 1835

The Election! The Election! that cry has rung even amongst our lonely hills like the blast of a trumpet. how has it roused the populous neighbourhood of Birstall? Ellen, under what banner have your brothers ranged themselves? the Blue or the Yellow? Use your influence with them entreat them if it be necessary on your knees to stand by their country and Religion in this day of danger . . . [Oh how I wish] Stuart Wortley the Son of the most patriotic Patrician Yorkshire owns would be elected the Representative of his native

Province, Lord Morpeth was at Haworth last week and I saw him, My opinion of his Lordship is recorded in a letter I wrote yesterday to Mary Taylor. it is not worth writing over again. so I will not trouble you with it here.

Charlotte to Ellen; Haworth, 2 July 1835

We are all about to divide, break up, separate, Emily is going to school Branwell is going to London, and I am going to be a Governess   This last determination I formed myself, knowing that I should have to take the step sometime, and 'better sune as syne' to use the Scotch proverb and knowing also that Papa would have enough to do with his limited income should Branwell be placed at the Royal Academy, and Emily at Roe-Head. Where am I going to reside? you will ask – within four miles of Yourself dearest at a place neither of us are wholly unacquainted with, being no other than the identical Roe-Head mentioned above. Yes I am going to teach in the very school where I was myself taught – Miss Wooler made me the offer and I preferred it to one or two proposals of Private Governesship which I had before received – I am sad, very sad at the thoughts of leaving home but Duty – Necessity – these are stern mistresses who will not be disobeyed. Did I not once say Ellen you ought to be thankful for your independence? I felt what I said at the time, and I repeat it now with double earnestness: if any thing would cheer me, it is the idea of being so near you – surely you and Polly will come, and see me – it would be wrong in me to doubt it – you were never unkind yet. Emily, and I leave home on the 29th of this month, the idea of being together consoles us both somewhat, and in truth since I must enter a situation 'my lines have fallen in pleasant places' – I both love and respect Miss Wooler.

The momentous changes announced so dramatically in this letter were not to be. Charlotte did indeed leave Haworth to take up her first job, a teaching post at Roe Head, in the summer of 1835. Miss Wooler had offered to educate Emily free of charge but her kindness was not to be rewarded. At seventeen, and having spent only seven months away at school as a child, Emily was too set in her ways to surrender to the discipline of Roe Head. She became physically ill and by October was back at Haworth, where the liberty to enjoy her imaginary world, Gondal, to the full was restored and, with it, her health. Her place at Roe Head was taken by the fifteen-year-old Anne, the youngest and most docile of the Brontës, who had never left home before. Less dependent on the need to give free rein to her imagination than Emily, and sharing Charlotte's determination to acquire a formal education, Anne adapted more easily to the routine of school life and, like her elder sister, even made a friend.

The grandiose plan to place Branwell at the Royal Academy which had prompted the family dispersal also came to nothing. For some years now Branwell had been pursuing the idea of becoming a portrait painter, a career which appealed to all the family's passion for the glamorous world of the arts. Fortunately, before their plans were too far advanced, Branwell's tutor, William Robinson, a Leeds-based artist, who had himself been a pupil of Sir Thomas Lawrence, pointed out that Branwell was not sufficiently versed in anatomical and classical painting to enable him to be admitted. More lessons with Robinson were therefore called for, but the Royal Academy plan, like an equally ambitious scheme for Branwell to go on a Continental tour to further his artistic education, fell through, probably because of lack of money.

Branwell to the Secretary of the Royal Academy; Haworth, c. July 1835

Sir,

Having an earnest desire to enter as Probationary Student in the Royal Academy but not being possessed of information as to the means of obtaining my desire I presume to request from you as Secretary to the Institution an answer to the questions –

Where am I to present my drawing?

At what time –?

And especialy

Can I do it in August or September

**Branwell and Patrick to William Robinson; Haworth,*
16 November 1835

Haworth nr Bradford
Novr 16th
1835

Dear Sir,

After repeated delays, for which I am ashamed to apologise I have at length nearly completed my picture, and shall be ready to appear with it before your bar of judgement on Monday next the 23d of this Month. But should this day prove inconvenient to yourself, my Father desires me to request that you would name by Letter any day and time you may think proper; since that which would be the most convenient to you would certainly prove the same to me.

And my Father likewise, being so sensible of the value of your instructions and so pleased with your manner of conveying them, has resolved upon my receiving (if it should prove agreeable to you) a course of Lessons during the ensuing Winter, in addition to those you have already given me – but upon this subject it may be most proper to speak when I see you Sir; which time is looked forward to with no little fear and doubting by – if he dare aspire to the title

Your Obedient Pupil
P B Brontē

Mr Robinson
Ivy Cottage
Little Woodhouse
    Leeds –

Dear Sir,

As my Son, has previously express'd nearly all I had to say, I would only observe in addition – That I am so much pleased with the progress he has made, under your tuition, and so fully impressed with the idea, that he should go to the Metropolis under the <u>most favourable circumstances</u>, that I have finally made up my mind, that by your permission, he shall have at least another course of lessons from you, during the season of Winter, and shall improve himself, in Anatomy, which is the grammar of painting, & also make some farther progress in Classics, and consequently defer his journey, to London, till next Summer – When, God willing – I intend he shall go – I esteem it a high privilege, to have for him, an opportunity of instruction from you – since, without flattery, I must say, that except the pictures of Sir Thomas Lawrence, and Sir Jos[h]ua Reynolds, I have seen none of the English School, which I like so well as your own. My Son joins with me, in very respectful regards to You, and Mrs Robinson, and your little Family – I remain, Dear Sir,

Yours, very respectfully,
and truly,
P. Bronté

Branwell's commitment to his artistic career seems to have been less than whole-hearted, despite the sacrifices that it necessitated from the rest of his family. Like Charlotte, he was unable to rid himself of a compulsion to write and, even while he trained as an artist, he expended a great deal of energy in trying to secure admission to the ranks of *Blackwood's Magazine* as a contributor, pursuing the editor with a stream of letters which did more credit to his enthusiasm than to his tact. The editor, unkindly if wisely, left them unanswered.

Branwell to the Editor of Blackwood's Magazine*; Haworth, [8] December 1835*

All, Sir, that I desire of you is that you. would in answer to this letter request a Specimen or Specimen's of my writing and I even wish that you would name the subject on which you would wish me to write – In letters previous to this I have perhaps spoken too openly respecting the extent of my powers, But I did so because I determined to say what I beleived; I <u>know</u> that I am not one of the wretched writers of the day, I know that I possess strength to assist you beyond some of your own contributors; but I wish to make you the Judge in this case and give you the benefit of its desiscion.

Now Sir, do not act like a common place person, but like a man willing to examine for himself. Do not turn from the naked truth of my letters but <u>prove me</u> – and if I do not stand the proof I will not farther press myself on you – If I do stand it – Why – You have lost an able writer in James Hogg and God grant you may gain one in

Patrick Branwell Brontë

★★*John Brown and Joseph Redman to the Secretary to the Provincial Lodge of Free Masons, Wakefield; Haworth, 8 February 1836*

We beg leave to inform you, that a Young Gentleman, the Rev P Bronte's son, has made Application to us, wishing to be admitted into Masonry, but is only about 20 Years of Age – in consequence of which – we, (in conformity with the constitutions) do hereby apply to you for a Dispensation for that purpose – The Rev P Bronte is the Minister of the Chapelry of Haworth, and always appears to be very favourable to Masonry –

★★*John Brown and Joseph Redman to the Deputy General Secretary to the Provincial Lodge of Free Masons, Wakefield; Haworth, 11 February 1836*

We received your letter of the 9th Inst. and was very much surprised at your answer, as we doubted not but our request would be complyed with, being, as we thought agreeable to the laws of the Craft . . . in fact, this young Gentleman is a Pourtrait Painter and for the purpose of acquiring information or instruction intends going on to the Continent this Summer – which in our former letter we did not think of stating as not necessary –

Charlotte, tied to the unrelenting and monotonous regime of teaching at Roe Head and without the prospect of escape, abroad or elsewhere, felt increasingly stifled and frustrated. There was neither the physical leisure nor the mental energy for Angrian imaginings; moments snatched for this indulgence were inevitably and rudely ended by the interruption of incomprehending pupils. Charlotte's anger vented itself in splenetic outbursts against the 'dolts' and 'scrubs' in her occasional diary papers, the mis-named Roe Head Journal, but Angria itself had increasingly become a poisoned chalice. A lengthy religious crisis, fostered if not actually prompted by Ellen, who seems to have toyed with Calvinistic doctrines of pre-destination and election at this time, led Charlotte to a growing sense of her own worthlessness and a recognition that she had turned her Angrian heroes into idols whom she worshipped more assiduously than her own God. Her only pleasure had now become a matter for self-reproach and shame. Unable to tell Ellen about Angria, Charlotte could only hint at the terrible secret which was now an obstacle to her own salvation and pour out her miseries in Ellen's ever sympathetic ear.

Mary Taylor to Mrs Gaskell; 18 January 1856

I heard that she had gone as teacher to Miss Wooler's. I went to see her, and asked how she could give so much for so little money, when she could live without it. She owned that, after clothing herself and Anne, there was nothing left, though she had hoped to be able to save something. She confessed it was not brilliant, but what could she do? I had nothing to answer. She seemed to have no interest or pleasure beyond the feeling of duty, and, when she could get the opportunity, used to sit alone and 'make out.' She told me afterwards that one evening she had sat in the dressing-room until it was quite dark, and then observing it all at once had taken sudden fright.

Charlotte, Roe Head Journal; autumn 1835

About a week since I got a letter from Branwell containing a most exquisitely characteristic epistle from Northangerland to his daughter – It is astonishing what a soothing and delightful tone that letter seemed to speak – I lived on its contents for days, in every pause of employment – it came chiming in like some sweet bar of music – bringing with it agreeable thoughts such as I had for many weeks been a stranger to . . .

Charlotte, Roe Head Journal; 4 February 1836

I cannot get used to the ongoings that surround me. I fulfil my duties strictly & well, I so to speak if the illustration be not profane as God was not in the wind nor the fire nor the earth-quake so neither is my heart in the task, the theme or the exercicese. it is the still small voices alone that comes to me at eventide, that which like a breeze with a voice in it over the deeply blue hills & out of the now leafless forests & from the cities on distant river banks of a far & bright continent, it is that which wakes my spirit & engrosses all my living feelings all my energies which are not merely mechanical & like Haworth & home wakes sensations which lie dormant elsewhere.

Charlotte to Ellen; Roe Head, 10 May 1836

Don't deceive yourself by imagining that I have a bit of real goodness about me. My Darling if I were like you I should have my face Zionward though prejudice and error might occasionally fling a mist over the glorious vision before me. for with all your single-hearted sincerity you have your faults. but I am not like you. If you knew my thoughts; the dreams that absorb me; and the fiery imagination that at times eats me up and makes me feel Society as it is, wretchedly insipid you would pity and I dare say despise me. But Ellen I know the treasures of the Bible I love and adore them. I can see the Well of Life in all its clearness and brightness; but when I stoop down to drink of the pure waters they fly from my lips as if I were Tantalus. I have written like a fool.

Charlotte to Ellen; Roe Head, c. 28 May 1836

You are far too kind and frequent in your invitations. You puzzle me; I hardly know how to refuse, and it is still more embarrassing to accept. At any rate I cannot come this week, for we are in the very thickest melee of the Repetitions. I was hearing the terrible fifth section when your note arrived. But Miss Wooler says I must go to Gomersal next Friday as she promised for me on Whit-Sunday; and on Sunday morning I will join you at church if it be convenient, and stay   at Rydings till Monday morning. There's a free and easy proposal! Miss Wooler has driven me to it; she says her character is implicated!

Charlotte to Ellen; Haworth, c. 7 July 1836

When I was at Huddersfield whom do you think I saw? Amelia Walker. She and her Sister and Mamma and Papa and Brother were all at the Vicarage when we arrived there on Friday. They were monstrously gracious, Amelia almost enthusiastic in her professions of friendship!! She is taller, thinner, paler and more delicate looking than she used to be – very pretty still, very lady-like and polished, but spoilt utterly spoilt by the most hideous affectation. I wish she would copy her Sister who is indeed an example: that affable unaffected manners and a sweet disposition may fascinate powerfully without the aid of beauty. We spent the Tuesday at Lascelles Hall and had on the whole a very pleasant day. Miss Amelia changed her character every half hour, now she assumed the sweet sentimentalist, now the reckless rattler. Sometimes the question was 'Shall I look prettiest lofty?' and again 'Would not tender familiarity suit me better?' At one moment she affected to inquire after her old school-acquaintance the next she was detailing anecdotes of High Life. At last I got so sick of this that I turned for relief from her to her Brother, but William Walker though now grown a tall – well built man is an incorrigible '<u>Booby</u>' from him I could not extract a word of sense.

Charlotte, Roe Head Journal; 11 August 1836

All this day I have been in a dream half-miserable & half-ecstatic miserable because I could not follow it out uninterruptedly, ecstatic because it shewed almost in the vivid light of reality the ongoings of the infernal world. I had been toiling for nearly an hour with Miss Lister, Miss Marriott & Ellen Cook striving to teach them the distinction between an article and a substantive. The parsing lesson was completed, a dead silence had succeeded it in the school-room & I sat sinking from irritation & weariness into a kind of lethargy.

The thought came over me am I to spend all the best part of my life in this wretched bondage, forcibly suppressing my rage at the idleness the apathy and the hyperbolical & most asinine stupidity of these fat headed oafs and on compulsion assuming an air of kindness, patience & assiduity? must I from day to day sit chained to this chair prisoned with in these four bare-walls, while these glorious summer suns are burning in heaven & the year is revolving in its richest glow & declaring at the close of every summer day the time I am losing will never come again? Stung to the heart with this reflection I started up & mechanically walked to the window – a sweet August morning was smiling without   The dew was not yet dried off the field. the early shadows were stretching cool & dim from the hay-stack & the roots of the grand old oaks & thorns scattered along the sunk fence. All was still except the murmur of the scrubs about me over their tasks, I flung up the sash. an uncertain sound of inexpressible sweetness came on a dying gale from the south, I looked in that direction Huddersfield & the hills beyond it were all veiled in blue mist, the woods of Hopton & Heaton Lodge were clouding the waters-edge & the Calder silent but bright was shooting among them like a – silver arrow. I listened the sound sailed full & liquid down the descent. it was the bells of Huddersfield Parish church. I shut the window & went back to my seat. Then came on me rushing impetuously. all the mighty phantasm that this had conjured from nothing to a system strong as some religious creed. I felt as if I could have written gloriously – I longed to write. The Spirit of all Verdopolis of all the mountainous North of all the woodland West of all the river-watered East came crowding into my mind. if I had had time to indulge it I felt that the vague sensations of that moment would have settled down into some narrative better at least than any thing I ever produced before. But just then a Dolt came up with a lesson. I thought I should have vomited

Charlotte to Ellen; Roe Head, 26 September 1836

You have been very kind to me of late, and gentle and you have spared me those little sallies of ridicule which owing to my miserable and wretched touchiness of character used formerly to make me wince as if I had been touched with a hot iron: things that nobody else cares for enter into my mind and rankle there like venom. I know these feelings are absurd and therefore I try to hide them but they only sting the deeper for concealment. I'm an idiot!

Charlotte to Ellen; Roe Head, ?October 1836

If I like people it is my nature to tell them so and I am not afraid of offering incense to your vanity. It is from Religion that you derive your chief charm and may its influence always preserve you as pure, as unassuming and as benevolent in thought and deed as you are now. What am I compared to you I feel my own utter worthlessness when I make the comparison. I'm a very coarse, common-place wretch! Ellen (I have some qualities that make me very miserable, some feelings that you can have no participation in – that few very few people in the world can at all understand. I don't pride myself on these peculiarities, I strive to conceal and suppress them as much as I can, but they burst out sometimes and then those who see the explosion despise me and I hate myself for days afterwards).

Charlotte, Roe Head Journal; c. October 1836

I'm just going to write, because I cannot help it Wiggins might indeed talk of scriblemania if he were to see me just now. encompassed by the bulls, (query calves of Bashan) all wondering why I write with my eyes shut – staring, gaping hang their astonishment – A C-k on one side of me E L-r on the other and Miss W-r in the background, Stupidity the atmostphere, school-books the employment, asses the society, what in all this is there to remind me of the divine, silent, unseen land of thought . . . That wind pouring in impetuous current through the air, sounding wildly unremittingly from hour, to hour, deepening its tone as the night advances, coming not in gusts, but with a rapid gathering stormy swell, that wind I know is heard at this moment far away on the moors at Haworth. Branwell & Emily hear it and as it sweeps over our house down the churchyard & round the old church, they think perhaps of me & Anne – Glorious! that blast was mighty it reminded me of

Northangerland, there was something so merciless in the heavier rush, that made the very house groan as if it could scarce bear this acceleration of impetus. O it has wakened a feeling that I cannot satisfy – a thousand wishes rose at its call which must die with me for they will never be fulfilled. now I should be agonized if I had not the dream to repose on. its existences, its' forms its scenes do fill a little of the craving vacancy . . .

Charlotte to Ellen; Roe Head, ?October/November 1836

Week after week I have lived on the expectation of your coming. Week after week I have been disappointed – I have not regretted what I said in my last note to you. The confession was wrung from me by sympathy and kindness such as I can never be sufficiently thankful for. I feel in a strange state of mind still gloomy but not despairing. I keep trying to do right, checking wrong feelings, repressing wrong thoughts – but still – every instant I find – myself going astray – I have a constant tendency to scorn people who are far better than I am – A horror at the idea of becoming one of a certain set – a dread lest if I made the slightest profession I should sink at once into Phariseeism, merge wholly into the ranks of the self-righteous. In writing at this moment I feel an irksome disgust at the idea of using a single phrase that sounds like religious cant – I abhor myself – I despise myself – if the Doctrine of Calvin be true I am already an outcast – You cannot imagine how hard rebellious and intractable all my feelings are – When I begin to study on the subject I almost grow blasphemous, atheistical in my sentiments, don't desert me – don't be horrified at me, you know what I am –

Charlotte to Ellen; Roe Head, 5–6 December 1836

I often plan the pleasant life which we might lead together, strengthening each other in that power of self-denial, that hallowed and glowing devotion which the first Saints of God often attained to – My eyes fill with tears when I contrast the bliss of such a state brightened by hopes of the future with the melancholy state I now live in, uncertain that I have ever felt true contrition, wandering in

41

thought and deed, longing for holiness which I shall <u>never</u>, <u>never</u> obtain – smitten at times to the heart with the conviction that your Ghastly Calvinistic doctrines are true – darkened in short by the very shadows of Spiritual Death! If Christian perfection be necessary to Salvation I shall never be saved, my heart is a real hot bed for sinful thoughts and as to practice when I decide on an action I scarcely remember to look to my Redeemer for direction.

The Christmas holidays at Haworth at the end of 1836, which would normally have restored Charlotte's spirits, were marred when Tabby Aykroyd, the much-loved servant who had been with the Brontë family for thirteen years, fell in Main Street and broke her leg so badly that her life was in danger. Happily for the Brontës, she survived, but the accident cast a shadow over the holidays which would only lengthen and deepen when Charlotte returned to Roe Head in the New Year.

Charlotte to Ellen; Haworth, 29 December 1836

I am sure you will have thought me very remiss in not sending my promised letter long before now, but I have a sufficient and a very melancholy excuse in an accident that befell our old faithful Tabby a few days after my return home – She was gone out into the village on some errand, when as she was descending the steep street her foot slipped on the ice, and she fell – it was dark and no one saw her mis-chance, till after a time her groans attracted the attention of a passer-by She was lifted up and carried into a druggist's near and after examination it was discovered, that she had completely shattered, and dislocated one leg Unfortunately the fracture could not be set till six o'clock the next morning as no Surgeon was to be had before that time, and she now lies at our house, in a very doubtful and dangerous state. Of course we are all exceedingly distressed at the circumstance for she was like one of our own family – Since the event we have been almost without assistance a person has dropped in now and then to do the drudgery but we have as yet been able to procure no regular Servant, and consequently the whole work of the house as well as the additional duty of nursing Tabby falls on ourselves . . . I would urge your visit yet, I would entreat and press it but the thought comes across me 'Should Tabby die while you are in the house?' I should never forgive myself – No it must not be – and in a thousand ways the Consciousness of that, mortifies and disappoints me most keenly. And I am not the only one who is disappointed, All in the house were looking forward to your visit with eagerness

Chapter Three

1837–9

By 1837, to all outward appearances, Branwell and Charlotte seemed established in their respective careers. Secretly, however, they longed not only to be able to support themselves by their writing but also to achieve literary fame. To that end, they both approached some of the leading literary figures of the day, sending examples of their work for critical appraisal. The hope was, of course, that a favourable opinion might influence a potential publisher. Branwell first approached *Blackwood's Magazine* but, to his ill-concealed frustration, his numerous assaults on the editor failed to achieve any response.

Branwell to the Editor of Blackwood's Magazine*; Haworth, 4 January 1837*

In a former letter, I hinted, that I was in possession of something the design of which, whatever might be its execution, would be superior to that of any <u>series</u> of articles which has yet appeared in Blackwood's Magazine – But, being prose, of course, and of great length, as well as peculiar in character, a description of it by letter would be impracticable. – So surely a journey of 300 miles shall not deter me from a knowledge of myself and a hope of enterance into the open world.

Now, Sir, all I ask of you is – To permit this interview, and, in answer to this letter, to say that you will <u>see</u> me, were it only for one half hour – the fault be mine should you have reason to repent your permission.

Now, is the trouble of writing a single line, to outweigh the certainty of doing good to a fellow Creature and the possibility of doing good to Yourself? – Will you Still so wearisomely refuse me a word, when You can neither know what you refuse or whom you are refusing? Do you think your Magazine so perfect that no addition to its power would be either possible or desirable? – Is it pride which actuates you – or custom – or prejudice? – Be a Man – Sir! and think no more of these things! Write to me – Tell me that you will receive a visit – and rejoicingly will I take upon myself the labour, which, if it suc[c]eed, will be an advantage both to you and me, and, if it fail, will still be an advantage, because I shall then be assured of the impossibility of succeeding.

The usual silence greeted this unwisely belligerent letter, so Branwell turned elsewhere, writing a similarly impassioned plea to one of the poets who had most influenced his own writing. William Wordsworth, however, was disgusted at Branwell's maladroit attempts at flattery (and his verse which was highly imitative of Wordsworth's own) and proved equally unresponsive.

Branwell to the poet William Wordsworth; Haworth, 10 January 1837

Sir,

I most earnestly entreat you to read and pass your judgement upon what I have sent you, because from the day of my birth to this the nineteenth year of my life I have lived among wild and secluded hills where I could neither know what I was or what I could do. – I read for the same reason that I eat or drank, – because it was a real craving of Nature. I wrote on the same principle as I spoke, – out of the impulse and feelings of the mind; – nor could I help it, for what came, came out and there was the end of it, for as to self conceit, that could not receive food from flattery, since to this hour Not half a dozen people in the world know that I have ever penned a line. – But a change has taken place now, Sir, and I am arrived at an age wherein I must do something for myself – the powers I possess must be excercised to a definite end, and as I dont know them myself I must ask of others what they are worth, – yet there is no one here to tell me, and still, if they are worthless, time will henceforth be too precious to be wasted on them.

Do pardon me, Sir, that I have ventured to come before one whose works I have most loved in our Literature and who most has been with me a divinity of the mind – laying before him one of my writings, and asking of him a judgement of its contents, – I must come before some one from whose sentence there is no appeal, and such an one he is who has developed the theory of Poetry as well as its Practice, and both in such a way as to claim a place in the memory of a thousand years to come.

My aim, Sir is to push out into the open world and for this I trust not poetry alone that might launch the vessel but could not bear her on --- Sensible and scientific Prose bold and vigourous efforts in my walk in Life would give a farther title to the notice of the world and then again Poetry ought to brighten and crown that name with glory – but nothing of all this can be even begun without means and as I don't posess these I must in every shape strive to gain them; Surely in this day when there is not a writing poet worth a sixpence the feild must be open if a better man can step forward.

Charlotte was more fortunate. Robert Southey, the Poet Laureate, in an extraordinarily percipient letter, praised the quality of her work but pointed out the inherent dangers in allowing herself to become absorbed in an imaginary world which was more attractive than the one in which she was compelled to live. His comments must have cut Charlotte to the quick, for they described her own struggles at Roe Head as vividly and accurately as if he had actually seen her drifting off into Angrian fantasy and being brought abruptly back to reality by the demands of her pupils. Charlotte was sincerely grateful for his advice which she not only accepted, shelving her literary ambitions and returning to her duties at Roe Head, but also carefully preserved, noting on Southey's letter that it was 'to be kept for ever'.

Robert Southey, the Poet Laureate, to Charlotte; Keswick, March 1837

What you are I can only infer from your letter, wh[ich] appears to be written in sincerity, tho' I may suspect that you have used a fictitious signature. Be that as it may, the letter & the verse bear the same stamp, & I can well understand the state of mind wh[ich] they indicate. What I am, you might have learnt by such of my publications as have come into your hands: but you live in a visionary world & seem to imagine that this is my case also, when you speak of my 'stooping from a throne of light & glory.' Had you happened to be acquainted with me, a little personal knowledge w[oul]d have tempered your enthusiasm. You who so ardently desire 'to be for ever known' as a poetess, might have had your ardour in some degree abated, by seeing a poet in the decline of life, & witnessing the effect wh[ich] age produces upon our hopes & aspirations. Yet I am neither a disappointed man, nor a discontented one, & you w[ould] never have heard from me any chilling sermonisings upon the text that all is vanity.

It is not my advice that you have asked as to the direction of your talents, but my opinion of them. and Yet the opinion may be worth little, & the advice much. You evidently possess & in no inconsiderable degree what Wordsworth calls 'the faculty of Verse.' I am not depreciating it when I say that in these times it is not rare. Many volumes of poems are now published every year without attracting public attention, any one of wh[ich] if it had appeared half a century ago, w[oul]d have obtained a high reputation for its author. Whoever therefore is ambitious of distinction in this way, ought to be prepared for disappointment.

But it is not with a view to distinction that you sh[oul]d cultivate this talent, if you consult your own happiness. I who have made literature my profession, & devoted my life to it, & have never for a moment repented of the deliberate choice, think myself nevertheless bound in duty to caution every young man who applies as an aspirant to me for encouragement & advice, against taking so perilous a course. You will say that a woman has no need of such a caution, there can be no peril in it for her: & in a certain sense this is true. But there is a danger of wh[ich] I w[oul]d with all kindness & all earnestness warn you. The daydreams in wh[ich] you habitually indulge are likely to induce a distempered state of mind, & in proportion as all the 'ordinary uses of the world' seem to you 'flat & unprofitable', you will be unfitted for them, without becoming fitted for anything else. Literature cannot be the business of a woman's life: & it ought not to be. The more she is engaged in her proper duties, the less leisure will she have for it, even as an accomplishment & a recreation. To those duties you have not yet been called, & when you are you will be less eager for celebrity. You will then not seek in imagination for excitement, of wh[ich] the vicissitudes of this life & the anxieties, from wh[ich] you must not hope to be exempted (be your station what it may) will bring with them but too much.

But do not suppose that I disparage the gift wh[ich] you possess, nor that I w[oul]d discourage you from exercising it, I only exhort you so to think of it & so to use it, as to render it conducive to your own permanent good. Write poetry for its own sake, not in a spirit of emulation, & not with a view to celebrity: the less you aim at that, the more likely you will be to deserve, & finally to obtain it. So written, it is wholesome both for the heart & soul. It may be made next to religion the surest means of soothing the mind & elevating it. You may embody in it your best thoughts & your wisest feelings, & in so doing discipline & strengthen them.

Farewell Madam! It is not because I have forgotten that I was once young myself that I write to you in this strain — but because I remember it. You will neither doubt my sincerity, nor my good will. And however ill what has been said may accord with your present views & temper, the longer you live the more reasonable it will appear to you. Tho' I may be but an ungracious adviser, you will allow me therefore to subscribe myself,

With the best wishes for your happiness, here & hereafter,
Your true friend
Robert Southey

Charlotte to Robert Southey; Roe Head, 16 March 1837

Sir,

I cannot rest till I have answered your letter, even though by addressing you a second time I should appear a little intrusive; but I must thank you for the kind, and wise advice you have condescended to give me. I had not ventured to hope for such a reply; so considerate in its tone, so noble in its spirit. I must suppress what I feel, or you will think me foolishly enthusiastic.

At the first perusal of your letter I felt only shame, and regret that I had ever ventured to trouble you with my crude rhapsody   I felt a painful heat rise to my face when – I thought of the quires of paper I had covered with what once gave me so much delight, but which now was only a source of confusion; but after I had thought a little and read it again, and again – the prospect seemed to clear   You do not forbid me to write; you do not say that what I write is utterly destitute of merit; you only warn me against the folly of neglecting real duties, for the sake of imaginative pleasures – of writing for the love of fame & for the selfish excitement of emulation: You kindly allow me to write poetry for its own sake provided I leave undone nothing which I ought to do in order to pursue that single, absorbing exquisite gratification: I am afraid Sir you think me very foolish – I know the first letter I wrote to you was all senseless trash from beginning to end but I am not altogether the idle, dreaming being it would seem to denote. My Father is a Clergyman of limited though competent income, and I am the eldest of his children – He expended quite as much in my education as he could afford in justice to the rest. I thought it therefore my duty when I left school to become a Governess – In that capacity I find enough to occupy my thoughts all day long, and my head and hands too, without having a moment's time for one dream of the imagination. In the evenings I confess I do think but I never trouble any one else with my thoughts   I carefully avoid every appearance of pre-occupation and eccentricity – which might lead those I live amongst to suspect the nature of my pursuits. Following my Father's advice who from my childhood has counselled me just in the wise, and kindly tone of your letter; I have endeavoured not only attentively to observe all the duties a woman ought to fulfil but to feel deeply interested in them – I don't always succeed for sometimes when I am teaching, and sewing I'd far rather be reading or writing – but I try to deny myself – and my father's approbation has hitherto amply rewarded me for the privation.

Once more allow me to thank you, with sincere gratitude. I trust I shall never more feel ambitious to see my name in print – if the wish should rise I'll look at Southey's autograph and suppress it: It is honour enough for me that I have written to him and received an answer. That letter is consecrated; no one shall ever see it but

Papa and my brother and Sisters – Again I thank you – this incident I suppose will be renewed no more. if I live to be an old woman I shall remember it thirty years hence as a bright dream – The signature which you suspected of being fictitious is my real name, again therefore I must sign myself

Charlotte Brontë

Pray Sir, excuse me for writing to you a second time; I could not help writing – partly to tell you how thankful I am for your kindness and partly to let you know that your advice shall not be wasted; however sorrowfully and reluctantly it may be at first followed. C.B–

Many years later, when she was herself a famous authoress, Charlotte was approached by Robert Southey's son, who wanted to include this correspondence in an edition of his late father's letters he was preparing for publication. Though too embarrassed by her own youthful enthusiasm to allow herself to be identified, Charlotte willingly gave her permission and, in doing so, acknowledged the debt of gratitude she owed to the former Poet Laureate.

★★*Charlotte to the Reverend Charles Cuthbert Southey; Haworth, 26 August 1850*

Haworth. Augt 26th/50

Dear Sir

Your note would have been sooner answered, had not absence from home prevented me from referring to the two letters to which it alludes, and I wished to look at them once more before deciding on their publication.

I have now read them and feel that – truly wise and kind as they are – they ought to be published; I must, however, beg you to suppress my name and likewise to omit the passage which I have marked with a pencil; my own letter to Mr Southey I do not remember but the passage quoted there seems to me now somewhat silly, and I would rather it was not preserved.

When I wrote to your Father I was very young; I needed the

benevolent yet stern advice he gives me, and fortunately I had just sense enough to feel its value and to resolve on its adoption. At this moment I am grateful to his memory for the well-timed check received in my girlhood at his hand.

May I add that the perusal of his Life and Correspondence arranged by yourself has much deepened the esteem and admiration with which I previously regarded him. You will kindly return the letter enclosed, for it is very precious to me.

I am, my dear Sir
Yours sincerely
C Brontë

The Revd C.C.Southey.

While Charlotte struggled to reconcile duty and inclination at Roe Head, her father laboured unremittingly at Haworth. His intimate knowledge of the problems of the wool trade, which alternated wildly between periods of boom and bust, led him to take a prominent public role in opposing the harsh new Poor Laws which did not distinguish between the causes of poverty and made relief dependent on committal to the workhouse. As one of the few men in the township entitled to vote, he also played an important part in the West Riding Parliamentary election which brought Lord Morpeth to Haworth.

★*Patrick to the Editor of the* Leeds Intelligencer*; Haworth, 17 April 1837*

A law has lately been passed called the Poor Law Amendment Bill; a greater misnomer I never read or heard. It is a monster of iniquity, a horrid and cruel deformity, even in regard to what before was no very shapely or symmetrical representation. I know that a committee is sitting to <u>amend</u> the bill – but let me tell you, my dear friends, that it <u>cannot be amended; it must be repealed altogether</u> . . . What, then, my friends are we to do under these circumstances? Why, verily, I see no plan better for us than that adopted by the Apostles, namely, <u>to obey God, rather than man. We will not</u> therefore submit to go to their <u>bastiles. We will not live</u> on their water gruel, and on their two ounces of cheese, and their fourteen ounces of bread per day. We will not suffer ourselves to be chained by their three tyrannical commissioners; and we never will endure the idea, of men rolling in affluence and luxury, prescribing to us the most extreme line which can keep soul and body together. We have religion, reason, justice and humanity, on our side, and by these we are determined to stand or fall . . . Then let me request you to do your duty – petition, remonstrate, and resist powerfully but legally, and God, the father and friend of the poor, will crown all your efforts with success.

Patrick to Mrs Taylor of Stanbury; Haworth, 19 July 1837

Haworth,
July 19th 1837

Dear Madam,

As Lord Morpeth is coming to Haworth, tomorrow evening at four O'Clock and Miss Branwell and my Children, wish to see and hear him – and it is likely that there will be a good deal of drunkness, and confusion on the roads, I must request that you will excuse us, for not accepting your kind invitation – On any other opportunity when most convenient to yourself, My Children will drink tea with you, previously to their going to school – Miss Branwell and my Children, join with me in kind regards to you and your family. I remain, Dear Madam,

Yours, truly,
P. Brontē

Benjamin Binns, son of the Haworth tailor, interviewed in the Bradford Observer, *17 February 1894*

Elections at Haworth in those days were very violent affairs. The voters, it is true, were not numerous, and they had to go to York to record their suffrages. The Tories, or 'Blues,' were very few in number, and dared hardly show their faces. On this occasion the platforms for the two parties were erected nearly opposite each other, the Liberals being located against a laithe which stood on the now open space in front of the Black Bull Inn. The vicar and his son Branwell were on the 'Blue' platform. The former took a great interest in political matters, often writing letters to the newspapers. The Liberals were there in great numbers, Robert Pickles, a noted politician, having brought a considerable body from the outskirts. When Mr Brontë began to question Lord Morpeth a regular 'hulla-bulloo' was set up. Branwell in his impetuous way, rushed to the front crying, 'If you won't let my father speak, you shan't speak.' After that election Branwell's effigy, bearing a herring in one hand and a potato in the other, in allusion to his nationality, was carried through the main street of Haworth and afterwards burned. Branwell witnessed the procession from a shop in the village.

Election fever may have seized Haworth and the Brontë men, but for Emily, happily cocooned in her fantasy world, these events were unworthy of notice. Her diary paper, written during Charlotte and Anne's school holiday, reveals the extent to which the imaginary world had already assumed a greater importance in the eighteen-year-old Emily's mind, at least, than the real one.

Emily, diary paper; Haworth, 26 June 1837

Monday evening June 26 1837

A bit past 4 o'Clock Charolotte working in Aunts room Branwell reading Eugene Aram to her Anne and I writing in the drawing room – Anne a poem beginning Fair was the Evening and brightly the Sun – I Agustus – Almedas life 1st vol – 4th page from the last a fine rather coolish thin grey cloudy but Sunny day Aunt working in the little Room papa – gone out. Tabby in the Kitchin – the Emperors and Empreses of Gondal and Gaaldine preparing to depart from Gaaldine to Gondal to prepare for the coranation which will be on the 12th of July Queen Victoria ascended the throne this month Northangerland in Monceys Isle – Zamorna at Eversham. all tight and right in which condition it is to be hoped we shall all be on this day 4 years at which time Charolotte will be 25 and 2 months – Branwell just 24 it being his birthday – myself 22 and 10

months and a peice Anne 21 and nearly a half   I wonder where we
shall be and how we shall be and what kind of a day it will be then
let us hope for the best
   Emily Jane Brontë – Anne Brontë

I guess that this day 4 years we shall all be in this drawing room
comfortable   I hope it may be so   Anne guesses we shall all be gone
somewhere together comfortable   We hope it may be either

Aunt. come Emily   Its past 4 o'Clock.
Emily Yes Aunt
Anne well do you intend to write in the evening
Emily well what think you
(we agreed to go out 1st to make sure if we get into a humor   we
may Stay [out?])

At the end of 1837 there was a crisis at Roe Head. Anne fell ill and
Charlotte, thinking that Miss Wooler was treating the matter too lightly,
had a blazing row with her headmistress which resulted in the Brontës
returning home. Charlotte may have been overwrought, but the testimony
of the Reverend James La Trobe, a Moravian minister who visited her
sister during her illness, suggests that she had not underestimated the
seriousness of Anne's complaint. Like Charlotte too, he recognized that
Anne was suffering from a crisis of faith which had added to the severity
of her illness. Interestingly, he attributed this to the underlying religious
tensions at the school, suggesting that the Calvinist doctrines which had
deeply troubled both the sisters were disseminated at Roe Head.

*Reverend James La Trobe, minister of the Moravian Church at Mirfield,
to William Scruton; c. 1898*

She was suffering from a severe attack of gastric fever which brought
her very low, and her voice was only a whisper; her life hung on a
slender thread. She soon got over the shyness natural on seeing a
perfect stranger. The words of love, from Jesus, opened her ear to
my words, and she was very grateful for my visits. I found her well
acquainted with the main truths of the Bible respecting our salvation,
but seeing them more through the law than the gospel, more as a

requirement from God than His gift in His Son, but her heart opened to the sweet views of salvation, pardon, and peace in the blood of Christ, and she accepted His welcome to the weary and heavy laden sinner, conscious more of her not loving the Lord her God than of acts of enmity to Him, and, had she died then, I should have counted her His redeemed and ransomed child.

Charlotte to Ellen; Haworth, 4 January 1838

You were right in your conjectures respecting the cause of my sudden departure – Anne continued – wretchedly ill – neither the pain nor the difficulty of breathing left her – and how could I feel otherwise than very miserable? I looked upon her case in a different light to what I could wish or expect any uninterested person to view it in – Miss Wooler thought me a fool – and – by way of proving her opinion treated me with marked coldness – we came to a little eclairsissement one evening – I told her one or two rather plain truths – which set her a crying – and the next day unknown to me she wrote to Papa – telling him that I had reproached her – bitterly – taken her severely to task &c. &c. -- Papa sent for us the day after he had received her letter – Meantime I had formed a firm resolution – to quit Miss Wooler and her concerns for ever – but just before I went away she took me into her room – and giving way to her feelings which in general she restrains far too rigidly – gave me to understand that in spite of her cold repulsive manners She had a considerable regard for me and would be very sorry to part with me – If any body likes me I can't help liking them – and remembering that she had in general been very kind to me – I gave in and said I – would come back if she wished me – so – we're settled again for the present – but I am not satisfied I should have respected her far more if she had turned me out of doors instead of crying for two days and two nights together – I was in a regular passion my 'warm temper' quite got the better of me – Of which I don't boast for it was a weakness – nor am I ashamed of it for I had reason to be angry – Anne is now much better – though she still requires a great deal of care – however I am relieved from my worst fears respecting her –

Safely back at home and supported by the more benign religion of her father, Anne quickly recovered, but did not return to school. Charlotte, however, was prevailed upon to mend her quarrel with Miss Wooler who, over the Christmas holidays of 1837–8, had moved from Roe Head to a less congenial spot a short distance away at Dewsbury Moor. For just a year, Charlotte struggled to retain her post, fighting a losing battle against a depression of spirits and consequent ill-health, which she termed hypochondria. In the summer, she almost gave up, returning home before the end of term, but a long holiday and a visit from the lively Taylor sisters restored her and the autumn found her back at her post again.

Charlotte to Ellen; Haworth, 9 June 1838

You will be surprised when you see the date of this letter. I ought to be at Dewsbury-Moor – you know – but I stayed as long as I was able and at length I neither could nor dared stay any longer. My health and spirits had utterly failed me and the medical man whom I consulted enjoined me if I valued my life to go home. So home I went, the change has at once roused and soothed me – and I am now I trust fairly in the way to be myself again – A calm and even mind like yours Ellen cannot conceive the feelings of the shattered wretch who is now writing to you.when after weeks of mental and bodily anguish not to be described something like tranquillity and ease began to dawn again. I will not enlarge on the subject to me every recollection of the past half year is painful – to you it cannot be pleasant – Mary Taylor is far from well – I have watched her narrowly during her visit to us – her lively spirits and bright colour might delude you into a belief that all was well – but she breathes short, has a pain in her chest, and frequent flushings of fever. I cannot tell you what agony these symptoms give me. they remind me so strongly of my two sisters. whom no power of medicine could save. I trust she may recover; her lungs certainly are not ulcerated yet, she has no cough, no pain in the side.and perhaps this hectic fever may be only the temporary effects of a severe winter and a late Spring on a delicate constitution – Martha is now very well – she has kept in a constant flow of good-humour during her stay here and has consequently been very fascinating . . . They are making such a noise about me I cannot write any more. Mary is playing on the piano. Martha is chattering as fast as her little tongue can run and Branwell is standing before her laughing at her vivacity.

Charlotte to Ellen; Dewsbury Moor, 24 August 1838

As you will perceive by the date of this letter I am again at Dewsbury-Moor engaged in the old business teach – teach – teach. Miss Eliza Wooler and Mrs Wooler are coming here next Christmas Miss Wooler will then relinquish the school in favour of her Sister Eliza – but I am happy to say the worthy dame will continue to reside in the house. with all her faults I should be sorry indeed to part with her.

<u>When will you come home?</u> Make haste you have been at Bath long enough for all purposes – by this time you have acquired polish enough I am sure. if the varnish is laid on much thicker I am afraid the good wood underneath will be quite concealed and your old Yorkshire friends won't stand that – <u>come</u> – <u>come</u> I am getting really tired of your absence. Saturday after Saturday comes round and I can have no hope of hearing your knock at the door and then being told that 'Miss Ellen Nussey is come.' O dear in this monotonous life of mine that was a pleasant event.

Charlotte's determination to stay at her post may have been strengthened by observing the difficulties facing her brother and sisters in their attempts to find congenial employment. Surprisingly, given the amount of time and money spent in training Branwell as a professional portrait painter, his choice of career seems to have been very much in doubt.

★★*Patrick to John Driver, Esquire, of Liverpool; Haworth,*
23 February 1838

Haworth – near
Bradford, Yorkshire,
Feby.23d.1838.

Dear Sir,

You are aware, that I have been looking out, during some time, in order to procure a respectable situation, for my Son

Branwell. As yet, however, I have not succeeded, according to my wishes, or his. I once thought that he might get into the Mercantile line – but there seem to be many and great difficulties in reference to this. I then, turned my attention to a University Education, but this would require great expense, and four or five years from hence, ere he could, in a pecuniary way, do Any thing for himself. These, are serious, and important considerations, which demand great precaution. I am now, of opinion, that it might be, the most prudent of all plans, under all the circumstances of the case, to endeavour to procure for him, a Situation, as Clerk, in a Bank. This would be respectable, and in time, should he conduct himself well, sufficiently lucrative, and might ultimately lead, to something more desirable. I have made no attempt – either in Halifax, Bradford, or Leeds, since, I think it would be to his advantage to go farther from home, And to see a little more of the World. London, Liverpool, or Manchester, would Answer better, on many accounts, and would open a wider field, for talent, and suitable connexions. On these grounds, I have taken the liberty of applying to You, as the most likely of any Gentleman, I know – requesting, that you would be so good, as to do what you can, Amongst your Friends, at home, and abroad in order to procure an opening for him, as Clerk in some Respectable Bank. I know not what the usual terms, are, on which a young man enters upon such a line of life, but I have heard, that they are comparatively easy, as far as money matters, are concerned. Trusting, that you will kindly excuse, this trouble, with our joint regards, to You and Your Brother, I remain, Dear Sir,

> Yours, very respectfully,
> And truly,
> P. Bronte.

No clerkship in a bank was forthcoming from Mr Driver, so it was as a last resort, rather than the culmination of all his training, that in the summer of 1838 Branwell set himself up as a professional portrait painter in a studio in Bradford and offered his services to potential patrons. The venture proved unsuccessful; Branwell was competing against not only

long-established artists but also a new and much cheaper form of portraiture, the daguerreotype photograph. By the following February, he
was back home in Haworth, his artistic career finally abandoned for
good. He was not alone in his short-lived attempt to earn a living. In
the autumn of 1838, Emily, now twenty years old, left home for her
first post.

Charlotte to Ellen; Dewsbury Moor, 2 October 1838

My Sister Emily is gone into a Situation as teacher in a large school
of near forty pupils near Halifax. I have had one letter from her since
her departure   it gives an appalling account of her duties – Hard
labour from six in the morning until near eleven at night. with only
one half hour of exercise between – this is slavery   I fear she will
never stand it –

Emily, 'A little while'; Law Hill, 4 December 1838

> A little while, a little while
> The noisy crowd are barred away;
> And I can sing and I can smile –
> A little while I've holyday!
>
> Where wilt thou go my harassed heart?
> Full many a land invites thee now;
> And places near, and far apart
> Have rest for thee, my weary brow –
>
> There is a spot mid barren hills
> Where winter howls and driving rain
> But if the dreary tempest chills
> There is a light that warms again
>
> The house is old, the trees are bare
> And moonless bends the misty dome
> But what on earth is half so dear –
> So longed for as the hearth of home?

The mute bird sitting on the stone,
The dank moss dripping from the wall,
The garden-walk with weeds o'e'r-grown
I love them – how I love them all!

Shall I go there? or shall I seek
Another clime, another sky –
Where tongues familiar music speak
In accents dear to memory?

Yes, as I mused, the naked room,
The flickering firelight died away
And from the midst of cheerless gloom
I passed to bright, unclouded day –

A little and a lone green lane
That opened on a common wide
A distant, dreamy, dim blue chain
Of mountains circling every side –

A heaven so clear, an earth so calm,
So sweet, so soft, so hushed an air
And, deepening still the dream like charm,
Wild moor-sheep feeding everywhere –

That was the scene – I knew it well
I knew the path-ways far and near
That winding o'er each billowy swell –
Marked out the tracks of wandering deer

Could I have lingered but an hour
It well had paid a week of toil
But truth has banished fancy's power
I hear my dungeon bars recoil –

Even as I stood with raptured eye
Absorbed in bliss so deep and dear
My hour of rest had fleeted by
And given me back to weary care

Only six months after taking up her post at Law Hill, Emily resigned and returned home to Haworth, telling her pupils that she preferred the house dog to any of them. All the family were now reunited at Haworth, for Charlotte too had come to the end of her endurance and left Miss Wooler's school again, this time for good.

Charlotte to Ellen; Haworth, 20 January 1839

My <u>dear</u>, <u>kind</u> Ellen

I can hardly help laughing when I reckon up the number of urgent invitations I have received from you during the last three months – had I accepted all, or even half of them – the Birstallians would certainly have concluded that I had come to make Brookroyd my permanent residence – When you set your mind upon a thing you have a peculiar way of hedging one in with a circle of dilemmas so that they hardly know how to refuse you – however I shall take a running leap and clear them all – Frankly my dear Ellen I <u>cannot come</u> – Reflect for yourself a moment – do you see nothing absurd in the idea of a person coming again into a neighbourhood within a month after they have taken a solemn and formal leave of all their acquaintance –?

Though Patrick seems to have been remarkably relaxed about the fact that he now had four adult children unemployed and living at home, the situation could not continue for long; his income simply could not support them all. A new and entirely unexpected avenue of escape opened for Charlotte when, in March 1839, her friend Ellen Nussey's brother, Henry, who had recently settled in a comfortable new curacy at Donnington in Sussex, wrote to her with a proposal of marriage.

Charlotte to the Reverend Henry Nussey, brother of her friend, Ellen; Haworth, 5 March 1839

Before answering your letter, I might have spent a long time in consideration of its subject; but as from the first moment of its reception and perusal I determined on which course to pursue, it seemed to me that delay was wholly unnecessary.

You are aware that I have many reasons to feel grateful to your family, that I have peculiar reasons for affection towards one at least of your Sisters, and also that I highly esteem yourself. do not therefore accuse me of wrong motives when I say that my answer to your proposal must be a <u>decided negative</u>. In forming this decision – I trust I have listened to the dictates of conscience more than to those [of] inclination; I have no personal repugnance to the idea of a union with you – but I feel convinced that mine is not the sort of disposition calculated to form the happiness of a man like you. It has always been my habit to study the characters of those amongst whom I chance to be thrown, and I think I know yours and can imagine what description of woman would suit you for a wife. Her character should not be too marked, ardent and original – her temper should be mild, her piety undoubted, her [spirits] even and cheerful, and her '<u>personal attractions</u>' sufficient to please your eye and gratify your just pride. As for me you do not know me, I am not the serious, grave, cool-headed individual you suppose – you would think me romantic and [eccentric – you would] say I was satirical and [severe – however I scorn] deceit and I will never for the sake of attaining the distinction of matrimony and escaping the stigma of an old maid take a worthy man whom I am conscious I cannot render happy.

Charlotte to Ellen; Haworth, 12 March 1839

Now my dear Ellen there were in this proposal some things that might have proved a strong temptation – I thought if I were to marry so, Ellen could live with me and how happy I should be. but again I asked myself two questions – Do I love Henry Nussey as much as a woman ought to love the man her husband? Am I the person best qualified to make him happy? – Alas Ellen my Conscience answered '<u>no</u>' to both these questions. I felt that though I esteemed Henry – though I had a kindly leaning towards him because he is an amiable – well-disposed man yet I had not, and never could have that intense attachment which would make me willing to die for him – and if ever I marry it must be in that light of adoration that I will regard my Husband   ten to one I shall never have the chance again but n'importe. Moreover I was aware that Henry knew so little of me he could hardly be conscious to whom he was writing – why it would startle him to see me in my natural home-character he would think I was a wild, romantic enthusiast indeed – I could not sit all day long making a grave face before my husband – I would laugh and satirize and say whatever came into my head first – and if he were a clever man & loved me the whole world weighed in the balance against his smallest wish should be as light as air –

With no other option now open, the Brontës had to face the prospect of securing new employment. Anne, the youngest at nineteen, was the first to set out, taking a post as a private governess to the Ingham family of Blake Hall, near her old school at Roe Head. She was soon followed by Charlotte who decided to try a similar post with the Sidgwicks at Stonegappe, in Lothersdale, in the vain hope that the task of managing two or three young children might prove more congenial than teaching classes of teenage girls. They were both to be swiftly disillusioned.

Charlotte to Ellen; Haworth, 15 April 1839

I could not very well write to you in the week you requested as about that time we were very busy in preparing for Anne's departure – poor child! She left us last Monday no one went with her – it was her own wish that she might be allowed to go alone – as she thought she could manage better and summon more courage if thrown entirely upon her own resources. We have had one letter from her since she went – she expresses herself very well satisfied – and says that Mrs Ingham is extremely kind, the two eldest children alone are under her care, the rest are confined to the nursery – with which and its occupants she has nothing to do. both her pupils are desperate little dunces – neither of them can read and sometimes they even profess a profound ignorance of their alphabet. the worst of it is the little monkies are excessively indulged and she is not empowered to inflict any punishment she is requested when they misbehave themselves to inform their Mamma – which she says is utterly out of the question as in that case she might be making complaints from morning till night – 'So she alternately scolds, coaxes and threatens – sticks always to her first word and gets on as well as she can' – I hope she'll do, you would be astonished to see what a sensible, clever letter she writes – it is only the talking part, that I fear – but I do seriously apprehend that Mrs Ingham will sometimes consider that she has a natural impediment of speech for my own part I am as yet 'wanting a situation – like a housemaid out of place' – by the bye Ellen I've lately discovered that I've quite a talent for cleaning – sweeping up hearths dusting rooms – making beds &c. so if everything else fails – I can turn my hand to that – if anybody will give me good wages, for little labour. I won't be a cook – I hate cooking – I won't be a nursery-maid – nor a lady's-maid far less a lady's companion – or a mantua-maker – or a straw-bonnet maker or a taker-in of plain-work – I will be nothing but a house-maid.

Charlotte to Emily; Stonegappe, 8 June 1839

I have striven hard to be pleased with my new situation. The country, the house, and the grounds are, as I have said, divine. But, alack-a-day! there is such a thing as seeing all beautiful around you – pleasant woods, winding white paths, green lawns, and blue sunshiny sky – and not having a free moment or a free thought left to enjoy them in. The children are constantly with me, and more riotous, perverse, unmanageable cubs never grew. As for correcting them, I soon quickly found that was entirely out of the question: they are to do as they like. A complaint to Mrs Sidgwick brings only black looks upon oneself, and unjust, partial excuses to screen the children. I have tried that plan once. It succeeded so notably that I shall try it no more. I said in my last letter that Mrs Sidgwick did not know me. I now begin to find that she does not intend to know me, that she cares nothing in the world about me except to contrive how the greatest possible quantity of labour may be squeezed out of me, and to that end she overwhelms me with oceans of needlework, yards of cambric to hem, muslin nightcaps to make, and, above all things, dolls to dress. I do not think she likes me at all, because I can't help being shy in such an entirely novel scene, surrounded as I have hitherto been by strange and constantly changing faces. I used to think I should like to be in the stir of grand folks' society but I have had enough of it – it is dreary work to look on and listen. I see now more clearly than I have ever done before that a private governess has no existence, is not considered as a living and rational being except as connected with the wearisome duties she has to fulfil. While she is teaching the children, working for them, amusing them, it is all right. If she steals a moment for herself she is a nuisance. Nevertheless, Mrs Sidgwick is universally considered an amiable woman. Her manners are fussily affable. She talks a great deal, but as it seems to me not much to the purpose. Perhaps I may like her better after a while. At present I have no call to her. Mr Sidgwick is in my opinion a hundred times better – less profession, less bustling condescension, but a far kinder heart. It is very seldom that he speaks to me, but when he does I always feel happier and more settled for some minutes after. He never asks me to wipe the children's smutty noses or tie their shoes or fetch their pinafores or set them a chair. One of the pleasantest afternoons I have spent here – indeed, the only one at all pleasant – was when Mr Sidgwick walked out with his children, and I had orders to follow a little behind. As he strolled on through his fields with his magnificent Newfoundland dog at his side, he looked very like what a frank, wealthy, Conservative gentleman ought to be. He spoke freely and unaffectedly to the people he met, and though he indulged his children and allowed them to tease himself far too much, he would not suffer them grossly to insult others.

Charlotte to Ellen; Swarcliffe, 30 June 1839

I am writing a letter to you with pencil because I cannot just now procure ink without going into the drawing-room – where I do not wish to go. I only received your letter yesterday: for we are not now residing at Stonegappe – but at Swarcliffe a summer residence of Mr Greenwood's Mrs Sidgwick's father. it is near Harrogate – & Ripon – a beautiful place in a beautiful country – rich and agricultural – . . . I must not bother you too much with my sorrows Ellen, of which I fear you have heard an exaggerated account – if you were near me perhaps I might be tempted to tell you all – to grow egotistical and pour out the long history of a Private Governesse's trials and crosses in her first Situation – As it is I will only ask you to imagine the miseries of a reserved wretch like me – thrown at once into the midst of a large Family – proud as peacocks & wealthy as Jews – at a time when they were particularly gay – when the house was filled with Company – all Strangers people whose faces I had never seen before – in this state of things having the charge given me of a set of pampered spoilt & turbulent children – whom I was expected constantly to amuse as well as instruct – I soon found that the constant demand on my stock of animal spirits reduced them to the lowest state of exhaustion – at times I felt and I suppose seemed depressed – to my astonishment I was taken to task on the subject by Mrs Sidgwick with a stern[n]ess of manner & a harshness of language scarcely credible – like a fool I cried most bitterly – I could not help it – my spirits quite failed me at first. I thought I had done my best – strained every nerve to please her – and to be treated in that way merely because I was shy – and sometimes melancholy was too bad. at first I was for giving all up and going home – But after a little reflection I determined – to summon what energy I had and to weather the Storm – I said to myself I have never yet quitted a place without gaining a friend – Adversity is a good school – the Poor are born to labour and the Dependent to endure. I resolved to be patient – to command my feelings and to take what came – the ordeal I reflected would not last many weeks – and I trusted it would do me good – I recollected the fable of the Willow and the Oak – I bent quietly and I trust now the Storm is blowing over me –

Charlotte to Emily; Swarcliffe, July 1839

Mine bonnie love,

I was as glad of your letter as tongue can express: it is a real, genuine pleasure to hear from home; a thing to be saved till bedtime, when one has a moment's quiet and rest to enjoy it thoroughly. Write whenever you can. I could like to be at home. I could like to work in a mill, I could like to feel mental liberty. I could like this weight of restraint to be taken off. But the holidays will come. Corragio.

Charlotte's post was only temporary and, by the middle of July, she was back at home. Her plans to go on a brief holiday – the first she had ever taken away from home – with Ellen were initially frustrated by Aunt Branwell's fears about the propriety of allowing two young women to travel alone. A second, but equally unexpected, proposal of marriage made by the Reverend David Pryce to Charlotte after only a single afternoon's acquaintance must have reinforced her aunt's objections. Eventually, however, Ellen carried the day and the friends spent three weeks together at Bridlington on the east coast of Yorkshire, where Charlotte was enraptured by her first sight of the sea.

Charlotte to Ellen; Haworth, 26 July 1839

Your proposal has almost driven me 'clean daft' – if you don't understand that ladylike expression you must ask me what it means when I see you – the fact is an excursion with you anywhere – whether to Cleethorpes or Canada just by ourselves – without any ninnies to annoy us – would be to me most delightful – I should indeed like to go – but I can't get leave of absence for longer than a week and I'm afraid that wouldn't suit you – must I then give it up entirely? I feel as if I could not – I never had such a chance of enjoyment before ... O Ellen rich people seem to have many pleasures – at their command which we are debarred from –

Charlotte to Ellen; Haworth, 4 August 1839

I have an odd circumstance to relate to you   prepare for a hearty laugh – the other day – Mr Hodgson – Papa's former Curate – now a Vicar came over to spend the day – with us – bringing with him his own Curate. The latter Gentleman by name Mr Price is a young Irish Clergyman – fresh from Dublin University – it was the first time we had any of us seen him, but however after the manner of his Countrymen he soon made himself at home his character quickly appeared in his conversation – witty – lively, ardent – clever too – but deficient in the dignity & discretion of an Englishman   at home you know Ellen I talk with ease and am never shy – never weighed down & oppressed by that miserable mauvaise honte which torments

& constrains me elsewhere – so I conversed with this Irishman & laughed at his jests – & though I saw faults in his character excused them because of the amusement his originality afforded – I cooled a little indeed & drew in towards the latter part of the evening – because he began to season his conversation with something of Hibernian flattery which I did not quite relish. however they went away and no more was thought about them.

A few days after I got a letter the direction of which puzzled me it being in a hand I was not accustomed to see – evidently it was neither from you nor Mary Taylor, my only Correspondents – having opened & read it it proved to be a declaration of attachment – & proposal of Matrimony – expressed in the ardent language of the sapient young Irishman! well thought I – I've heard of love at first sight but this beats all. I leave you to guess what my answer would be – convinced that you will not do me the injustice of guessing wrong.

When we meet I'll show you the letter. I hope you are laughing heartily. this is not like one of my adventures is it? it more nearly resembles Martha Taylor's – I'm certainly doomed to be an old maid Ellen – I can't expect another chance – never mind I made up my mind to that fate ever since I was twelve years old.

Charlotte to Ellen; Haworth, 14 August 1839

I have in vain packed my box – and prepared everything for our anticipated journey   it so happens that I can get no conveyance this week nor the next. The only gig let out to hire in Haworth is at Harrogate & likely to remain there for aught I can hear – Papa decidedly objects to my going by the coach and walking to Birstal[l] though I am sure I could manage it. Aunt exclaims against the weather and the roads and the four winds of Heaven. so I'm in a fix and what is worse so are <u>You</u> . . . The elders of the House have never cordially acquiesced in the measure, & now that impediments seem to start up at every step opposition grows more open – Papa indeed would willingly indulge me, but this very kindness of his makes me doubt whether I ought to draw upon it – & though I could battle out Aunt's dis-content I yield to Papa's indulgence –

He does not say so but I know he would rather I stayed at home – Aunt means well too I daresay but I am provoked that she reserved the expression of her decided dis-approval till all was settled between you and myself.

Charlotte to Ellen; Haworth, 24 October 1839

Have you forgot the Sea by this time Ellen? is it grown dim in your mind? or you can still see it dark blue and green and foam-white and hear it – roaring roughly when the wind is high or rushing softly when it is calm? How is your health – have good effects resulted from the change? I am as well as need be, and very fat.

Charlotte to the Reverend Henry Nussey; Haworth, 28 October 1839

I enjoyed my late excursion with Ellen with the greater zest because such pleasures have not often chanced to fall in my way – I will not tell you what I thought of the Sea – because I should fall into my besetting sin of enthusiasm. I may however say that its glorious changes – its ebb and flow – the sound of its restless waves – formed a subject for contemplation that never wearied either the eye the ear or the mind.

Christmas found the family reunited once more at Haworth. Though Anne had been dismissed from Blake Hall and Tabby Aykroyd, the much loved servant, was to leave them temporarily because of ill health, the Brontës ended the year in cheerful mood.

Charlotte to Ellen; Haworth, 21 December 1839

We are at present and have been during the last month rather busy as for that space of time we have been without a Servant except a little girl to run errands   poor Tabby – became so lame from a large ulcer in her leg that she was at length obliged to leave us – She is residing with her Sister in a little house of her own, which she bought with her savings a year or two since. She is very comfortable and wants nothing: as she is near we see her very often – In the meantime Emily and I are sufficiently busy as you may suppose – I manage the ironing and keep the rooms clean – Emily does the baking and attends to the Kitchen – We are such odd animals that we prefer this mode of contrivance to having a new face among us. Besides we do not despair of Tabby's return and she shall not be supplanted by a stranger in her absence. I excited Aunt's wrath very much by burning the clothes the first time I attempted to Iron but I do better now. Human feelings are queer things – I am much happier – black-leading the stoves – making the beds and sweeping the floors at home, than I should be living like a fine lady anywhere else.

Chapter Four

1840–42

The new year which ushered in a new decade did not begin on an auspicious note. Through Ellen Nussey, the Brontës learnt of the death of fifteen-year-old Ann Cook, who had been Charlotte's pupil at Roe Head. This was a particular blow for Anne Brontë, as the girl had been and was to be the only friend she ever made outside her own family.

Charlotte to Ellen; Haworth, 12 January 1840

Your letter, which I received this morning, was one of painful interest. Anne C[ook] it seems, is <u>dead</u>; when I saw her last, she was a young, beautiful, and happy girl; and now 'life's fitful fever' is over with her, and she 'sleeps well.' I shall never see her again. It is a sorrowful thought; for she was a warm-hearted, affectionate being, and I cared for her. Wherever I seek for her now in this world, she cannot be found, no more than a flower or a leaf, which withered twenty years ago. A bereavement of this kind gives one a glimpse of the feeling those must have, who have seen all drop round them, friend after friend, and are left to end their pilgrimage alone. But tears are fruitless and I try not to repine.

Charlotte may not have repined, but she was in low spirits, not least because she knew that she must make an effort to find a new situation. This was not an attractive prospect and when Ellen sought her advice about whether she too should go out as a governess, Charlotte made no effort to disguise her feelings on the subject.

Charlotte to Ellen; Haworth, 24 January 1840

I know not whether to encourage you in your plan of going out or not – your health seems to me the great obstacle – if you could obtain a Situation like Mary Brooke you might do very well – But you could never live in an unruly, violent family of modern children such for instance as those at Blake Hall – Anne is not to return – Mrs Ingham is a placid mild woman – but as for the children it was one struggle of life-wearing exertion to keep them in anything like decent order.

I am miserable when I allow myself to dwell on the necessity of spending my life as a Governess. The chief requisite for that station seems to me to be the power of taking things easily as they come and of making oneself comfortable and at home wherever we may chance to be – qualities in which all our family are singularly deficient. I know I cannot live with a person like Mrs Sidgwick – but I hope all women are not like her – and my motto is 'Try again.'

While Charlotte and Anne reluctantly sought new employment as governesses, Branwell too embarked upon the teaching profession. On the last day of 1839, he set out for Broughton-in-Furness, on the fringes of the Lake District, where he had secured an appointment as private tutor to the two sons of Robert Postlethwaite.

Charlotte to Ellen; Haworth, 28 December 1839

How he will like, or settle remains yet to be seen, at present he is full of Hope and resolution. I who know his variable nature, and his strong turn for active life, dare not be too sanguine.

Branwell to John Brown, sexton of Haworth; Broughton-in-Furness,
13 March 1840

Old Knave of Trumps,

Don't think I have forgotten you, though I have delayed so long in writing to you. It was my purpose to send you a yarn as soon as I could find materials to spin one with, and it is only just now that

I have had time to turn myself round and know where I am. If you saw me now, you would not know me, and you would laugh to hear the character people give me. Oh, the falsehood and hypocrisy of this world! I am fixed in a little retired town by the sea-shore, among wild woody hills that rise round me – huge, rocky, and capped with clouds. My employer is a retired county magistrate, a large landowner, and of a right hearty and generous disposition. His wife is a quiet, silent, and amiable woman, and his sons are two fine, spirited lads. My landlord is a respectable surgeon, and six days out of seven is as drunk as a lord! His wife is a bustling, chattering, kind-hearted soul; and his daughter! – oh! death and damnation! Well, what am I? That is, what do they think I am? A most calm, sedate, sober, abstemious, patient, mild-hearted, virtuous, gentlemanly philosopher, – the picture of good works, and the treasure-house of righteous thoughts – Cards are shuffled under the tablecloth, glasses are thrust into the cupboard, if I enter the room. I take neither spirits, wine, nor malt liquors, I dress in black and smile like a saint or martyr. Everybody says, 'What a good young Gentleman is Mr Postlethwaites tutor!' This is fact, as I am a living soul and right comfortably do I laugh at them. I mean to continue in their good opinion.

In Branwell's absence, life at Haworth was enlivened by the presence of Patrick's new curate, the Reverend William Weightman. A gentle, kind and lively young man, good-looking and pleasant mannered, he rapidly became a family favourite and was on intimate terms with the Parsonage household when Ellen visited in the spring of 1840. The girls nick-named him Miss Celia Amelia, in a transparent attempt to play down his sexual attraction, but the atmosphere was highly flirtatious. Gossip was inevitable.

Charlotte to Ellen; Haworth, 17 March 1840

My dear Mrs Eleanor

I wish to scold you with a forty horse power for having told Martha Taylor that I had requested you 'not to tell <u>her</u> everything' which piece of information of course has thrown Martha into a tremendous ill-humour besides setting the teeth of her curiosity on edge with the notion, that there is something very important in the wind which you and I are especially desirous to conceal from her.

Such being the state of matters I desire to take off any embargo I may have laid on your tongue which I plainly see will not be restrained and to enjoin you to walk up to Gomersal and tell her forthwith every individual occurrence you can recollect, including Valentines, 'Fair Ellen, Fair Ellen' – 'Away fond love' 'Soul divine' and all – likewise if you please the painting of Miss Celia Amelia Weightman's portrait and that young lady's frequent and agreeable visits –

Ellen, Reminiscences; 1871

'Celia Amelia,' Mr Brontë's curate, a lively, handsome young man fresh from Durham University, an excellent classical scholar. He gave a very good lecture on the Classics at Keighley. The young ladies at the Parsonage must hear his lecture, so he went off to a married clergyman to get him to write to Mr Brontë and invite the young ladies to tea, and offer his escort to the lecture, and back again to the Parsonage. Great fears were entertained that permission would not be given – it was a walk of four miles each way. The Parsonage was not reached till 12p.m. The two clergymen rushed in with their charges, deeply disturbing Miss Branwell, who had prepared hot coffee for the home party, which of course fell short when two more were to be supplied. Poor Miss Branwell lost her temper, Charlotte was troubled, and Mr Weightman, who enjoyed teazing the old lady, was very thirsty. The great spirits of the walking party had a trying suppression, but twinkling fun sustained some of them.

There was also a little episode as to valentines. Mr Weightman discovered that none of the party had ever received a valentine – a great discovery! Whereupon he indited verses to each one, and walked ten miles to post them, lest Mr Brontë should discover his dedicatory nonsense, and the quiet liveliness going on under the sedate espionage of Miss Branwell and Mr Brontë himself.

Charlotte to Ellen; Haworth, 7 April 1840

Little Haworth has been all in a bustle about Church-rates since you were here – we had a most stormy meeting in the School-room – Papa took the chair and Mr Collins and Mr Weightman acted as his supporters one on each side – There was violent opposition – which set Mr Collins' Irish blood in a ferment and if Papa had not kept him quiet partly by persuasion, and partly by compulsion he would have given the Dissenters their Kail through the reek (a Scotch proverb which I'll explain another time) – He and Mr Weightman both bottled up their wrath for that time but it was only to explode with redoubled force at a future period – We had two sermons on Dissent and its consequences preached last Sunday one in the afternoon by Mr Weightman and one in the evening by Mr Collins – all the Dissenters were invited to come and hear and they actually shut up their chapels and came in a body; of course the church was crowded. Miss Celia Amelia delivered a noble, eloquent high-Church, Apostolical succession discourse – in which he banged the Dissenters most fearlessly and unflinchingly – I thought they had got enough for one while, but it was nothing to the dose that was thrust down their throats in the evening – a keener, cleverer, bolder and more heart-stirring harangue I never heard than that which Mr Collins delivered from Haworth Pulpit last Sunday Evening – he did not rant – he did not cant he did not whine, he did not snivel, he just got up and spoke with the boldness of a man who is impressed with the truth of what he is saying who has no fear of his enemies and no dread of consequences – his Sermon lasted an hour yet I was sorry when it was done

Charlotte to Ellen; Haworth, 15 May 1840

Do not be over-persuaded to marry a man you can never respect – I do not say <u>love</u>, because, I think, if you can respect a person before marriage, moderate love at least will come after; and as to intense <u>passion</u>, I am convinced that that is no desirable feeling. In the first place, it seldom or never meets with a requital; and, in the second place, if it did, the feeling would be only temporary: it would last the honeymoon, and then, perhaps, give place to disgust, or indifference, worse perhaps than disgust. Certainly this would be the case on the man's part; and on the woman's – God help her, if she is left to love passionately and alone.

Our letters are assuming an odd tone. We write of little else but love and marriage, and [verily?], I have a sort of presentiment that you will be married before you are many years older. I do not wish you to reciprocate the compliment, because I am tolerably well convinced that I shall never marry at all. Reason tells me so, and I am not so utterly the slave of feeling but that I can <u>occasionally hear</u> her voice.

Charlotte to the Reverend Henry Nussey; Haworth, 26 May 1840

In looking over my papers this morning I found a letter from you of the date of last Feby. with the mark upon it <u>unanswered</u> your sister Ellen often accuses me of want of punctuality in answering letters, and I think her accusation is here justified . . . You must not again ask me to write in a regular literary way to you on some particular topic – I cannot do it at all – do you think I am a Blue-stocking? I feel half-inclined to laugh at you for the idea, but perhaps you would be angry what was the topic to be – Chemistry? or Astronomy? or Mechanics? or Chonchology or Entomology or what other ology? I know nothing at all about any of these – I am not scientific, I am not a Linguist – you think me far more learned than I am – If I told you all my Ignorance I am afraid you would be shocked – however as I wish still to retain a little corner in your good opinion I will hold my tongue

Believe me
Yours respectfully
C Brontë

While Charlotte remained at home 'in very good health and spirits and uneasy only because I cannot yet hear of a Situation', Anne had succeeded in finding a new post. In May 1840 she went to join the household of the Reverend Edmund Robinson at Thorp Green, a large country house on an estate just outside York, where she was to be governess to three girls and a boy. Branwell, meanwhile, had been making the most of his proximity to the Lake District by contacting one of the eminent poets who still lived there. Hartley Coleridge, son of the more famous Samuel Taylor Coleridge, lived at Nab Cottage on the shores of Rydal Water. Unlike William Wordsworth, Coleridge responded not only with an invitation to visit him but also with encouraging advice on Branwell's literary ambitions.

Branwell to Hartley Coleridge; Broughton-in-Furness, 20 April 1840

It is with much reluctance that I venture to request, for the perusal of the following lines, a portion of the time of one upon whom I can have no claim, and should not dare to intrude; but I do not, personally, know a man on whom to rely for an answer to the question I shall put, and I could not resist my longing to ask a man from whose judgement there would be little hope of appeal.

Since my childhood I have been wont to devote the hours I could spare from other and very different employments to efforts at literary composition, always keeping the results to myself, nor have they in more than two or three instances been seen by any other. But I am about to enter active life, and prudence tells me not to waste the time which must make my independence; yet, sir, I love writing too well to fling aside the practice of it without an effort to ascertain whether I could turn it to account, not in <u>wholly</u> maintaining myself, but in <u>aiding</u> my maintenance, for I do not sigh after fame and am not ignorant of the folly or the fate of those who, without ability, would depend for their lives upon their pens; but I seek to know, and venture, though with shame, to ask from one whose word I must respect: whether, by periodical or other writing, I could please myself with writing, and make it subservient to living.

Branwell to Hartley Coleridge; Haworth, 27 June 1840

Sir,

You will, perhaps, have forgotten me, but it will be long before I forget my first conversation with a man of real intellect, in my first visit to the classic lakes of Westmoreland.

77

During the delightful day which I had the honour of spending with you at Ambleside, I received permission to transmit to you, as soon as finished, the first book of a translation of Horace, in order that, after a glance over it, you might tell me whether it was worth further notice or better fit for the fire.

I have – I fear most negligently, and amid other very different employments – striven to translate 2 books, the first of which I have presumed to send you, and will you, sir, stretch your past kindness by telling me whether I should amend and pursue the work or let it rest in peace?

Great corrections I feel it wants, but till I feel that the work might benefit me, I have no heart to make them; yet if your judgement prove in any way favourable, I will re-write the whole, without sparing labour to reach perfection . . . Excuse my unintelligibility, haste, and appearance of presumption, and – Believe me to be, Sir, your most humble and grateful servant,

P B Brontē

If anything in this note should displease you, lay it, sir, to the account of inexperience and <u>not</u> impudence.

At Haworth, Charlotte's infatuation with William Weightman had cooled into something like pique as she realized that he had not singled her out for any special attentions and that she had been in danger of making a fool of herself over him. This was brought sharply home to her as she watched her friend, Ellen, and many of the other young ladies in the neighbourhood falling for his charms.

Charlotte to Ellen; Haworth, June 1840

Mary Taylor's visit has been a very pleasant one to us, and I believe to herself also – She and Mr Weightman have had several games at chess which generally terminated in a species of mock hostility – Mr Weightman is better in health, but don't set your heart on him   I'm afraid he is very fickle – not to you in particular but to half a dozen other ladies   he has just cut his inamorata at Swansea and sent her back all her letters – his present object of Devotion is

Caroline Dury to whom he has just despatched a most passionate copy of verses   poor lad, his sanguine temperament bothers him grievously

Charlotte to Ellen; Haworth, 14 July 1840

I am very glad you continue so heart-whole   I rather feared our mutual nonsense might have made a deeper impression on you than was safe   Mr Weightman – left Haworth this morning, we do not expect him back again for some weeks – I am fully convinced Ellen that he is a thorough male-flirt   his sighs are deeper than ever – and his treading on toes more assiduous – I find he has scattered his impressions far and wide – K[e]ighley has yielded him a fruitful field of conquest, Sarah Sugden is quite smitten   so is Caroline Dury – She however has left – and his Reverence has not yet ceased to idolize her memory – I find he is perfectly conscious of his irresistibleness & is as vain as a peacock on the subject – I am not at all surprised at all this – it is perfectly natural – a handsome – clever – prepossessing – good-humoured young man – will never want troops of victims amongst young ladies – So long as you are not among the number it is all right –

Charlotte to Ellen; Haworth, c.14 August 1840

As you only sent me a note I shall only send you one, and that not out of revenge – but because like you I have but little to say – The freshest news in our house is that we had about a fortnight ago – a visit from some of our South of England relations. John Branwell Williams and his Wife and daughter – they have been staying above a month with Uncle Fennell at Crosstone – They reckon to be very grand folks indeed – and talk largely – I thought assumingly   I cannot say I much admired them – To my eyes there seemed to be an attempt to play the great Mogul down in Yorkshire – Mr Williams himself was much less assuming than the womenites – he seemed a frank, sagacious kind of man – very tall and vigorous with a keen active look – the moment he saw me he exclaimed that I was the very image of my Aunt Charlotte. Mrs Williams sets up for being a woman of great talents, tact and accomplishment – I thought there was much more noise than work. my cousin Eliza is a young lady intended by nature to be a bouncing good-looking girl Art has trained her to be a languishing affected piece of goods. I would have been friendly with her; but I could get no talk except about the Low-Church Evangelical Clergy the Millennium, Baptist Noel – Botany, and her own Conversion. A Mistaken Education has utterly spoiled the lass, her face tells that she is naturally goodnatured – though perhaps indolent – in manner she is something of a sanctified Amelia Walker – affecting at times a saintly child-like innocence so utterly out of keeping with her round rosy face and tall, bouncing figure – that I could hardly refrain from laughing as I watched her – Write a long letter to me next time and I'll write you ditto Good-bye

Charlotte to Ellen; Haworth, 20 August 1840

Our August Relations as you choose to call them are gone back to London, they never stayed with us they only spent one day at our house – they were visitors of Uncle Fennell's – I fancy Uncle Fennell would be very glad to get rid of them ... I have got another bale of French books from Gomersal, containing upwards of 40 volumes – I have read about half – they are like the rest clever wicked sophistical and immoral – the best of it is, they give one a thorough idea of France and Paris – and are the best substitute for French Conversation I have met with.

Charlotte to Ellen; Haworth, 29 September 1840

A woman of the name of Mrs B[rooke], it seems, wants a teacher. I wish she would have me; and I have written to another woman denominated Peg Wooler, to tell her so. Verily, it is a delightful thing to live here at home, at full liberty to do just what one pleases. But I recollect some fable or other about grasshoppers and ants by a scrubby old knave, yclept Aesop; the grasshoppers sung all the summer and starved all the winter.

A distant relation of mine, one Patrick Boanerges, has set off to seek his fortune, in the wild, wandering, adventurous, romantic, knight-errant-like capacity of clerk on the Leeds and Manchester Railroad. Leeds and Manchester, where are they? Cities in the wilderness – like Tadmor, alias Palmyra – are they not? I know Mrs Ellen is burning with eagerness to hear something about W[illiam] W[eightman], whom she adores in her heart, and whose image she cannot efface from her memory. I think I'll plague her by not telling her a word. To speak heaven's truth, I have precious little to say, inasmuch as I seldom see him, except on a Sunday, when he looks as handsome, cheery and good tempered as usual. I have indeed had the advantage of one long conversation since his return from Westmoreland, when he poured out his whole warm fickle soul in fondness and admiration of Agnes Walton. Whether he is in love with her or not I can't say; I can only observe that it sounds very like it. He sent us a prodigious quantity of game while he was away. A brace of wild ducks, a brace of black grouse, a brace of partridges, ditto of snipes, ditto of curlews, and a large salmon. There is one little trait respecting him which lately came to my knowledge, which gives a glimpse of the better side of his character. Last Saturday night he had been sitting an hour in the parlour with Papa; and as he went away, I heard Papa say to him – 'what is the matter with you? You seem in very low spirits to-night.' 'Oh, I don't know. I've been to see a poor young girl, who, I'm afraid, is dying.' 'Indeed, what is her name?' 'Susan Bland, the daughter of John Bland, the super-intendent.' Now Susan Bland is my oldest and best scholar in the Sunday-school; and when I heard that, I thought I would go as soon as I could to see her. I did go, on Monday afternoon, and found her very ill and weak, and seemingly far on her way to that bourne whence no traveller returns. After sitting with her some time, I happened to ask her mother if she thought a little port wine would do her good. She replied that the doctor had recommended it, and that when Mr Weightman was last there, he had sent them a bottle of wine and a jar of preserves. She added, that he was always good-natured to poor folks, and seemed to have a deal of feeling and kind-heartedness about him. This proves that he is not all selfishness and vanity. No doubt, there are defects in his character, but there are also good qualities. God bless him!

Charlotte to Ellen; Haworth, 12 November 1840

You remember Mr and Mrs C[ollins]? Mrs C- came here the other day, with a most melancholy tale of her wretched husband's drunken, extravagant, profligate habits. She asked Papa's advice; there was nothing, she said, but ruin before them. They owed debts which they could never pay. She expected Mr C-'s immediate dismissal from his curacy; she knew from bitter experience, that his vices were utterly hopeless. He treated her and her child savagely; with much more to the same effect. Papa advised her to leave him for ever, and go home, if she had a home to go to. She said this was what she had long resolved to do; and she would leave him directly, as soon as Mr B[usfeild] dismissed him. She expressed great disgust and contempt towards him, and did not affect to have the shadow of regard in any way. I do not wonder at this, but I <u>do</u> wonder she should ever marry a man towards whom her feelings must always have been pretty much the same as they are now. I am morally certain no decent woman could experience anything but aversion towards such a man as Mr C-. Before I knew, or suspected his character, and when I rather wondered at his versatile talents, I felt it in an uncontrollable degree. I hated to talk to him, – hated to look at him; though, as I was not certain that there was substantial reason for such a dislike, and thought it absurd to trust to mere instinct, I both concealed and repressed the feeling as much as I could; and, on all occasions, treated him with as much civility as I was mistress of. I was struck with Mary's expression of a similar feeling at first sight; she said when we left him, 'That is a hideous man, Charlotte!' I thought 'He is indeed.' In what precise way he has committed himself in Ireland I know not, but Mrs C. says he dare not follow her there.

Towards the end of the year, it appeared that Mr Vincent, Ellen's dilatory suitor, was at last going to make a formal proposal of marriage. Ellen was undecided and sought advice from her friend. Charlotte responded in a remarkably pragmatic, even cynical, way, revealing in the process that there had been an attraction between Branwell and Mary Taylor during her visit in the summer which had come to nothing. Mary's subsequent shame at allowing her feelings to be so publicly displayed, echoing

Charlotte's own experiences earlier in the year, may account for some of the latter's increasing sarcasm at William Weightman's expense.

Charlotte to Ellen; Haworth, 20 November 1840

. . . now I'll tell you a word of truth: at which you may be offended or not as you like – From what I know of your character – and I think I know it pretty well – I should say you will never <u>love before marriage</u> – After that ceremony is over, and after you have had some months to settle down, and to get accustomed to the creature you have taken for your worse half – you will probably make a most affectionate and happy wife – even if the individual should not prove <u>all</u> you could wish – you will be indulgent towards his little follies and foibles – and will not feel much annoyance at them. this will especially be the case if he should have sense sufficient to allow you to guide him in important matters. Such being the case Nell – I hope you will not have the romantic folly to wait for the awakening of what the French call '<u>Une grande passion</u>' – My good girl 'une grande passion' is '<u>une grande folie.</u>' I have told you so before – and I tell it you again Mediocrity in all things is wisdom – mediocrity in the sensations is superlative wisdom. When you are as old as I am Nell – (I am sixty at least being your Grandmother) you will find that the majority of those worldly precepts – whose seeming coldness – shocks and repels us in youth – are founded in wisdom. Did you not once say to me in all childlike simplicity 'I thought Charlotte – no young ladies should fall in love, till the offer was actually made' I forget what answer I made at the time – but I now reply after due consideration – 'Right as a glove' – the maxim is just – and I hope you will always attend to it – I will even extend and confirm it – no young lady should fall in love till the offer has been made, accepted – the marriage ceremony performed and the first half year of wedded life has passed away – a woman may then begin to love, but with great precaution – very coolly – very moderately – very rationally – If she ever loves so much that a harsh word or a cold look from her husband cuts her to the heart – she is a fool – if she ever loves so much that her husband's will is her law – and that she has got into a habit of watching his looks in order that she may anticipate his wishes she will soon be a neglected fool – Did I not once tell you of an instance of a Relative of mine who cared for a young lady till he began to suspect that she cared more for him and then instantly conceived a sort of contempt for her? You know to what I allude – never as you value your ears mention the circumstance – but I have two studies – <u>you</u> are my study for the success the credit, and the respectability of a quiet, tranquil character – Mary is my study – for the contempt, the remorse – the misconstruction which follow the development of feelings in themselves noble, warm – generous – devoted and profound – but which being too freely revealed – too frankly bestowed – are not estimated at their real value. God bless her – I never hope to see in this world a character more truly noble – she would <u>die</u> willingly for one she loved – her intellect and her attainments are of the very highest standard – yet during her last visit here – she so conducted herself on one or two occasions that Mr Weightman thought her mad – do not for a moment suspect that she acted in a manner really wrong – her conduct was merely wrought to a pitch of great intensity and irregularity seldom equalled – but it produced a most unfortunate impression. I did not value her the less for it, because I understood it, yet I doubt whether Mary will ever marry.

Neither Charlotte nor Branwell had abandoned their literary ambitions. Both were still writing stories and poems inspired by Angria and, following Branwell's meeting with Hartley Coleridge in the summer, both contacted him with examples of their work. The draft of Coleridge's reply to Branwell – which, ironically, may never have been sent – was full of praise for his translations of Horace, but Charlotte's acknowledgement of his reply to her suggests that his comments on her prose tale had been less than enthusiastic. The extraordinary tone of Charlotte's letter, which is flippant to the point of rudeness, can only be explained by the fact that she was writing under what she hoped would appear to be a masculine persona.

*Hartley Coleridge to Branwell, draft letter, 30 November–
1 December 1840*

Dear Bronte

I fear you have thought me unkind or forgetful in neglecting so
long to notice your letter and the enclosed translations. Believe me,
I would not be the one, and could not be the other – but I am a sad
Procrastinator . . . You are by no means the first or the only person
who has applied to me for judgement upon their writings. I smile
to think that so small an asteroid as myself should have satellites. But
you have heard the distich –

> Fleas that bite little dogs have lesser fleas that bite em –
> The lesser fleas – have fleas still less – so on – ad infinitum.

Howbeit, you are – with one exception – the only young Poet in
whom I could find merit enough to comment without flattery – on
stuff enough to be worth finding fault with. I think, I told you how
much I was struck with the power and energy of the lines you sent
before I had the pleasure of seeing you. Your translation of Horace
is a work of much greater promise, and though I do not counsel a
publication of the whole – I think many odes might appear with
very little alteration. Your versification is often masterly – and you
have shown skill in great variety of measures – There is a racy english
in your language which is rarely to be found even in the original –
that is to say – untranslated, and certainly untranslateable effusions
of many of our juveniles, which considering how thorough[ly] Latin
Horace is in his turns of phrase, and collocation of words – is a proof
of sound scholarship – and command of both languages –

Charlotte to Hartley Coleridge; Haworth, 10 December 1840

I was almost as much pleased to get your letter as if it had been
one from Professor Wilson containing a passport of admission to
Blackwood['s Magazine] – You do not certainly flatter me very
much nor suggest very brilliant hopes to my imagination – but on
the whole I can perceive that you write like an honest man and a
gentleman – and I am very much obliged to you both for the candour

and civility of your reply. It seems then Messrs Percy and West are not gentlemen likely to make an impression upon the heart of any Editor in Christendom? well I commit them to oblivion with several tears and much affliction but I hope I can get over it.

Your calculation that the affair might have extended to three Vols is very moderate – I felt myself actuated by the pith and perseverance of a Richardson and could have held the distaff and spun day and night till I had lengthened the thread to thrice that extent – but you, like a most pitiless Atropos, have cut it short in its very commencement – I do not think you would have hesitated to do the same to the immortal Sir Charles Grandison if Samuel Richardson Esqr had sent you the first letters of Miss Harriet Byron – and Miss Lucy Selby for inspection – very good letters they are Sir, Miss Harriet sings her own praises as sweetly as a dying swan – and her friends all join in the chorus, like a Company of wild asses of the desert. It is very edifying and profitable to create a world out of one's own brain and people it with inhabitants who are like so many Melchisedecs – 'Without father, without mother, without descent, having neither beginning of days, nor end of life'. By conversing daily with such beings and accustoming your eyes to their glaring attire and fantastic features – you acquire a tone of mind admirably calculated to enable you to cut a respectable figure in practical life – If you have ever been accustomed to such society Sir you will be aware how distinctly and vividly their forms and features fix themselves on the retina of that 'inward eye' which is said to be 'the bliss of solitude' Some of them are so ugly – you can liken them to nothing but the grotesque things carved by a besotted pagan for his temple – and some of them so preternaturally beautiful that their aspect startles you as much as Pygmalion's Statue must have startled him – when life began to animate its chiselled features and kindle up its blind, marble eyes.

I am sorry Sir I did not exist forty or fifty years ago when the Lady's magazine was flourishing like a green bay tree – In that case I make no doubt my aspirations after literary fame would have met with due encouragement – Messrs Percy and West should have stepped forward like heroes upon a stage worthy of their pretensions and I would have contested the palm with the Authors of Derwent

Priory – of the Abbey and of Ethelinda. – You see Sir I have read the Lady's Magazine and know something of its contents – though I am not quite certain of the correctness of the titles I have quoted for it is long, very long since I perused the antiquated print in which those tales were given forth – I read them before I knew how to criticize or object – they were old books belonging to my mother or my Aunt; they had crossed the Sea, had suffered ship-wreck and were discoloured with brine – I read them as a treat on holiday afternoons or by stealth when I should have been minding my lessons – I shall never see anything which will interest me so much again – One black day my father burnt them because they contained foolish love-stories. With all my heart I wish I had been born in time to contribute to the Lady's magazine . . . I am pleased that you cannot quite decide whether I belong to the soft or the hard sex – and though at first I had no intention of being enigmatical on the subject – yet as I accidentally omitted to give the clue at first, I will venture purposely to withhold it now – as to my handwriting, or the ladylike tricks you mention in my style and imagery – you must not draw any conclusion from those – Several young gentlemen curl their hair and wear corsets – Richardson and Rousseau – often write exactly like old women – and Bulwer and Cooper and Dickens and Warren like boarding-school misses. Seriously Sir, I am very much obliged to you for your kind and candid letter – and on the whole I wonder you took the trouble to read and notice the demi-serious novelette of an anonymous scribe who had not even the manners to tell you whether he was a man or woman or whether his commonplace 'CT' meant Charles Tims or Charlotte Tomkins.

Charlotte to Ellen, on the death of Mary Taylor's father; Haworth, 3 January 1841

I received the news in your last with no surprise and with the feeling that this removal must be a relief to Mr Taylor himself and even to his family – The bitterness of death was past a year ago when it was first discovered that his illness must terminate fatally – all between has been lingering suspense – this is at an end now and the present certainty however sad is better than the former doubt. What will be the consequences of his death is another question – for my own part I look forward to a dissolution and dispersion of the family perhaps not immediately but in the course of a year or two – It is true causes may arise to keep them together awhile longer – but they are restless active spirits and will not be restrained always. – Mary alone has more energy and power in her nature than any ten men you can pick out in the united parishes of Birstal[l] and Gomersal   It is vain to limit a character like hers within ordinary boundaries – she will overstep them – I am morally certain Mary will establish her own landmarks – So will the rest of them.

Charlotte to the Reverend Henry Nussey; Haworth, 11 January 1841

I shall be glad to receive the poetry which you offer to send me – you ask me to return the gift in kind – How do you know that I have it in my power to comply with that request? Once indeed I was very poetical, when I was sixteen, seventeen, eighteen and nineteen years old – but I am now twenty-four approaching twenty-five – and the intermediate years are those which begin to rob life of some of its superfluous colouring. At this age it is time that the imagination should be pruned and trimmed – that the judgement should be cultivated – and a few at least, of the countless illusions of early youth should be cleared away. I have not written poetry for a long while.

Just over a year and a half after leaving her last post, Charlotte finally accepted a new position as a governess in the family of John White, a wealthy Bradford merchant, who lived on the outskirts of the town at Upperwood House, Rawdon. Though her circumstances were in every way preferable to those of her earlier appointments, Charlotte was temperamentally unsuited to living with strangers in a house where, though treated with kindness, she was neither a member of the family nor one of the servants.

Charlotte to Ellen; Upperwood House, Rawdon, 3 March 1841

The house is not very large, but exceedingly comfortable and well regulated; the grounds are fine and extensive. In taking the place I have made a large sacrifice in the way of salary, in the hope of securing comfort – by which word I do not mean to express good eating and drinking, or warm fire, or a soft bed, but the society of cheerful faces, and minds and hearts not dug out of a lead mine, or cut from a marble quarry. My salary is not really more than £16 per annum, though it is nominally £20, but the expense of washing will be deducted therefrom. My pupils are two in number, a girl of eight and a boy of six . . . [they] are wild and unbroken, but apparently well disposed. I wish I may be able to say as much next time I write to you. My earnest wish and endeavour will be to please them. If I can but feel that I am giving satisfaction, and if at the same time I can keep my health, I shall, I hope, be moderately happy. But no one but myself can tell how hard a governess's work is to me – for no one but myself is aware how utterly averse my whole mind and nature are to the employment. Do not think that I fail to blame myself for this, or that I leave any means unemployed to conquer this feeling. Some of my greatest difficulties lie in things that would appear to you comparatively trivial. I find it so hard to repel the rude familiarity of children. I find it so difficult to ask either servants or mistress for anything I want, however much I want it. It is less pain to me to endure the greatest inconvenience than to request its removal. I am a fool. Heaven knows I cannot help it!

Charlotte to Ellen; Upperwood House, Rawdon, 21 March 1841

You must excuse a very short answer to your last most welcome letter – for my time is entirely occupied – Mrs White expects a good deal of sewing from me – I cannot sew much during the day on account of the children – who require the closest attention. I am obliged therefore to devote the evenings to this business . . . this place is better than Stonegappe but God knows I have enough to do to keep a good heart on the matter what you said has cheered me a little – I wish I could always act according to your advice – Home-sickness afflicts me sorely – I like Mr White extremely – respecting Mrs White I am for the present silent – I am trying hard to like her. The children are not such little devils incarnate as the Sedgwicks – but they are over-indulged & at times hard to manage.

Charlotte to Ellen; Upperwood House, Rawdon, 1 April 1841

My dear Nelly

It is 12 o'clock at night but I must just write you a word before I go to-bed – If you think I'm going to refuse your invitation – or if you sent it me with that idea – you're mistaken – as soon as I had read your shabby little note – I gathered up my spirits directly – walked on the impulse of the moment into Mrs White's presence – popped the question – and for two minutes received no answer – will she refuse me when I work so hard for her? thought I. Ye -es -es, drawled Madam – in a reluctant cold tone – thank you Madam said I with extreme cordiality, and was marching from the room – when she recalled me with – 'You'd better go, on Saturday afternoon then – when the children have holiday – & if you return in time for them to have all their lessons on Monday morning – I don't see that much will be lost' you are a genuine Turk thought I but again I assented & so the bargain was struck – . . . God bless you – I want to see you again Huzza for Saturday afternoon after next! I'll snap my fingers at Mrs W & her imps. Good night my lass!

C. Brontë

Charlotte to Emily; Upperwood House, 2 April 1841

I had a letter from Anne yesterday; she says she is well. I hope she speaks absolute truth. I had written to her and Branwell a few days before. I have not heard from Branwell yet. It is to be hoped that his removal to another station will turn out for the best. As you say, it looks like getting on at any rate . . . Matters are progressing very strangely at Gomersal. Mary Taylor and Waring have come to a singular determination, but I almost think under the peculiar circumstances a defensible one, though it sounds outrageously odd at first. They are going to emigrate – to quit the country altogether. Their destination unless they change is Port Nicholson, in the northern island of New Zealand!!! Mary has made up her mind that she can not and will not be a governess, a teacher, a milliner, a bonnet-maker nor housemaid. She sees no means of obtaining employment she would like in England, so she is leaving it. I counselled her to go to France likewise and stay there a year before she decided on this strange unlikely-sounding plan of going to New Zealand, but she is quite resolved. I cannot sufficiently comprehend what her views and those of her brothers may be on the subject, or what is the extent of their information regarding Port Nicholson, to say whether this is rational enterprise or absolute madness.

Charlotte to Ellen; Upperwood House, 4 May 1841

During the last three weeks that hideous operation called 'A Thorough Clean' has been going on in the house – it is now nearly completed for which I thank my stars – as during its progress I have fulfilled the twofold character of Nurse and Governess – while the nurse has been transmuted into Cook & housemaid. That nurse by the bye is the prettiest lass you ever saw & when dressed has much more the air of a lady than her Mistress. Well can I believe that Mrs W has been an exciseman's daughter – and I am convinced also that Mr W's extraction is very low – yet Mrs W talks in an amusing strain of pomposity about his & her family & connexions & affects to look down with wondrous hauteur on the whole race of 'Tradesfolk' as she terms men of business – I was beginning to think Mrs W– a good sort of body in spite of all her bouncing, and boasting – her bad grammar and worse orthography – but I have had experience of one little trait in her character which condemns her a long way with me – After treating a person on the most familiar terms of equality for a long time – If any little thing goes wrong she does not scruple to give way to anger in a very coarse unladylike manner – though in justice no blame could be attached where she ascribed it all – I think passion is the true test of vulgarity or refinement – Mrs W– when put out of her way is highly offensive – She must not give me any more of the same sort – or I shall ask for my wages & go.

This place looks exquisitely beautiful just now – The grounds are certainly lovely – and all is as green as an emerald – I wish you would just come and look at it – Mrs W– would be as proud as Punch to shew it you. Mr W– has been writing an urgent invitation to papa entreating him to come and spend a week here. I don't at all wish papa to come – it would be like incurring an obligation – which I have no wish to do because in my secret soul I mean to leave Upperwood House when I can get a better place. Somehow I have managed to get a good deal more control over the children lately – This makes my life a good deal easier – Also by dint of nursing the fat baby it has got to know me & be fond of me – occasionally I suspect myself of growing rather fond of it – but this suspicion clears away the moment its mamma takes it & makes a fool of it – from a bonny, rosy little morsel – it sinks in my estimation into a small, petted nuisance – Ditto with regard to the other children.

Charlotte to the Reverend Henry Nussey; Upperwood House, Rawdon,
9 May 1841

It seems Ellen has told you that I am become a Governess again – as you say it is indeed a hard thing for flesh and blood to leave home – especially a <u>good</u> home – not a wealthy or splendid one – my home is humble and unattractive to strangers but to me it contains what I shall find nowhere else in the world – the profound, and intense affection which brothers and sisters feel for each other when their minds are cast in the same mould, their ideas drawn from the same source – when they have clung to each other from childhood and when family disputes have never sprung up to divide them.

We are all separated now, and winning our bread amongst strangers as we can – my sister Anne is near York, my brother in a situation near Halifax. I am here, Emily is the only one left at home where her usefulness and willingness make her indispensable. Under these circumstances should we repine? I think not – our mutual affection ought to comfort us under all difficulties – if the God on whom we must all depend will but vouchsafe us health and the power to continue in the strict line of duty, so as never under any temptation to swerve from it an inch – we shall have ample reason to be grateful and contented.

The Leeds Intelligencer, *5 June 1841*

HAWORTH CHURCH SUNDAY SCHOOL. – On Whit-
Monday the teachers and scholars of the Church Sunday School,
Haworth, held their annual festival, when the children, to the number
of upwards of two hundred, walked in procession through the town,
when they returned to the school room, and were regaled with
buns, beer, &c. Great praise is due to the Rev. Wm. Weightman,
the respected curate of the church, for his praiseworthy exertions in
behalf of the school, and for his activity and perseverance in establishing a parochial and lending library, for the good of those in
particular who are connected with the Church and Sunday school,
and for the general edification of the parishioners in the principles
of the Church of England.

Charlotte to Ellen; Haworth, 1 July 1841

Dear Nell

I was not at home when I got your letter – but I am at home
now – and it feels like Paradise.

I came last night – . . . When I asked for a Vacation – Mrs W
offered a week or ten days – but I demanded three weeks and stood
to my tackle with a tenacity worthy of yourself lassie. I gained the
point – but I don't like such victories.

I have gained another point – you are <u>unanimously</u> requested to
come here next Tuesday and stay as long as you can Write to me
directly – say if that day is convenient and whether we are to meet
you at Keighley – Aunt is in high good humour – I hope she will
keep so. I need not write a long letter now

Good bye dear Nell
CB.

July 1st.

I have lost the chance of seeing Anne She is gone back to 'the Land
of Egypt and the House of Bondage' also little black Tom [the
family cat] is dead – every cup however sweet has its drop of bitter
in it –

93

Probably you will be at a loss to ascertain the identity of that gentleman but don't fret about it   I'll tell you when you come. Keeper is as well, big – and grim as ever – I'm too happy to write – Come lassie –

Charlotte to Ellen; Haworth, 19 July 1841

. . . there is a project hatching in this house – which both Emily and I anxiously wished to discuss with you – The project is yet in its infancy – hardly peeping from its shell – and whether it will ever come out – a fine, full-fledged chicken – or will turn addle and die before it cheeps, is one of those considerations that are but dimly revealed by the oracles of futurity   Now dear Nell don't be nonplussed by all this metaphorical mystery – I talk of a plain and every day occurrence – though in Delphic style – I wrap up the information in figures of speech concerning eggs, chickens, etcetera etceterorum.

To come to the point – Papa and Aunt talk by fits & starts of our – id est – Emily Anne & myself commencing a School –! I have often you know said how much I wished such a thing – but I never could conceive where the capital was to come from for making such a speculation – I was well aware indeed, that Aunt <u>had</u> money – but I always considered that she was the last person who would offer a loan for the purpose in question – A loan however she <u>has</u> offered or rather intimates that she perhaps <u>will</u> offer in case pupils can be secured, – an eligible situation obtained &c. &c.

Emily, diary paper; Haworth, 30 July 1841

A Paper to be opened
when Anne is
25 years old
or my next birthday after –
if
– all be well –

————

Emily Jane Brontë July the 30th 1841..

It is Friday evening – near 9 o'clock – wild rainy weather   I am seated in the dining room alone – having just concluded tidying our desk-boxes – writing this document – Papa is in the parlour. Aunt up stairs in her room – she has been reading Blackwood's Magazine to papa – Victoria and Adelaide are ensconced in the peat-house – Keeper is in the kitchen – Nero in his cage – We are all stout and hearty as I hope is the case with Charlotte, Branwell, and Anne, of whom the first is at John White Esqre upperwood House, Rawden The second is at Luddenden foot and the third is I beleive at – Scarborough – enditing perhaps a paper corresponding to this – A scheme is at present in agitation for setting us up in a school of our own   as yet nothing is determined but I hope and trust it may go on and prosper and answer our highest expectations. This day 4 – years I wonder whether we shall still be dragging on in our present condition or established to our heart's content   Time will show –

I guess that at the time appointed for the opening of this paper – we (i.e.) Charlotte, Anne and I – shall be all merrily seated in our own sitting-room in some pleasant and flourishing seminary having just gathered in for the midsummer holydays   our debts will be paid off and we shall have cash in hand to a considerable amount. papa Aunt and Branwell will either have been – or be coming – to visit us – it will be a fine warm summery evening. very different from this bleak look-out   Anne and I will perchance slip out into the garden a minutes to peruse our papers. I hope either this [o]r something better will be the case –

The Gondalians are at present in a threatening state but there is no open rupture as yet – all the princes and princesses of the royal royalty are at the palace of In-struction – I have a good many books on hands but I am sorry to say that as usual I make small progress with any – however I have just made a new regularity paper! and I mean verb sap – to do great things – and now I close sending from far an exhortation of courage courage! to exiled and harassed Anne wishing she was here

Anne, diary paper; Scarborough, 30 July 1841

July the 30th, A.D. 1841

This is Emily's birthday. She has now completed her 23rd year, and is, I believe, at home. Charlotte is a governess in the family of Mr White. Branwell is a clerk in the railroad station at Luddenden Foot, and I am a governess in the family of Mr Robinson. I dislike the situation and wish to change it for another. I am now at Scarborough. My pupils are gone to bed and I am hastening to finish this before I follow them.

We are thinking of setting up a school of our own, but nothing definite is settled about it yet, and we do not know whether we shall be able to or not. I hope we shall. And I wonder what will be our condition and how or where we shall all be on this day four years hence; at which time, if all be well, I shall be 25 years and 6 months old, Emily will be 27 years old, Branwell 28 years and 1 month, and Charlotte 29 years and a quarter. We are now all separate and not likely to meet again for many a weary week, but we are none of us ill that I know of and all are doing something for our own livelihood except Emily, who, however, is as busy as any of us, and in reality earns her food and raiment as much as we do.

> How little know we what we are
> How less what we may be!

Four years ago I was at school. Since then I have been a governess at Blake Hall, left it, come to Thorp Green, and seen the sea and York Minster. Emily has been a teacher at Miss Patchet's school, and left it. Charlotte has left Miss Wooler's, been a governess at Mrs Sidgwick's, left her, and gone to Mrs White's. Branwell has given up painting, been a tutor in Cumberland, left it, and become a clerk on the railroad. Tabby has left us, Martha Brown has come in her place. We have got Keeper, got a sweet little cat and lost it, and also got a hawk. Got a wild goose which has flown away, and three tame ones, one of which has been killed. All these diversities, with many others, are things we did not expect or foresee in the July of 1837. What will the next four years bring forth? Providence only knows.

But we ourselves have sustained very little alteration since that time. I have the same faults that I had then, only I have more wisdom and experience, and a little more self-possession than I then enjoyed. How will it be when we open this paper and the one Emily has written? I wonder whether the Gondalians will still be flourishing, and what will be their condition. I am now engaged in writing the fourth volume of Solala Vernon's Life.

For some time I have looked upon 25 as a sort of era in my existence. It may prove a true presentiment, or it may be only a superstitious fancy; the latter seems most likely, but time will show.

Anne Brontë

The Brontë sisters' plans for establishing their own school — a scheme which would have allowed them to live and work together again, as well as giving them the relative freedom of self-employment — were suddenly disrupted in an unexpected fashion. Charlotte received a letter from Mary Taylor, who had put off her decision to emigrate to New Zealand and was visiting her sister, Martha, at her school in Brussels. It was to transform Charlotte's ambitions.

Charlotte to Ellen; Upperwood House, Rawdon, 7 August 1841

Mary's letter spoke of some of the pictures & cathedrals she had seen — pictures the most exquisite — & cathedrals the most venerable — I hardly know what swelled to my throat as I read her letter — such a vehement impatience of restraint & steady work. such a strong wish for wings — wings such as wealth can furnish — such an urgent thirst to see — to know — to learn — something internal seemed to expand boldly for a minute — I was tantalized with the consciousness of faculties unexercised — then all collapsed and I despaired.

Charlotte to Aunt Elizabeth Branwell; Upperwood House, Rawdon, 29 September 1841

My friends recommend me, if I desire to secure permanent success, to delay commencing the school for six months longer, and by all means to contrive, by hook or by crook, to spend the intervening time in some school on the Continent. They say schools in England are so numerous, competition so great, that without some such step towards attaining superiority we shall probably have a very hard struggle, and may fail in the end . . . I would not go to France or to Paris. I would go to Brussels, in Belgium. The cost of the journey there, at the dearest rate of travelling, would be £5; living is there little more than half as dear as it is in England, and the facilities for education are equal or superior to any other place in Europe. In half a year, I could acquire a thorough familiarity with French. I could improve greatly in Italian, and even get a dash of German, *i.e.* providing my health continued as good as it is now. Martha Taylor is now staying in Brussels, at a first-rate establishment there. I should not think of going to the Chateau de Kockleburg, where she is resident, as the terms are much too high; but if I wrote to her, she, with the assistance of Mrs Jenkins, the wife of the British Consul, would be able to secure me a cheap and decent residence and respectable protection. I should have the opportunity of seeing her frequently, she would make me acquainted with the city; and, with the assistance of her cousins, I should probably in time be introduced to connections far more improving, polished, and cultivated, than any I have yet known.

These are advantages which would turn to vast account, when we actually commenced a school – and, if Emily could share them with me, only for a single half-year, we could take a footing in the world afterwards which we can never do now. I say Emily instead of Anne; for Anne might take her turn at some future period, if our school answered. I feel certain, while I am writing, that you will see the propriety of what I say; you always like to use your money to the best advantage; you are not fond of making shabby purchases; when you do confer a favour, it is often done in style; and depend upon it £50, or £100, thus laid out, would be well employed. Of course, I know no other friend in the world to whom I could apply on this subject except yourself. I feel an absolute conviction that, if this advantage were allowed us, it would be the making of us for life. Papa will perhaps think it a wild and ambitious scheme; but who ever rose in the world without ambition? When he left Ireland to go to Cambridge University, he was as ambitious as I am now. I want us <u>all</u> to go on. I know we have talents, and I want them to be turned to account. I look to you, aunt, to help us. I think you will not refuse. I know, if you consent, it shall not be my fault if you ever repent your kindness.

Charlotte to Ellen; Upperwood House, Rawdon, 2 November 1841

Miss Wooler did most kindly propose that I should come to Dewsbury Moor & attempt to revive the school her sister had relinquished – she offered me the use of her furniture for the consideration of her board – at first I received the proposal cordially & prepared to do my utmost to bring about success – but a fire was kindled in my very heart which I could not quench – I so longed to increase my attainments to become something better than I am – a glimpse of what I felt I shewed to you in one of my former letters – only a glimpse – Mary Taylor cast oil on the flames – encouraged me & in her own strong energetic language heartened me on – I longed to go to Brussels – but how could I get? I wished for one at least of my Sisters to share the advantage with me   I fixed on Emily – she deserved the reward I knew – How could this point be managed? – In extreme excitement I wrote a letter home which carried the point – I made an appeal to Aunt for assistance which was answered by consent – Things are not settled. Yet it is sufficient to say we have a <u>chance</u> of going for half a year –

Charlotte to Emily; Upperwood House, Rawdon, 7 November 1841

Anne seems omitted in the present plan, but if all goes right I trust she will derive her full share of benefit from it in the end. I exhort all to hope. I believe in my heart this is acting for the best; my only fear is lest others should doubt and be dismayed. Before our half year in Brussels is completed, you and I will have to seek employment abroad. It is not my intention to retrace my steps home till twelve months, if all continues well and we and those at home retain good health.

Charlotte to Ellen; Haworth, 10 January 1842

I got home on Christmas Eve. The parting scene between me and my late employers was such as to efface the memory of much that annoyed me while I was there, but indeed, during the whole of the last six months they only made too much of me. Anne has rendered herself so valuable in her difficult situation that they have entreated her to return to them, if it be but for a short time. I almost think she will go back . . .

Chapter Five

1842–4

At the beginning of February 1842, Patrick escorted Charlotte and Emily to Brussels, where they had been accepted as pupils at the Pensionnat Heger. They travelled to London, took the Channel crossing to Ostend and then completed the journey by coach. Patrick stayed a few days to see his daughters settled, then returned to England, pausing only to visit the site of the battle of Waterloo. Though they felt their isolation at the school, the Brontës were not without friends in Brussels. Mary and Martha Taylor were already established at the Château de Koekelberg and the Dixon family, who were cousins to the Taylors, also lived in the city; the English chaplain, Mr Jenkins, was a brother of one of Patrick's former colleagues in the Dewsbury area. Despite their language difficulties, Charlotte and Emily seem to have adapted quickly to their new surroundings and were soon producing work of such quality that they attracted the attention of Monsieur Heger. Though Emily rebelled against his teaching methods, believing that they encouraged derivative work, Charlotte blossomed; her two years in Brussels were to transform her life and her work.

Charlotte to Ellen; Pensionnat Heger, Rue d'Isabelle, Brussels, May 1842

I was twenty-six years old a week or two since – and at that ripe time of life I am a schoolgirl – a complete school-girl and on the whole very happy in that capacity   It felt very strange at first to submit to authority instead of exercising it – to obey orders instead of giving them – but I like that state of things – I returned to it with the same avidity that a cow that has long been kept on dry hay returns to fresh grass – don't laugh at my simile – it is natural to me to submit and very unnatural to command.

This is a large school in which there are about 40 externes or day-pupils and 12 pensionnaires or boarders – Madame Heger the head is a lady of precisely the same cast of mind degree of cultivation & quality of character as Miss Catherine Wooler – I think the severe points are a little softened because she has not been disappointed & consequently soured – in a word – she is a married instead of a maiden lady – there are 3 teachers in the school Mademoiselle Blanche – mademoiselle Sophie and Mademoiselle Marie – The two first have no particular character – one is an old maid & the other will be one – Mademoiselle Marie is talented & original – but of repulsive & arbitrary manners which have made the whole school except myself and Emily her bitter enemies – no less than seven masters attend to teach the different branches of education – French drawing – music, singing, writing, arithmetic, and German.

All in the house are Catholics except ourselves one other girl and the gouvernante of Madame's children – an Englishwoman in rank something between a lady's maid and a nursery governess   the difference in Country & religion makes a broad line of demarcation between us & all the rest   we are completely isolated in the midst of numbers – yet I think I am never unhappy – my present life is so delightful so congenial to my nature compared to that of a Governess – my time constantly occupied passes too rapidly – hitherto both Emily and I have had good health and therefore we have been able to work well. There is one individual of whom I have not yet spoken Monsieur Heger the husband of Madame – he is professor of Rhetoric a man of power as to mind but very choleric & irritable in temperament – a little black, ugly being with a face that varies in expression, sometimes he borrows the lineaments of an insane Tom-cat – sometimes those of a delirious Hyena – occasionally – but very seldom he discards these perilous attractions and assumes an air not above a hundred degrees removed from what you would call mild & gentleman-like   he is very angry with me just at present because I have written a translation which he chose to stigmatize as peu correct – not because it was particularly so in reality but because he happened to be in a bad humour when he read it – he did not tell me so – but wrote the accusation in the margin of my book and asked in brief stern phrase how it happened that my compositions were always better than my translations – adding that the thing seemed to him inexplicable   the fact is some weeks ago in a high-flown humour he forbade me to use either dictionary or grammar – in translating the most difficult English compositions into French this makes the task rather arduous – & compels me every now and then to introduce an English word which nearly plucks the eyes out of his head when he sees it.

Emily and he don't draw well together at all – when he is very ferocious with me I cry – & that sets all things straight.

Emily works like a horse and she has had great difficulties to contend with – far greater than I have had   indeed those who come to a French school for instruction ought previously to have acquired a considerable knowledge of the French language – otherwise they will lose a great deal of time for the course of instruction is adapted to natives & not to foreigners and in these large establishments they will not change their ordinary course for one or two strangers – the few private lessons that monsieur Heger has vouchsafed to give us are I suppose to be considered a great favour & I can perceive they have already excited much spite & jealousy in the school –

While two of his sisters resumed their schooling on the Continent and Anne quietly laboured on as a governess at Thorp Green, Branwell's promising career on the railway suddenly came to an ignominious end. At the end of March, a company audit revealed that there was a deficit of some eleven pounds in Branwell's accounts and, though he was not suspected of theft, he was summarily dismissed from the railway. Hoping for reinstatement, or employment with another railway company, he kept in contact with Francis Grundy, a railway engineer, who had become his friend.

Branwell to Francis Grundy; Haworth, 22 May 1842

I cannot avoid the temptation to cheer my spirits by scribbling a few lines to you, while I sit alone – all the household being at church – the sole occupant of an ancient parsonage, among lonely hills which probably will never hear the whistle of an Engine till yourself and I are in the grave.

After experiencing, since my return home, extreme pain and

illness, with mental depression worse than either, I have at length regained health strength and soundness of mind far superior, I trust, to any thing shewn by that miserable wreck which you used to know under my name. I can now speak cheerfully and enjoy the company of another without the stimulus of six glasses of whiskey: I can write, think, and act with some approach to resolution; and I only want a <u>motive</u> for exertion to be happier than I have been for years before: But I feel my recovery from <u>almost Insanity</u>, to be retarded by having nothing to listen to except the wind moaning among old chimneys and older Ash Trees – nothing to look at except heathy hills walked over when life had all to hope for and nothing to regret with me – no one to speak to except crabbed old Greeks and Romans who have been dust these two thousand years: And yet this quiet life – from its contrast, makes the year passed at Luddenden foot appear like a Night mare; for I would rather give a hand than undergo again the grovelling carelessness – the malignant yet cold debauchery – the determination to find out how far the mind could carry the body without both being chucked into Hell, which marked my conduct while there – lost as I was to all that I really liked; and seeking relief from the indulgence of feelings which form the black spot in my character.

The rapidity of my recovery from such a state of ruin proves – I trust that I have still something left in me which may do me service, but I ought not to remain too long in solitude, for the world soon forgets a man who has bidden it 'good by'; and, though quiet is an excellent cure for a diseased mind, no medicine should be continued after the patient's recovery.

Convinced of the necessity, and anxious for the opportunity of active life, I am about – though ashamed of the business – to dun you for an answer to the following questions.

1st – Can I obtain a chance of some situation, under English Engineers, on one of the lines commencing abroad, either in Russia – Sweden – Belgium – France – or the Sardinian Dominions – such as I could properly fill, if possessed of the qualifications mentioned below – viz.

The usual branches of a gentlemans education – including some acquaintance with French and such a notion of Drawing and the excecution of plans &c as might perhaps with proper instruction be turned to some useful account in office or out of door employment.–

Recommendations from any necessary number of individuals, and these of the most respectable order.–

Securities to any amount requisite.–

Branwell to Francis Grundy; Haworth, 9 June 1842

Any feeling of disappointment which the perusal of your letter might otherwise have caused, was allayed by its kindly and considerate tone; but I should have been a fool to entertain, under present circumstances, any very sanguine hopes respecting situations connected with Railways; since I could not but be aware of the great glut in that market.

I had only hoped that, from the few who are generally found willing to take them, and from so many Railways being contemplated, in France &c; situations abroad would be more attainable.

You ask me, Sir; why I don't turn my attention in another direction? and so I would but that most of my relations, and more immediate connections, are Clergymen, or, by a private life, somewhat removed from this busy world – And, as for the church, I have not one mental quality – except perhaps hypocrisy – whi[c]h would make me cut a figure in it's pulpits.

Mr James. Montgomery, and another literary gentleman, who have lately seen some thing of my 'head work', wish me to turn some attention to literature, sending me, along with their advice, plenty of puff and praise; and this may be all very well; but I have little conceit of myself, and great desire for activity.

Charlotte to Ellen; Brussels, July 1842

I consider it doubtful whether I shall come home in September or not – Madame Heger has made a proposal for both me and Emily to stay another half year – offering to dismiss her English master and take me as English teacher – also to employ Emily some part of each day as in teaching music to a certain number of the pupils – for these services we are to be allowed to continue our studies in French and

German – and to have board &c. without paying for it – no salaries however are offered – the proposal is kind and in a great selfish city like Brussels and a great selfish school containing nearly ninety pupils (boarders & day-pupils included) implies a degree of interest which demands gratitude in return – I am inclined to accept it – what think you? . . . I don't deny that I sometimes wish to be in England or that I have brief attacks of home-sickness – but on the whole I have borne a very valiant heart so far – and I have been happy in Brussels because I have always been fully occupied with the employments that I like – Emily is making rapid progresse in French, German, Music and Drawing – Monsieur & Madame Heger begin to recognize the valuable points of her character under her singularities.

Laetitia Wheelwright, friend and fellow pupil of Charlotte at the Pensionnat Heger, to Clement Shorter, biographer of Charlotte Brontë; January 1896

I am afraid my recollections of Emily Brontë will not aid you much. I simply disliked her from the first, her tallish ungainly ill-dressed figure contrasting so strangely with Charlotte's small, neat trim person, although their dresses were alike; always answering our jokes with 'I wish to be as God made me'. She taught my three youngest sisters music for four months to my annoyance, as she would only take them in their play hours, so as not to curtail her own school hours, naturally causing many tears to small children, the eldest 10, the youngest not seven. Fortunately she was summoned home in November and did not return to Brussels. Charlotte was devotedly attached to her, and thought so highly of her talents.

Monsieur Heger, quoted by Mrs Gaskell in her Life of Charlotte Brontë

Emily had a head for logic, and a capability of argument, unusual in a man, and rare indeed in a woman, according to M. Heger. Impairing the force of this gift, was her stubborn tenacity of will, which rendered her obtuse to all reasoning where her own wishes, or her own sense of right, was concerned. 'She should have been a man –

a great navigator,' said M. Heger in speaking of her. 'Her powerful reason would have deduced new spheres of discovery from the knowledge of the old; and her strong, imperious will would never have been daunted by opposition or difficulty; never have given way but with life.' And yet, moreover, her faculty of imagination was such that, if she had written a history, her view of scenes and characters would have been so vivid, and so powerfully expressed, and supported by such a show of argument, that it would have dominated over the reader, whatever might have been his previous opinions, or his cooler perceptions of its truth.

Mary Taylor to Ellen; Brussels, 24 September 1842

Charlotte & Emily are well; not only in health but in mind & hope. They are content with their present position & even gay & I think they do quite right not to return to England though one of them at least could earn more at the beautiful town of Bradford than she is now doing.

Madame Heger's offer to the sisters had dovetailed neatly with Charlotte's own schemes to stay on in Brussels after their aunt's money ran out, but a crisis at home put paid to all their plans. First William Weightman, the young curate, died of cholera and then Aunt Branwell fell ill of a bowel obstruction; Branwell, still at home after losing his job in the spring, nursed them both devotedly and watched helplessly as they died agonizing deaths.

Patrick, funeral sermon for the late Reverend William Weightman; Haworth, 2 October 1842

In his preaching, and practising, he was, as every clergyman ought to be, neither distant nor austere, timid nor obtrusive, nor bigoted, exclusive, nor dogmatical. He was affable, but not familiar; open, but not too confiding. He thought it better, and more scriptural, to make the love of God, rather than the fear of hell, the ruling motive for obedience. He did not see why true believers, having the promise of the life that now is, as well as that which is to come, should create unto themselves artificial sorrows, and disfigure the garment of gospel peace with the garb of sighing and sadness. Pondering on, and rejoicing in the glad tidings of salvation, he wished others to rejoice from the same principles, and though he preached the necessity of sincere repentance, and heart-felt sorrow for sin, he believed that the convert, in his freedom from its thraldom, should rejoice evermore in the glorious liberty of the gospel . . . His character wore well; the surest proof of real worth. He had, it is true, some peculiar advantages. Agreeable in person and manners, and constitutionally cheerful, his first introduction was prepossessing. But what he gained at first, he did not lose afterwards. He had those qualities which enabled him rather to gain ground. He had classical attainments of the first order, and above all, his religious principles were sound and orthodox . . . In visiting, and cottage lectures, a most important part of a minister's duty, he . . . was as active and sedulous as health and circumstances would permit; and in the Sunday School, especially, he was useful in more than an ordinary degree. He had the rare art of communicating information with diligence and strictness, without austerity, so as to render instruction, even to the youngest and most giddy, a pleasure, and not a task . . . Thus, our reverend friend lived – but, it may be asked, how did he die? During his illness, I generally visited him twice a day, joined with him in prayer, heard his request for the prayers of this congregation, listened to him whilst he expressed his entire dependence on the merits of the Saviour, heard of his pious admonitions to his attendants, and saw him in tranquility close his eyes on this bustling, vain, selfish world; so that I may truly say, his end was peace, and his hope glory.

Branwell to Francis Grundy; Haworth, 25 October 1842

There is no misunderstanding. I have had a long attendance at the death-bed of the Rev Mr Weightman, one of my dearest friends, and now I am attending at the death-bed of my aunt, who has been for twenty years as my mother. I expect her to die in a few hours. As my sisters are far from home, I have had much on my mind, and these things must serve as an apology for what was never intended as neglect of your friendship to us . . .

Branwell to Francis Grundy; Haworth, 29 October 1842

As I don't want to lose a <u>real</u> friend, I write in deprecation of the tone of your letter. Death only has made me neglectful of your kindness, and I have lately had so much experience with him, that your sister would not <u>now</u> blame me for indulging in gloomy visions either of this world or another. I am incoherent, I fear, but I have been waking two nights witnessing such agonising suffering as I would not wish my worst enemy to endure; and I have now lost the guide and director of all the happy days connected with my childhood.

Charlotte to Ellen; Haworth, 10 November 1842

I was not yet returned to England when your letter arrived – We received the first news of Aunt's illness – Wednesday Novbr 2nd – we decided to come home directly – next morning a second letter informed us of her death. We sailed from Antwerp on Sunday – we travelled day & night and got home on Tuesday morning – of course the funeral and all was over. We shall see her no more – Papa is pretty well We found Anne at home she is pretty well also – . . . Martha Taylor's illness was unknown to me till the day before she died – I hastened to Kokleberg the next morning – unconscious that she was in great danger – and was told that it was finished, she had died in the night – Mary was taken away to Bruxelles – I have seen Mary frequently since – she is in no way crushed by the event – but while Martha was ill she was to her, more than a Mother – more than a Sister watching – nursing – cherishing her – so tenderly, so unweariedly – she appears calm and serious now – no bursts of violent emotion – no exaggeration of distress – I have seen Martha's grave – the place where her ashes lie in a foreign country. Aunt – Martha – Taylor – Mr Weightman are now all gone – how dreary & void everything seems – Mr Weightman's illness was exactly what Martha's was – he was ill the same length of time & died in the same manner – Aunts disease was internal obstruction. she also was ill a fortnight.

Monsieur Heger to Patrick; Brussels, 5 November 1842

I have not the honour of knowing you personally, yet I feel a sincere esteem for you, because there is no risk of being mistaken in judging a father of a family by his children and, from this point of view, the education and sentiments that we have found in your daughters can only give us a very high idea of your merit and your character. You will learn, no doubt with pleasure, that your children have made quite remarkable progress in all the branches of education, and that that progress is entirely due to their love of work and their perseverance; we have had to do little for such pupils; their improvement is more your work than ours; we have not had to teach them the value of time and education, they had learnt all that in their paternal home and we, for our part, have only had the slight merit of directing their efforts and supplying suitable sustenance for the laudable activity that your daughters have derived from your example and your teaching. May the well-earned praises we have given your children be a consolation to you in the sorrow which afflicts you; that is our hope in writing to you and it will be, for Miss Charlotte and Miss Emily, a sweet and fine recompense for their labours.

In losing our two dear pupils, we should not hide from you that we feel both regret and anxiety; we are grieved because this sudden separation is going to cut short the almost paternal affection we feel for them and our pain increases at the thought of so much work interrupted, so many good things begun, which only required time to be brought to a favourable conclusion. In a year each of your daughters would have been completely prepared for all future eventualities; each of them was acquiring both learning and, at the same time, a knowledge of teaching; Miss Emily was about to learn the piano, to receive lessons from the best professor that we have in Belgium, and already she had little pupils herself; she was at the same time losing the remnants of her ignorance and the more embarrassing remnants of her timidity. Miss Charlotte was beginning to give lessons in French and to acquire that confidence, that aplomb so necessary to teaching; another year or more and the work would have been done and done well. Then, if you had agreed, we could have offered your daughters, or at least one of them, a position which would have been to her taste and which would have given her that delightful independence which is so difficult for a young person to find.

Monsieur Heger's letter to Patrick gave Charlotte the ammunition she needed to persuade him to allow her to return to Brussels. Emily had apparently no wish to do so and, as Anne still had her job at Thorp Green, she was the obvious person to assume the role of family housekeeper in Aunt Branwell's stead. The family spent Christmas quietly together at home, enlivened by a visit from Ellen Nussey, then separated once more. Emily remained at home with her father; Branwell went to join Anne at Thorp Green, where he was to take sole charge of the only boy in the Robinson family, young Edmund, who had outgrown Anne's care. Charlotte returned alone to Brussels.

Mary Taylor to Ellen; Germany, 16 February 1843

I know well how you would spend the month you talk of when Miss Brontë was with you & how you would discuss all imaginable topics & all imaginable people all day & half the night. Tell me something about Emily Brontë. I can't imagine how the newly acquired qualities can _fit_ in, in the same head & heart that is occupied by the old ones. Imagine Emily turning over prints or 'taking wine' with any stupid fop & preserving her temper & politeness! . . . I have heard from Charlotte since her arrival – she seems content at least but [I] fear her sister's absence will have a bad effect. When people have so little amusement they cannot afford to lose _any_. However we shall see.

Charlotte to Ellen; Brussels, 6 March 1843

I am settled by this time of course – I am not too much overloaded with occupation and besides teaching English I have time to improve myself in German. I ought to consider myself well off and to be thankful for my good fortune – I hope I am thankful – and if I could always keep up my spirits – and never feel lonely or long for companionship or friendship or whatever they call it, I should do very well – As I told you before Msieur and Mde Heger are the only two persons in the house for whom I really experience regard and esteem and of course I cannot always be with them nor even often – They told me when I first returned that I was to consider their sitting-room my sitting-room also and to go there whenever I was not engaged in the school-room – this however I cannot do – in the day-time it is a public-room – where music-masters and mistresses are constantly passing in and out and in the evening I will not and ought not to intrude on Mr & Mde Heger & their children – thus I am a good deal by myself out of school-hours – but that does not signify –

I now regularly give English lessons to Mr Heger and his brother-in-law Mr Chappelle (Mr H's first wife was the sister of Mr C's present wife) they get on with wonderful rapidity – especially the first – he already begins to speak English very decently – if you could see and hear the efforts I make to teach them to pronounce like Englishmen and their unavailing attempts to imitate, you would laugh to all eternity.

The Carnival is just over and we have entered upon the gloom and abstinence of Lent – the first day of Lent we had coffee without milk for breakfast – vinegar & vegetables with a very little salt-fish for dinner and bread for supper – The carnival was nothing but masking and mum[m]ery – Mr Heger took me and one of the pupils into the town to see the masks – it was animating to see the immense crowds & the general gaiety – but the masks were nothing –

Charlotte to Ellen; Brussels, April 1843

Is there ever any talk now of your coming to Brussels? During the bitter cold weather we had through February and the principal part of March – I did not regret that you had not accompanied me – If I had seen you shivering as I shivered myself – if I had seen your hands and feet as red and swelled as mine were – my discomfort would just have been doubled – I can do very well under this sort of thing – it does not fret me – it only makes me numb and silent – but if you were to pass a winter in Belgium you would be ill – However, more genial weather is coming now and I wish you were here — yet I never have pressed you & never would press you too warmly to come — there are privations & humiliations to submit to — there is monotony and uniformity of life — and above all there is a constant sense of solitude in the midst of numbers — the Protestant the Foreigner is a solitary being whether as teacher or pupil — I do not say this by way of complaining of my own lot — for though I acknowledge that there are certain disadvantages in my present position, what position on earth is without them? and whenever I turn back to compare what I am with what I was — my place here with my place at Mrs Sedgwick's or Mrs White's — I am thankful.

Charlotte to Branwell; Brussels, 1 May 1843

Are you in better health and spirits and does Anne continue to be pretty well —? I understand papa has been to see you — did he seem cheerful and well? Mind when you write to me you answer these questions as I wish to know — Also give me a detailed account as to how you get on with your pupil and the rest of the family I have received a general assurance that you do well and are in good odour — but I want to know particulars —

As for me I am very well and wag on as usual, I perceive however that I grow exceedingly misanthropic and sour — you will say this is no news, and that you never knew me possessed of the contrary qualities, philanthropy & sugariness — das ist wahr (which being translated means that is true) but the fact is the people here are no go whatsoever — amongst 120 persons, which compose the daily population of this house I can discern only 1 or 2 who deserve anything like regard — This is not owing to foolish fastidiousness on my part — but to the absence of decent qualities on theirs — they have not intellect or politeness or good-nature or good-feeling — they are nothing — I don't hate them — hatred would be too warm a feeling — They have no sensations themselves and they excite none — but one wearys from day to day of caring nothing, fearing nothing, liking nothing hating nothing — being nothing, doing nothing — yes, I teach & sometimes get red-in-the-face with impatience at their stupidity — but don't think I ever scold or fly into a passion — if I spoke warmly, as warmly as I sometimes used to do at Roe-Head they would think me mad – nobody ever gets into a passion here – such a thing is not known – the phlegm that thickens their blood is too gluey to boil – they are very false in their relations with each other – but they rarely quarrel & friendship is a folly they are unacquainted with – The black swan Mr Heger is the sole veritable exception to this rule (for Madame, always cool & always reasoning is not quite an exception) but I rarely speak to Mr now for not being a pupil I have little or nothing to do with him – from time to time he shews his kind-heartedness by loading me with books – so that I am still indebted to him for all the pleasure or amusement I have – . . . It is a curious metaphysical fact that always in the evening when I am in the great Dormitory alone – having no other company than a number of beds with white curtains I always recur as fanatically as ever to the old ideas the old faces & the old scenes in the world below

Increasingly lonely and disillusioned with life in Brussels, Charlotte was rapidly becoming more emotionally dependent on Monsieur Heger. What had begun as simple admiration of the qualities which made him such an outstanding teacher was turning into an unhealthy and obsessive love for the man. Ironically, her brother was also embarking on the great love affair of his life and the object of his passion was also married; unlike Charlotte, however, Branwell received every encouragement.

Branwell to John Brown, sexton of Haworth; extracts made in 1859 by Lord Houghton from a letter by Branwell written at Thorp Green, May 1843

In May 1843 he writes from Mr Robinson's near York – (Thorpe) to say he is living in a palace, with a delightful pupil – I curl my hair & scent my handkerchief like a Squire – I am the favourite of all the household – my master is generous – but my mistress is DAMN-ABLY TOO FOND OF ME She is a pretty woman, about 37. with a darkish skin & bright glancing eyes. – He asks his friend seriously to advise him what to do – tells him to consult two other grave men, who will understand him. is it worth-while for him to go on to extremities, which she evidently desires – the husband is sick & emaciated – she is always making him presents, talking to his sister (the governess) about him – telling him she does not care a farthing for him – asking him if he loves her & so on

Emily to Ellen; Haworth, 22 May 1843

Dear Miss Ellen,

I should be wanting in common civility if I did not thank you for your kindness in letting me know of an opportunity to send 'postage-free.'

I have written as you directed though if 'next Tuesday' means tomorrow I fear it will be too late to go with Mr Taylor.

Charlotte has never mentioned a word about coming home if you would go over for half a year perhaps you might be able to bring her back with you otherwise she may vegetate there till the age of Methuselah for mere lack of courage to face the voyage.

All here are in good health so was Anne according to the last accounts – the holydays will be here in a week or two and then if she be willing I will get her to write you a proper letter – a feat that I have never performed.

With love and good wishes,
E J Brontë

Charlotte to Emily; Brussels, 29 May 1843

I have now the entire charge of the English lessons. I have given two lessons to the first class. Hortense Lannoy was a picture on these occasions, her face was black as a 'blue-piled thunder-loft,' and her two ears were red as raw beef. To all questions asked her reply was, 'je ne sais pas.' It is a pity but her friends could meet with a person qualified to cast out a devil. I am richly off for companionship in these parts. Of late days, Mr and Mde Heger rarely speak to me, and I really don't pretend to care a fig for any body else in the establishment. You are not to suppose by that expression that I am under the influence of <u>warm</u> affection for Mde Heger. I am convinced she does not like me – why, I can't tell, nor do I think she herself has any definite reason for the aversion; but for one thing, she cannot comprehend why I do not make intimate friends of Mesdames Blanche, Sophie, and Haussé. M. Heger is wondrously influenced by Madame, and I should not wonder if he disapproves very much of my unamiable want of sociability. He has already given me a brief lecture on universal bienveillance, and, perceiving that I don't improve in consequence, I fancy he has taken to considering me as a person to be let alone – left to the error of her ways; and consequently he has in a great measure withdrawn the light of his countenance, and I get on from day to day in a Robinson-Crusoe-like condition – very lonely.

Charlotte to Ellen; Brussels, 6 August 1843

If I complain in this letter have mercy and don't blame me for I forewarn you that I am in low spirits and that Earth and Heaven seem dreary and empty to me at this moment – In a few days our vacations will begin – everybody is joyous and animated at the prospect because everybody is to go home – I know that I am to stay here during the 5 weeks that the holidays last and that I shall be much alone and consequently get downcast and find both days & nights of a weary length – It is the first time in my life that I have really dreaded the vacation.

Charlotte to Emily; Brussels, 2 September 1843

Yesterday I went on a pilgrimage to the cemetery, and far beyond it on to a hill where there was nothing but fields as far as the horizon. When I came back it was evening; but I had such a repugnance to return to the house, which contained nothing that I cared for, I still kept threading the streets in the neighbourhood of the Rue d'Isabelle and avoiding it. I found my self opposite Ste Gudule, and the bell, whose voice you know, began to toll for evening salut. I went in, quite alone (which procedure you will say is not much like me), wandered about the aisles where a few old women were saying their prayers, till vespers begun. I stayed till they were over. Still I could not leave the church or force myself to go home – to school I mean.

An odd whim came into my head. In a solitary part of the Cathedral six or seven people still remained kneeling by the confessionals. In two confessionals I saw a priest. I felt as if I did not care what I did, provided it was not absolutely wrong, and that it served to vary my life and yield a moment's interest. I took a fancy to change myself into a Catholic and go and make a real confession to see what it was like. Knowing me as you do, you will think this odd, but when people are by themselves they have singular fancies. A penitent was occupied in confessing. They do not go into the sort of pew or cloister which the priest occupies, but kneel down on the steps and confess through a grating. Both the confessor and the penitent whisper very low, you can hardly hear their voices. After I had watched two or three penitents go and return, I approached at last and knelt down in a niche which was just vacated. I had to kneel there ten minutes waiting, for on the other side was another penitent invisible to me. At last that went away and a little wooded door inside the grating opened, and I saw the priest leaning his ear towards me. I was obliged to begin, and yet I did not know a word of the formula with which they always commence their confessions. It was a funny position. I felt precisely as I did when alone on the Thames at midnight. I commenced with saying I was a foreigner and had been brought up a Protestant. The priest asked if I was a Protestant then. I somehow could not tell a lie, and said 'yes.' He replied that in that case I could not 'jouir du bonheur de la confesse'; but I was determined to confess, and at last he said he would allow me because it might be the first step towards returning to the true church. I actually did confess – a real confession. When I had done he told me his address, and said that every morning I was to go to the rue du Parc – to his house – and he would reason with me and try to convince me of the error and enormity of being a Protestant!!! I promised faithfully to go. Of course, however, the adventure stops there, and I hope I shall never see the priest again. I think you had better not tell papa of this. He will not understand that it was only a freak, and will perhaps think I am going to turn Catholic.

Charlotte to Emily; Brussels, 1 October 1843

This is Sunday morning. They are at their idolatrous 'messe,' and I am here – that is, in the réfectoire. I should like uncommonly to be in the dining-room at home, or in the kitchen, or the back kitchen. I should like even to be cutting up the hash, with the clerk and some register people at the other table, and you standing by, watching that I put enough flour, and not too much pepper, and, above all, that I save the best pieces of the leg of mutton for Tiger and Keeper, the first of which personages would be jumping about the dish and carving-knife, and the latter standing like a devouring flame on the kitchen floor. To complete the picture, Tabby blowing the fire, in order to boil the potatoes to a sort of vegetable glue! How divine are these recollections to me at this moment! Yet I have no thought of coming home just now. I lack a real pretext for doing so . . . Tell me whether papa really wants me very much to come home, and whether you do likewise. I have an idea that I should be of no use there – a sort of aged person upon the parish.

Charlotte to Ellen; Brussels, 13 October 1843

It is a curious position to be so utterly solitary in the midst of numbers – sometimes this solitude oppresses me to excess – one day lately I felt as if I could bear it no longer – and I went to Mde Heger and gave her notice – If it had depended on her I should certainly have soon been at liberty but Monsieur Heger – having heard of what was in agitation – sent for me the day after – and pronounced with vehemence his decision that I should not leave – I could not at that time have persevered in my intention without exciting him to passion – so I promised to stay a while longer – how long that while will be I do not know – I should not like to return to England to do nothing – I am too old for that now – but if I could hear of a favourable occasion for commencing a school – I think I should embrace it.

Charlotte to Emily; Brussels, 19 December 1843

Dear E.J.

I have taken my determination. I hope to be at home the day after New Year's Day. I have told Mde Heger. But in order to come home I shall be obliged to draw on my cash for another £5. I have only £3 at present, and as there are several little things I should like to buy before I leave Brussels – which you know cannot be got as well in England – £3 would not suffice. Low spirits have afflicted me much lately, but I hope all will be well when I get home – above all, if I find papa and you and B. and A. well. I am not ill in body. It is only the mind which is a trifle shaken – for want of comfort.

I shall try to cheer up now. – Good-bye.

C.B.

Charlotte to Ellen; Haworth, January 1844

I cannot tell what occupies your thoughts and time – are you ill? is some one of your family ill? are you married? are you dead? if it be so you may as well write a word to let me know – for my part I am again in old England . . .

Charlotte to Ellen; Haworth, 23 January 1844

Everyone asks me what I am going to do now that I am returned home and every one seems to expect that I should immediately commence a school – In truth Ellen it is what I should wish to do . . . I suffered much before I left Brussels – I think however long I live I shall not forget what the parting with Monsr Heger cost me – It grieved me so much to grieve him who has been so true and kind and disinterested a friend – at parting he gave me a sort of diploma certifying my abilities as a teacher – sealed with the seal of the Athenée Royal of which he is professor. He wanted me to take one of his little girls with me – this however I refused to do as I knew it would not have been agreeable to Madame – I was surprised also at the degree of regret expressed by my Belgian pupils when they knew I was going to leave   I did not think it had been in their phlegmatic natures – . . . I do not know whether you feel as I do Ellen – but there are times now when it appears to me as if all my ideas and feelings except a few friendships and affections are changed from what they used to be – something in me which used to be enthusiasm is tamed down and broken – I have fewer illusions – what I wish for now is active exertion – a stake in life – Haworth seems such a lonely, quiet spot, buried away from the world – I no longer regard myself as young, indeed I shall soon be 28 – and it seems as if I ought to be working and braving the rough realities of the world as other people do – It is however my duty to restrain this feeling at present and I will endeavour to do so

Though she had torn herself away from Brussels, Charlotte found it impossible to sever her links with Monsieur Heger. She wrote to him, pouring out on paper the things which she could not say to his face.

Charlotte to Monsieur Heger; Haworth, 24 July 1844

I have just been offered a position as first mistress in a large boarding-school in Manchester, with a salary of 100£ i.e. 2500 frs a year – I cannot accept it – for in accepting it I would have to leave my father and that I cannot do – However I have a plan (when one lives in seclusion the brain works all the time – one longs for occupation – one longs to begin active life) Our Parsonage is quite a large house – with some alterations – there will be room for five or six boarders – if I can find that number of children of good family I will devote myself to their education – Emily does not like teaching much but she would occupy herself with the housekeeping and, although a little anti-social, she is too good hearted not to do her utmost for the well-being of the children – she is also very generous and as for order, economy, organisation – hard work – all those things which are essential in a boarding school – I willingly take responsibility

There is my plan Monsieur, which I have already explained to my father and which he approves – It only remains to find pupils – rather a difficult thing – for we live far from towns and people do not willingly cross the mountains which form a barrier round us –

but a task which is without difficulty is almost without merit – there is great interest in overcoming obstacles – I do not say that I will succeed but I will <u>try</u> to succeed – the effort itself will do me good – there is nothing I fear as much as idleness – unemployment – inertia – lethargy of the faculties – when the body is idle, the spirit suffers cruelly. I would not feel this lethargy if I could write – once I spent days, weeks, entire months writing and not all in vain because Southey, and Coleridge – two of our best writers, to whom I sent some manuscripts, were pleased to give their approbation – but at present my sight is too weak to write – if I write too much I will go blind. This weakness of sight is a terrible privation for me – without it, do you know what I would do Monsieur? – I would write a book and dedicate it to my literature master – to the only master I have ever had – to you Monsieur. I have often told you in French how much I respect you – how much I owe to your goodness, to your advice, I would like to say it once in English – that cannot be – it must not be thought of – a literary career is closed to me – that of teaching alone is open to me – it does not offer the same attractions – it does not matter, I will enter it and if I do not go far, it will not be through lack of diligence.

Charlotte to Ellen; Haworth, ?10 August 1844

I have seriously entered into the enterprise of keeping a school – or rather taking a limited number of pupils at home   that is I have begun to seek in good earnest for pupils – I wrote to Mrs White, not asking her for her daughter – I cannot do that – but informing her of my intentions I received an answer from Mr White expressive of, I believe, sincere regret that I had not informed them a month sooner in which case, he said, they would gladly have sent me their own daughter and also Colonel Stott's – but that now both were promised to Miss Cockhills' –

I was partly disappointed by this answer – and partly gratified – indeed I derived quite an impulse of encouragement from the warm assurance that if I had but applied a little sooner they would certainly have sent me Sarah Louise   I own I had misgivings that nobody would be willing to send a child for education to Haworth – these

The Misses Bronte's Establishment

FOR

THE BOARD AND EDUCATION

OF A LIMITED NUMBER OF

YOUNG LADIES.

THE PARSONAGE, HAWORTH,

NEAR BRADFORD.

TERMS.

	£.	s.	d.
BOARD AND EDUCATION, including Writing, Arithmetic, History, Grammar, Geography, and Needle Work, per Annum, ...	35	o	o
French, .. ⎫ German, .. ⎬ .. .. each per Quarter .. .. Latin .. .. ⎭	I	I	o
Music, ... ⎫ Drawing, .. ⎭ .. .. each per Quarter	I	I	o
Use of Piano Forte, per Quarter, ...	o	5	o
Washing, per Quarter, ...	o	I5	o

---

Each Young Lady to be provided with One Pair of Sheets, Pillow Cases, Four Towels, a Dessert and Tea-spoon.

A Quarter's Notice, or a Quarter's Board, is required previous to the Removal of a Pupil.

misgivings are partly done away with – . . . As soon as I can get an assurance of only <u>one</u> pupil – I will have cards of terms printed – and will commence the repairs necessary in the house – I wish all that to be done before winter –

Charlotte to Ellen; Haworth, 2 October 1844

I – Emily & Anne are truly obliged to you for the efforts you have made in our behalf – and if you have not been successful you are only like ourselves – every one wishes us well – but there are no pupils to be had – We have no present intention however of breaking our hearts on the subject – still less of feeling mortified at defeat – The effort must be beneficial whatever the result may be – because it teaches us experience and an additional knowledge of the world . . .

Charlotte to Ellen; Haworth, 14 November 1844

We have made no alterations yet in our house – it would be folly to do so while there is so little likelihood of our ever getting pupils – I fear you are giving yourself far too much trouble on our account – Depend upon it Ellen if you were to persuade a mamma to bring her child to Haworth – the aspect of the place would frighten her and she would probably take the dear thing back with her instanter We are all glad that we have made the attempt and we are not cast down because it has not succeeded.

Chapter Six

1845

Anxious not to encourage his former pupil's all too obvious infatuation with him, Monsieur Heger had gradually distanced himself from Charlotte, initially by restricting their correspondence to once every six months and then by neglecting to answer her letters. This had the opposite effect to the one he had intended. Charlotte became increasingly desperate and correspondingly indiscreet. The passion for him that she had nurtured in silence during the last year of her residence in Brussels had still to be stifled at home. She could speak of her illicit love to no one, not even to Emily, so, in the few letters Monsieur Heger permitted her to send him, she became more overt in her expressions of affection. As he did not reciprocate her feelings, Monsieur Heger attempted to destroy the letters but his wife, who had had her suspicions about Charlotte for some time, found them in his waste-paper bin, carefully sewed back together the torn fragments and stored them away for future reference.

Charlotte to Monsieur Heger; Haworth, 8 January 1845

Day and night I find neither rest nor peace – if I sleep I have tortured dreams in which I see you always severe, always gloomy and annoyed with me –

Forgive me then Monsieur if I take the course of writing to you again – How can I endure life if I make no effort to alleviate my sufferings?

I know that you will be impatient when you read this letter – you will say again that I am over-excited – that I have black thoughts &c. It may be so Monsieur – I do not seek to justify myself, I submit to every kind of reproach – all that I know – is that I cannot –

that I will not resign myself to losing the friendship of my master completely – I would rather undergo the greatest physical sufferings than always have my heart torn apart by bitter regrets. If my master withdraws his friendship entirely from me I will be completely without hope – if he gives me a little – very little – I will be content – happy, I will have a reason for living – for working –

Monsieur, the poor do not need much to live – they only ask for the crumbs of bread which fall from the rich man's table – but if one refuses them these crumbs of bread – they die of hunger – Nor do I need much affection from those I love – I would not know what to do with an absolute and complete friendship – I am not used to such a thing – but you once showed me a little interest when I was your pupil in Brussels – and I cling on to preserving that little interest – I cling on to it as I cling on to life . . .

I do not wish to reread this letter – I will send it as I have written it – Nevertheless, I have the vague feeling that there are cold and rational people who would say on reading this – 'she is raving' – The only revenge I would wish on such people is a single day of the torments I have suffered for eight months – we would see then if they did not rave too.

Unable to conquer her feelings for Monsieur Heger and, after the failure of the school scheme, deprived of an outlet for her energies, Charlotte sank further into depression. In February 1845 there was another parting, this time with her old school-friend and closest confidante outside the family, Mary Taylor, who finally set sail for a new life in New Zealand with her brother Waring. Charlotte, paying a farewell visit to Mary at Hunsworth, could not fail to contrast her friend's activity and courage with her own paralysing inertia of body and mind.

Mary Taylor to Mrs Gaskell; 18 January 1856

When I last saw Charlotte [February 1845] she told me she had quite decided to stay at home. She owned she did not like it. Her health was weak. She said she would like any change at first, as she had liked Brussels at first, and she thought that there must be some possibility for some people of having a life of more variety and more communion with human kind, but she saw none for her. I told her very warmly that she ought not to stay at home; that to spend the next five years at home, in solitude and weak health, would ruin her; that she would never recover it. Such a dark shadow came over her face when I said, 'Think of what you'll be five years hence!' that I stopped, and said, 'Don't cry, Charlotte!' She did not cry, but went on walking up and down the room, and said in a little while, 'But I intend to stay, Polly.'

Charlotte to Ellen; Haworth, 20 February 1845

I spent a week at Hunsworth not very pleasantly; headache, sickliness, and flatness of spirits made me a poor companion, a sad drag on the vivacious and loquacious gaiety of all the other inmates of the house. I never was fortunate enough to be able to rally, for so much as a single hour, while I was there. I am sure all, with the exception perhaps of Mary, were very glad when I took my departure. I begin to perceive that I have too little life in me, nowadays, to be fit company for any except very quiet people. Is it age, or what else, that changes one so?

Charlotte to Ellen; Haworth, 24 March 1845

I can hardly tell you how time gets on here at Haworth – There is no event whatever to mark its progress – one day resembles another – and all have heavy lifeless physiognomies – Sunday – baking day & Saturday are the only ones that bear the slightest distinctive mark – meantime life wears away – I shall soon be 30 – and I have done nothing yet – Sometimes I get melancholy – at the prospect before and behind me – yet it is wrong and foolish to repine – undoubtedly my Duty directs me to stay at home for the present – There was a time when Haworth was a very pleasant place to me, it is not so now – I feel as if we were all buried here – I long to travel – to work to live a life of action – Excuse me my dear Ellen for troubling you with my fruitless wishes – I will put by the rest and not bother you with them.

You <u>must</u> write to me – if you knew how welcome your letters are – you would write very often. Your letters and the French Newspapers – are the only messengers that come to me from the outer world – beyond our Moors; and very welcome messengers they are.

Charlotte to Ellen; Haworth, 2 April 1845

Ten years ago I should have laughed heartily at your account of the blunder you made in mistaking the bachelor doctor of Burlington for a Married Man   I should have certainly thought you scrupulous over-much – and wondered how you could possibly regret being civil to a decent individual merely because he happened to be single instead of double. Now however I can perceive that your scruples are founded on common-sense. I know that if women wish to escape the stigma of husband-seeking they must act & look like marble or clay – cold – expressionless, bloodless – for every appearance of feeling of joy – sorrow – friendliness, antipathy, admiration – disgust are alike construed by the world into an attempt to hook in a husband – Never mind Nell – well meaning women have their own Consciences to comfort them after all – do not therefore be too much afraid of shewing yourself as you are – affectionate and good-hearted – do not too harshly repress sentiments & feelings excellent in themselves because you fear that some puppy may fancy that you are letting them come out to fascinate him – Do not condemn yourself to live only by halves because if you shewed too much animation some pragmatical thing in breeches (excuse the expression) might take it into its pate to imagine that you designed to dedicate your precious life to its inanity – Still, a composed – decent, equable deportment is a capital treasure and that you possess.

Charlotte to Ellen; Haworth, 24 April 1845

I was amused with your allusions to individuals at Hunsworth – I have little doubt of the truth of the report you mention about Mr Joe [Taylor] paying assiduous attention to Isabella Nussey – whether it will ever come to a match is another thing – <u>Money</u> would decide that point as it does most others of a similar nature – You are perfectly right in saying that Mr Joe is more influenced by Opinion than he, himself suspects – I saw his lordship in a new light last time I was at Hunsworth – sometimes I could scarcely believe my ears when I heard the stress he laid on wealth – Appearance Family – and all those advantages which are the acknowledged idols of the world – His conversation on Marriage (and he talked much about it) differed in no degree from that of any hackneyed Fortune-Hunter – except that with his own peculiar and native audacity he avowed views & principles which more timid individuals conceal. Of course I raised no argument against anything he said I listened and laughed inwardly to think how indignant I should have been 8 years since if any one had accused Joe Taylor of being a worshipper of Mam[m]on and of Interest. Indeed I still believe that the Joe Taylor of 10 years ago – is not the Joe Taylor of to-day – The world with its hardness and selfishness has utterly changed him – He thinks himself grown wiser than the wisest – in a worldly sense he is wise his feelings have gone through a process of petrification which will prevent them from ever warring against his interest – but Ichabod! all glory of principle and much elevation of character is gone!

The arrival of a new curate in Haworth, a belated replacement for the much-lamented William Weightman, was barely noticed by Charlotte at the time. Arthur Bell Nicholls was fortunate in being spared her usual sarcasms at the expense of curates but neither of them suspected then the major role he would later play in the Brontës' lives.

Charlotte to Mrs Rand, wife of the former National School Master of Haworth; Haworth, 26 May 1845

Papa has got a new Curate lately a Mr Nicholls from Ireland – he did duty for the first time on Sunday – he appears a respectable young man, reads well, and I hope will give satisfaction.

Some prospect of escape from Haworth was offered Charlotte by Ellen, who invited her to join her at Hathersage, in the Peak District of Derbyshire. Ellen's brother, Henry, was about to be married and she was supervising repairs to his vicarage in preparation for the arrival of the newly-weds.

1. 'Oh! Those high, wild, desolate moors, up above the whole world, and the very realms of silence!': Mrs Gaskell, describing Haworth moors in a letter to a friend after her first visit to the Parsonage in September 1853.

2. One of the earliest photographs of Church Lane, Haworth, taken across the churchyard in about 1860, before the present trees were planted. The Parsonage is at the top of the lane and the church (demolished in 1879) at the bottom. Between them is the Sunday school, built by Patrick in 1832, and at its lower end is the Sexton's cottage, where Arthur Bell Nicholls lodged with John Brown's family before his marriage to Charlotte.

3. Moorland surrounded Haworth in the Brontës' day. One of their favourite walks from childhood followed the valley of Sladen Beck, seen in this photograph, past a few scattered upland farms and up on to the moorland wilderness behind the Parsonage.

4. A typical moorland farmhouse, sketched in 1833 by the sixteen-year-old Branwell.

5. Built in 1779, Haworth Parsonage remained virtually unchanged for almost a century. This photograph, probably taken from the church tower in about 1860, splendidly illustrates the exposed position of the Parsonage on the hilltop above the township. Note the pristine steps to the front door, which Patrick had had turned because they were worn, and on the far right the washing draped over the lane wall to dry.

6. E. M. Wimperis was chosen to illustrate Smith, Elder & Co.'s 1872 edition of the Brontës' works and produced this picture of Lowood for *Jane Eyre*. It actually depicts Charlotte's model for Lowood Institution, the Clergy Daughters' School at Cowan Bridge, which the four eldest Brontë daughters attended in 1824–5.

7. The Brontës were all great animal lovers and always had as many pets as their Aunt Branwell would allow them to keep. This is the fifteen-year-old Emily's portrait 'from life' of her dog Grasper, drawn in pencil in January 1834.

8. Ellen Nussey (1817–97), Charlotte's schoolfriend, as a young girl in an undated portrait.

9. Anne Brontë (1820–49), a watercolour painted by her sister Charlotte in about 1833.

10. Roe Head School, Mirfield, a drawing done as a school exercise by Charlotte, probably in 1832.

11. (Above) Upperwood House at Rawdon, where Charlotte was a governess to the White family in 1841. Charlotte described the house as 'not very large, but exceedingly comfortable and well regulated' with extensive and 'exquisitely beautiful' grounds.

12. (Left) Joseph Bentley Leyland (1811–51), a Halifax-based sculptor who became a close friend and correspondent of Branwell. He actively encouraged Branwell's artistic and poetic ambitions and introduced him to his own literary circles.

13. William Robinson (1799–1838), RA, a former pupil of Sir Thomas Lawrence, whom Patrick engaged to teach Branwell the art of portraiture.

14. A thumbnail self-portrait of Branwell Brontë (1817–48), sketched in pencil on the back of his 1840 drawing of Broughton church.

15. Branwell's famous portrait of his sisters, (left to right) Anne, Emily and Charlotte, painted as an exercise for William Robinson in 1834. It is usually known as the 'Pillar Portrait' because of the light-coloured column between Emily and Charlotte. In fact, this 'pillar' was actually Branwell's attempt to cover up his own self-portrait, probably on Robinson's advice because the composition was too crowded. As the paint has become transparent with age, Branwell's figure, with its distinctive red hair and cravat, can once again be dimly made out, as can the pencil under-drawing of the other portraits. The picture was folded into four by Arthur Bell Nicholls and stored for over forty years on top of a wardrobe, hence the dramatic cracks in the paint.

16. A previously unpublished letter (see pp. 33–4), written jointly by Branwell and Patrick to William Robinson on 16 November 1835. Asking Robinson to give Branwell a further course of lessons, the letter supports the theory that, contrary to Brontë legend. Branwell never made an abortive attempt to enter the Royal Academy.

Charlotte's lethargy was such that she did not immediately leap at the chance, using Patrick's failing eyesight as an excuse not to stir from home. Anne's decision to resign from Thorp Green, no doubt combined with robust encouragement from both her sisters, finally persuaded her to change her mind.

Charlotte to Ellen; Haworth, 13 June 1845

How long are you going to stay at Hathersage   As to my going to see you there, it is quite out of the question. It is hardly worth while to take so long a journey for a week or a fortnight and longer I could not stay – I feel reluctant indeed to leave papa for a single day – his sight diminishes weekly and can it be wondered at – that as he sees the most precious of his faculties leaving him, his spirits sometimes sink? t is so hard to feel that his few and scanty pleasures must all soon go – he now has the greatest difficulty in either reading or writing – and then he dreads the state of dependence to which blindness will inevitably reduce him – He fears that he will be nothing in his parish – I try to cheer him, sometimes I succeed temporarily – but no consolation can restore his sight or atone for the want of it. Still he is never peevish – never impatient only anxious and dejected.

Charlotte to Ellen; Haworth, 18 June 1845

You thought I refused you coldly did you? It was a queer sort of coldness when I would have given my ears to be able to say yes, and felt obliged to say no.

Matters are now however a little changed, Branwell and Anne are both come home. and Anne I am rejoiced to say has decided not to return to Mr Robinson's – <u>her</u> presence at home certainly makes me feel more at liberty – Then dear Ellen if all be well I will come and see you at Hathersage – tell me only when I must come – . . . Of course when I come you will let me enjoy your own company in peace and not drag me out a visiting.

I have no desire at all to see your medical-clerical curate – I think he must be like all the other curates I have seen – and they seem to me a self-seeking, vain, empty race. At this blessed moment we have no less than three of them in Haworth-Parish – and God knows there is not one to mend another.

The other day they all three . . . dropped or rather rushed in unexpectedly to tea. It was Monday and I was hot & tired – still if they had behaved quietly and decently – I would have served them out their tea in peace – but they began glorifying themselves and abusing Dissenters in such a manner – that my temper lost its balance and I pronounced a few sentences sharply & rapidly which struck them all dumb – Papa was greatly horrified also – I don't regret it.

Ellen to her friend Mary Gorham; Hathersage, 22 July 1845

Charlotte Brontè says I am to give her respects & say you are a subject of daily annoyance to her for I am so often talking of you She has great regrets she has not seen you. We have been to Castleton & the Miss Halls accompanied us through the caverns & were very lively & noisy . . . Charlotte was very much pleased with the caverns but the mirth of [the] Miss Halls was rather displeasing to her – We had Mrs Eyre's pony & we went a little way up cave dale. We shall not see Chatsworth again whilst Charlotte is here . . . C.B. leaves me on Saturday –

Emily, diary paper; Haworth, 31 July 1845

Haworth – Thursday – July 30th 1845

My birthday – showery – breezy – cool – I am twenty seven years old to day – this morning Anne and I opened the papers we wrote 4 years since on my twenty third birthday – this paper we intend, if all be well, to open on my 30th three years hence in 1848 – since the 1841 paper the following events have taken place

Our school scheme has been abandoned and instead Charlotte and I went to Brussels on the 8th of Febr[u]ary 1842

Branwell left his place at Luddenden Foot

C and I returned from Brussels November 8th 1842 in consequence of Aunt's death –

Branwell went to Thorpgreen as a tutor where Anne still continued January 1843

Charlotte returned to Brussels the same month and after staying a year came back again on new years day 1844

Anne left her situation at Thorp Green of her own accord – June 1845

Branwell left – July 1845

Anne and I went our first long Journey by ourselves together – leaving Home on the 30th of June – monday – sleeping at York – returning to Keighley Tuesday evening sleeping there and walking home on Wedensday morning – though the weather was broken, we enjoyed ourselves very much except during a few hours at Bradford and during our excursion we were Ronald Macelgin, Henry Angora, Juliet Augusteena, Rosobelle Esraldan, Ella and Julian Egramont Catherine Navarre and Cordelia Fitzaphnold escaping from the palaces of Instruction to join the Royalists who are hard driven at present by the victorious Republicans – The Gondals still flo[u]rish bright as ever   I am at present writing a work on the First Wars – Anne has been writing some articles on this and a book by Henry Sophona – We intend sticking firm by the rascals as long as they delight us which I am glad to say they do at present – I should have mentioned that last summer the school scheme was revived in full vigo[u]r – we had prospectuses printed despatched letters to all acquaintances imparting our plans and did our little all – but it was found no go – now I dont desire a school at all and none of us have any great longing for it – we have cash enough for our present wants with a prospect of accumolation – we are all in decent health – only that papa has a complaint in his eyes and with the exception of B who I hope will be better and do better, hereafter. I am quite contented for myself – not as idle as formerly, altogether as hearty and having learnt to make the most of the present and hope for the future with less fidget[i]ness that I cannot do all I wish – seldom or ever troubled with nothing to do and merely desiring that every body could be as comfortable as myself and as undesponding and then we should have a very tolerable world of it –

By mistake I find we have opened the paper on the 31st instead of the 30th   Yesterday was much such a day as this but the morning was devine –

Tabby who was gone in our last paper is come back and has lived with us – two years and a half and is in good health – Martha who also departed is here too – We have got Flossey, got and lost Tiger – lost the Hawk Nero which with the geese was given away and is doubtless dead for when I came back from Brussels I enquired on all hands and could hear nothing of him – Tiger died early last year – Keeper and Flossey are well also the canary acquired 4 years since –

We are now all at home and likely to be there some time – Branwell went to Liverpool on Tuesday to stay a week – Tabby has just been teasing me to turn as formerly to 'pilloputate' – Anne and I should have picked the black currants if it had been fine and sunshiny – I must hurry off now to my turning and ironing I have plenty of work on hands and writing and am altogether full of business with best wishes for the whole House till 1848 – July 30th and as much longer as may be I conclude
E.J. Brontë

Anne, diary paper; Haworth, 31 July 1845

Thursday July the 31st 1845. Yesterday was Emily's birthday and the time when we should have opened our 1845 paper but by mistake we opened it to day instead – How many things have happened since it was written – some pleasant some far otherwise – Yet I was then at Thorp Green and now I am only just escaped from it – I was wishing to leave it then and if I had known that I had four years longer to stay how wretched I should have been but during my stay I have had some very unpleasant and undreamt of experience of human nature – Others have seen more changes Charlotte has left Mr White's and been twice to Brussels where she stayed each time nearly a year – Emily has been there too and stayed nearly a year – Branwell has left Luddenden foot and been a Tutor at Thorp Green and had much tribulation and ill health he was very ill on Tuesday but he went with John Brown to Liverpool where he now is I suppose and we hope he will be better and do better in future – This is a dismal cloudy wet evening we have had so far a very cold wet summer – Charlotte has lately been to Hathersage in Derbyshire on a visit of three weeks to Ellen Nuss[e]y – she is now sitting sewing in the Dining-Room Emily is ironing upstairs I am sitting in the Dining Room in the Rocking chair before the fire with my feet on the fender Papa is in the parlour Tabby and Martha are I think in the Kitchen Keeper and Flossy are I do not know where little Dick is hopping in his cage – When the last paper was written we were thinking of setting up a School – the scheem has been dropt and long after taken up again and dropt again because we could not get pupils – Charlotte is thinking about getting another situation – she wishes to go to Paris – will she go? she has let Flossy in by the bye and he is now lying on the sopha – Emily is engaged in writing the Emperor Julius's life She has read some of it and I want very much to hear the rest – She is writing some poetry too I wonder what it is about – I have begun the third volume of passages in the life of an Individual, I wish I had finished it – This afternoon I began to set about making my grey figured silk frock that was dyed at Keigthley – What sort of a hand shall I make of it? E. and I have a great deal of work to do – when shall we sensibly diminish it? I want to get a habit of early rising shall I succeed? We have not yet finished our Gondal chronicles that we began three years and a half ago when will they be done? – The Gondals are at present in a sad state the Republicans are uppermost but the Royalists are not quite overcome – the young sovereigns with their brothers and sisters are still at the palace of Instruction – The Unique Society above half a year ago were wrecked on a dezart Island as they were returning from Gaaldin – they are still there but we have not played at them much yet – The Gondals in general are not in first rate playing condition – will they improve?

I wonder how we shall all be and where and how situated on the thirtyeth of July 1848 when if we are all alive Emily will be just 30 I shall be in my 29th year Charlotte in her 33rd and Branwell in his 32nd and what changes shall we have seen and known and shall we be much changed ourselves? I hope not – for the worse at least – I for my part cannot well be <u>flatter</u> or older in mind than I am now – Hoping for the best I conclude

Anne Brontë

What both the diary papers glossed over was the scandal of Branwell's unexpected dismissal from Thorp Green. His affair with Mrs Robinson had been discovered and, though Branwell himself was convinced otherwise, she had managed to avert her husband's wrath by laying all the blame at Branwell's door.

Charlotte to Ellen; Haworth, 31 July 1845

It was ten o'clock at night when I got home – I found Branwell ill – he is so very often owing to his own fault – I was not therefore shocked at first – but when Anne informed me of the immediate cause of his present illness I was greatly shocked, he had last Thursday received a note from Mr Robinson sternly dismissing him intimating that he had discovered his proceedings which he characterised as bad beyond expression and charging him on pain of exposure to break off instantly and for ever all communication with every member of his family – We have had sad work with Branwell since – he thought of nothing but stunning, or drowning his distress of mind – no one in the house could have rest – and at last we have been obliged to send him from home for a week with some one to look after him – he has written to me this morning and expresses some sense of contrition for his frantic folly – he promises amendment on his return – but so long as he remains at home I scarce dare hope for peace in the house – We must all I fear prepare for a season of distress and disquietude –

Branwell to his friend from Halifax, the sculptor J. B. Leyland; Haworth, 4 August 1845

I returned yesterday from a week's journey to Liverpool and North Wales, but I found during my absence that wherever I went a certain woman robed in black, and calling herself 'MISERY' walked by my side, and leant on my arm as affectionately as if she were my legal wife.

Like some other husbands, I could have spared her presence.

In an attempt to rouse himself, Branwell began work on a novel which drew heavily on his experiences of the past two years; Mrs Robinson would be its tragic heroine. Writing could only be a temporary distraction for his unhappiness and, as all his efforts to find another post proved ineffective, his presence at home made life increasingly difficult for his family.

Branwell to J. B. Leyland; Haworth, 10 September 1845

I have, since I saw you at Halifax, devoted my hours of time snatched from downright illness, to the composition of a three volume <u>Novel</u> – one volume of which is completed – and along with the two forthcoming ones, has been really the result of half a dozen by past years of thoughts about, and experience in, this crooked path of life.

I felt that I must rouse myself to attempt some thing while roasting daily and nightly over a slow fire – to wile away my torment and I knew that in the present state of the publishing and reading world a Novel is the most saleable article so that where ten pounds would be offered for a work the production of which would require the utmost stretch of a man's intellect – two hundred pounds would be a refused offer for three volumes whose composition would require the smoking of a cigar and the humming of a tune.

My Novel is the result of years of thought and if it gives a vivid picture of human feelings for good and evil – veiled by the cloak of deceit which must enwrap man and woman – If it records as faithfully as the pages that unveil man's heart in Hamlet or Lear the conflicting feelings and clashing pursuits in our uncertain path through life I shall be as much gratified (and as much astonished) as I should be if in betting that I could jump over the Mersey I jumped over the Irish Sea. It would not be more pleasant to light on Dublin instead of Birkenhead than to leap from the present bathos of fictitious literature on to the firmly fixed rock honoured by the foot of a Smollet or Feilding.

**★★*Branwell to ?Richard Metcalfe, Solicitor of Keighley, local agent for the projected Manchester, Hebden Bridge and Keighley Junction Railway; Haworth, [October 1845]*

Haworth.
Bradford.
Yorks.

Dear Sir,

I respectfully beg leave to offer myself as candidate for the situation of Secretary to the Manchester and Hebden Bridge and K[e]ighley and Carlisle Junction Railway.

I trust to be able to produce full testimonials as to my qualifications and Securities, if required, to any probable amount.

I am,
Dear Sir,
Your most respectful and
obedt Servt,
P.B. Bronté –

*★*Branwell to Francis Grundy; Haworth, October 1845*

When I say that since I shook hands with you in Halifax two summers ago my life till lately has been one of apparent happiness and indulgence you will ask why should I now complain? And I can only reply by shewing the under current of distress that bore my bark toward a whirlpool despite the surface waves of life that seemed wafting me toward peace.

In a letter begun in the spring of 1843 and never finished owing to incessant attacks of illness, I tried to tell you how I was situated – As Tutor to the only son of a wealthy Gentleman whose wife was sister to Mr Thos Gisborne M.p. for Nottingham, and – Mrs Evans the wife of the member for one division of Derbyshire – and the cousin of Mr Macaulay. This Lady (though her husband detested me) shewed toward me a degree of kindness which – when I was deeply grieved one day at her husbands conduct opened into an unexpected declaration of more than ordinary feeling. My admiration

of her mental and personal attractions which, though she is 17 years
older than myself, are both very great, my knowledge of her totally
unselfish generosity, sweet temper and unwearied care for all others
with ill requital in return, my horror at the heartless and unmanly
manner in which she was treated by an eunuch like fellow who
though possessed of such a treasure never even occupied the same
apartment with her – All combined to make me reciprocate an
attachment I had little dared to look for. During nearly three years
I had daily 'troubled pleasure soon chastised by fear' in the society
of one whom I must, till death, call my <u>wife</u>.

Three months since, while at home, I received a furious letter
from my Employer threat[e]ning to shoot me if I returned from the
vacation – and letters from her ladies maid and her physician informed
me of the outbreak and threatened proceedings only checked by her
firm courage and resolution that come what harm might to her none
should come to me – The wretchedly broken health and want of
energy in her bloodless mock husband made him put up with the
simple joy of daily torturing her while I was left uninjured.

Had I strength to return and meet him the results would be serious
to one or both, but providence has hitherto denied me the power
for I have lain during nine long weeks utterly shattered in body and
broken down with mental despair. The probability of his state of
health ere long leaving her free to give me herself and her estate as
was her hearts resolve never rose to drive off the prospect of her
decline under her present grief and sufferings and I dreaded too the
wreck of my mind and body which God knows have both during
a short life been severely tried.

Eleven continued nights of sleepless horrors reduced me to almost
blindness and while taken into Wales to rouse me the sweet scenery,
the sea, the sound of music only caused fits of unspeakable distress
and irrepressible tears. I implored for society and comfort but could
neither be pleasant to one or blessed by the other, and wine or other
stimulants caused not exhiliration but deeper dejection.

You will say 'What a fool!' but if you knew the many causes I
have had for sorrow which I cannot hint at here you would perhaps
pity as well as blame.

I am better now but though at the kind request of Mr Macaulay and Mr Baines I have striven to rouse my mind by writing something that I ought to make deserving of being read, I find I really cannot yet do so with effect for one line of poetry like one note of music produces in my frame a sick[e]ning thrill of despair.

I know you will – if you read it at all – despise this letter and its writer, but I can only answer the writer does the same, and he would not wish to live if he did not hope that active exertion and change of scene may yet restore him to the by past manhood which used to boast of unconquerable health, where for 3 years he has known no interval of one week from agonizing sickness, and latterly not even one day.

Charlotte to Ellen; Haworth, 4 November 1845

You do not reproach me in your last but I fear you must have thought me unkind in being so long without answering you – The fact is I had hoped to be able to ask you to come to Haworth – Branwell seemed to have a prospect of getting employment, and I waited to know the result of his efforts in order to say, 'dear Ellen come and see us' – but the place (a Secretaryship to a Railroad Committee) is given to another person   Branwell still remains at home and while <u>he</u> is here – <u>you</u> shall not come – I am more confirmed in that resolution the more I know of him – I wish I could say one word to you in his favour – but I cannot – therefore I will hold my tongue.

Charlotte's disgust at her brother's lack of self-control was all the more poignant because she was herself unable to overcome her own feelings for Monsieur Heger. At least she nursed her humiliation and hurt in private, saving her emotional outbursts for the letters she continued to write to her Brussels professor.

Charlotte to Monsieur Heger; Haworth, 18 November 1845

I tell you frankly . . . that I have tried to forget you, for the remembrance of a person whom one believes one will never see again but whom, nevertheless, one esteems highly, harasses the spirit too much and when one has suffered this kind of anxiety for one or two years, one is ready to do anything to recover calmness. I have done everything, I have sought occupations, I have forbidden myself completely the pleasure of speaking about you – even to Emily, but I cannot conquer either my regrets or my impatience – and that is humiliating – not to be master of one's own thoughts, to be slave to a regret, a memory, slave to a dominant and fixed idea which tyrannises the spirit. Why cannot I have exactly as much friendship for you as you have for me – neither more nor less? I would then be so calm, so liberated – I could keep silence for ten years without effort.

Chapter Seven

1846-7

Charlotte, Biographical Notice of Ellis and Acton Bell, *1850*

One day, in the autumn of 1845, I accidentally lighted on a MS. volume of verse in my sister Emily's handwriting. Of course, I was not surprised, knowing that she could and did write verse: I looked it over, and something more than surprise seized me, – a deep conviction that these were not common effusions, nor at all like the poetry women generally write. I thought them condensed and terse, vigorous and genuine. To my ear, they had also a peculiar music – wild, melancholy, and elevating.

My sister Emily was not a person of demonstrative character, nor one, on the recesses of whose mind and feelings, even those nearest and dearest to her could, with impunity, intrude unlicensed; it took hours to reconcile her to the discovery I had made, and days to persuade her that such poems merited publication. I knew, however, that a mind like hers could not be without some latent spark of honourable ambition, and refused to be discouraged in my attempts to fan that spark to a flame.

Meantime, my younger sister quietly produced some of her own compositions, intimating that since Emily's had given me pleasure, I might like to look at hers. I could not but be a partial judge, yet I thought that these verses too had a sweet sincere pathos of their own.

We had very early cherished the dream of one day becoming authors. This dream, never relinquished even when distance divided and absorbing tasks occupied us, now suddenly acquired strength and consistency; it took the character of a resolve. We agreed to arrange a small selection of our poems, and, if possible, get them printed.

Charlotte's discovery of Emily's poems was to save her sanity. It gave her new hope and new purpose at a time when her morale was lower than it had ever been. She launched into the business of getting the sisters' poems published with enthusiasm, taking all the responsibility for the arrangements on herself. Emily and Anne were less involved, but it was apparently at Emily's insistence that the three sisters, retaining their own initials, adopted the androgynous pseudonyms of Currer, Ellis and Acton Bell. It was also stipulated that no one else was to know about the venture, so Charlotte entered upon a sort of double life in which all reference to her main preoccupation was omitted from her letters to her friends. Not even Patrick and Branwell were admitted to the secret, though the latter may have guessed it when he accidentally received a parcel of proofs intended for Charlotte. Aylott & Jones, a small publishing house in Paternoster Row which was better known for its religious publications, offered to print the book if the sisters would bear all the costs involved. This they agreed to do, hoping that the sales would justify the expense; at the very least they hoped that the little book would bring them critical acclaim.

Charlotte to Aylott & Jones; Haworth, 28 January 1846

Gentlemen

May I request to be informed whether you would undertake the publication of a Collection of short poems in I vol. oct[avo] –

If you object to publishing the work at your own risk – would you undertake it on the Author's account? –

I am Gentlemen
Your obdt. hmble. Servt.
C Brontë

Address
   Revd P Brontë
   Haworth Bradford – Yorkshire

Charlotte to Margaret Wooler; Haworth, 30 January 1846

I thought you would wonder how we were getting on when you heard of the Railway Panic and you may be sure that I am very glad to answer your kind enquiries by an assurance that our small capital is as yet undiminished. The York and N. Midland is, as you say, a very good line – yet I confess to you I should wish, for my own part, to be wise in time – I cannot think that even the very best lines will continue for many years at their present premiums and I have been most anxious for us to sell our shares ere it be too late – and to secure the proceeds in some safer if, for the present, less profitable investment. I cannot however persuade my Sisters to regard the affair precisely from my point of view and I feel as if I would rather run the risk of loss than hurt Emily's feelings by acting in direct opposition to her opinion – she managed in a most handsome and able manner for me when I was at Brussels and prevented by distance from looking after my own interests – therefore I will let her manage still and take the consequences. Disinterested and energetic she certainly is and if she be not quite so tractable or open to conviction as I could wish I must remember perfection is not the lot of humanity and as long as we can regard those we love and to whom we are closely allied, with profound and never-shaken esteem, it is a small thing that they should vex us occasionally by, what appear to us unreasonable and headstrong notions. You my dear Miss Wooler know full as well as I do the value of sisters' affection to each other; there is nothing like it in this world, I believe, when they are nearly equal in age and similar in education, tastes and sentiments.

You ask about Branwell; he never thinks of seeking employment and I begin to fear that he has rendered himself incapable of filling any respectable station in life, besides, if money were at his disposal he would use it only to his own injury – the faculty of self-government is, I fear almost destroyed in him You ask me if I do not think that men are strange beings – I do indeed, I have often thought so – and I think too that the mode of bringing them up is strange, they are not half sufficiently guarded from temptation – Girls are protected as if they were something very frail and silly indeed while boys are turned loose on the world as if they – of all beings in existence, were the wisest and the least liable to be led astray.

Charlotte to Aylott & Jones; Haworth, 31 January 1846

Since you agree to undertake the publication of the work respecting which I applied to you – I should wish now to know as soon as possible the cost of paper and printing, I will then send the necessary remittance together with the manuscript.

I should like it to be printed in I octavo volume of the same quality of paper and size of type as Moxon's last edition of Wordsworth. The poems will occupy – I should think from 200 to 250 pages. They are not the production of a Clergyman nor are they exclusively of a religious character – but I presume these circumstances will be immaterial

Charlotte to Aylott & Jones; Haworth, 6 February 1846

Gentlemen

I send you the M.S. as you desired.

You will perceive that the Poems are the work of three persons – relatives – their separate pieces are distinguished by their respective signatures –

I am Gentlemen

Yrs truly

C Brontë

Feby. 6th./46

I am obliged to send it in two parcels on account of the weight –

In the latter part of February, Charlotte went to stay with Ellen Nussey at Brookroyd in Birstall. As letters from Aylott & Jones had still to be dealt with and were forwarded to her from Haworth, it must have been difficult for Charlotte to keep the secret from Ellen but, at this stage at least, she does not appear to have suspected that the Brontës were publishing.

Emily to Ellen; Haworth, 25 February 1846

Haworth.

25th. Feb. 1846

Dear Miss Ellen,

I fancy this note will be too late to decide one way or the other with respect to Charlotte's stay – yours only came this morning (Wedensday) and unless mine travels faster you will not receive it till Friday – Papa, of course misses C and will be glad to have her back. Anne and I ditto – but as she goes from home so seldom you may keep her a day or two longer if your eloquence is equal to the task of persuading her – that is if she be still with you when you get this permission

Yours truly E J Bronte

love from Anne

Branwell to John Frobisher, conductor of the Halifax Concerts and organist of Halifax Parish Church; Haworth, March 1846

Dear Sir,

I dare say you have forgotten both myself and a conversation in which, some years ago, I alluded to a favourite air – Glucks 'Mater divinae gratiae' as it is called in Novello's voluntaries, and 'Non vi turbate no' in Knights Musical Library.

I have ventured to compose English words on the recent stirring events in India adapted to the original air, and I do not know whether or not it would be worth your while to look over the manuscript and make what use you think best of it – or publish it as Glucks Air adapted to English words by myself – or arranged by Yourself – or under any title if it would deserve a title at all.

As I write in utter ignorance – and the stanzas were written to amuse an hour of long illness – excuse my intrusion upon your patience and believe me,

Your most respectful and ob't Servt,
P. Branwell Brontë

N.B. From the number of stanzas (eight) the air would have to be sung just twice over.

Charlotte to Ellen; Haworth, 3 March 1846

I reached home a little after 2 o'clock all safe and right – yesterday – I found papa very well – his sight much the same – Emily & Anne were gone to Keighley to meet me – unfortunately I had returned by the old road while they were gone by the new – and we missed each other – they did not get home till ½ past 4 – and were caught in the heavy shower of rain which fell in the afternoon – I am sorry to say Anne has taken a little cold in consequence – but I hope she will soon be well – . . . I went into the room where Branwell was to speak to him about an hour after I got home – it was very forced work to address him – I might have spared myself the trouble as he took no notice & made no reply – he was stupified – My fears were not in vain   Emily tells me that he got a sovereign from Papa while I have been away under pretence of paying a pressing debt – he went immediately & changed it at a public-house – and has employed it as was to be expected – she concluded her account with saying he was 'a hopeless being' – it is too true – In his present state it is scarcely possible to stay in the room where he is – what the future has in store – I do not know –

Charlotte to Aylott & Jones; Haworth, 3 March 1846

I send a draft for £31-10s – being the amount of your Estimate –

I suppose there is nothing now to prevent your immediately commencing the printing of the work – When you acknowledge the receipt of the draft – will you state how soon it will be completed –

Charlotte to Aylott & Jones; Haworth, 28 March 1846

As the proofs have hitherto always come safe to hand – under the direction of C Brontë Esqre. – I have not thought it necessary to request you to change it, but a little mistake having occurred yesterday – I think it will be better to send them to me in future under my real address which is
Miss Brontë
    Revd P Brontë's &c,

Spurred on by their success in getting the book of poems to the point of publication, the sisters now embarked on a much more ambitious project. Perhaps it would be possible to earn a living from their writing – a career that would enable them to do what they most loved and also allow them to stay together at home. They each began to write a novel, Charlotte *The Professor*, Emily *Wuthering Heights* and Anne *Agnes Grey*, and Charlotte undertook what was to become the long and dreary process of finding a publisher.

Charlotte to Aylott & Jones; Haworth, 6 April 1846

C. E & A Bell are now preparing for the Press a work of fiction – consisting of three distinct and unconnected tales which may be published either together as a work of 3 vols. of the ordinary novel-size, or separately as single vols – as shall be deemed most advisable.

It is not their intention to publish these tales on their own account.

They direct me to ask you whether you would be disposed to undertake the work – after having of course by due inspection of the M.S. ascertained that its contents are such as to warrant an expectation of success.

An early answer will oblige as in case of your negativing the proposal – inquiry must be made of other Publishers –

Charlotte to Aylott & Jones; Haworth, 11 April 1846

It is evident that unknown authors have great difficulties to contend with before they can succeed in bringing their works before the public, can you give me any hint as to the way in which these difficulties are best met. For instance, in the present case, where a work of fiction is in question, in what form would a publisher be most likely to accept the M.S. – ? whether offered as a work of 3 vols or as tales which might be published in numbers or as contributions to a periodical?

What publishers would be most likely to receive favourably a proposal of this nature?

Would it suffice to write to a publisher on the subject or would it be necessary to have recourse to a personal interview?

Your opinion and advice on these three points or on any other which your experience may suggest as important – would be esteemed by us a favour

Branwell to J. B. Leyland; Haworth, 28 April 1846

I cannot, without a smile at myself, think of my stay for three days in Halifax on a business which need not have occupied three hours; but in truth when I fall back <u>on</u> myself I suffer so much wretchedness that I cannot withstand any temptations to get <u>out</u> of myself – and for that reason I am prosecuting enquiries about situations suitable to me whereby I could have a voyage abroad. The quietude of home, and the inability to make my family aware of the nature of most of my sufferings makes me write

> 'Home thoughts are not, with me
> Bright, as of yore;
> Joys are forgot by me,
> Taught to deplore!
>
> <u>My</u> home has taken rest
> In an afflicted breast
> Which I have often pressed
> But – may no more!

Troubles never come alone – and I have some little troubles astride the shoulders of the big one.

Literary exertion would seem a resource, but the depression attendant on it, and the almost hopelessness of bursting through the barriers of literary circles, and getting a hearing among publishers, make me disheartened and indifferent; for I cannot write what would be thrown, unread, into a library fire. Otherwise I have the materials for a respectably sized volume, and if I were in London personally I might perhaps try Henry Moxon – a patronizer of the sons of rhyme; though I dare say the poor man often smarts for his liberality in publishing hideous trash.

As I know that, while here, I might send a manuscript to London, and say goodbye to it I feel it folly to feed the flames of a printers fire.

So much for egotism!

Charlotte to Aylott & Jones; Haworth, 11 May 1846

The books may be done up in the style of Moxon's duodecimo edition of Wordsworth.

The price may be fixed at 5s. or if you think that too much for the size of the volume – say 4s.

On 26 May 1846, the Reverend Edmund Robinson died. When the news eventually filtered through to Haworth, Branwell was ecstatic: marriage with Mrs Robinson and the culmination of all his hopes at last seemed within his grasp. Mrs Robinson, however, had no intention of throwing herself away on the unemployed son of an impoverished clergyman and, through various confidantes, soon made it clear that there was no question of her marrying Branwell. The tale she told him – which was untrue – was that her husband's will had stipulated that she would inherit nothing if she ever made contact with Branwell again. For Branwell this was the final straw. With nothing to hope for and nothing to gain, he sank into the oblivion of alcoholism. Mrs Robinson, on the other hand, skilfully played on his feelings by appearing distraught at this enforced separation from her lover whilst also playing the public role of a grieving widow. In the meantime, she began to make plans for her own future, which included securing a titled husband.

Charlotte to Ellen; Haworth, 17 June 1846

We – I am sorry to say – have been somewhat more harrassed than usual lately – The death of Mr Robinson – which took place about three weeks or a month ago – served Branwell for a pretext to throw all about him into hubbub and confusion with his emotions – &c. &c. Shortly after came news from all hands that Mr Robinson had altered his will before he died and effectually prevented all chance of a marriage between his widow and Branwell by stipulating that she should not have a shilling if she ever ventured to reopen any communication with him – Of course he then became intolerable – to papa he allows rest neither day nor night – and he is continually screwing money out of him sometimes threatening that he will kill himself if it is withheld from him – He says Mrs R- is now insane

– that her mind is a complete wreck – owing to remorse for her conduct towards Mr R– (whose end it appears was hastened by distress of mind) – and grief for having lost him.

I do not know how much to believe of what he says but I fear she is very ill – Branwell declares now that he neither can nor will do anything for himself – good situations have been offered more than once – for which by a fortnight's work he might have qualified himself – but he will do nothing – except drink, and make us all wretched –

Branwell to Francis Grundy; Haworth, June 1846

The gentleman with whom I have been is dead. His property is left in trust for the family, provided I do not see the widow; and if I do, it reverts to the executing trustees, with ruin to her. She is now distracted with sorrows and agonies; and the statement of her case, as given by her coachman, who has come to see me at Haworth, fills me with inexpressible grief. Her mind is distracted to the verge of insanity, and mine is so wearied that I wish I were in my grave. –

Branwell to J. B. Leyland; Haworth, c. June/July 1846

Well, my dear Sir, I have got my finishing stroke at last – and I feel stunned into marble by the blow.

I have this morning received a long, kind and faithful letter from the medical gentleman who attended Mr R. in his last illness and who has since had an interview with one whom I can never forget.

He knows me <u>well</u>, and he pities my case most sincerely – for he declares that though used to the rough ups and downs of this weary world, he shed tears from his heart when he saw the state of that lady and knew what I should feel.

When he mentioned my name she stared at him and fainted. When she recovered she in turns dwelt on her inextinguishable love for me – her horror at having been the first to delude me into wretchedness, and her agony at having been the cause of the death of her husband, who, in his last hours, bitterly repented of his treatment of her.

Her sensitive mind was totally wrecked. She wandered into talking of entering a nunnery; and the Doctor fairly debars me from hope in the future.

It's hard work for me dear Sir; I would bear it – but my health is so bad that the body seems as if it could not bear the mental shock.

I never cared one bit about the property. I cared about herself – and always shall do.

May God bless her but I wish I had never known her!

My appetite is lost; my nights are dreadful, and having nothing to do makes me dwell on past scenes – on her own self, her voice – her person – her thoughts – till I could be glad if God would take me. In the next world I could not be worse than I am in this.

I am not a whiner dear Sir, but when a young man like myself has fixed his soul on a being <u>worthy</u> of all love – and who for years, has <u>given</u> him all love, pardon him for boring a friend with a misery that has only one black end.

I fully expected a change of the will – and difficulties placed in my way by powerful and wealthy men, but I <u>hardly</u> expected the hopeless ruin of the mind that I loved even more than its body.

Excuse my egotism, and believe me,

Dear Sir,
Yours,
P.B. Brontë.

The little volume of *Poems*, on which such high hopes rested, had been published in May. It sold only two copies and was barely noticed by the reviewers. Those reviews that did appear were encouraging, spurring Charlotte to greater efforts in her search for a publisher for the novels.

Review of Poems *from the* Critic*; 4 July 1846*

. . . it is long since we have enjoyed a volume of such genuine poetry as this. Amid the heaps of trash and trumpery in the shape of verses, which lumber the table of the literary journalist, this small book of some 170 pages only has come like a ray of sunshine, gladdening the eye with present glory, and the heart with promise of bright hours in store . . . To those whose love of poetry is more a matter of education than of heart, it is probable that these poems may not prove attractive; they too much violate the conventionalities of poetry for such as look only to form, and not to substance; but they in whose hearts are chords strung by nature to sympathize with the beautiful and the true in the world without, and their embodiments by the gifted among their fellow men, will recognize in the compositions of Currer, Ellis and Acton Bell, the presence of more genius than it was supposed this utilitarian age had devoted to the loftier exercises of the intellect.

Review of Poems *from the* Athenaeum; *4 July 1846*

The second book on our list furnishes another example of a family in whom appears to run the instinct of song. It is shared, however, by the three brothers — as we suppose them to be — in very unequal proportions; requiring in the case of Acton Bell, the indulgences of affection . . . and rising, in that of Ellis, into an inspiration, which may yet find an audience in the outer world. A fine quaint spirit has the latter, which may have things to speak that men will be glad to hear, — and an evident power of wing that may reach heights not here attempted.

Charlotte to Henry Colburn, a London publisher; Haworth, 4 July 1846

I request permission to send for your inspection the M.S. of a work of fiction in 3 vols. It consists of three tales, each occupying a volume and capable of being published together or separately, as thought most advisable. The authors of these tales have already appeared before the public . . .

I am Sir
Yours respectfully,
C Bell

Address   Mr Currer Bell
       Parsonage
       Haworth
       Bradford
       Yorkshire

Charlotte to Ellen; Haworth, 10 July 1846

Who gravely asked you 'whether Miss Brontë was not going to be married to her papa's Curate'?

I scarcely need say that never was rumour more unfounded – it puzzles me to think how it could possibly have originated – A cold, far-away sort of civility are the only terms on which I have ever been with Mr Nicholls – I could by no means think of mentioning such a rumour to him even as a joke – it would make me the laughing-stock of himself and his fellow-curates for half a year to come – They regard me as an old maid, and I regard them, one and all, as highly uninteresting, narrow and unattractive specimens of the 'coarser sex'.

Review from the Bradford Observer, *23 July 1846*

ORATORIO AT HAWORTH – On Monday last, being the first day of Haworth rush bearing, a good musical performance took place in St Michael's church, for the benefit of the celebrated Mr Parker, of Haworth. That gentleman, with Mrs Sunderland, Mr Hargreaves, & Mr Baldwin, were the principal vocal performers. The instrumental & chorus performers were very numerous and efficient. Mr Parker being of the Baptist persuasion the Puseyite clergy of the district did not attend, nor any of the few laity whom they have made proselytes to their doctrines & practices. Nevertheless, the church was crowded to suffocation, & in the west gallery was seated the venerable incumbent, the Rev P Bronte, B A, who is now totally blind, & near him the rev preacher of the day before, as well as another clergyman, the son of a deceased & highly respected incumbent, & Joseph Greenwood, Esq, a magistrate.

Charlotte to Aylott & Jones; Haworth, 23 July 1846

The Messrs Bell would be obliged to you to post the enclosed note in London. It is an answer to the letter you forwarded, which contained an application for their autographs from a person who professed to have read and admired their poems. I think I before intimated that the Messrs Bell are desirous for the present of remaining unknown, for which reason they prefer having the note posted in London to sending it direct, in order to avoid giving any clue to residence or identity by post-mark, etc.

I am Gentlemen
Yours truly,
C Brontë

While it was gratifying that one reader had thought highly enough of their poems to request their autographs, the sisters had rather lost interest in the fate of the little volume of *Poems*. The manuscripts of *The Professor*, *Wuthering Heights* and *Agnes Grey* were doing the rounds of the publishers, Branwell's histrionics were disrupting the equilibrium of family life and as Patrick's cataracts reduced him almost to blindness, an operation to restore his sight before it was too late became more urgent.

Charlotte to Ellen; 9 August 1846

In a fortnight I hope to go with papa to Manchester to have his eyes couched – Emily and I made a pilgrimage there a week ago to search out an operator and we found one in the person of a Mr Wilson – He could not tell from description whether the eyes were ready for an operation – Papa must therefore necessarily take a journey to Manchester to consult him – if he judges the cataract ripe – we shall remain – if on the contrary he thinks it not yet sufficiently hardened we shall have to return – and papa must remain in darkness a while longer.

Charlotte to Ellen; Manchester, 21 August 1846

I just scribble a line to you to let you know where I am – in order that
you may write to me here for it seems to me that a letter from you would
relieve me from the feelings of strangeness I have in this big town.

Papa and I came here on Wednesday, we saw Mr Wilson the
Oculist the same day; he pronounced papa's eyes quite ready for an
operation and has fixed next Monday for the performance of it –
Think of us on that day dear Nell –

We got into our lodgings yesterday – I think we shall be comfortable, at least our rooms are very good, but there is no Mistress of
the house (she is very ill and gone out into the country) and I
am somewhat puzzled in managing about provisions – we board
ourselves – I find myself excessively ignorant – I can't tell what the
deuce to order in the way of meat – &c I wish you or your Sister
Ann could give me some hints about how to manage – For ourselves
I could contrive – papa's diet is so very simple – but there will be a
nurse coming in a day or two – and I am afraid of not having things
good enough for her – Papa requires nothing you know but plain
beef & mutton, tea and bread and butter but a nurse will probably
expect to live much better – give me some hints if you can –

Mr Wilson says we shall have to stay here for a month at least –
it will be dreary – I wonder how poor Emily and Anne will get on
at home with Branwell – they too will have their troubles –

Charlotte to Ellen; Manchester, 26 August 1846

The operation is over – it took place yesterday – Mr Wilson performed it, two other surgeons assisted – Mr Wilson says he considers
it quite successful but papa cannot yet see anything – The affair
lasted precisely a quarter of an hour – it was not the simple operation
of couching Mr Carr described but the more complicated one of
extracting the cataract – Mr Wilson entirely disapproves of couching.

Papa displayed extraordinary patience and firmness – the surgeons
seemed surprised. I was in the room all the time, as it was his wish
that I should be there – of course I neither spoke nor moved till the
thing was done – and then I felt that the less I said either to papa or

the surgeons, the better – papa is now confined to his bed in a dark room and is not to be stirred for four days – he is to speak and to be spoken to as little as possible –

Patrick, marginal notes in his copy of Graham's Domestic Medicine; *Haworth, January 1847*

In Augt 1846 – Mr Wilson, surgeon – 72, Mosley St, Manchester, operated for cataract, in one of my eyes – the left one – He informed me, and others, also, that, generally, they do not operate on both eyes – for fear of inflammation, which, would destroy the sight, Belladonna a virulent poison – was first applied, twice, in order to expand the pupil – this occasioned very acute pain for only about five seconds – The feeling, under the operation – which lasted fifteen minutes, was of a burning nature – but not intolerable – as I have read is generally the case, in surgical operations. My <u>lens</u> was <u>extracted</u> so that cataract can never return in that eye – I was confined on my back – a month in a dark room, with bandages over my eyes for the greater part of the time – and had a careful nurse to attend me both night, & day – I was bled with 8 leeches, at one time, & 6, on another, (these caused but little pain) in order to prevent, inflammation – Through divine mercy, and the skill of the surgeon, as well as my D[aughte]r Ch[arlotte]'s attention, and the assiduity of the nurse – after a year of nearly total blindness – I was so far restored to sight, as to be able to read, and write, and find my way, without a guide – The operation is critical, and ought not to be ventured upon without due precaution. P.B.

It was in the unpromising confines of the lodging-house rooms in Manchester, attending on her invalid father and suffering herself from a raging toothache which kept her awake at night, that Charlotte began to write *Jane Eyre*. In contrast to her later novels, she was caught up immediately in the story, writing fast and furiously without interruption until she had carried Jane away from Thornfield Hall. The impetus was only lost when she returned home, where the rest of the book would be written more slowly and with greater effort. Unable to recapture her initial enthusiasm and, in any case, having failed to secure either a publisher for *The Professor* or sales for *Poems*, Charlotte's frustration threatened to overpower her.

Charlotte to Ellen; Haworth, 14 October 1846

. . . if I <u>could</u> leave home Ellen − I should not be at Haworth now
− I know life is passing away and I am doing nothing − earning
nothing   a very bitter knowledge it is at moments − but I see no
way out of the mist − More than one very favourable opportunity
has now offered which I have been obliged to put aside − probably
when I am free to leave home I shall neither be able to find place
nor employment − perhaps too I shall be quite past the prime of life
− my faculties will be rusted − and my few acquirements in a great
measure forgotten − These ideas sting me keenly sometimes − but
whenever I consult my Conscience it affirms that I am doing right
in staying at home − and bitter are its upbraidings when I yield to
an eager desire for release − I returned to Brussels after Aunt's death
against my conscience − prompted by what then seemed an irresistible
impulse − I was punished for my selfish folly by a total withdrawal
for more than two year[s] of happiness and peace of mind − I could
hardly expect success if I were to err again in the same way −

Charlotte to Margaret Wooler; Haworth, November 1846

I pity Mr Thomas from my heart. For ten years − he has now, I
think, been a sufferer from nervous complaints − For ten years he
has felt the tyranny of Hypochondria − A most dreadful doom, far
worse than that of a man with healthy nerves buried for the same
length of time in a subterranean dungeon − I endured it but a year
− and assuredly I can never forget the concentrated anguish of certain
insufferable moments and the heavy gloom of many long hours −
besides the preternatural horror which seemed to clothe existence
and Nature − and which made Life a continual waking Night-mare
− Under such circumstances the morbid Nerves can know neither
peace nor enjoyment − whatever touches − pierces them − sensation
for them is all suffering − A weary burden nervous patients consequently become to those about them − they know this and it
infuses a new gall − corrosive in its extreme acritude, into their bitter
cup − When I was at Dewsbury-Moor − I could have been no better
company for you than a stalking ghost − and I remember I felt my

incapacity to <u>impart</u> pleasure fully as much as my powerlessness to <u>receive</u> it – Mr Thomas, no doubt feels the same –

Charlotte to Ellen; Haworth, 13 December 1846

I hope you are not frozen up in Northamptonshire – the cold here is dreadful   I do not remember such a series of North-Pole-days – England might really have taken a slide up into the Arctic Zone – the sky looks like ice – the earth is frozen, the wind is as keen as a two-edged blade – I cannot keep myself warm – We have all had severe colds and coughs in consequence of the severe weather – Poor Anne has suffered greatly from asthma – but is now I am glad to say rather better – she had two nights last week when her cough and difficulty of breathing were painful indeed to hear and witness and must have been most distressing to suffer – she bore it as she does all affliction – without one complaint – only sighing now and then when nearly worn out – she has an extraordinary heroism of endurance. I admire but I certainly could not imitate her . . . You say I am 'to tell you plenty' – What would you have me to say – nothing happens at Haworth – nothing at least of a pleasant kind – one little incident indeed occurred about a week ago to sting us to life – but if it gives no more pleasure for you to hear than it did for us to witness – you will scarcely thank me for adverting to it –

It was merely the arrival of a Sheriff's Officer on a visit to Branwell – inviting him either to pay his debts or to take a trip to York – Of course his debts had to be paid – it is not agreeable to lose money time after time in this way but it is ten times worse – to witness the shabbiness of his behaviour on such occasions – But where is the use of dwelling on this subject   it will make him no better.

Branwell to J. B. Leyland; Haworth, January 1847

I wish Mr Thos Nicholson of the 'Old Cock' would send me my bill of what I owe to him, and, the moment that I recieve my outlaid cash, or any sum which may fall into my hands through the hands of one whom I may never see again, I shall settle it.

That settlement, I have some reason to hope, will be <u>shortly</u>.

Branwell to J. B. Leyland; Haworth, 24 January 1847

This last week an honest and kindly friend has warned me that concealed hopes about one lady should be given up let the effort to do so cost what it may. He is the Family Medical attendant, and was commanded by Mr Evans, M.P. for North Derbyshire to return me, unopened, a letter which I addressed to Throp Green and which the Lady was not permitted to see . . . I had reason to hope that ere very long I should be the husband of a Lady whom I loved best in the world and with whom, in more than competence, I might live at leisure to try to make myself a name in the world of posterity, without being pestered by the small but countless botherments, which like mosquitoes sting us in the world of work-day toil. That hope, and herself are <u>gone</u> – <u>She</u> to wither into patiently pining decline – <u>It</u>, to make room for drudgery falling on one now ill fitted to bear it . . . I have been in truth too much petted through life, and in my last situation I was so much master, and gave myself so much up to enjoyment that now when the cloud of ill health and adversity has come upon me it will be a disheart[e]ning job to work myself up again through a new lifes battle, from the position of five years ago to which I have been compelled to retreat with heavy loss and no gain. My army stands now where it did then, but mourning the slaughter of Youth, Health, Hope, and both mental and physical elasticity.

The last two losses are indeed important to one who once built his hopes of rising in the world on the possession of them. Noble writings, works of art, music or poetry now instead of rousing my imagination, cause a whirlwind of blighting sorrow that sweeps over my mind with unspeakable dreariness, and if I sit down and try to write all ideas that used to come clothed in sunlight now press round me in funeral black; for really every pleasurable excitement that I used to know has changed to insipidity or pain.

I shall never be able to realize the too sanguine hopes of my friends, for at 28 I am a thouroghly <u>old man</u> – mentally and bodily – Far more so indeed than I am willing to express. God knows I do not scribble like a poetaster when I quote Byron's terribly truthful words –

'No more, no more, oh! never more on me
The freshness of the heart shall fall like dew,
Which, out of all the lovely things we see
Extracts emotions beautiful and new!'

I used to think that if I could have for a week the free range of the British Museum – the Library included – I could feel as though I were placed for seven days in paradise, but now really, dear Sir, my eyes would roam over the Elgin marbles, the Egyptian saloon and the most treasured volumes like the eyes of a dead cod fish.

My rude rough acquaintances here ascribe my unhappiness solely to causes produced by my sometimes irregular life, because they have known no other pains than those resulting from excess or want of ready cash – They do not know that I would rather want a shirt than want a springy mind, and that my total want of happiness, were I to step into York Minster now, would be far, far worse than their want of an hundred pounds when they might happen to need it; and that if a dozen glasses or a bottle of wine drives off their cares, such cures only make me outwardly passable in company but never drive off mine.

I know, only that it is time for me to be something when I am nothing. That my father cannot have long to live, and that when he dies my evening, which is already twilight, will become night – That I shall then have a constitution still so strong that it will keep me years in torture and despair when I should every hour pray that I might die.

Charlotte to Ellen; Haworth, 1 March 1847

Dear Nell – as you wish to avoid making me uneasy – say nothing more about my going to Brookroyd at present – Let your visit to Sussex be got over – let the summer arrive – and then we shall see how matters stand by that time. To confess the truth I really should like you to come to Haworth before I again go to Brookroyd – and it is natural and right that I should have this wish – to keep friendship in proper order the balance of good offices must be preserved – otherwise a disquieting and anxious feeling creeps in and destroys mutual comfort – In summer – and in fine weather your visit here might be much better managed than in winter – we could go out more   be more independent of the house and of one room – Branwell has been conducting himself very badly lately – I expect from the extravagance of his behaviour and from mysterious hints he drops – (for he never will speak out plainly) that we shall be hearing news of fresh debts contracted by him soon –

The Misses Robinson – who had entirely ceased their correspondence with Anne for half a year after their father's death have lately recommenced it – for a fortnight they sent her a letter almost every day – crammed with warm protestations of endless esteem and gratitude – they speak with great affection too of their Mother – and never make any allusion intimating acquaintance with her errors – It is to be hoped they are and always will remain in ignorance on that point – especially since – I think – she has bitterly repented them. We take special care that Branwell does not know of their writing to Anne.

Charlotte to Ellen; Haworth, 24 March 1847

I shall be 31 next birthday – My Youth is gone like a dream – and very little use have I ever made of it – What have I done these last thirty years –? Precious little –

At the beginning of April, the Brontës had a visitor whose story seems to have inspired Anne with the plot of her second novel, *The Tenant of Wildfell Hall*. Mrs Collins was the wife of the former curate of Keighley and the fact that both she and her husband were both so well known to the Brontës gave added poignancy to the dramatic tale she had to tell.

Charlotte to Ellen; Haworth, 4 April 1847

Do you remember my telling you or did I ever tell you about that wretched and most criminal Mr Collins – after running an infamous career of vice both in England and France – abandoning his wife to disease and total destitution in Manchester – with two children and without a farthing in a strange lodging-house? Yesterday evening

Martha came up stairs to say – that a woman 'rather lady-like' as she said wished to speak to me in the kitchen – I went down – there stood Mrs Collins pale and worn but still interesting looking and cleanly and neatly dressed as was her little girl who was with her – I kissed her heartily – I could almost have cryed to see her for I had pitied her with my whole soul – when I heard of her undeserved sufferings, agonies and physical degradation – she took tea with us stayed about two hours and entered frankly into the narrative of her appalling distresses – her constitution has triumphed over the hideous disease – and her excellent sense – her activity and perseverance have enabled her to regain a decent position in society and to procure a respectable maintenance for herself and her children – She keeps a lodging-house in a very eligible part of the suburbs of Manchester (which I know) and is doing very well – she does not know where Mr Collins is and of course can never more endure to see him – She is now staying for a few days at Eastwood House with the Sugdens who I believe have been all along very kind to her – and the circumstance is greatly to their credit –

Charlotte to Ellen; Haworth, 12 May 1847

We shall all be glad to see you on the Thursday or Friday of next week, whichever day will suit you best . . . Branwell is quieter now – and for a good reason – he has got to the end of a considerable sum of money of which he became possessed in the Spring – and consequently is obliged to restrict himself in some degree – You must expect to find him weaker in mind and the complete rake in appearance – I have no apprehension of his being at all uncivil to you, on the contrary, he will be as smooth as oil

Charlotte to Ellen; Haworth, 14 May 1847

Your letter and its contents were most welcome. It will however suit us better if you can come on Wednesday in next week – we fix this day because it is the only one on which there is a carrier who can take charge of your luggage from Keighley Station – You must direct it to Mr Brontë's Haworth – and we will tell the carrier to inquire for it – The railroad has been opened some time but it only comes as far as Keighley – the remaining distance you will have to walk – there are trains from Leeds – I believe at all hours – if you can arrive at Keighley by about 4 o'clock in the afternoon Emily, Anne & I will all three meet you at the Station – we can take tea jovially together at the Devonshire Arms and walk home in the cool of the evening – this, with fine weather will I think be a much better arrangement than fagging through four miles in the heat of noon

Ellen's long-promised visit failed to materialize, prevented by her elder sister's decision to visit the wealthy Swaine family at the same time. Charlotte could not contain her bitterness.

Charlotte to Ellen; Haworth, 20 May 1847

Your letter of yesterday did indeed give me a cruel chill of disappointment. I can not blame you – for I know it was not your fault – but I must say I do not altogether exempt your sister Anne from reproach – I do not think she considers it of the least consequence whether little people like us of Haworth are disappointed or not, provided great nobs like the Briar Hall gentry are accommodated – this is bitter, but I feel bitter –

As to going to Brookroyd – it is absurd – I will not go near the place till you have been to Haworth –

My respects to all and sundry accompanied with a large amount of wormwood and gall – from the effusion of which you and your Mother alone are excepted –

C B-

Just over a year after its publication, *Poems* by Currer, Ellis and Acton Bell had still sold only two copies. As further sales were extremely unlikely, the Brontës decided to make a grand gesture and send complimentary copies to some of the authors whose work they most admired. The poets William Wordsworth, Alfred Tennyson, Hartley Coleridge and Ebenezer Elliott and the writers Thomas de Quincey and J. G. Lockhart were among the recipients.

Charlotte to Hartley Coleridge; Haworth, 16 June 1847

Sir

My relatives Ellis and Acton Bell and myself, heedless of the repeated warnings of various respectable publishers, have committed the rash act of printing a volume of poems.

The consequences predicted have, of course, overtaken us; our book is found to be a drug; no man needs it or heeds it; in the space of a year our publisher has disposed but of two copies and by what painful efforts, he succeeded in getting rid of those two himself only knows.

Before transferring the edition to the Trunk-makers, we have decided on distributing as presents, a few copies of what we cannot sell. We beg to offer you one in acknowledgment of the pleasure and profit we have often derived from your writings.

I am, Sir
Yours respectfully
Currer Bell.

The failure of *Poems*, combined with the seeming impossibility of getting their novels accepted by any publisher, led Emily and Anne to compromise. Rather than never see *Wuthering Heights* and *Agnes Grey* in print, they decided to contribute towards the cost of publication and, on these terms, the two books were accepted by Thomas Newby, a London publisher, who agreed to publish them in the usual format as a three-volume set. *The Professor*, which filled only a single volume, was now even less likely to find a publisher, but Charlotte refused to admit defeat.

Charlotte, Biographical Notice of Ellis and Acton Bell;
19 September 1850

At last *Wuthering Heights* and *Agnes Grey* were accepted on terms somewhat impoverishing to the two authors; Currer Bell's book found acceptance nowhere, nor any acknowledgment of merit, so that something like the chill of despair began to invade his heart. As a forlorn hope, he tried one publishing house more – Messrs Smith and Elder. Ere long, in a much shorter space than that on which experience had taught him to calculate – there came a letter, which he opened in the dreary expectation of finding two hard hopeless lines, intimating that Messrs Smith and Elder 'were not disposed to publish the MS.,' and, instead, he took out of the envelope a letter of two pages. He read it trembling. It declined, indeed, to publish that tale, for business reasons, but it discussed its merits and demerits so courteously, so considerately, in a spirit so rational, with a discrimination so enlightened, that this very refusal cheered the author better than a vulgarly-expressed acceptance would have done. It was added, that a work in three volumes would meet with careful attention.

Charlotte to Smith, Elder & Co; Haworth, 7 August 1847

Your objection to the want of varied interest in the tale is, I am aware, not without grounds – yet it appears to me that it might be published without serious risk if its appearance were speedily followed up by another work from the same pen of a more striking and exciting character. The first work might serve as an introduction and accustom the public to the author's name, the success of the second might thereby be rendered more probable.

I have a second narrative in 3 vols. now in progress and nearly completed, to which I have endeavoured to impart a more vivid interest than belongs to the Professor; in about a month I hope to finish it – so that if a publisher were found for 'the Professor', the second narrative might follow as soon as was deemed advisable – and thus the interest of the public (if any interest were roused) might not be suffered to cool.

Will you be kind enough to favour me with your judgement on this plan –

Smith, Elder & Co., a small but dynamic publishing house co-owned and run by the young George Smith, remained unconvinced by Charlotte's argument and politely, but firmly, declined to publish *The Professor*. Less than three weeks later, Charlotte posted to them the completed manuscript of *Jane Eyre*. It caused a sensation.

George Smith, A Memoir *(London, 1902)*

The MS. of 'Jane Eyre' was read by Mr Williams in due course. He brought it to me on a Saturday, and said that he would like me to read it. There were no Saturday half-holidays in those days, and, as was usual, I did not reach home until late. I had made an appointment with a friend for Sunday morning; I was to meet him about twelve o'clock, at a place some two or three miles from our house, and ride with him into the country.

After breakfast on Sunday morning I took the MS. of 'Jane Eyre' to my little study, and began to read it. The story quickly took me captive. Before twelve o'clock my horse came to the door, but I could not put the book down. I scribbled two or three lines to my friend, saying I was very sorry that circumstances had arisen to prevent my meeting him, sent the note off by my groom, and went on reading the MS. Presently the servant came to tell me that luncheon was ready; I asked him to bring me a sandwich and a glass of wine, and still went on with 'Jane Eyre'. Dinner came; for me the meal was a very hasty one, and before I went to bed that night I had finished reading the manuscript.

The next day we wrote to 'Currer Bell' accepting the book for publication.

Charlotte to Smith, Elder & Co.; Haworth, 12 September 1847

In accepting your terms, I trust much to your equity and sense of justice. You stipulate for the refusal of my two next works at the price of one hundred pounds each. One hundred pounds is a small sum for a year's intellectual labour, nor would circumstances justify me in devoting my time and attention to literary pursuits with so narrow a prospect of advantage did I not feel convinced that in case the ultimate result of my efforts should prove more successful than you now anticipate, you would make some proportionate addition to the remuneration you at present offer. On this ground of confidence in your generosity and honour, I accept your conditions.

Charlotte to Smith, Elder & Co.; Haworth, 24 September 1847

I have to thank you for punctuating the [proof]sheets before sending them to me as I found the task very puzzling – and besides I consider your mode of punctuation a great deal more correct and rational than my own.

Even though she was on the brink of achieving her life's ambition, Charlotte's promise to her sisters prevented her from sharing her excitement with Ellen. No hint could be given of what was taking place.

Charlotte to Ellen; Haworth, 25 September 1847

My boxes came safe this morning – I have distributed the presents. Papa says I am to remember him most kindly to you – the screen will be very useful and he thanks you for it – Tabby was charmed with her cap she said she never thought of naught o' t' sort as Miss Nussey sending her aught – and she is sure she can never thank her enough for it –
    I was infuriated on finding a jar in my trunk – at first I hoped it was empty but when I found it heavy and replete I could have hurled it all the way back to Birstal[l] – however the inscription A- B- softened me much – it was at once kind and villanous in you to send it – you ought first to be tenderly kissed and then afterwards as tenderly whipped – Emily is just now sitting on the floor of the bed-room where I am writing, looking at her apples – she smiled when I gave them and the collar to her as your presents with an expression at once well-pleased and slightly surprised – Anne thanks you much – All send their love –

Anne to Ellen; Haworth, 4 October 1847

My dear Miss Ellen,
    Many thanks to you for your unexpected and welcome epistle. Charlotte is well, and meditates writing to you. Happily for all parties the east wind no longer prevails – during its continuance she complained of its influence as usual. I too suffered from it, in some

degree, as I always do, more or less; but this time, it brought me no reinforcement of colds and coughs which is what I dread the most. Emily considers it a 'dry uninteresting wind', but it does not affect her nervous system.

Charlotte to Ellen; Haworth, 7 October 1847

Anne was very much pleased with her letter – I presume she has answered it before now – I would fain hope that her health is a little stronger than it was – and her spirits a little better – but she leads much too sedentary a life, and is continually sitting stooping either over a book or over her desk – it is with difficulty one can prevail on her to take a walk or induce her to converse – I look forward to next Summer with the confident intention that she shall – if possible – make at least a brief sojourn at the sea-side.

Charlotte to Ellen; Haworth, 15 October 1847

We are getting on here the same as usual – only that Branwell has been more than ordinarily troublesome and annoying of late – he leads papa a wretched life. Mr Nicholls is returned [from holiday in Ireland] just the same – I cannot for my life see those interesting germs of goodness in him you discovered, his narrowness of mind always strikes me chiefly – I fear he is indebted to your imagination for his hidden treasures.

Chapter Eight

1847–8

Jane Eyre was published on 16 October 1847 to instant acclaim. At least one critic, G. H. Lewes, wrote to Charlotte through her publishers, prompting an occasional correspondence that would continue for some years, even though Charlotte was irritated and sometimes offended by his reviews.

Charlotte to G. H. Lewes; Haworth, 6 November 1847

Your letter reached me yesterday; I beg to assure you that I appreciate fully the intention with which it was written, and I thank you sincerely both for its cheering commendation and valuable advice.

You warn me to beware of Melodrame and you exhort me to adhere to the real. When I first began to write, so impressed was I with the truth of the principles you advocate that I determined to take Nature and Truth as my sole guides and to follow in their very footprints; I restrained imagination, eschewed romance, repressed excitement: over-bright colouring too I avoided, and sought to produce something which should be soft, grave and true.

My work (a tale in I vol.) being completed, I offered it to a publisher. He said it was original, faithful to Nature, but he did not feel warranted in accepting it, such a work would not sell. I tried six publishers in succession; they all told me it was deficient in 'startling incident' and 'thrilling excitement', that it would never suit the circulating libraries, and as it was on those libraries the success of works of fiction mainly depended they could not undertake to publish what would be over-looked there – 'Jane Eyre' was rather objected to at first [on] the same grounds – but finally found acceptance.

I mention this to you, not with a view of pleading exemption from censure, but in order to direct your attention to the root of certain literary evils – if in your forthcoming article in 'Frazer' you would bestow a few words of enlightenment on the public who support the circulating libraries, you might, with your powers, do some good.

You advise me too, not to stray far from the ground of experience as I become weak when I enter the region of fiction; and you say 'real experience is perennially interesting and to all men.'

I feel that this also is true, but, dear Sir, is not the real experience of each individual very limited? and if a writer dwells upon that solely or principally is he not in danger of repeating himself, and also of becoming an egotist?

Then too, Imagination is a strong, restless faculty which claims to be heard and exercised, are we to be quite deaf to her cry and insensate to her struggles? When she shews us bright pictures are we never to look at them and try to reproduce them? – And when she is eloquent and speaks rapidly and urgently in our ear are we not to write to her dictation? I shall anxiously search the next number of 'Frazer' for your opinion on these points.

Believe me, dear Sir,
Yours gratefully
C Bell

Most critics fell over themselves to bestow accolades on 'decidedly the best novel of the season' though Charlotte's most treasured tribute came privately, through her publishers, from her great hero, the novelist, William Makepeace Thackeray.

G. H. Lewes, *Review of* Jane Eyre *in* Fraser's Magazine, *December 1847*

After laughing over the *Bachelor of the Albany*, we wept over *Jane Eyre*. This, indeed, is a book after our own heart; and, if its merits have not forced it into notice by the time this paper comes before our readers, let us, in all earnestness, bid them lose not a day in sending for it. The writer is evidently a woman, and, unless we are deceived, new in the world of literature. But, man or woman, young or old, be that as it may, no such book has gladdened our eyes for a long while. Almost all that we require in a novelist she has: perception of character, and power of delineating it; picturesqueness; passion; and knowledge of life. The story is not only of singular interest, naturally evolved, unflagging to the last, but it fastens itself upon your attention, and will not leave you. The book closed, the enchantment continues . . . Reality – deep, significant reality – is the great characteristic of the book. It *is* an autobiography, – not, perhaps, in the naked facts and circumstances, but in the actual suffering and experience . . . This gives the book its charm: it is soul speaking to soul; it is an utterance from the depths of a struggling, suffering, much-enduring spirit: *suspiria de profundis!*

Review of Jane Eyre *from the* Westminster Review, *1847*

Decidedly the best novel of the season; and one, moreover, from the natural tone pervading the narrative, and the originality and freshness of its style, possessing the merit so rarely met with now-a-days in works of this class, of amply repaying a second perusal. Whoever may be the author, we hope to see more such books from her pen; for that these volumes are from the pen of a lady, and a clever one too, we have not the shadow of a doubt.

Review of Jane Eyre *from the* Era, *November 1847*

This is an extraordinary book. Although a work of fiction, it is no mere novel, for there is nothing but nature and truth about it, and its interest is entirely domestic; neither is it like your familiar writings, that are too close to reality. There is nothing morbid, nothing vague, nothing improbable about the story of Jane Eyre; at the same time it lacks neither the odour of romance nor the hue of sentiment . . . The story is, therefore, unlike all that we have read, with very few exceptions; and for power of thought and expression, we do not know its rival among modern productions . . . all the serious novel writers of the day lose in comparison with Currer Bell.

W. M. Thackeray to William Smith Williams; 23 October 1847

I wish you had not sent me *Jane Eyre*. It interested me so much that I have lost (or won if you like) a whole day in reading it at the busiest period with the printers I know wailing for copy. Who the author can be I can't guess, if a woman she knows her language better than most ladies do, or has had a 'classical' education. It is a fine book though, the man and woman capital, the style very generous and upright so to speak . . . The plot of the story is one with wh[ich] I am familiar. Some of the love passages made me cry, to the astonishment of John, who came in with the coals. St John the Missionary is a failure I think but a good failure, there are parts excellent. I don't know why I tell you this but that I have been exceedingly moved and pleased by *Jane Eyre*. It is a woman's writing, but whose? Give my respects and thanks to the author, whose novel is the first English one (and the French are only romances now) that I've been able to read for many a day.

Charlotte to William Smith Williams; Haworth, 28 October 1847

You are right in having faith in the reality of Helen Burns's character: she was real enough: I have exaggerated nothing there: I abstained from recording much that I remember respecting her, lest the narrative should sound incredible. Knowing this, I could not but smile at the quiet, self-complacent dogmatism with which one of the journals lays it down that 'such creations as Helen Burns are very beautiful but very untrue.'

The plot of 'Jane Eyre' may be a hackneyed one; Mr Thackeray remarks that it is familiar to him; but having read comparatively few novels, I never chanced to meet with it, and I thought it original –

Charlotte to Smith, Elder & Co.; Haworth, 1 December 1847

'The Examiner' reached me to-day; it had been missent on account of the direction which was to Currer Bell, Care of Miss Brontë. Allow me to intimate that it would be better in future not to put the name of Currer Bell on the outside of communications; if directed simply to Miss Brontë they will be more likely to reach their destination safely. Currer Bell is not known in this district and I have no wish that he should become known.

Review from the Halifax Guardian, *7 November 1847*

Jane Eyre is a work of far different kind. Without the conventionalities and cant of the novel-school, it wins upon the reader with scenes of pathos, which mark the true artist. It is not the least remarkable evidence of the ability of the writer, that even in positions which our calmer reason must condemn as improbable, all seems natural and truthful! What could not such a writer do, were his talents devoted to some more useful and some better line of literature!

Charlotte to William Smith Williams; Haworth, 11 December 1847

There are moments when I can hardly credit that anything I have done should be found worthy to give even transitory pleasure to such men as Mr Thackeray, Sir John Herschel, Mr Fonblanque, Leigh Hunt and Mr Lewes – that my humble efforts should have had such a result is a noble reward.

I was glad and proud to get the Bank Bill Mr Smith sent me yesterday – but I hardly ever felt delight equal to that which cheered me when I received your letter containing an extract from a note by Mr Thackeray in which he expressed himself gratified with the perusal of 'Jane Eyre.' Mr Thackeray is a keen, ruthless satirist – I had never perused his writings but with blended feelings of admiration and indignation – Critics, it appears to me, do not know what an intellectual boa-constrictor he is – they call him 'humerous', 'brilliant' – his is a most scalping humour, a most deadly brilliancy – he does not play with his prey – he coils round it and crushes it in his rings. He seems terribly in earnest in his war against the falsehood and follies of 'the World' – I often wonder what that 'World' thinks of him.

The success of *Jane Eyre* prompted Thomas Newby to publish *Wuthering Heights* and *Agnes Grey* which had languished for many months in his care.

He did not fail to observe that there must be some link between the now-famous Currer Bell and the Ellis and Acton Bell who had entrusted their works to him. He scurried about with uncharacteristic haste and had the two books in print before the end of the year. His authoresses, whom he had not the courtesy to keep informed, were obliged to assume that publication had actually taken place when they received their bound copies. While Charlotte pondered the subject of her next novel, Emily and Anne waited anxiously for the reviews of their own work.

Charlotte to William Smith Williams; Haworth, 14 December 1847

Of course a second work has occupied my thoughts much. I think it would be premature in me to undertake a serial now; I am not yet qualified for the task: I have neither gained a sufficiently firm footing with the public, nor do I possess sufficient confidence in myself, nor can I boast those unflagging animal spirits, that even command of the faculty of composition, which, as you say and I am persuaded, most justly, is an indispensable requisite to success in serial literature. I decidedly feel that ere I change my ground, I had better make another venture in the 3 vol. novel form.

Respecting the plan of such a work, I have pondered it, but as yet with very unsatisfactory results. Three commencements have I essayed, but all three displease me. A few days since I looked over 'The Professor.' I found the beginning very feeble, the whole narrative deficient in incident and in general attractiveness; yet the middle and latter portion of the work, all that relates to Brussels, the Belgian school &c. is as good as I can write; it contains more pith, more substance, more reality, in my judgement, than much of 'Jane Eyre'. It gives, I think, a new view of a grade, an occupation, and a class of characters – all very common-place, very insignificant in themselves, but not more so than the materials composing that portion of 'Jane Eyre' which seems to please most generally –.

My wish is to recast 'the Professor', add as well as I can, what is deficient, retrench some parts, develop others – and make of it a 3-vol. work; no easy task, I know, yet I trust not an impracticable one . . . 'Wuthering Heights' is, I suppose, at length published – at least Mr Newby has sent the authors their six copies – I wonder how it will be received. I should say it merits the epithets of 'vigorous' and 'original' much more decidedly than 'Jane Eyre' did. 'Agnes Grey' should please such critics as Mr Lewes – for it is 'true' and 'unexaggerated' enough.

The books are not well got up – they abound in errors of the press. On a former occasion I expressed myself with perhaps too little reserve regarding Mr Newby – yet I cannot but feel, and feel painfully that Ellis and Acton have not had the justice at his hands that I have had at those of Messrs Smith & Elder

Charlotte to William Smith Williams; Haworth, 18 December 1847

Your advice merits and shall have my most serious attention. I feel the force of your reasoning. It is my wish to do my best in the career on which I have entered; So I shall study and strive, and by dint of time, thought and effort, I hope yet to deserve in part the encouragement you and others have so generously accorded me. But <u>Time</u> will be necessary: that I feel more than ever . . . The Observer has just reached me. I always compel myself to read the Analysis in every newspaper-notice. It is a just punishment – a due though severe humiliation for faults of plan and construction. I wonder if the analyses of other fictions read as absurdly as that of 'Jane Eyre' always does

Charlotte to William Smith Williams; Haworth, 21 December 1847

I cannot thank you sufficiently for your letters, and I can give you but a faint idea of the pleasure they afford me; they seem to introduce such light and life to the torpid retirement where we lie like dormice. But – understand this distinctly, you must never write to me except when you have both leisure and inclination. I know your time is too fully occupied and too valuable to be often at the service of any one individual.

You are not far wrong in your judgement respecting 'Wuthering Heights' & 'Agnes Grey.' Ellis has a strong, original mind, full of strange though sombre power: when he writes poetry that power speaks in language at once condensed, elaborated and refined – but in prose it breaks forth in scenes which shock more than they attract – Ellis will improve, however, because he knows his defects. 'Agnes Grey' is the mirror of the mind of the writer. The orthography and punctuation of the books are mortifying to a degree – almost all the errors that were corrected in the proof-sheets appear intact in what should have been the fair copies. If Mr Newby always does business in this way, few authors would like to have him for their publisher a second time.

Believe me, dear Sir,
Yours respectfully
C Bell.

The Brontës' (and Mr Newby's) hopes for the success of *Wuthering Heights* and *Agnes Grey* were soon to be dashed. Few critics deigned to notice *Agnes Grey* but the reviews of *Wuthering Heights* were either baffled or hostile; at best they admitted the power of Ellis Bell's writing. The appearance of three books by the Bells in such a short time naturally increased speculation about the identity and sex of the mysterious authors, whom many believed to be a single person. More insidiously, the increasingly savage criticism of the coarseness and brutality of *Wuthering Heights* eventually began to infect reviews of *Jane Eyre*.

Review of Wuthering Heights & Agnes Grey *from the* Athenaeum, *25 December 1847*

'Jane Eyre', it will be recollected, was *edited* by Mr Currer Bell. Here are two tales so nearly related to 'Jane Eyre' in cast of thought, incident, and language as to excite some curiosity. All three might be the work of one hand, – but the first issued remains the best. In spite of much power and cleverness; in spite of its truth to life in the remote nooks and corners of England 'Wuthering Heights' is a disagreeable story. The Bells seem to affect painful and exceptional subjects: – the misdeeds and oppressions of tyranny – the eccentricities of 'woman's fantasy.' They do not turn away from dwelling on those physical acts of cruelty which we know to have their warrant in the real annals of crime and suffering, – but the contemplation of which true taste rejects. The brutal master of the lonely house on 'Wuthering Heights' – a prison which might be pictured from life – has doubtless had his prototype in those uncongenial and remote districts where human beings, like the trees, grow gnarled and dwarfed and distorted by the inclement climate; but he might have been indicated with far fewer touches, in place of so entirely filling the canvas that there is hardly a scene untainted by his presence . . . Enough of what is mean and bitterly painful and degrading gathers round every one of us during the course of his pilgrimage through this vale of tears to absolve the Artist from choosing his incidents and characters out of such a dismal catalogue; and if the Bells, singly or collectively, are contemplating future or frequent utterances in Fiction, let us hope that they will spare us further interiors so gloomy as the one here elaborated with such dismal minuteness

J. G. Lockhart to a friend; Sussex Place, 29 December 1847

I have finished the adventures of Miss Jane Eyre, and think her far the cleverest that was written since Austen and Edgeworth were in their prime. Worth fifty Trollopes and Martineaus rolled into one counterpane, with fifty Dickenses and Bulwers to keep them company; but rather a brazen Miss. The two heroines exemplify the duty of taking the initiative, and illustrate it under the opposite cases as to worldly goods of all sorts, except wit. One is a vast heiress, and beautiful as angels are everywhere but in modern paintings. She asks a handsome curate, who will none of her, being resolved on a missionary life in the far East. The other is a thin, little, unpretty slip of a governess, who falls in love with a plain stoutish Mr Burnand, aged twenty years above herself, sits on his knee, lights his cigar for him, asks him flat one fine evening, and after a concealed mad wife is dead, at last fills that awful lady's place. Lady Fanny will easily extract the moral of this touching fable.

Charlotte to William Smith Williams; Haworth, 4 January 1848

'Jane Eyre' has got down into Yorkshire; a copy has even penetrated into this neighbourhood: I saw an elderly clergyman reading it the other day, and had the satisfaction of hearing him exclaim 'Why – they have got ---- school, and Mr ---- here, I declare! and Miss ---- ' (naming the original of Lowood, Mr Brocklehurst and Miss Temple) He had known them all: I wondered whether he would recognize the portrait, and was gratified to find that he did and that moreover he pronounced them faithful and just – he said too that Mr ---- (Brocklehurst) 'deserved the chastisement he had got.'

He did not recognize 'Currer Bell' – What author would be without the advantage of being able to walk invisible? One is thereby enabled to keep such a quiet mind.

Review of Wuthering Heights *from the* Examiner, *8 January 1848*

This is a strange book. It is not without evidences of considerable power; but, as a whole, it is wild, confused, disjointed, improbable; and the people who make up the drama, which is tragic enough in its consequences, are savages ruder than those who lived before the days of Homer . . . Heathcliff may be considered as the hero of the book, if a hero there be. He is an incarnation of evil qualities; implacable hate, ingratitude, cruelty, falsehood, selfishness, and revenge. He exhibits, moreover, a certain stoical endurance in early life, which enables him to 'bide his time,' and nurse up his wrath till it becomes mature and terrible; and there is one portion of his nature, one only, wherein he appears to approximate to humanity. Like the Corsair, and other such melodramatic heroes, he is

'Linked to one virtue and a thousand crimes;'

and it is with difficulty that we can prevail upon ourselves to believe in the appearance of such a phenomenon, so near our own dwellings as the summit of a Lancashire or Yorkshire moor.

Review of Wuthering Heights *from* Douglas Jerrold's Weekly
Newspaper, *15 January 1848*

'Wuthering Heights' is a strange sort of book, – baffling all regular
criticism; yet, it is impossible to begin and not finish it; and quite as
impossible to lay it aside afterwards and say nothing about it . . . In
'Wuthering Heights' the reader is shocked, disgusted, almost
sickened by details of cruelty, inhumanity, and the most diabolical
hate and vengeance, and anon come passages of powerful testimony to the supreme power of love – even over demons in the
human form. The women in the book are of a strange fiendish-
angelic nature, tantalizing, and terrible, and the men are indescribable out of the book itself . . . We strongly recommend all our
readers who love novelty to get this story, for we can promise
them that they never have read anything like it before. It is
very puzzling and very interesting, and if we had space we would
willingly devote a little more time to the analysis of this remarkable
story, but we must leave it to our readers to decide what sort of
book it is.

Review of Wuthering Heights *from the* Atlas, *22 January 1848*

Wuthering Heights is a strange, inartistic story. There are evidences
in every chapter of a sort of rugged power – an unconscious strength
– which the possessor seems never to think of turning to the best
advantage. The general effect is inexpressibly painful. We know
nothing in the whole range of our fictitious literature which presents
such shocking pictures of the worst forms of humanity . . . There is
not in the entire *dramatis personae* a single character which is not
utterly hateful or thoroughly contemptible. If you do not detest the
person, you despise him; and if you do not despise him, you detest
him with your whole heart. Hindley, the brutal, degraded sot, strong
in the desire to work all mischief, but impotent in his degradation;
Linton Heathcliff, the miserable, drivelling coward, in whom we
see selfishness in its most abject form; and Heathcliff himself, the
presiding evil genius of the piece, the tyrant father of an imbecile
son, a creature in whom every evil passion seems to have reached a

gigantic excess – form a group of deformities such as we have rarely seen gathered together on the same canvas.

Though they were disappointed with the reviews, the Brontës had other and more pressing problems than the critical reception of *Wuthering Heights* and *Agnes Grey*. All the family had been ill at the beginning of the year with persistent coughs and colds. More seriously, Branwell's slide into alcoholism after the death of Mr Robinson had now reached the point at which his health was suffering; he began to have fits and showed all the symptoms of *delirium tremens*. Had he been forced to rely on his own and his family's resources, he could not have afforded to drink to excess but the money which Mrs Robinson continued to send him periodically enabled him to finance his habit.

Branwell to J. B. Leyland; Haworth, January 1848

I was <u>really</u> far enough from well when I saw you last week at Halifax, and if you should happen shortly to see Mrs Sugden of the Talbot you would greatly oblige me by telling her that I consider her conduct towards me as most kind and motherly, and that if I did anything, during temporary illness, to offend her I deeply regret it, and beg her to take my regret as my apology till I see her again, which, I trust will be ere long.

I was not intoxicated when I saw you last, Dear Sir, but I was so much broken down and embittered in heart that it did not need much extra stimulus to make me experience the fainting fit I had, after you left, at the Talbot, and another, more severe at Mr Crowthers – the Commercial Inn near the Northgate.

Charlotte to Ellen; Haworth, 11 January 1848

We have not been very comfortable here at home lately – Far from it indeed – Branwell has contrived by some means to get more money from the old quarter – and has led us a sad life with his absurd and often intolerable conduct – Papa is harassed day and night – we have little peace – he is always sick, has two or three times fallen down in fits – what will be the ultimate end God knows –

Though Charlotte was still prohibited by the vow of secrecy that the 'Bell brothers' had taken from sharing anything of her new and burgeoning literary life with Ellen, she had at least the consolation and stimulation of being able to correspond with her publishers and other writers on literary topics.

★*Charlotte to G. H. Lewes; Haworth, 12 January 1848*

If I ever <u>do</u> write another book, I think I will have nothing of what you call 'melodrame'; I <u>think</u> so, but I am not sure. I <u>think</u> too I will endeavour to follow the counsel which shines out of Miss Austen's 'mild eyes'; 'to finish more, and be more subdued'; but neither am I sure of that. When authors write best, or at least, when they write most fluently, an influence seems to waken in them which becomes their master, which will have its own way, putting out of view all behests but its own, dictating certain words, and insisting on their being used, whether vehement or measured in their nature; new moulding characters, giving unthought-of turns to incidents, rejecting carefully elaborated old ideas, and suddenly creating and adopting new ones. Is it not so? And should we try to counteract this influence? Can we indeed counteract it? . . . Why do you like Miss Austen so very much? I am puzzled on that point.

What induced you to say that you would rather have written 'Pride & Prejudice' or 'Tom Jones' than any of the Waverley novels?

I had not seen 'Pride & Prejudice' till I read that sentence of yours, and then I got the book and studied it. And what did I find? An accurate daguerreotyped portrait of a common-place face; a carefully-fenced, highly cultivated garden with neat borders and delicate flowers – but no glance of a bright vivid physiognomy – no open country – no fresh air – no blue hill – no bonny beck. I should hardly like to live with her ladies and gentlemen in their elegant but confined houses. These observations will probably irritate you, but I shall run the risk.

Charlotte to G. H. Lewes; Haworth, 18 January 1848

What a strange sentence comes next in your letter! You say I must familiarize my mind with the fact that 'Miss Austen is not a poetess, has no sentiment (you scornfully enclose the word in inverted commas) no eloquence, none of the ravishing enthusiasm of poetry' – and then you add, I <u>must</u> 'learn to acknowledge her as <u>one of the greatest artists, of the greatest painters of human character</u>, and one of the writers with the nicest sense of means to an end that ever lived.'

The last point only will I ever acknowledge.

Can there be a great Artist without poetry?

What I call – what I will bend to as a great Artist, there cannot be destitute of the divine gift. But by <u>poetry</u> I am sure you understand something different to what I do – as you do by 'sentiment'. It is <u>poetry</u>, as I comprehend the word which elevates that masculine George Sand, and makes out of something coarse, something godlike. It is 'sentiment', in my sense of the term, sentiment jealously hidden, but genuine, which extracts the venom from that formidable Thackeray, and converts what might be only corrosive poison into purifying elixir. If Thackeray did not cherish in his large heart deep feeling for his kind, he would delight to exterminate; as it is, I believe he wishes only to reform.

Miss Austen, being as you say without 'sentiment', without <u>poetry</u>, may be – <u>is</u> sensible, real (more <u>real</u> than <u>true</u>) but she cannot be great.

. . . I have something else to say. You mention the authoress of 'Azeth the Egyptian': you say you think I should sympathize 'with her daring imagination and pictorial fancy.' Permit me to undeceive you: with infinitely more relish can I sympathize with Miss Austen's clear common sense and subtle shrewdness. If you find no inspiration in Miss Austen's page, neither do you find there windy wordiness: to use your words once again, she exquisitely adapts her means to her end: both are very subdued, a little contracted, but never absurd. I have not read 'Azeth', but I did read or begin to read a tale in the 'New Monthly' from the same pen, and harsh as the opinion may sound to you, I must cordially avow that I thought it both turgid and feeble: it reminded me of some of the most inflated and emptiest parts of Bulwer's novels: I found in it neither strength, sense nor originality.

All three sisters were now writing another novel. Anne, answering a note from Ellen, had to suppress the fact that she was now working hard on *The Tenant of Wildfell Hall*. Unable to tell a deliberate lie, she simply said that they had done nothing 'to speak of' since Ellen's previous visit. Emily, meanwhile, had written to her publisher, Thomas Newby, to inform him that her second novel was in preparation and asking him if he would be prepared to publish it. His reply, preserved in her writing desk, is one of the few tantalizing glimpses we have of Emily's lost successor to *Wuthering Heights*.

Anne to Ellen; Haworth, 26 January 1848

You do not tell us how <u>you</u> bear the present unfavourable weather. We are all cut up by this cruel east wind: most of us, e.i. Charlotte, Emily, and I, have had the inf[l]uenza, or a bad cold instead, twice over within the space of a few weeks; Papa has had it once. Tabby has hitherto escaped it altogether. – I have no news to tell you, for we have been nowhere, seen no one, and done nothing (to <u>speak</u> of) since you were here – and yet we contrive to be busy from morning to night. Flossy is fatter than ever, but still active enough to relish a sheep hunt –

★Charlotte to Ellen; Haworth, 28 January 1848

It is very kind in you to continue to write occasionally to Anne – for I think your letters both do her good and give her pleasure – the Robinsons still amaze me by the continued frequency and constancy of their correspondence – poor girls – they still complain of their Mother's proceedings – that woman is a hapless being; calculated to bring a curse wherever she goes by the mixture of weakness, perversion & deceit in her nature. Sir Edward Scott's wife is said to be dying – if she goes I suppose they will marry – that is if Mrs R. can marry — She affirmed her husband's will bound her to remain single — but I do not believe anything she says.

Charlotte to William Smith Williams; Haworth, 15 February 1848

I should much — very much like to take that quiet view of the 'great world' you allude to, but I have as yet won no right to give myself such a treat: it must be for some future day — when — I don't know. Ellis, I imagine, would soon turn aside from the spectacle in disgust; I do not think he admits it as his creed that 'the proper study of mankind is man'; at least not the artificial man of cities. In some points I consider Ellis somewhat of a theorist: now and then he broaches ideas which strike my sense as much more daring and original than practical; his reason may be in advance of mine, but certainly it often travels a different road. I should say Ellis will not be seen in his full strength till he is seen as an essayist.

Thomas Cautley Newby, publisher, to Emily as 'Ellis Bell'; London, 15 February 1848

Dear Sir,

I am much obliged by your kind note & shall have great pleasure in making arrangements for your next novel. I would not hurry its completion, for I think you are quite right not to let it go before the world until well satisfied with it, for much depends on your new work if it be an improvement on your first you will have established yourself as a first rate novelist, but if it fall short the Critics will be too apt to say that you have expended your talent in your first novel. I shall therefore, have pleasure in accepting it upon the understanding that its completion be at your own time.

Believe me
My dear Sir
Yrs sincerely
T C Newby

Feb. 15. 1848

Charlotte to William Smith Williams; Haworth, 11 March 1848

I have, in my day, wasted a certain quantity of Bristol board and drawing-paper, crayons and cakes of colour, but when I examine the contents of my portfolio now, it seems as if during the years it has been lying closed, some fairy had changed what I once thought sterling coin into dry leaves, and I feel much inclined to consign the whole collection of drawings to the fire; I see they have no value. If then 'Jane Eyre' is ever to be illustrated, it must be by some other hand than that of its author. But I hope no one will be at the trouble to make portraits of my characters: Bulwer and Byron — heroes and heroines are very well — they are all of them handsome — but my personages are mostly unattractive in look and therefore ill-adapted to figure in ideal portraits — At the best, I have always thought such representations futile.

Charlotte to Margaret Wooler; Haworth, 31 March 1848

I remember well wishing my lot had been cast in the troubled times of the late war, and seeing in its exciting incidents a kind of stimulating charm which it made my pulses beat fast only to think of: I remember even, I think, being a little impatient that you would not fully sympathize with my feelings on those subjects, that you heard my aspirations and speculations very tranquilly, and by no means seemed to think the flaming sword could be any pleasant addition to the joys of Paradise.

I have now outlived youth; and, though I dare not say that I have outlived all its illusions — that the romance is quite gone from Life, the veil fallen from Truth, and that I see both in naked reality — yet certainly many things are not to me what they were ten years ago; and amongst the rest, 'the pomp and circumstance of war' have quite lost in my eyes their factitious glitter —

Speculation about the real identity of the three Bells continued apace. Charlotte's publishers, at her request, continued to fend off queries about their famous author, but suspicions were already being aroused among the Brontës' own circle of acquaintance. Charlotte moved quickly to stamp out the rumours, but in her anxiety to do so, she compromised the integrity of her friend Ellen.

Charlotte to William Smith Williams; Haworth, 20 April 1848

I trust your firm will not lose by the 3rd edition of 'Jane Eyre' what has been made by the first, but I must say I think you enterprising to run the risk; however you have all along been the reverse of timid in the business. Success to the fearless!

It is very kind and right in you to answer 'Currer Bell' to all queries respecting the authorship of 'Jane Eyre': that is the only name I wish to have mentioned in connection with my writings. 'Currer Bell' only – I am and will be to the Public; if accident or design should deprive me of that name, I should deem it a misfortune – a very great one; mental tranquillity would then be gone; it would be a task to write – a task which I doubt whether I could continue. If I were known – I should ever be conscious in writing that my book must be read by ordinary acquaintances – and that idea would fetter me intolerably.

Charlotte to Ellen; Haworth, 22 April 1848

I had quite forgotten – till your letter reminded me, that it was the anniversary of your birthday and mine – I am now 32. Youth is gone – gone – and will never come back: can't help it. I wish you many returns of your birthday and increase of happiness with increase of years.

Charlotte to Ellen; Haworth, 3 May 1848

All I can say to you about a certain matter is this: the report – if report there be – and if the lady, who seems to have been rather mystified, had not dreamt what she fancied had been told to her – must have had its origin in some absurd misunderstanding. I have given <u>no one</u> a right either to affirm, or hint, in the most distant manner, that I am 'publishing' – (humbug!) Whoever has said it – if any one has, which I doubt – is no friend of mine. Though twenty books were ascribed to me, I should own none. I scout the idea utterly. Whoever, after I have distinctly rejected the charge, urges it upon me, will do an unkind and an ill-bred thing. The most profound obscurity is infinitely preferable to vulgar notoriety; and that notoriety I neither seek nor will have. If then any Birstallian or Gomersallian should presume to bore you on the subject, – to ask you what 'novel' Miss Brontë has been 'publishing' – you can just say, with the distinct firmness of which you are perfect mistress, when you choose, that you are authorized by Miss Brontë to say, that she repels and disowns every accusation of the kind. You may add, if you please, that if any one has her confidence, you believe you have, and she has made no drivelling confessions to you on the subject.

The subject of her next novel had troubled Charlotte for some time but ideas had begun to evolve which would later have considerable influence on *Shirley*. These she tentatively put forward in her correspondence with William Smith Williams, her confidant on literary matters, in a couple of long and revealing letters prompted by the discovery that his daughters were contemplating careers as governesses.

Charlotte to William Smith Williams; Haworth, 12 May 1848

Some remarks in your last letter on teaching commanded my attention. I suppose you never were engaged in tuition yourself, but if you had been, you could not have more exactly hit on the great qualification – I had almost said – the <u>one</u> great qualification necessary to the task: the faculty, not merely of <u>acquiring</u> but of <u>imparting</u> knowledge; the power of influencing young minds; that natural fondness for – that innate sympathy with children, which, you say, Mrs Williams is so happy as to possess. He or She who possesses this faculty, this sympathy – though perhaps not otherwise highly accomplished – need never fear failure in the career of instruction. Children will be docile with them, will improve under them; parents will consequently repose in them confidence; their task will be comparatively light, their path comparatively smooth. If the faculty be absent, the life of a teacher will be a struggle from beginning to end. No matter how amiable the disposition, how strong the sense of duty, how active the desire to please; no matter how brilliant and varied the accomplishments; if the governess has not the power to win her young charge, the secret to instil gently and surely her own knowledge into the growing mind entrusted to her, she will have a wearing, wasting existence of it. To educate a child as, I daresay Mrs Williams has educated her children, probably with as much pleasure to herself as profit to them, will indeed be impossible to the teacher who lacks this qualification; but, I conceive, should circumstances – as in the case of your daughters – compel a young girl notwithstanding to adopt a governesses' profession, she may contrive to instruct and even to instruct well. That is – though she cannot form the child's mind, mould its character, influence its disposition and guide its conduct as she would wish, she may give lessons – even good, clear, clever lessons in the various branches of knowledge, she may earn and doubly earn her scanty salary; as a daily governess, or a school-teacher she may succeed, but as a resident governess she will never (except under peculiar and exceptional circumstances) be happy. Her deficiency will harass her not so much in school-time as in play-hours; the moments that would be rest and recreation to the governess who understood and could adapt herself to children, will be almost torture to her who has not that power; many a time, when her charge turns unruly on her hands, when the responsibility which she would wish to discharge faithfully and perfectly, becomes unmanageable to her, she will wish herself a housemaid or kitchen-girl, rather than a baited, trampled, desolate, distracted governess.

The Governesses' Institution may be an excellent thing in some points of view – but it is both absurd and cruel to attempt to raise still higher the standard of acquirements. Already Governesses are not half nor a quarter paid for what they teach – nor in most instances is half or a quarter of their attainments required by their pupils. The young Teacher's chief anxiety, when she sets out in life, always is, to know a great deal; her chief fear that she should not know enough; brief experience will, in most instances, shew her that this anxiety has been misdirected. She will rarely be found too ignorant for her pupils; the demand on her knowledge will not often be larger than she can answer; but on her patience – on her self-control the requirement will be enormous; on her animal spirits (and woe be to her if these fail!) the pressure will be immense.

I have seen an ignorant nursery-maid who could scarcely read or write – by dint of an excellent, serviceable sanguine – phlegmatic temperament which made her at once cheerful and unmovable; of a robust constitution and steady, unimpressionable nerves which kept her firm under shocks, and unharassed under annoyances – manage with comparative ease a large family of spoilt children, while their Governess lived amongst them a life of inexpressible misery; tyrannized over, finding her efforts to please and teach utterly vain, chagrined, distressed, worried – so badgered so trodden-on, that she ceased almost at last to know herself, and wondered in what despicable, trembling frame her oppressed mind was prisoned – and could not realise the idea of evermore being treated with respect and regarded with affection – till she finally resigned her situation and went away quite broken in spirit and reduced to the verge of decline in health.

Those who would urge on Governesses more acquirements do not know the origin of their chief sufferings. It is more physical and mental strength, denser moral impassibility that they require, rather than additional skill in arts or sciences. As to the forcing system, whether applied to Teachers or Taught – I hold it to be a cruel system.

It is true the world demands a brilliant list of accomplishments; for £20 per ann. it expects in one woman the attainments of several professors – but the demand is insensate – and I think should rather be resisted than complied with. If I might plead with you in behalf of your daughters – I should say – Do not let them waste their young lives in trying to attain manifold accomplishments. Let them try rather to possess thoroughly, fully one or two talents, then let them endeavour to lay in a stock of health, strength, cheerfulness; let them labour to attain self-control, endurance, fortitude, firmness; if possible, let them learn from their mother something of the precious art she possesses – these things, together with sound principles, will be their best supports – their best aids through a governess's life.

As for that one who - you say has a nervous horror of exhibition – I need not beg you to be gentle with her – I am sure you will not be harsh – but she must be firm with herself, or she will repent it in after-life – She should begin by degrees to endeavour to overcome her diffidence. Were she destined to enjoy an independent, easy existence she might respect her natural disposition to seek retirement and even cherish it as a shade-loving virtue – but since that is not her lot; since she is fated to make her way in the crowd – and to depend on herself, she should say – I will try and learn the art of self-possession – not that I may display my accomplishments – but that I may have the satisfaction of feeling that I am my own mistress – and can move and speak, undaunted by the fear of man. While however – I pen this piece of advice – I confess that it is much easier to give than to follow. What the sensations of the nervous are under the gaze of publicity none but the nervous know – and how powerless Reason and Resolution are to control them would sound incredible except to the actual sufferers . . .

Believe me
yours sincerely
Currer Bell

P.S. I must, after all, add a morsel of paper – for I find – on glancing over yours, that I have forgotten to answer a question you ask respecting my next work – I have not therein so far treated of governesses, as I do not wish it to resemble its predecessor. I often wish to say something about the 'condition of women' question – but it is one respecting which so much 'cant' has been talked, that one feels a sort of repugnance to approach it. It is true enough that the present market for female labour is quite overstocked – but where or how could another be opened? Many say that the professions now filled only by men should be open to women also – but are not their present occupants and candidates more than numerous enough to answer every demand? Is there any room for female lawyers, female doctors, female engravers, for more female artists, more authoresses? One can see where the evil lies – but who can point out the remedy? When a woman has a little family to rear and educate and a household to conduct, her hands are full, her vocation is evident – when her destiny isolates her – I suppose she must do what she can – live as she can – complain as little – bear as much – work as well as possible. This is not high theory – but I believe it is sound practice – good to put into execution while philosophers and legislators ponder over the better ordering of the Social System. At the same time, I conceive that when Patience has done its utmost and Industry its best, whether in the case of Women or Operatives, and when both are baffled and Pain and Want triumphant – the Sufferer is free – is entitled – at last to send up to Heaven any piercing cry for relief – if by that cry he can hope to obtain succour.

Charlotte to William Smith Williams; Haworth, 15 June 1848

I have always been accustomed to think that the necessity of earning one's subsistence is not in itself an evil; but I feel it may become a heavy evil if health fails, if employment lacks; if the demand upon our efforts made by the weakness of others dependent upon us, becomes greater than our strength suffices to answer. In such a case I can imagine that the married man may wish himself single again, and that the married woman, when she sees her husband over-exerting himself to maintain her and her children, may almost wish – out of the very force of her affection for him – that it had never been her lot to add to the weight of his responsibilities. Most desirable then is it that all – both men and women – should have the power and the will to work for themselves; most advisable that both Sons and Daughters should early be inured to habits of independence and industry . . . Should your daughter, however, go out as a governess, she should first take a firm resolution not to be too soon daunted by difficulties, too soon disgusted by disagreeables; and if she has a high spirit, sensitive feelings, she should tutor the one to submit the other to endure for the sake of those at home. That is the governesses' best talisman of patience – it is the best balm for wounded suscep- tibility – When tried hard she must say 'I will be patient not out of servility – but because I love my parents – and wish through my perseverance, diligence, and success, to repay their anxieties and tenderness for me'. With this aid the least deserved insult may often be swallowed quite calmly, like a bitter pill with a draught of fair water.

I think you speak excellent sense when you say that girls without fortune should be brought up and accustomed to support themselves; and that if they marry poor men, it should be with a prospect of being able to help their partners. If all parents thought so, girls would not be reared on speculation with a view to their making mercenary marriages – and consequently women would not be so piteously degraded as they now too often are.

The Brontë sisters had always been conscious of the importance of being able to earn their own livings. That duty seems never to have been instilled in Branwell who, three years after his dismissal from Thorp Green, had still not found paid employment and, indeed, by this time, had ceased to seek it. His two surviving last letters suggest that he was now unemployable; the once brilliant, ambitious and adored brother was now simply a drunken sot, barely capable of writing coherently, even to his closest friends.

Branwell to J. B. Leyland; Haworth, 22 June 1848

Mr Nicholson has sent to my Father a demand for the settlement of my bill owed to him immediately, under penalty of a Court Summons.

I have written to inform him that I shall soon be able to pay him the balance left in full – for that I will write to Dr Crosby and request an advance through his hands which I am sure to obtain, when I will remit my amount owed, at once, to the Old Cock.

I have also given John Brown this morning Ten shillings which John will certainly place in Mr N.'s hands on Wednesday next.

If he refuses my offer and presses me with law I am RUINED. I have had five months of such utter sleeplessness violent cough and frightful agony of mind that jail would destroy me for ever.

I earnestly beg you to see Nicholson and tell him that my receipt of money on asking, through Dr Crosby, is morally certain.

If you conveniently can, see Mrs Sugden of the Talbot, and tell her that on receipt of the money I expect so shortly I will transmit her the whole or part of the account I owe her.

Excuse this scrawl – Long have I resolved to write to you a letter of five or six pages, but intolerable mental wretchedness and corporeal weakness have utterly prevented me.

I shall bother you again if this painful business only gets settled.

At present believe me
Dear Sir,
Yours, Sincerely but nearly worn out,
P.B. Brontë

Branwell to John Brown, sexton of Haworth; Haworth, undated

Sunday.
Noon.

Dear John,

I shall feel very much obliged to you if [you] can contrive to get me Five pence worth of Gin in a proper measure.

Should it be speedily got I could perhaps take it from you or Billy at the lane top or what would be quite as well, sent out for, to you.

I anxiously ask the favour because I know the good it will do me.

Punctual[l]y at Half-past-Nine in the morning you will be paid the 5d out of a shilling given me then. Yours, P.B.B.

At the end of June 1848, Anne's second novel, *The Tenant of Wildfell Hall*, was published by Thomas Newby. Like *Wuthering Heights* it was condemned by the critics for dwelling 'inartistically' on scenes of brutality and debauchery, but unlike that book or *Agnes Grey*, it enjoyed a moderate success in terms of sales, requiring a reprint only six weeks after its first appearance. It was preceded by a review of *Jane Eyre* which stung Charlotte to the quick and which set the tone for those of *The Tenant of Wildfell Hall*.

Review of Jane Eyre *from the* Christian Remembrancer, *April 1848*

. . . we cannot wonder that the hypothesis of a male author should have been started, or that ladies especially should still be rather determined to uphold it. For a book more unfeminine both in its excellences and defects, it would be hard to find in the annals of female authorship. Throughout there is masculine power, breadth and shrewdness, combined with masculine hardness, coarseness, and freedom of expression. Slang is not rare. The humour is frequently produced by a use of Scripture, at which one is rather sorry to have smiled. The love-scenes glow with a fire as fierce as that of Sappho, and somewhat more fuliginous. There is an intimate acquaintance with the worst parts of human nature, a practised sagacity in discovering the latent ulcer, and a ruthless rigour in exposing it, which must command our admiration, but are almost startling in one of the softer sex. Jane Eyre professes to be an autobiography, and we think it likely that in some essential respects it is so. If the authoress has not been, like her heroine, an oppressed orphan, a starved and bullied charity-school girl, and a despised and slighted governess (and the intensity of feeling which she shows in speaking of the wrongs of this last class seems to prove that they have been her own), at all events we fear she is one to whom the world has not been kind. And, assuredly, never was unkindness more cordially repaid. Never was there a better hater. Every page burns with moral Jacobinism. 'Unjust, unjust,' is the burden of every reflection upon the things and powers that be. All virtue is but well masked vice, all religious profession and conduct is but the whitening of the sepulchre, all self-denial is but deeper selfishness.

Review of The Tenant of Wildfell Hall *from the* Spectator;
8 July 1848

The Tenant of Wildfell Hall, like its predecessor, suggests the idea of considerable abilities ill applied. There is power, effect, and even nature, though of an extreme kind, in its pages; but there seems in the writer a morbid love for the coarse, not to say the brutal; so that his level subjects are not very attractive, and the more forcible are displeasing or repulsive, from their gross, physical, or profligate substratum.

Review of The Tenant of Wildfell Hall *from* Sharpe's London Magazine; *August 1848*

. . . so revolting are many of the scenes, so coarse and disgusting the language put into the mouths of some of the characters, that the reviewer to whom we entrusted it returned it to us, saying it was unfit to be noticed in the pages of *Sharpe*; and we are so far of the same opinion, that our object in the present paper is to warn our readers, and more especially our lady-readers, against being induced to peruse it, either by the powerful interest of the story, or the talent with which it is written . . . we cannot but express our deep regret that a book in many respects eminently calculated to advance the cause of religion and right feeling, the moral of which is unimpeachable and most powerfully wrought out, should be rendered unfit for the perusal of the very class of persons to whom it would be most useful, (namely, imaginative girls likely to risk their happiness on the forlorn hope of marrying and reforming a captivating rake,) owing to the profane expressions, inconceivably coarse language, and revolting scenes and descriptions by which its pages are disfigured.

Chapter Nine

1848

'Acton Bell' has published another book – it is in 3 vols but I do not like it quite as well as 'Agnes Grey' the subject not being such as the author had pleasure in handling – it has been praised by some reviews and blamed by others – as yet only £25 have been realised for the copyright – and as 'Acton Bell's' publisher is a shuffling scamp – I expect no more.

About 2 months since, I had a letter from my publishers, Smith & Elder – saying that 'Jane Eyre' had had a great run in America – and that a publisher there had consequently bid high for the first sheets of the next work by 'Currer Bell' which they had promised to let him have. Presently after came a second missive from Smith & Elder – all in alarm, suspicion and wrath – their American correspondent had written to them complaining that the first sheets of a new work by 'Currer Bell' had been already received and not by their house but by a rival publisher – and asking the meaning of such false play – it inclosed an extract from a letter from Mr Newby (A. & E. Bell's publisher) affirming that 'to the best of his belief "Jane Eyre" "Wuthering Heights" – "Agnes Grey" – and "The Tenant of Wildfell Hall" (the new work) were all the production of one writer.'

This was a lie, as Newby had been told repeatedly that they were the productions of 3 different authors – but the fact was he wanted to make a dishonest move in the game – to make the Public and 'the Trade' believe that he had got hold of 'Currer Bell' & thus cheat Smith & Elder by securing the American publisher's bid.

The upshot of it was that on the very day I received Smith & Elder's letter – Anne and I packed up a small box, sent it down to

Keighley – set out ourselves after tea – walked through a thunder-storm to the station, got to Leeds and whirled up by the night train to London – with the view of proving our separate identity to Smith & Elder and confronting Newby with his lie –

We arrived at the Chapter Coffee House – (our old place Polly – we did not well know where else to go) about eight o'clock in the morning – We washed ourselves – had some breakfast – sat a few minutes and then set off in queer, inward excitement, to 65. Cornhill. Neither Mr Smith nor Mr Williams knew we were coming – they had never seen us – they did not know whether we were men or women – but had always written to us as men.

We found 65 – to be a large bookseller's shop in a street almost as bustling as the Strand – we went in – walked up to the counter – there were a great many young men and lads here and there – I said to the first I could accost – 'May I see Mr Smith –?' – he hesitated, looked a little surprised – but went to fetch him – We sat down and waited awhile – looking at some books on the counter – publications of theirs well known to us – many of which they had sent us copies as presents. At last somebody came up and said dubiously 'Did you wish to see me, Ma'am?' 'Is it Mr Smith?' I said looking up through my spectacles at a young, tall, gentlemanly man. 'It is.' I then put his own letter into his hand directed to 'Currer Bell.' He looked at it – then at me – again – yet again – I laughed at his queer perplexity – a recognition took place – I gave my real name – 'Miss Brontë' – We were both hurried from the shop into a little back room – ceiled with a great skylight and only large enough to hold 3 chairs and a desk – and there explanations were rapidly gone into – Mr Newby being anathematized, I fear with undue vehemence. Smith hurried out and returned quickly with one whom he introduced as Mr Williams – a pale, mild, stooping man of fifty – very much like a faded Tom Dixon – Another recognition – a long, nervous shaking of hands – then followed talk – talk – talk – Mr Williams being silent – Mr Smith loquacious –

'Allow me to introduce you to my mother & sisters – How long do you stay in Town? You must make the most of the time – to-night you must go to the Italian opera – you must see the Exhibition – Mr Thackeray would be pleased to see you – If Mr

Lewes knew "Currer Bell" was in town – he would have to be shut up – I will ask them both to dinner at my house &c.' I stopped his projects and discourses by a grave explanation – that though I should very much like to see both Mr Lewes and still more Mr Thackeray – we were as resolved as ever to preserve our incognito – We had only confessed ourselves to our publisher – in order to do away with the inconveniences that had arisen from our too well preserved mystery – to all the rest of the world we must be 'gentlemen' as heretofore.

Williams understood me directly – Smith comprehended by slower degrees – he did not like the quiet plan – he would have liked some excitement, eclat &c.

He then urged us to meet a literary party incognito – he would introduce us a[s] 'Country Cousins' The desire to see some of the personages whose names he mentioned – kindled in me very strongly – but when I found on further examination that he could not venture to ask such men as Thackeray &c. at a short notice, without giving them a hint as to whom they were to meet, I declined even this – I felt it would have ended in our being made a show of – a thing I have ever resolved to avoid.

Then he said we must come and stay at his house – but we were not prepared for a long stay & declined this also – as we took leave – he told us he should bring his sisters to call on us that evening – We returned to our Inn – and I paid for the excitement of the interview by a thundering head-ache & harrassing sickness – towards evening as I got no better & expected the Smiths to call – I took a strong dose of sal volatile – it roused me a little – still I was in grievous bodily case when they were announced – They came in two elegant, young ladies in full dress – prepared for the Opera – Smith himself in evening costume – white gloves, &c a distinguished, handsome fellow enough – We had by no means understood that it was settled that we were to go to the Opera – and were not ready – Moreover we had no fine, elegant dresses either with us or in the world – However on brief rumination, I though[t] it would be wise to make no objections – I put my headache in my pocket – we attired ourselves in the plain – high-made, country garments we possessed – and went with them to their carriage – where we found Williams likewise in full dress. They must have thought us queer, quizzical-looking beings, especially me with my spectacles – I smiled inwardly at the contrast which must have been apparent between me and Mr Smith as I walked with him up the crimson carpeted staircase of the Opera House and stood amongst a brilliant throng at the box-door – which was not yet open. Fine ladies & gentlemen glanced at us with a slight, graceful superciliousness quite warranted by the circumstances – Still I felt pleasurably excited – in spite of headache and sickness & conscious clownishness; and I saw Anne was calm and gentle – which she always is –

The performance was Rossini's opera of the 'Barber of Seville' – very brilliant though I fancy there are things I should like better – We got home after one o'clock – we had never been in bed the night before – had been in constant excitement for 24 hours – you may imagine we were tired.

The next day – (Sunday) Mr Williams came early to take us to church – he was so quiet but so sincere in his attentions – one could not but have a most friendly leaning towards him – he has a nervous hesitation in speech and a difficulty in finding appropriate language in which to express himself – which throws him into the background in conversation – but I had been his correspondent – and therefore knew with what intelligence he could write – so that I was not in danger of underrating him. In the afternoon – Mr Smith came in his carriage with his Mother – to take us to his house to dine   I should mention by the way that neither his Mother nor his Sisters knew who we were – and their strange perplexity would have been ludicrous if anyone had dared to laugh – To be brought down to a part of the city into whose obscure, narrow streets they said they had never penetrated before – to an old, dark strange-looking Inn – to take up in their fine carriage a couple of odd-looking country-women – to see their elegant, handsome son & brother treating with scrupulous politeness these insignificant spinsters – must have puzzled them thoroughly. Mr Smith's residence is at Bayswater, 6 miles from Cornhill – a very fine place – the rooms – the drawing-room especially – looked splendid to us. There was no company – only his mother his two grown up sisters – and his brother a lad of 12–13 and a little sister – the youngest of the family – very like himself

– They are all dark-eyed – dark-haired and have clear & pale faces – the mother is a portly, handsome woman of her age – and all the children more or less well-looking – one of the daughters decidedly pretty – except that the expression of her countenance – is not equal to the beauty of her features. We had a fine dinner – which neither Anne nor I had appetite to eat – and were glad when it was over – I always feel under awkward constraint at table. Dining out would be a hideous bore to me.

Mr Smith made himself very pleasant – he is a firm, intelligent man of business though so young – bent on getting on – and I think desirous to make his way by fair, honourable means – he is enterprising – but likewise cool & cautious. Mr Smith is a practical man – I wish Mr Williams were more so – but he is altogether of the contemplative, theorizing order – Mr Williams lives too much in abstractions –

On Monday we went to the Exhibition of the Royal Academy – the National Gallery, and dined again at Mr Smith's – then went home with Mr Williams to tea – and saw his comparatively humble but neat residence and his fine family of eight children – his wife was ill. A daughter of Leigh Hunt's was there – she sang some little Italian airs which she had picked up among the peasantry in Tuscany, in a manner that charmed me – for herself she was a rattling good-natured personage enough –

On Tuesday Morning we left London – laden with books Mr Smith had given us – and got safely home. A more jaded wretch than I looked when I returned, it would be difficult to conceive – I was thin when I went but was meagre indeed when I returned; my face looked grey & very old – with strange, deep lines ploughed in it – my eyes stared unnaturally – I was weak and yet restless. In a while, however these bad effects of excitement went off and I regained my normal condition – We saw Newby – but of him more another time. Good bye. God bless you – write. CB

Charlotte and Anne's 'pop visit', as Mary Taylor called it, took place at the beginning of the second week in July 1848. Though it materially altered Charlotte's relationship with her publishers, it did not change anything else. As far as the general public were aware, the identity of the notorious Bells remained as mysterious as ever. Out of all the Brontës' friends and acquaintances, only Mary, always Charlotte's closest confidante and now, living on the other side of the world, somewhat detached from events, was admitted to the secret.

Charlotte to William Smith Williams; Haworth, 13 July 1848

We reached home safely yesterday, and in a day or two I doubt not we shall get the better of the fatigues of our journey.

It was a somewhat hasty step to hurry up to Town as we did, but I do not regret having taken it. In the first place, mystery is irksome, and I was glad to shake it off with you and Mr Smith, and to shew myself to you for what I am, neither more nor less; thus removing any false expectations that may have arisen under the idea that 'Currer Bell' had a just claim to the masculine cognomen he, perhaps somewhat presumptuously, adopted – that he was, in short, of the 'nobler sex.'

Mary Taylor to Charlotte; Wellington, New Zealand, 24 July 1848

About a month since I received and read *Jane Eyre*. It seemed to me incredible that you had actually written a book. Such events did not happen while I was in England. I begin to believe in your existence much as I do in Mr Rochester's. In a believing mood I don't doubt either of them . . . Your novel surprised me by being so perfect as a work of art. I expected something more changeable and unfinished. You have polished to some purpose . . . You are very different from me in having no doctrine to preach. It is impossible to squeeze a moral out of your production. Has the world gone so well with you that you have no protest to make against its absurdities? Did you never sneer or declaim in your first sketches? I will scold you well when I see you. I don't believe in Mr Rivers. There are no good men of the Brocklehurst species. A missionary either goes into his office for a piece of bread, or he goes from enthusiasm, and that is both too good and too bad a quality for St John. It's a bit of your absurd charity to believe in such a man. You have done wisely in choosing to imagine a high class of readers. You never stop to explain or defend anything and never seem bothered with the idea – if Mrs Fairfax or any other well-intentioned fool gets hold of this what will she think? And yet you know the world is made up of such, and worse. Once more, how have you written through 3 vols. without declaring war to the knife against a few dozen absurd do[c]trines each of which is supported by 'a large and respectable class of readers?' Emily seems to have had such a class in her eye when she wrote that strange thing <u>Wuthering Heights</u>. Ann too stops repeatedly to preach commonplace truths. She has had a still lower class in her mind's eye. Emily seems to have followed the bookseller's advice.

Charlotte to Ellen; Haworth, 28 July 1848

Anne continues to hear constantly – almost daily from her old pupils, the Robinsons – They are both now engaged to different gentlemen – and if they do not change their minds – which they have done already two or three times – will probably be married in a few months. Not one spark of love does either of them profess for her future husband – one of them openly declares that interest alone guides her – and the other, poor thing! is acting according to her mother's wish, and is utterly indifferent herself to the man chosen for her. The lighter-headed of the two sisters takes a pleasure in the spectacle of her fine wedding-dresses and costly bridal presents – the more thoughtful can derive no gratification from these things and is much depressed at the contemplation of her future lot – Anne does her best to cheer and counsel her – and she seems to cling to her quiet, former governess as her only true friend. Of Mrs R– I have not patience to speak – a worse mother a worse woman, I may say I believe, hardly exists – the more I hear of her the more deeply she revolts me – but I do not like to talk about her in a letter.

Branwell is the same in conduct as ever – his constitution seems much shattered – Papa – and sometimes all of us have sad nights with him – he sleeps most of the day, and consequently will lie awake at night – But has not every house its trial?

Charlotte to William Smith Williams; Haworth, 31 July 1848

You will have seen some of the notices of 'Wildfell Hall'. I wish my Sister felt the unfavourable ones less keenly. She does not <u>say</u> much, for she is of a remarkably taciturn, still, thoughtful nature, reserved even with her nearest of kin, but I cannot avoid seeing that her spirits are depressed sometimes. The fact is neither she nor any of us expected that view to be taken of the book which has been taken by some critics: that it had faults of execution, faults of art was obvious; but faults of intention or feeling could be suspected by none who knew the writer. For my own part I consider the subject unfortunately chosen – it was one the author was not qualified to handle at once vigorously and truthfully – the simple and natural – quiet description and simple pathos are, I think, Acton Bell's forte. I liked 'Agnes Grey' better than the present work.

Permit me to caution you not to speak of my Sister<u>s</u> when you write to me – I mean do not use the word in the plural. 'Ellis Bell' will not endure to be alluded to under any other appellation than the '<u>nom de plume</u>.' I committed a grand error in betraying [her: deleted] his identity to you and Mr Smith – it was inadvertent – the words 'we are three Sisters' escaped me before I was aware – I regretted the avowal the moment I had made it; I regret it bitterly now, for I find it is against every feeling and intention of 'Ellis Bell.'

Charlotte to William Smith Williams; Haworth, 14 August 1848

My sister Anne thanks you, as well as myself, for your just critique on 'Wildfell Hall.' It appears to me that your observations exactly hit both the strong and weak points of the book, and the advice which accompanies them is worthy of, and shall receive our most careful attention.

The first duty of an Author is – I conceive – a faithful allegiance to Truth and Nature; his second, such a conscientious study of Art as shall enable him to interpret eloquently and effectively the oracles delivered by those two great deities. The 'Bells' are very sincere in their worship of Truth, and they hope so to apply themselves to the consideration of Art as to attain, one day, the power of speaking the language of conviction in the accents of persuasion; though they rather apprehend that whatever pains they take to modify and soften, an abrupt word or vehement tone will now and then occur to startle ears polite, whenever the subject shall chance to be such as moves their spirits within them . . . You say, Mr Huntingdon reminds you of Mr Rochester – does he? Yet there is no likeness between the two; the foundation of each character is entirely different. Huntingdon is a specimen of the naturally selfish sensual, superficial man whose one merit of a joyous temperament only avails him while he is young and healthy, whose best days are his earliest, who never profits by experience, who is sure to grow worse, the older he grows. Mr Rochester has a thoughtful nature and a very feeling heart; he is neither selfish nor self-indulgent; he is ill-educated, misguided, errs, when he does err, through rashness and inexperience: he lives for a time as too many other men live – but being radically better than most men he does not like that degraded life, and is never happy in it. He is taught the severe lessons of Experience and has sense to learn wisdom from them – years improve him – the effervescence of youth foamed away, what is really good in him remains – his nature is like wine of a good vintage, time cannot sour – but only mellows him. Such at least was the character I meant to pourtray.

Heathcliff, again, of 'Wuthering Heights' is quite another creation. He exemplifies the effects which a life of continued injustice and hard usage may produce on a naturally perverse, vindictive and inexorable disposition. Carefully trained and kindly treated, the black gipsy-cub might possibly have been reared into a human being, but tyranny and ignorance made of him a mere demon. The worst of it is, some of his spirit seems breathed through the whole narrative in which he figures: it haunts every moor and glen, and beckons in every fir-tree of the 'Heights.'

In contrast to her letters with Smith Williams, in which she delighted to explore literary and intellectual ideas, Charlotte had to maintain the façade of her old life in her letters to friends. The exploits of Mrs Robinson and her daughters provided much bitter fodder for discussion with Ellen, but a letter from her former headmistress, Margaret Wooler, asking for information about the Clergy Daughters' School was more awkward to answer for the author who had so savagely portrayed the school in *Jane Eyre*.

★★*Charlotte to Ellen; Haworth, 18 August 1848*

The Robinsons go on as usual – they are not married yet – but expect to be married (or rather sacrificed) in the course of a few months: the unhappy Lady Scott is dead – after long suffering both mental and physical, I imagine, she expired two or three weeks ago. The Misses R– say that their mother does not care in the least what becomes of them; she is only anxious to get them husbands of any kind that they may be off her hands, and that she may be free to marry Sir E. Scott – whose infatuated slave, it would appear, she is. They assert that she does not appear to have the least affection for them now – formerly she professed a great deal, and was even servilely submissive to them – but now she treats them quite harshly – and they are often afraid to speak to her.

Charlotte to Margaret Wooler; Haworth, 28 August 1848

You said Mrs Carter had some thoughts of sending Ellen to school and wished to know whether the Clergy Daughters' School at Casterton was an eligible place.

My personal knowledge of that institution is very much out of date, being derived from the experience of twenty years ago; the establishment was at that time in its infancy, and a sad ricketty infancy it was. Typhus fever decimated the school periodically, and consumption and scrofula in every variety of form, [which] bad air and water, and bad and insufficient diet can generate, preyed on the ill-fated pupils. It would not <u>then</u> have been a fit place for any of Mrs Carter's children. But, I understand, it is very much altered for the better since those days. The school is removed from Cowan Bridge (a situation as unhealthy as it was picturesque, low, damp, beautiful with wood and water) to Casterton: the accommodations, the diet, the discipline, the system of tuition, all are, I believe, entirely altered and greatly improved. I was told that such pupils as behaved well and remained at the School till their educations were finished, were provided with situations as governesses, if they wished to adopt that vocation, and that much care was exercised in the selection; it was added they were also furnished with an excellent wardrobe on quitting Casterton.

Anne, Preface to the second edition of The Tenant of Wildfell Hall; *Haworth, 22 July 1848*

My object in writing the following pages, was not simply to amuse the Reader, neither was it to gratify my own taste, nor yet to ingratiate myself with the Press and the Public: I wished to tell the truth, for truth always conveys its own moral to those who are able to receive it ... As the story of 'Agnes Grey' was accused of extravagant over-colouring in those very parts that were carefully copied from the life, with a most scrupulous avoidance of all exaggeration, so, in the present work, I find myself censured for depicting con amore, with 'a morbid love of the coarse, if not of the brutal,' those scenes which, I will venture to say, have not been more painful for the most fastidious of my critics to read, than they were for me to describe. I may have gone too far, in which case I shall be careful not to trouble myself or my readers in the same way again; but when we have to do with vice and vicious characters, I maintain it is better to depict them as they really are than as they would wish to appear. To represent a bad thing in its least offensive light, is doubtless the most agreeable course for a writer of fiction to pursue; but is it the most honest, or the safest? Is it better to reveal the snares and pitfalls of life to the young and thoughtless traveller, or to cover them with branches and flowers? O Reader! if there were less of this delicate concealment of facts – this whispering 'Peace, peace,' when there is no peace, there would be less of sin and misery to the young of both sexes who are left to wring their bitter knowledge from experience ... if I have warned one rash youth from following in their steps, or prevented one thoughtless girl from falling into the very natural error of my heroine, the book has not been written in vain ... Such humble talents as God has given me I will endeavour to put to their greatest use; if I am able to amuse I will try to benefit too; and when I feel it my duty to speak an unpalatable truth, with the help of God, I *will* speak it, though it be to the prejudice of my name and to the detriment of my reader's immediate pleasure as well as my own . . . I am satisfied that if a book is a good one, it is so whatever the sex of the author may be. All novels are or should be written for both men and women to read, and I am at a loss to conceive how a man should permit himself to write anything that would be really disgraceful to a woman, or why a woman should be censured for writing anything that would be proper and becoming for a man.

Charlotte to William Smith Williams; Haworth, September 1848

Defects there are in both 'Jane Eyre' and 'Wildfell Hall' which it will be the authors' wisdom and duty to endeavour to avoid in future; other points there are to which they deem it incumbent on them firmly to adhere, whether such adherence bring popularity or unpopularity, praise or blame. The standard hero[e]s and heroines of novels, are personages in whom I could never, from childhood upwards, take an interest, believe to be natural, or wish to imitate: were I obliged to copy these characters, I would simply – not write at all. Were I obliged to copy any former novelist, even the greatest, even Scott, in anything, I would not write – Unless I have something of my own to say, and a way of my own to say it in, I have no business to publish; unless I can look beyond the greatest Masters, and study Nature herself, I have no right to paint; unless I can have the courage to use the language of Truth in preference to the jargon of Conventionality, I ought to be silent.

I am glad you have seen and approve of the preface to the 2nd editn of 'Wildfell Hall'; I, too, thought it sensible . . . I am glad the little vol- of the Bells' poems is likely to get into Mr Smith's hands. I should feel unmixed pleasure in the chance of its being brought under respectable auspices before the public, were Currer Bell's share in its contents absent – but of that portion I am by no means proud – much of it was written in early youth – I feel it now to be crude and rhapsodical. Ellis. Bell's is of a different stamp – of its sterling excellence I am deeply convinced, and have been from the moment the M.S. fell by chance into my hands. The pieces are short, but they are very genuine: they stirred my heart like the sound of a trumpet when I read them alone and in secret. The deep excitement I felt forced from me the confession of the discovery I had made – I was sternly rated at first for having taken an unwarrantable liberty – this I expected – for Ellis Bell is of no flexible or ordinary materials – but by dint of entreaty and reason – I at last wrung out a reluctant consent to have the 'rhymes' (as they were contemptuously termed) published – The author never alludes to them – or when she does – it is with scorn – but I know – no woman that ever lived – ever wrote such poetry before – Condensed energy, clearness, finish – strange, strong pathos are their characteristics – utterly different from the weak diffusiveness – the laboured yet most feeble wordiness which dilute the writings of even very popular poetesses. This is my deliberate and quite impartial opinion to which I should hold if all the critics in the periodical press held a different one – as I should to the supremacy of Thackeray in fiction –

Believe me
Yours sincerely
C Bell

Towards the end of September an event occurred which, in retrospect, seemed entirely predictable. At the time, however, it came as a cataclysmic shock, one for which none of the family was prepared. Branwell had been shattered in constitution for so long, and complained of illness for so much longer, that his sudden collapse in the street at first seemed nothing out of the ordinary. It was not until the doctor examined him that it was discovered that he was on the point of death from tuberculosis, a disease whose symptoms had been masked by those of dissipation. Only two days later, on Sunday, 24 September 1848, he died, at the age of only thirty-one. His distraught family could only console themselves with the knowledge that, at the end, he had shown some contrition for the folly of his final years.

Francis Leyland, brother of Branwell's friend J. B. Leyland, from his
The Brontë Family *(London, Hurst & Blackett, 1886)*

Some time before the end, John Brown entered Branwell's room, and they were alone. The young man, though faint and dying, spoke of the life they had led together. He took a short retrospect of his past excesses, in which the grave-digger had often partaken; but in it he made no mention of the lady whose image had distracted his brain. He appeared, in the calmness of approaching death, and the self-possession that preceded it, to be unconscious that he had ever loved any but the members of his family, for the depth and tenderness of which affection he could find no language to express. But, presently, seizing Brown's hand, he uttered the words: 'Oh, John, I am dying!' then, turning, as if within himself, he murmured: 'In all my past life I have done nothing either great or good.'

Anne to William Smith Williams; Haworth, 29 September 1848

My sister wishes me to thank you for your two letters, the receipt of which gave her much pleasure, though coming in a season of severe domestic affliction, which has so wrought upon her too delicate constitution as to induce a rather serious indisposition that renders her unfit for the slightest exertion. Even the light task of writing to a friend is at present too much for her, though, I am happy to inform you, she is now recovering; and I trust, ere long, she will be able to assure you herself of her complete restoration, and to give you her own sentiments upon the contents of your letters.

Charlotte to William Smith Williams; Haworth, 2 October 1848

My dear Sir

'We have buried our dead out of our sight.' A lull begins to succeed the gloomy tumult of last week. It is not permitted us to grieve for him who is gone as others grieve for those they lose; the removal of our only brother must necessarily be regarded by us rather in the light of a mercy than a chastisement: Branwell was his

Father's and his Sisters' pride and hope in boyhood, but since Manhood, the case has been otherwise. It has been our lot to see him take a wrong bent; to hope, expect, wait his return to the right path; to know the sickness of hope deferred, the dismay of prayer baffled, to experience despair at last; and now to behold the sudden early obscure close of what might have been a noble career.

I do not weep from a sense of bereavement — there is no prop withdrawn, no consolation torn away, no dear companion lost — but for the wreck of talent, the ruin of promise, the untimely dreary extinction of what might have been a burning and a shining light. My brother was a year my junior. I had aspirations and ambitions for him once — long ago — they have perished mournfully — nothing remains of him but a memory of errors and sufferings — There is such a bitterness of pity for his life and death — such a yearning for the emptiness of his whole existence as I cannot describe — I trust time will allay these feelings.

My poor Father naturally thought more of his <u>only</u> Son than of his daughters, and much and long as he had suffered on his account — he cried out for his loss like David for that of Absalom — my Son! my Son! And refused at first to be comforted — and then when I ought to have been able to collect my strength, and be at hand to support him — I fell ill with an illness whose approaches I had felt for some time previously — and of which the crisis was hastened by the awe and trouble of the death-scene — the first I had ever witnessed. The past has seemed to me a strange week — Thank God — for my Father's sake — I am better now — though still feeble — I wish indeed I had more general physical strength — the want of it is sadly in my way. I cannot do what I would do, for want of sustained animal spirits and efficient bodily vigour.

Charlotte to William Smith Williams; Haworth, 6 October 1848

When I looked on the noble face and forehead of my dead brother (Nature had favoured him with a fairer outside, as well as a finer constitution than his Sisters) and asked myself what had made him go ever wrong, tend ever downwards, when he had so many gifts to induce to, and aid in an upward course – I seemed to receive an oppressive revelation of the feebleness of humanity; of the inadequacy of even genius to lead to true greatness if unaided by religion and principle. In the value, or even the reality of these two things he would never believe till within a few days of his end, and then all at once he seemed to open his heart to a conviction of their existence and worth. The remembrance of this strange change now comforts my poor Father greatly. I myself, with painful, mournful joy, heard him praying softly in his dying moments, and to the last prayer which my father offered up at his bedside, he added 'amen.' How unusual that word appeared from his lips – of course you who did not know him, cannot conceive. Akin to this alteration was that in his feelings towards his relatives – all bitterness seemed gone.

When the struggle was over – and a marble calm began to succeed the last dread agony – I felt as I had never felt before that there was peace and forgiveness for him in Heaven. All his errors – to speak plainly – all his vices seemed nothing to me in that moment; every wrong he had done, every pain he had caused, vanished; his sufferings only were remembered; the wrench to the natural affections only was felt. If Man can thus experience total oblivion of his fellow's imperfections – how much more can the Eternal Being who made man, forgive his creature!

Had his sins been scarlet in their dye – I believe now they are white as wool – He is at rest – and that comforts us all   long before he quitted this world – Life had no happiness for him.

Charlotte to Ellen; Haworth, 9 October 1848

The past three weeks have been a dark interval in our humble home. Branwell's constitution had been failing fast all the summer – but still neither the Doctors nor himself thought him so near his end as he was – he was entirely confined to his bed but for one single day – and was in the village two days before his death.

He died after 20 minutes struggle on Sunday Morning 24th Septbr. He was perfectly conscious till the last agony came on – His mind had undergone the peculiar change which frequently precedes death, two days previously – the calm of better feelings filled it – a return of natural affection marked his last moments – he is in God's hands now – and the all-powerful – is likewise the all-merciful – a deep conviction that he rests at last – rests well after his brief, erring, suffering, feverish life fills and quiets my mind now.

The final separation – the spectacle of his pale corpse gave more acute, bitter pain than I could have imagined – Till the last hour comes we never know how much we can forgive, pity, regret a near relation – All his vices were and are nothing now – we remember only his woes.

Papa was acutely distressed at first but on the whole has borne the event well – Emily and Anne are pretty well – though Anne is always delicate, and Emily has a cold & cough at present –

All too soon it became apparent that Emily's symptoms masked the onset of the tuberculosis which had killed her brother. Her sisters and father could only watch helplessly as, refusing any medication or assistance, she grew daily weaker.

Charlotte to William Smith Williams; Haworth, 18 October 1848

I am afraid I shall not write a cheerful letter to you. A letter, however, of some kind I am determined to write, for I should be sorry to appear a neglectful correspondent to one from whose communications I have derived, and still derive, so much pleasure. Do not talk about not being on a level with Currer Bell, or regard him as 'an awful person'; if you saw him now, sitting muffled at the fireside, shrinking before the east wind (which for some days has been blowing wild and keen over our cold hills), and incapable of lifting a pen for any more formidable task than that of writing a few lines to an indulgent friend, you would be sorry not to deem yourself greatly his superior, for you would feel him to be a poor creature.

Charlotte to Ellen; Haworth, 29 October 1848

I feel much more uneasy about my sisters than myself just now. Emily's cold and cough are very obstinate; I fear she has pain in the chest – and I sometimes catch a shortness in her breathing when she has moved at all quickly – She looks very, very thin and pale. Her reserved nature occasions one great uneasiness of mind – it is useless to question her – you get no answers – it is still more useless to recommend remedies – they are never adopted.

Nor can I shut my eyes to the fact of Anne's great delicacy of constitution. The late sad event has I feel made me more apprehensive than common – I cannot help feeling much depressed sometimes – I try to leave all in God's hands, and to trust in his goodness – but faith and resignation are difficult to practise under some circumstances.

Charlotte to William Smith Williams; Haworth, 2 November 1848

I am better – but others are ill now: Papa is not well; my sister Emily has something like a slow inflammation of the lungs, and even our old servant, who has lived with us nearly a quarter of a century is suffering under serious indisposition.

I would fain hope that Emily is a little better this evening, but it is difficult to ascertain this: she is a real stoic in illness, she neither seeks nor will accept sympathy; to put any question, to offer any aid is to annoy; she will not yield a step before pain or sickness till forced; not one of her ordinary avocations will she voluntarily renounce: You must look on, and see her do what she is unfit to do, and not dare to say a word; a painful necessity for those to whom her health and existence are as precious as the life in their veins. When she is ill there seems to be no sunshine in the world for me; the tie of sister is near and dear indeed, and I think a certain harshness in her powerful, and peculiar character only makes me cling to her more. But this is all family egotism (so to speak) excuse it – and above all, never allude to it, or to the name, Emily, when you write to me; I do not always shew your letters, but I never withhold them when they are inquired after.

Charlotte to William Smith Williams; Haworth, 22 November 1848

I put your most friendly letter into Emily's hands as soon as I had myself perused it, taking care however not to say a word in favour of homoeopathy, that would not have answered; it is best usually to

leave her to form her own judgement and <u>especially</u> not to advocate the side you wish her to favour; if you do she is sure to lean in
the opposite direction, and ten to one will argue herself into
non-compliance. Hitherto she has refused medicine, rejected medical
advice. no reasoning, no entreaty has availed to induce her to see a
physician; after reading your letter she said 'Mr Williams' intention
was kind and good, but he was under a delusion – Homoeopathy
was only another form of Quackery.' Yet she may reconsider this
opinion and come to a different conclusion; her second thoughts
are often the best.

The North American Review is worth reading – there is no
mincing the matter there – what a bad set the Bells must be! What
appalling books they write! To-day as Emily appeared a little easier,
I thought the Review would amuse her so I read it aloud to her and
Anne. As I sat between them at our quiet but now somewhat
melancholy fireside, I studied the two ferocious authors. Ellis the
'man of uncommon talents but dogged, brutal and morose,' sat
leaning back in his easy chair drawing his impeded breath as he best
could, and looking, alas! piteously pale and wasted – it is not his
wont to laugh – but he smiled half-amused and half in scorn as he
listened – Acton was sewing, no emotion ever stirs him to loquacity,
so he only smiled too, dropping at the same time a single word of
calm amazement to hear his character so darkly portrayed. I wonder
what the Reviewer would have thought of his own sagacity, could
he have beheld the pair, as I did. Vainly too might he have looked
round for the masculine partner in the firm of 'Bell & Co.' How I
laugh in my sleeve when I read the solemn assertions that 'Jane Eyre'
was written in partnership, and that it 'bears the marks of more than
one mind, and one sex.'

★*Charlotte to Ellen; Haworth, 23 November 1848*

I told you Emily was ill in my last letter – she has not rallied yet –
She is <u>very</u> ill: I believe if you were to see her your impression would
be that there is no hope: a more hollow, wasted pallid aspect I have
not beheld. The deep tight cough continues; the breathing after the
least exertion is a rapid pant – and these symptoms are accompanied

by pain in the chest and side. Her pulse, the only time she allowed it to be felt, was found to be at 115 per minute. In this state she resolutely refuses to see a doctor; she will give no explanation of her feelings, she will scarcely allow her illness to be alluded to. Our position is, and has been for some weeks, exquisitely painful. God only knows how all this is to terminate. More than once I have been forced boldly to regard the terrible event of her loss as possible and even probable. But Nature shrinks from such thoughts. I think Emily seems the nearest thing to my heart in this world.

Miss Mary Robinson is just married to Mr Henry Clapham, a relation of the Sugdens – a low match for her – she feels it so – she does not, in writing to Anne, even profess to be happy.

Mrs Robinson is married too – She is now Lady Scott – her daughters say she is in the highest spirits –

Charlotte to William Smith Williams; Haworth, 7 December 1848

I can give no favourable report of Emily's state. My Father is very despondent about her. Anne and I cherish hope as well as we can – but her appearance and her symptoms tend to crush that feeling. Yet I argue that the present emaciation, cough, weakness, shortness of breath are the results of inflammation now, I trust, subsided, and that with time, these ailments will gradually leave her, but my father shakes his head and speaks of others of our family once similarly afflicted, for whom he likewise persisted in hoping against hope, and who are now removed where hope and fear fluctuate no more. There were, however, differences between their case and hers – important differences I think – I must cling to the expectation of her recovery; I cannot renounce it . . . I am indeed surprised that Mr Newby should say that he is to publish another work by Ellis and Acton Bell. Acton has had quite enough of him. I think I have before intimated that that author never more intends to have Mr Newby for a publisher . . . Ellis Bell is at present in no condition to trouble himself with thoughts either of writing or publishing; should it please Heaven to restore his health and strength he reserves to himself the right of deciding whether or not Mr Newby has forfeited every claim to his second work

Charlotte to Ellen; Haworth, 10 December 1848

I hardly know what to say to you about the subject which now interests me the most nearly of anything in this world – for in truth I hardly know what to think myself – Hope and fear fluctuate daily. The pain in her side and chest is better – the cough – the shortness of breath, the extreme emaciation continue. Diarrhoea commenced nearly a fortnight ago and continues still – of course it greatly weakens her, but she thinks herself it will tend to good, and I hope so. I have endured however such tortures of uncertainty on this subject that at length I could endure it no longer – and as her repugnance to seeing a medical man continues immutably as she declares 'no poisoning doctor' shall come near her – I have written, unknown to her, to an eminent physician in London, giving as minute a statement of her case and symptoms as I could draw up and requesting an opinion – I expect an answer in a day or two.

I am thankful to say that my own health is at present very tolerable – it is well such is the case – for Anne, with the best will in the world to be useful, is really too delicate to do or bear much: She too has at present frequent pains in the side. Papa is also pretty well – though Emily's state renders him very anxious.

The Robinsons were here about a week ago – they are attractive and stylish looking girls – they seemed overjoyed to see Anne; when I went into the room they were clinging round her like two children – she, meantime, looking perfectly quiet and passive. Their manner evinced more levity and giddiness than pretension or pomposity. They say Mr Clapham deceived them with his account of his fortune, establishment, connexions &c. I do not expect the pair will ever be particularly happy – and I fear neither of the young ladies has the power to make herself much respected wherever she goes.

Charlotte to Ellen; Haworth, 19 December 1848

Dear Ellen

I should have written to you before if I had had one word of hope to say – but I have not – She grows daily weaker. The physician's opinion was expressed too obscurely to be of use – he sent some medicine which she would not take. Moments so dark as these I have never known – I pray for God's support to us all. Hitherto he has granted it

Yours faithfully
C Brontë

Tuesday

Charlotte to William Smith Williams; Haworth, 20 December 1848

My dear Sir

When I wrote in such haste to Dr Epps, disease was making rapid strides, nor has it lingered since, the gallopping consumption has merited its name – neither physician nor medicine are needed now. Tuesday night and morning saw the last hours, the last agonies, proudly endured till the end. Yesterday Emily Jane Brontë died in the arms of those who loved her.

Thus the strange dispensation is completed – it is incomprehensible as yet to mortal intelligence. The last three months – ever since my brother's Death seem to us like a long, terrible dream. We look for support to God – and thus far he mercifully enables us to maintain our self-control in the midst of affliction whose bitterness none could have calculated on

Believe me   yours sincerely
C Brontë

Wednesday

William Smith Williams to Charlotte; London, 21 December 1848

How to address you, my Dear Madam, on this distressing occasion I know not. To describe the astonishment & pain that the mournful intelligence has caused me, & the deep concern at the loss to her family & to the world of your gifted sister Emily, which Mr Smith shares with me, is beyond my power. We feel for you & for your surviving – oh! what a world of sadness there is in that word! – your only sister, & for your bereaved father, & would fain shew our

216

sympathy in other ways than words, if we knew how . . . To mitigate your grief for such a loss, the only way is to think of the gain to her who has been taken from you, & of the duties that now devolve upon you to support your bereaved father & comfort your sister & be comforted by her. But how superfluous it is of me to remind you of the duties that your strong sense of rectitude & energy of will prompt you to perform, and which only bodily weakness – and may God give you strength to bear this heavy affliction! – can prevent you from fulfilling. And when after the first dread shock of losing one who was your other self has passed off, & left your mind calm enough to reflect with serene sorrowful contemplation on the great and good qualities of her who is now a memory of the past and a hope for the future, you cannot but find sweet consolation in re-calling those noble traits of character & high intelligence for which she was distinguished: for she being dead yet liveth & speaketh . . . Great griefs are life-lasting 'tis true; but their influences are as refreshing and beneficial to the soul as the night to the earth, & sleep to the body. May your night of sorrow be brief & relieved by the blessed rays of consolation that no grief is devoid of, and may the morning of peace & resignation dawn upon you both with the refreshing serenity of hopeful and affectionate feelings. You and your sister must be more & more endeared to each other now that you are left alone on earth, and having the same hopes, & sorrows, & pursuits, your sympathies will be more & more closely entwined.

God Bless and comfort you both, my dear friends, is the devout prayer of

Your sincere and attached
Wm Smith Williams.

Miss Brontë

It was a measure of how close a confidant William Smith Williams had become that Charlotte informed him of Emily's death several days before she wrote to tell Ellen. Emily was buried in the family vault under Haworth Church, alongside her mother, aunt, two sisters and brother, on 22 December 1848. The next day Charlotte wrote to Ellen, not just to give her the terrible news, but also to ask her old friend to stay with them; the comfort of her presence was to be needed more than either of them guessed, for yet another crushing blow was about to be dealt the grieving Brontës.

Charlotte to Ellen; Haworth, 23 December 1848

Dear Ellen

Emily suffers no more either from pain or weakness now. She never will suffer more in this world – She is gone after a hard, short conflict. She died on Tuesday, the very day I wrote to you. I thought it very possible then she might be with us still for weeks and a few hours afterwards she was in Eternity – Yes – there is no Emily in Time or on Earth now – yesterday – we put her poor, wasted mortal frame quietly under the Church pavement. We are very calm at present. why should we be otherwise? – the anguish of seeing her suffer is over – the spectacle of the pains of Death is gone by – the funeral day is past – we feel she is at peace – no need now to tremble for the hard frost and keen wind – Emily does not feel them. She has died in a time of promise – we saw her taken from life in its prime – but it is God's will and the place where she is gone is better than that she has left.

God has sustained me in a way that I marvel at through such agony as I had not conceived. I now look at Anne and wish she were well and strong – but she is neither, nor is papa – Could you now come to us for a few days? I would not ask you to stay long. Write and tell me if you could come next week and what day – and by what train I would try to send a gig for you to Keighley – You will I trust find us tranquil.

C Brontë

Try to come – I never so much needed the consolation of a friend's presence Pleasure, of course, there would be none for you in the visit, except what your kind heart would teach you to find in doing good to others.

Chapter Ten

1848–9

My dear Sir

I will write to you more at length when my heart can find a little rest – now I can only thank you very briefly for your letter which seemed to me eloquent in its sincerity.

Emily is nowhere here now – her wasted mortal remains are taken out of the house; we have laid her cherished head under the church-aisle beside my mother's, my two sisters', dead long ago, and my poor, hapless brother's. But a small remnant of the race is left – so my poor father thinks.

Well – the loss is ours – not hers, and some sad comfort I take, as I hear the wind blow and feel the cutting keenness of the frost, in knowing that the elements bring her no more suffering – their severity cannot reach her grave – her fever is quieted, her rest-lessness soothed, her deep, hollow cough is hushed for ever; we do not hear it in the night or listen for it in the morning; we have not the conflict of the strangely strong spirit and the fragile frame before us – relentless conflict – once seen, never to be forgotten. A dreary calm reigns round us, in the midst of which we seek resignation.

My father and my sister Anne are far from well – as to me, God has hitherto most graciously sustained me – so far I have felt adequate to bear my own burden and even to offer a little help to others – I am not ill – I can get through daily duties – and do something towards keeping hope and energy alive in our mourning household. My father says to me almost hourly, 'Charlotte, you must bear up – I shall sink if you fail me.' These words – you can conceive are a stimulus to nature. The sight too of my sister Anne's very still but deep sorrow wakens in me such fear for her that I dare not falter. Somebody <u>must</u> cheer the rest.

So I will not now ask why Emily was torn from us in the fulness of our attachment, rooted up in the prime of her own days, in the promise of her powers – why her existence now lies like a field of green corn trodden down – like a tree in full bearing – struck at the root; I will only say, sweet is rest after labour and calm after tempest, and repeat again and again that Emily knows that now.

Yours sincerely,
C Brontë

Even as she mourned one sister, Charlotte's worst fears for the youngest were about to be realized. Patrick had insisted that a specialist from Leeds should be sent for. He came on 5 January 1849, examined Anne and pronounced her doom; she had advanced tuberculosis and but a short time to live. Patient and long-suffering by nature, Anne drew strength and courage from her faith. A letter from a Liverpool clergyman, praising her for her quiet preaching of the doctrine of universal salvation – the idea that all men, no matter how sinful, would eventually find salvation in Heaven – had prompted the longest of all her few surviving letters.

**★★*Anne to the Reverend David Thom of Edge Hill, Liverpool; Haworth, 30 December 1848*

December 30th 1848

Sir,

Ill health must plead my excuse for this long delay in acknowledging your flattering communication; but, believe me, I am not the less gratified at the pleasure you have derived from my own and my relatives' works, especially from the opinions they express. I have seen so little of controversial Theology that I was not aware the doctrine of Universal Salvation had so able and ardent an advocate as yourself; but I have cherished it from my very childhood – with a trembling hope at first, and afterwards with a firm and glad conviction of its truth. I drew it secretly from my own heart not from the word of God before I knew that any other held it. And since then it has ever been a source of true delight to me to find the same views either timidly suggested or boldly advocated by benevolent and thoughtful minds; and I now believe there are many more believers than professors in that consoling creed. Why good men should be so averse to admit it, I know not; – into their own hearts at least, however they might object to its promulgation among the bulk of mankind. But perhaps the world is not ripe for it yet. I have frequently thought that since it has pleased God to leave it in darkness so long respecting this particular truth, and often to use such doubtful language as to admit of such a general misconception thereupon, he must have some good reason for it. We see how liable men are to yield to the temptations of the passing hour; how little the dread of future punishment – how still less the promise of future reward can avail to make them forbear and wait; and if so many thousands rush into destruction with (as they suppose) the prospect of Eternal Death before their eyes, – what might not the consequence be, if that prospect were changed for one of a limited season of punishment, far distant and unseen, – however protracted and terrible it might be?

I thankfully cherish this belief; I honour those who hold it; and I would that all men had the same view of man's hopes and God's unbounded goodness as he has given to us, if it might be had with safety. But does not that if require some consideration? should we not remember the weak brother and the infatuated slave of satan, and beware of revealing these truths too hastily to those as yet unable to receive them? But in these suggestions I am perhaps condemning myself, for in my late novel, 'The Tenant of Wildfell Hall', I have given as many hints in support of the doctrine as I could venture to introduce into a work of that description. They are however mere suggestions, and as such I trust you will receive them, believing that I am well aware how much may be said in favour of boldly disseminating God's truth and leaving that to work its way. Only let our zeal be tempered with discretion, and while we labour, let us humbly look to God who is able and certain to bring his great work to perfection in his own good time and manner.

Accept my best wishes in behalf of yourself and your important undertakings, and believe me to remain with sincere esteem

Yours truly
Acton Bell

Ellen, Reminiscences; c. 1871

I made my visit to Haworth and found the family wonderfully calm and sustained, but anxious respecting Anne. Mr Brontë enquired for the best doctor in Leeds. Mr Teale was recommended; and came to Haworth. Anne was looking sweetly pretty and flushed, and in capital spirits for an invalid. While consultations were going on in Mr Brontë's study, Anne was very lively in conversation, walking round the room supported by me. Mr Brontë joined us after Mr Teale's departure, and seating himself on the couch, he drew Anne towards him and said, 'My <u>dear</u> little Anne.' That was all – but it was understood.

Charlotte afterwards told me that Mr Teale said – The disease of consumption had progressed too far for cure; and he thought so seriously of the case, he took the trouble to acquaint my friends and urge them to call me home from my visit.

Charlotte to William Smith Williams; Haworth, 2 January 1849

My letters had better be brief at present – they cannot be cheerful. I am however still sustained, and still, while looking with dismay on the desolation sickness and death have wrought in our home I can combine with awe of God's judgements a sense of gratitude for his mercies. Yet life has become very void, and hope has proved a strange traitor: when I shall again be able to put confidence in her suggestions, I know not; she kept whispering that Emily would not – <u>could</u> not die – and where is she now? Out of my reach, – out of my world, torn from me.

Charlotte to Ellen; Haworth, 15 January 1849

I can scarcely say that Anne is worse, nor can I say she is better. She varies often in the course of a day yet each day is passed pretty much the same – the morning is usually the best time – the afternoon and evening the most feverish – Her cough is the most troublesome at night but it is rarely violent – the pain in her arm still disturbs her. She takes the cod-liver oil and the carbonate of iron regularly – she finds them both nauseous but especially the oil – her appetite is small indeed. Do not fear that I shall relax in my care of her – she is too precious to me not to be cherished with all the fostering strength I have. Papa – I am thankful to say – has been a good deal better this last day or two.

Charlotte to William Smith Williams; Haworth, 18 January 1849

In sitting down to write to you I feel as if I were doing a wrong and a selfish thing; I believe I ought to discontinue my correspondence with you till times change and the tide of calamity which of late days has set so strongly in against us, takes a turn. But the fact is, sometimes I feel it absolutely necessary to unburden my mind. To papa I must only speak cheeringly, to Anne only encouragingly, to you I may give some hint of the dreary truth.

Anne and I sit alone and in seclusion as you fancy us, but we do not study; Anne cannot study now, she can scarcely read; she occupies Emily's chair – she does not get well. A week ago we sent for a Medical Man of skill and experience from Leeds to see her; he examined her with the stethoscope; his report I forbear to dwell on for the present; even skilful physicians have often been mistaken in their conjectures.

My first impulse was to hasten her away to a warmer climate, but this was forbidden – she must not travel – she is not to stir from the house this winter – the temperature of her room is to be kept constantly equal.

Had leave been given to try change of air and scene, I should hardly have known how to act – I could not possibly leave papa – and when I mentioned his accompanying us the bare thought distressed him too much to be dwelt upon. Papa is now upwards of seventy years of age, his habits for nearly thirty years have been those of absolute retirement – any change in them is most repugnant to him and probably could not at this time especially – when the hand of God is so heavy upon his old age, be ventured upon without danger.

When we lost Emily I thought we had drained the very dregs of our cup of trial but now when I hear Anne cough as Emily coughed, I tremble lest there should be exquisite bitterness yet to taste. However I must not look forwards, nor must I look backwards. Too often I feel like one crossing an abyss on a narrow plank – a glance round might quite unnerve.

So circumstanced, my dear Sir, what claim have I on your friendship – what right to the comfort of your letters? My literary character is effaced for the time – and it is by that alone you know me – care of Papa and Anne is necessarily my chief present object in life to the exclusion of all that could give me interest with my Publishers or their connexions – Should Anne get better, I think I could rally and become Currer Bell once more – but if otherwise – I look no farther – sufficient for the day is the evil thereof.

Anne is very patient in her illness – as patient as Emily was unflinching. I recall one sister and look at the other with a sort of reverence as well as affection – under the test of suffering neither have faltered.

All the days of this winter have gone by darkly and heavily like a funeral train; since September sickness has not quitted the house – it is strange – it did not use to be so – but I suspect now all this has been coming on for years: unused any of us to the possession of robust health, we have not noticed the gradual approaches of decay; we did not know its symptoms; the little cough, the small appetite, the tendency to take cold at every variation of atmosphere have been regarded as things of course – I see them in another light now.

Charlotte to Ellen; Haworth, 30 January 1849

During the mild weather Anne really seemed something better; I began to flatter myself she was gathering strength. But the change to frost has told upon her – she suffers more of late – Still, her illness shews none of the fearful, rapid symptoms which appalled in Emily's case. Could she only get over the Spring I hope Summer may do much for her, and then early removal to a warmer locality for the winter might at least prolong her life. Could we only reckon upon another year I should be thankful – but can we do this even for the healthy?

Patrick to Mr Rand, former headmaster of the National School at Haworth; Haworth, 26 February 1849

I have indeed had my ample share of trouble – But it has been the Lord's will – and it is my duty, to resign – My only son has died, and soon after him, a beloved daughter, died also – For these things we may weep, since Christ himself wept over his dead freind – and also over the living inhabitants of Jerusalem – Yet, whilst we grieve, it should not be without hope . . . All my Family that remain, join me, in kind regards to you all.

I remain, Dear Sir,
Yours, truly,
P.Brontē

Letters and books from Smith, Elder & Co. now provided Charlotte with almost the only relief she could obtain from the relentless train of domestic tragedy. This had prevented her from continuing with her new novel, *Shirley*, but in February she sent her publishers a fair copy of the first volume, seeking their opinion of it. Their approval, qualified as it was, gave her the incentive she needed to start work again in the hours she could spare from nursing Anne.

Charlotte to James Taylor, of Smith, Elder & Co.; Haworth, 1 March 1849

The parcel arrived on Saturday evening. Permit me to express my sense of the judgement and kindness which have dictated the selection of its contents. They appear to be all good books, and good books are, we know, the best substitute for good society;   if circumstances debar me from the latter privilege, the kind attentions of my friends supply me with ample measure of the former.

Thank you for your remarks on 'Shirley.' Some of your strictures tally with some by Mr Williams. You both complain of the want of distinctness and impressiveness in my heroes. Probably you are right. In delineating male character I labour under disadvantages: intuition and theory will not always adequately supply the place of observation and experience. When I write about women I am sure of my ground – in the other case, I am not so sure.

Charlotte to William Smith Williams; Haworth, 2 March 1849

I am glad that you and Mr Smith like the commencement of my present work – I wish it were more than a commencement, for how it will be reunited after the long break, or how it can gather force of flow when the current has been checked – or rather drawn off so long – I know not.

I sincerely thank you both for the candid expression of your objections – what you say with reference to the first chapter shall be duly weighed – At present I feel reluctant to withdraw it – because as I formerly said of the Lowood-part of 'Jane Eyre,' – it is true – the curates and their ongoings are merely photographed from the life – I should like you to explain to me more fully the ground of your objections – is it because you think this chapter will render the work liable to severe handling by the press? Is it because knowing as you now do the identity of 'Currer Bell' – this scene strikes you as unfeminine? Is it because it is intrinsically defective and inferior –? I am afraid the first two reasons would not weigh with me – the last would.

Any thoughts Charlotte may have entertained about resuming her writing were swiftly quashed. Anne's health was deteriorating slowly but inexorably and Charlotte could think of nothing else. Anne herself was increasingly anxious to go to the Yorkshire coast, where she hoped that fresh air and sea-bathing might grant her a respite from her disease, if not a cure, but Charlotte, afraid of the consequences of a long journey, was reluctant to allow the invalid to go from home. An opportune legacy from

Anne's godmother, Fanny Outhwaite, finally allowed the scheme to go ahead.

Charlotte to Margaret Wooler; Haworth, 24 March 1849

I have delayed answering your letter in the faint hope that I might be able to reply favourably to your enquiries after my Sister's health. This, however, it is not permitted me to do. Her decline is gradual and fluctuating, but its nature is not doubtful. The symptoms of cough, pain in the side and chest, wasting of flesh, strength, and appetite – after the sad experience we have had – cannot be regarded by us as equivocal. In spirit she is resigned: at heart she is – I believe – a true Christian: She looks beyond this life – and regards her Home and Rest as elsewhere than on Earth. May God support her and all of us through the trial of lingering sickness – and aid her in the last hour when the struggle which separates soul from body must be gone through!

Charlotte to Ellen; Haworth, 29 March 1849

I read your kind note to Anne and she wishes me to thank you sincerely for your friendly proposal. She feels, of course, that it would not do to take advantage of it by quartering an invalid upon the inmates of Brookroyd – but she intimates that there is another way in which you might serve her perhaps with some benefit to yourself as well as her. Should it, a month or two hence, be deemed advisable that she should go either to the sea-side or to some inland watering-place – and should papa still be disinclined to move and I – consequently – be obliged to remain at home – she asks could you be her companion? Of course I need not add that in case of such an arrangement being made you would be put to no expense.

This, dear Ellen, is Anne's proposal – I make it to comply with her wish – but for my own part – I must add that I see serious objections to your accepting it – objections I cannot name to her. She continues to vary – is sometimes worse and sometimes better, as the weather changes – but on the whole I fear she loses strength.

Papa says her state is most precarious – she may be spared for some time – or a sudden alteration might remove her ere we were aware – were such an alteration to take place while she was far from home and alone with you – it would be too terrible – the idea of it distresses me inexpressibly, and I tremble whenever she alludes to the project of a journey . . . Write such an answer to this note as I can shew Anne – you can write any additional remarks to me on a separate piece of paper –

Anne to Ellen; 5 April 1849

My dear Miss Nussey,

I thank you greatly for your kind letter, and your ready compliance with my proposal as far as the <u>will</u> can go at least. I see however that your friends are unwilling that you should undertake the responsibility of accompanying me: under present circumstances. But I do not think there would be any great responsibility in the matter. I know, and everybody knows that you would be as kind and helpful as any one could possibly be; and I hope I should not be very troublesome. It would be as a companion not as a nurse that I should wish for your company; otherwise, I should not venture to ask it. As for your kind and often repeated invitation to Brookroyd, pray give my sincere thanks to your mother and sisters, but tell them I could not think of inflicting my presence upon them as I now am. It is very kind of them to make so light of the trouble but trouble, there must be, more or less, – and certainly no pleasure from the society of a silent invalid stranger. – I hope however that Charlotte will by some means make it possible to accompany me after all, for she is certainly very delicate and greatly needs a change of air and scene to renovate her constitution. And then your going with me before the end of May is apparently out of the question, unless you are disappointed in your visitors, but I should be reluctant to wait till then if the weather would at all permit an earlier departure. You say May is a trying month, and so say others. The earlier part is often cold enough I acknowledge, but, according to my experience, we are almost certain of some fine warm days in the latter half when the laburnums and lilacs are in bloom; whereas June is often cold and July gener[a]lly wet. But I have a more serious reason than this for my impatience of delay: the doctors say that change of air or removal to a better climate would hardly ever fail of success in consumptive cases if the remedy were taken in <u>time</u>, but the reason why there are so many disappointments is, that it is generally deferred till it is too late. Now I would not commit this error; and to say the truth, thouhg I suffer much less from pain and fever than I did when you were with us, I am decidedly weaker and very much thinner   my cough still troubles me a good deal, especially in the night, and, what seems worse than all, I am subject to great shortness of breath on going up stairs or any slight exertion. Under these circumstances I think there is no time to be lost. I have no horror of death: if I thought it inevitable I think I could quietly resign myself to the prospect, in the hope that you, dear Miss Nussey, would give as much of your company as you possibly could to Charlotte and be a sister to her in my stead. But I wish it would please God to spare me not only for Papa's and Charlotte's sakes, but because I long to do some good in the world before I leave it. I have many schemes in my head for future practise – humble and limited indeed – but still I should not like them all to come to nothing, and myself to have lived to so little purpose. But God's will be done. Remember me respectfully to your mother and sisters, and believe, me dear Miss N.

Yours most affectionately
Anne Brontë

Charlotte to Ellen; Haworth, 12 April 1849

I read Anne's letter to you; it was touching enough – as you say. If there were no hope beyond this world – no eternity – no life to come – Emily's fate and that which threatens Anne would be heart-breaking. I cannot forget Emily's death-day; it becomes a more fixed – a darker, a more frequently recurring idea in my mind than ever: it was very terrible, she was torn conscious, panting, reluctant though resolute out of a happy life. But it <u>will not do</u> to dwell on these things – I am glad your friends object to your going with Anne – it would never do: to speak truth – even if your Mother and Sisters had consented I never could – it is not that there is any laborious attention to pay her – she requires and will accept but little nursing – but there would be hazard and anxiety of mind beyond what you ought to be subjected to.

If, a month or six weeks hence, she continues to wish for a change as much as she does now – I shall – D.V. – go with her myself.– It will certainly be my paramount duty – other care must be made subservient to that – I have consulted Mr Teale – he does not object and recommends Scarbro' which was Anne's own choice. I trust affairs may be so ordered that you may be able to be with us at least part of the time.

Charlotte to Ellen; Haworth, 1 May 1849

I am glad to hear that when we go to Scarbro' you will be at liberty to go with us; but the journey and its consequences still continue a source of great anxiety to me: I must try to put it off two or three weeks longer if I can; perhaps by that time the milder season may have given Anne more strength, perhaps it will be otherwise – I cannot tell. The change to finer weather has not proved beneficial so far; she has sometimes been so weak and suffered so much from pain in her side during the last few days – that I have not known what to think. It may however be only a temporary aggravation of symptoms; she may rally again and be much better – but there must be some improvement before I can feel justified in taking her away from home. Yet to delay is painful – for as is always the case I believe under her circumstances – she seems herself but half conscious of the necessity for such delay: she wonders I believe why I do not talk more about the journey: it grieves me to think she may even be hurt by my seeming tardiness. She is very much emaciated – far more so than when you were here – her arms are no thicker than a little child's. The least exertion brings a shortness of breath – She goes out a little every day – but we creep rather than walk.

Charlotte to Ellen; Haworth, 12 May 1849

We have engaged lodgings at Scarbro – We stipulated for a good sized sitting-room and an airy double-bedded lodging room – with a sea view – and – if not deceived – have obtained these desiderata at No 2 Cliff – Anne says it is one of the best situations in the place – It would not have done to have taken lodgings either in the town or on the bleak, steep coast where Miss Wooler's house is situated – If Anne is to get any good she must have every advantage. Miss Outhwaite left her in her will a small legacy of 200£ and she cannot employ her money better than in obtaining what may prolong existence if it does not restore health –

Charlotte to Margaret Wooler; Haworth, 16 May 1849

Next Wednesday is the day fixed for our departure; Ellen Nussey accompanies us at her own kind and friendly wish: I would not refuse her society – but I dared not urge her to go, for I have little hope that the excursion will be one of pleasure or benefit to those engaged in it. Anne is extremely weak. She, herself, has a fixed impression that the sea-air will give her a chance of regaining strength – that chance therefore she must have.

Having resolved to try the experiment – misgivings are useless – and yet – when I look at her – misgivings will rise. She is more emaciated than Emily was at the very last – her breath scarcely serves her to mount the stairs however slowly – She sleeps very little at night – and often passes most of the forenoon in a semi-lethargic state – Still she is up all day – and even goes out a little when it is fine – fresh air usually acts as a temporary stimulus – but its reviving power diminishes.

Charlotte to Ellen; Haworth, 16 May 1849

We have now made our arrangements for the journey. We shall leave Keighley about ½ 1 o'clock and expect to reach Leeds soon after two – Wednesday 23rd that is next week . . . I fear you will be shocked when you see Anne – but be on your guard – dear Ellen –

to not express your feelings – indeed I can trust both your self-possession and your kindness.

I wish my judgement sanctioned this step of going to Scarbro' more fully than it does.

You ask how I have arranged about leaving papa – I could make no special arrangement – he wishes me to go with Anne – and would not hear of Mr Nicholls coming – or anything of that kind – so I do what I believe is for the best and leave the result to Providence.

Ellen, Reminiscences; c. 1871

The start for Scarbro' was delayed, owing to the increased illness of the dear invalid, but she declared herself far better the next day, and was still bent upon going, so that, in spite of poor Charlotte's conviction, (unselfishly kept to herself) that her beloved sister would never return to Haworth, they actually started on May 25th.

Their friend, who had waited for them in vain, the day before at Leeds, and had had the pain of witnessing the arrival of no fewer than three funerals from the platforms on which she was eagerly looking for her friends, in terrible anxiety, determined to go to the Parsonage, as soon as possible, to enquire for dear Anne, and she arrived just in time the next day to start with them . . . On our way to Scarborough we stopped at York, and after a rest at the George Hotel, and partaking of dinner, which she enjoyed, Anne went out in a bath–chair, and made purchases, along with Charlotte, of bonnets and dresses, besides visiting the minster . . . Her visit to York Minster was an overpowering pleasure not for its own imposing & impressive grandeur only, but because it brought to her susceptible nature a vital & overwhelming sense of Omnipotence. She said while gazing at the structure 'If finite power can do this what is the?' & here emotion stayed her speech & she was hastened to a less exciting scene.

Charlotte to William Smith Williams; Haworth, 27 May 1849

I am thankful to say we reached our destination safely, having rested one night at York. We found assistance wherever we needed it; there was always an arm ready to do for my sister what I was not quite strong enough to do: lift her in and out of the carriages, carry her across the line, etc.

It made her happy to see both York and its Minster, and Scarbro' and its bay once more. There is yet no revival of bodily strength – I fear indeed the slow ebb continues. People who see her tell me I must not expect her to last long – but it is something to cheer her mind.

Our lodgings are pleasant. As Anne sits at the window she can look down on the sea, which this morning is calm as glass. She says if she could breathe more freely she would be comfortable at this moment – but she cannot breathe freely.

Ellen, Reminiscences; c. 1855–71

The morning after her arrival at Scarborough, she insisted on going to the baths, and would be left there with only the attendant in charge. She walked back alone to her lodgings, but fell exhausted as she reached the garden-gate. She never named this, but it was discovered afterwards . . . On the 26th she drove on the sands for an hour & lest the poor donkey should be urged by its driver to a greater speed than her tender heart thought right she took the reins & drove herself – When she was joined by her friend she was charging the boy-master of the donkey to treat the poor animal well – she was ever fond of dumb things & would give up her own comfort for them.

On Sunday 27th she wished to go to Church & her eye brightened with the thought of once more worshipping her God among her fellow creatures but her sister & friend thought it prudent to dissuade her from the attempt – she submitted, though it was evident her heart was longing to join some public [act of] devotion & praise – She walked a little in the afternoon & meeting with a sheltered comfortable seat near the beach she begged her companions would leave her & enjoy the various scenes near [at] hand for the place was new to them but not to her – she loved the place & wanted her relative & friend to share her preference – The even[in]g closed in with the most glorious sunset ever witnessed . . . the dear invalid was drawn in her easy chair to the window to enjoy the scene with her friends. Her face became illumined almost as much as the glorious scene she gazed upon – little was said – for it was plain our dear invalid's thoughts were driven by the imposing view before her to penetrate forwards to the regions of unfading glory – She again thought of public worship & wished us to leave her & join those who were assembling at the House of God   we declined urging gently the duty & pleasure of staying with the invalid – On returning to her place near the fire she conversed with her sister on the propriety of returning to their home – she did not wish it for her own sake she said – she was fearing others might suffer more if her decease occurred where she was – she probably thought that the task of accompanying her lifeless remains on a long journey was more than her bereaved sister could bear – Her night was passed without any apparent accession of illness – she rose at 7 & performed most of her toilet herself by her expressed wish. Her sister always yielded such points as being the truest kindness not to press inability where it was not acknowledged . . . She was the first of the little party to be ready to go downstairs: but when she reached the head of the stairs, she felt fearful of descending. Charlotte went to her and discovered this. I fancying there was some difficulty, left my room to see what it was, when Anne smilingly told me she felt afraid of the steps downward. I immediately said: 'Let me try to carry you;' she looked pleased, but feared for me. Charlotte was angry at the idea, and greatly distressed, I could see, at this new evidence of Anne's weakness. Charlotte was at last persuaded to go to her room and leave us. I then went a step or two below Anne, and begged her to put her arms round my neck, and I said: 'I will carry you like a baby.' She still feared, but on my promising to put her down if I could not do it, she consented to trust herself to me. Strength seemed to be given for the effort, but on reaching the foot of the stairs, poor Anne's head fell like a leaden weight upon the top of mine. The shock was terrible, for I felt it could only be death that was coming. I just managed to bear her to the front of her easy-chair and drop her into it, falling myself on my knees before her, very miserable at the fact, and letting her fall at last, though it was into her chair. She was shaken, but she put out her arms to comfort me, and said: 'You know it could not be helped, you did your best.' After this she sat at the breakfast-table and partook of a basin of boiled milk prepared for her. Nothing occurred to excite alarm till about 11 am. The dear Invalid then spoke of feeling a change She believed she had not long to live could she reach home alive if prepared immediately for departure[?] a physician was sent for – Her address to him was made with perfect composure – she begged him to say how long he thought she might live – not to fear speaking the truth for she was not afraid to die – The doctor being thus urged reluctantly admitted that the angel of death was already arrived that life was ebbing fast – she thanked him for his truthfulness & he departed to come again very soon – She still occupied her easy chair looking so serene & reliant there was no opening for grief as yet though all knew the separation was at hand. She clasped her hands & reverently invoked a blessing from Heaven first upon her sister then upon her friend & thanked each for their kindness & attentions. Ere long the restlessness of death appeared & she was borne to the sofa On being asked if she were easier she looked gratefully at her questioner & said 'It is not you who can give me ease but soon all will be well through the merits of my Redeemer.' Shortly after this, seeing that her sister could hardly restrain her grief she said 'Take courage Charlotte! Take courage'. Her faith never failed & her eye never dimmed till about 2 o'clock when she calmly & without sigh breathed her last – So still & so hallowed were her last hours and moments there was no thought of assistance or of dread.

Anne Brontë died on 28 May 1849; she was twenty-nine years old. To avoid the trauma of Charlotte having to escort the coffin home and Patrick having to bury his third child in nine months, Anne was buried at Scarborough, in the cliff-top churchyard of St Mary's, beneath the walls of the ruined castle. Miss Wooler, who had taken a house on the other side of the town, discreetly joined Charlotte and Ellen for the funeral but did not otherwise intrude her presence. At Patrick and Ellen's insistence, Charlotte agreed to remain at the sea-side for a few weeks more; her own health had been severely tried by the strain of the last few months and she needed to recuperate and steel herself for the return home. Scarborough soon proved to be unbearable because of its associations with Anne's death, so, shortly after the funeral, the two friends moved a few miles away to the little resort of Filey.

**⋆⋆*Ellen to Mrs Ward; 2 The Cliff, Scarborough, 30 May 1849*

You will I am sure be sorry to hear that poor Miss Anne Brontë is departed this life – She died about 2 o'clock on Monday – very calmly – she <u>desired</u> death the last morn[in]g, & through all evinced the greatest fortitude & strength of mind. She was perfectly sensible to the last moment. her journey apparently had a beneficial effect – she drove out in a Donkey chaise on Saturday & on Sunday she walked on the Bridge – We inter her remains here this afternoon – Miss Brontë thinks it right to spare her Papa the misery of another interment so soon after the two previous ones.

Charlotte to William Smith Williams; Scarborough, 30 May 1849

My dear Sir

My poor Sister is taken quietly home at last. She died on Monday – With almost her last breath she said she was happy – and thanked God that death was come, and come so gently. I did not think it would be so soon. You will not expect me to add more at present.

Yours faithfully
C Brontë

Charlotte to William Smith Williams; Scarborough, 4 June 1849

I hardly know what I said when I wrote last – I was then feverish and exhausted – I am now better and – I believe – quite calm.

You have been informed of my dear Sister Anne's death – let me now add that she died without severe struggle – resigned – trusting in God – thankful for release from a suffering life – deeply assured that a better existence lay before her – She believed – she hoped, and declared her belief and hope with her last breath. – Her quiet – Christian death did not rend my heart as Emily's stern, simple, undemonstrative end did – I let Anne go to God and felt He had a right to her I could hardly let Emily go – I wanted to hold her back then – and I want her back now – Anne, from her childhood seemed preparing for an early death – Emily's spirit seemed strong enough to bear her to fulness of years – They are both gone – and so is poor Branwell – and Papa has now me only – the weakest – puniest – least promising of his six children – Consumption has taken the whole five.

Charlotte to William Smith Williams; Filey, 13 June 1849

When I wrote to you last I thought it probable I might not address you again soon – but this evening I will write because I feel in the mood to do so without, I trust, paining you.

You have been kind enough to take a certain interest in my afflictions, and I feel it a sort of duty to tell you how I am enabled to sustain them. The burden is lightened far beyond what I could expect by more circumstances than one. Papa is resigned and his health is not shaken. An immediate change of scene has done me good. All I meet are kind – my friend Ellen is affectionately so. You – on whom I have no claim – write to me in the strain best tending to consolation.

Then – my Sister died happily; nothing dark, except the inevitable shadow of Death overclouded her hour of dissolution the doctor – a stranger – who was called in – wondered at her fixed tranquillity of spirit and settled longing to be gone. He said in all his experience he had seen no such death-bed, and that it gave evidence of no common mind – yet to speak the truth – it but half consoles to remember this calm – there is piercing pain in it. Anne had had enough of life such as it was – in her twenty-eighth year she laid it down as a burden I hardly know whether it is sadder to think of that than of Emily turning her dying eyes reluctantly from the pleasant sun. Had I never believed in a future life before, my Sisters' fate would assure me of it. There must be Heaven or we must despair

– for life seems bitter, brief – blank. To me – these two have left in their memories a noble legacy. Were I quite solitary in the world – bereft even of Papa – there is something in the past I can love intensely and honour deeply – and it is something which cannot change – which cannot decay – which immortality guarantees from corruption.

They have died comparatively young – but their short lives were spotless – their brief career was honourable – their untimely death befel amidst all associations that can hallow, and not one that can desecrate.

A year ago – had a prophet warned me how I should stand in June 1849 – how stripped and bereaved – had he foretold the autumn, the winter, the spring of sickness and suffering to be gone through – I should have thought – this can never be endured. It is over. Branwell – Emily – Anne are gone like dreams – gone as Maria and Elizabeth went twenty years ago. One by one I have watched them fall asleep on my arm – and closed their glazed eyes – I have seen them buried one by one – and – thus far – God has upheld me. from my heart I thank Him.

I thank too the friends whose sympathy has given me inexpressible comfort and strength – you, amongst the number.

Filey, where, we have been for the last week – is a small place with a wild rocky coast – its sea is very blue – its cliffs are very white – its sands very solitary – it suits Ellen and myself better than Scarborough which is too gay. I would stay here another week – but Ellen says I must go to-morrow to Bridlington – and after I have been a week there, I intend to return home to Papa. May I retain strength and cheerfulness enough to be a comfort to him and to bear up against the weight of the solitary life to come – it will be solitary – I cannot help dreading the first experience of it – the first aspect of the empty rooms which once were tenanted by those dearest to my heart – and where the shadow of their last days must now – I think – linger for ever.

Charlotte to Ellen; Haworth, 23 June 1849

I got home a little before eight o'clock. All was clean and bright waiting for me – Papa and the servants were well – and all received me with an affection which should have consoled. The dogs seemed in strange ecstacy. I am certain they regarded me as the harbinger of others – the dumb creatures thought that as I was returned – those who had been so long absent were not far behind.

I left Papa soon and went into the dining-room – I shut the door – I tried to be glad that I was come home – I have always been glad before – except once – even then I was cheered. but this time joy was not to be the sensation. I felt that the house was all silent – the rooms were all empty – I remembered where the three were laid – in what narrow dark dwellings – never were they to reappear on earth. So the sense of desolation and bitterness took possession of me – the agony that <u>was to be undergone</u> – and <u>was not</u> to be avoided came on – I underwent it & passed a dreary evening and night and a mournful morrow – to-day I am better.

I do not know how life will pass – but I certainly do feel confidence in Him who has upheld me hitherto. Solitude may be cheered and made endurable beyond what I can believe. The great trial is when evening closes and night approaches – At that hour we used to assemble in the dining-room – we used to talk – Now I sit by myself – necessarily I am silent. – I cannot help thinking of their last days – remembering their sufferings and what they said and did and how they looked in mortal affliction – perhaps all this will become less poignant in time.

Charlotte to William Smith Williams; Haworth, 25 June 1849

I am now again at home – where I returned last Thursday. I call it <u>home</u> still – much as London would be called London if an earthquake should shake its streets to ruins. But let me not be ungrateful: Haworth parsonage is still a home for me, and not quite a ruined or desolate home either. Papa is there – and two most affectionate and faithful servants – and two old dogs, in their way as faithful and affectionate – Emily's large house-dog which lay at the side of her dying-bed, and followed her funeral to the vault, lying in the pew couched at our feet while the burial service was being read – and Anne's little spaniel. The ecstasy of these poor animals when I came in was something singular – at former returns from brief absences they always welcomed me warmly – but not in that strange, heart-touching way – I am certain they thought that, as I was returned, my sisters were not far behind – but here my Sisters will come no more. Keeper may visit Emily's little bedroom – as he still does day by day – and Flossy may look wistfully round for Anne – they will never see them again – nor shall I – at least the human part of me –

I must not write so sadly – but how can I help thinking and feeling sadly? In the day-time effort and occupation aid me – but when evening darkens something in my heart revolts against the burden of solitude – the sense of loss and want grows almost too much for me. I am not good or amiable in such moments – I am rebellious – and it is only the thought of my dear Father in the next room, or of the kind servants in the kitchen – or some caress from the poor dogs which restores me to softer sentiments and more rational views. As to the night – could I do without bed – I would never seek it – waking – I think – sleeping – I dream of them – and I cannot recall them as they were in health – still they appear to me in sickness and suffering – Still my nights were worse after the first shock of Branwell's death – they were terrible then – and the impressions experienced on waking were at that time such as we do not put into language. Worse seemed at hand than was yet endured – in truth worse awaited us.

All this bitterness must be tasted – perhaps the palate will grow used to the draught in time and find its flavour less acrid – this pain must be undergone – its poignancy – I trust – will be blunted one day. Ellen would have come back with me but I would not let her – I knew it would be better to face the desolation at once – later or sooner the sharp pang must be experienced.

Labour must be the cure, not sympathy – Labour is the only radical cure for rooted sorrow – The society of a calm, serenely cheerful companion – such as Ellen – soothes pain like a soft opiate – but I find it does not probe or heal the wound – sharper – more severe means are necessary to make a remedy. Total change might do much – where that cannot be obtained – work is the best substitute.

Chapter Eleven

1849–50

Charlotte had long been searching for a subject for her second novel; in the fate of single women, she at last found one which was dear to her heart. She returned to *Shirley* with something akin to desperation. Painful as it was to write, especially without the companionship and stimulus her sisters had always provided, work was to be her salvation. It enabled her to retreat from the terrible reality of her own loss and the desolation of the life she was compelled to lead. Now, as never before, she lived through her letters, pouring out her emotions and thoughts to friends, old and new.

Charlotte to William Smith Williams; Haworth, 3 July 1849

Come what may afterwards, an education secured is an advantage gained – a priceless advantage. Come what may – it is a step towards independency – and one great curse of a single female life is its dependency. It does credit both to Louisa's heart and head that she herself wishes to get this presentation: encourage her in the wish. Your daughters – no more than your sons – should be a burden on your hands: your daughters – as much as your sons – should aim at making their way honourably through life. Do not wish to keep them at home. Believe me – teachers may be hard-worked, ill-paid and despised – but the girl who stays at home doing nothing is worse off than the hardest-wrought and worst paid drudge of a school. Whenever I have seen, not merely in humble, but in affluent homes – families of daughters sitting waiting to be married, I have pitied them from my heart. It is doubtless well – very well – if Fate decrees them a happy marriage – but if otherwise – give their existence some object – their time some occupation – or the peevishness of disappointment and the listlessness of idleness will infallibly degrade their nature . . . Lonely as I am – how should I be if Providence had never given me courage to adopt a career – perseverance to plead through two long, weary years with publishers till they admitted me? – How should I be with youth past – sisters lost – a resident in a moorland parish where there is not a single educated family? In that case I should have no world at all: the raven, weary of surveying the deluge and without an ark to return to, would be my type. As it is, something like a hope and motive sustains me still. I wish all your daughters – I wish every woman in England had also a hope and motive: Alas! there are many old maids who have neither.

Charlotte to Ellen; Haworth, 14 July 1849

My life is what I expected it to be – sometimes when I wake in the morning – and know that Solitude, Remembrance and Longing are to be almost my sole companions all day through – that at night I shall go to bed with them, that they will long keep me sleepless – that next morning I shall wake to them again – Sometimes – Nell – I have a heavy heart of it.

But crushed I am not – yet: nor robbed of elasticity nor of hope nor quite of endeavour – Still I have some strength to fight the battle of life. I am aware and can acknowledge I have many comforts – many mercies – still I can get on.

But I do hope and pray – that never may you or any one I love, be placed as I am. To sit in a lonely room – the clock ticking loud through a still house – and to have open before the mind's eye the record of the last year with its shocks, sufferings losses – is a trial –

Charlotte to William Smith Williams; Haworth, 16 August 1849

The North British Review duly reached me. I read attentively all it says about E. Wyndham, J. Eyre, and F. Hervey. Much of the article is clever – and yet there are remarks which – for me – rob it of importance.

To value praise or stand in awe of blame we must respect the source whence the praise and blame proceed –: and I do not respect an inconsistent critic. He says 'if "Jane Eyre" be the production of a woman – she must be a woman unsexed.'

In that case the book is an unredeemed error and should be un-reservedly condemned. 'Jane Eyre' is a woman's autobiography – by a woman it is professedly written – if it is written as no woman would write – condemn it – with spirit and decision – say it is bad – but do not first eulogise and then detract. I am reminded of the 'Economist.' The literary critic of that paper praised the book if written by a man – and pronounced it 'odious' if the work of a woman

To such critics I would say – 'To you I am neither Man nor Woman – I come before you as an Author only – it is the sole standard by which you have a right to judge me – the sole ground on which I accept your judgement'.

Charlotte to Ellen; Haworth, 23 August 1849

Papa has not been well at all lately. He has had another attack of bronchitis. I felt very uneasy about him for some days, more wretched indeed than I care to tell you. After what has happened, one trembles at any appearance of sickness; and when anything ails papa, I feel too keenly that he is the <u>last</u>, the <u>only</u> near and dear relation I have in the world. Yesterday and to-day he has seemed much better, for which I am truly thankful.

Charlotte to William Smith Williams; Haworth, 29 August 1849

The book is now finished (thank God!) and ready for Mr Taylor – but I have not yet heard from him. I thought I should be able to tell whether it was equal to 'Jane Eyre' or not – but I find I cannot – it may be better – it may be worse – I shall be curious to hear your opinion – my own is of no value – . . . Whatever now becomes of the work – the occupation of writing it has been a boon to me – it took me out of dark and desolate reality to an unreal but happier region – The worst of it is my eyes are grown somewhat weak and my head somewhat weary and prone to ache with close work. You can write nothing of value unless you give yourself wholly to the theme – and when you so give yourself – you lose appetite and sleep – it cannot be helped –

Charlotte to George Smith; Haworth, 14 September 1849

I am truly glad to learn that the result of my labours is such as to satisfy you and my other kind friends in Cornhill; I hope the public will think with you, and indeed after the opinions expressed by yourself, Mr Williams and Mr Taylor, I now feel a degree of confidence on the subject.

The Bank-Bill reached me safely: I assure you I felt rather proud of its amount; I am pleased to be able to earn so much, for Papa will be pleased too when I tell him. I should like to take care of this money: it is Papa's great wish that I should realize a small independency if you could give me a word of advice respecting the wisest and safest manner of investing this £500, I should be very much obliged to you. I have already a few shares in a Railway, but these are so much fallen in value of late that I hardly like to venture on so uncertain an investment a second time. A hint on the subject – provided it costs you no trouble – would be very acceptable to me.

Charlotte to William Smith Williams; Haworth, 17 September 1849

Your letter gave me great pleasure. An author who has shewn his book to none, held no consultation about plan, subject, characters or incidents, asked and had no opinion from one living being, but fabricated it darkly in the silent workshop of his own brain – such an author awaits with a singular feeling the report of the first impression produced by his creation in a quarter where he places confidence, and truly glad he is when that report proves favourable.

Do you think this book will tend to strengthen the idea that Currer Bell is a woman – or will it favour a contrary opinion?

★★*Charlotte to William Smith Williams; Haworth, 19 September 1849*

I am sorry to say Newby <u>does</u> know my real name. I wish he did not – but that cannot be helped – Meantime, though I earnestly wish to preserve my incognito, I live under no slavish fear of discovery – I am ashamed of nothing I have written – not a line.

Charlotte to William Smith Williams; Haworth, 21 September 1849

I am obliged to you for preserving my secret, being at least as anxious as ever (<u>more</u> anxious, I cannot well be) to keep quiet. You asked me in one of your letters lately whether I thought I should escape identification in Yorkshire. I am so little known, that I think I shall. Besides the book is far less founded on the Real – than perhaps appears. It would be difficult to explain to you how little actual experience I have had of life, how few persons I have known and how very few have known me.

As an instance how the characters have been managed – take that of Mr Helstone. If this character had an original, it was in the person of a clergyman who died some years since at the advanced age of eighty. I never saw him except once – at the Consecration of a Church – when I was a child of ten years old. I was then struck with his appearance and stern, martial air. At a subsequent period I heard him talked about in the neighbourhood where he had resided – some mentioned him with enthusiasm – others with detestation – I listened to various anecdotes, balanced evidence against evidence and drew an inference. The original of Mr Hall I have seen – he knows me slightly, but he would as soon think I had closely observed him or taken him for a character – he would as soon, indeed, suspect me of writing a book – a novel – as he would his dog – Prince.

Charlotte was soon to be disabused of her sanguine belief that she could escape detection and preserve her anonymity as an author. *Shirley* was published on 26 October 1849, while she was staying with Ellen Nussey at Birstall. As the novel had drawn heavily on the history, landscape and inhabitants of that area, it was not surprising that Ellen's friends and neighbours began to put two and two together. 'Mr Hall' not only recognized himself and his portrayer but would write to Ellen demanding to know 'from headquarters' the identity of other characters in Charlotte's novel. Ellen herself had been let into the secret of the Bells' identity during her visit to Haworth at the beginning of the year, but it was Mary Taylor's brother, Joe, who actively spread the gossip.

Charlotte to William Smith Williams; Haworth, 1 November 1849

I have permitted myself the treat of spending the last week with my friend Ellen – Her residence is in a far more populous and stirring neighbourhood than this – whenever I go there I am unavoidably forced into society – clerical society chiefly.

During my late visit I have too often had reason – sometimes in a pleasant – sometimes in a painful form to fear that I no longer walk invisible – 'Jane Eyre' – it appears has been read all over the district – a fact of which I never dreamt – a circumstance of which the possibility never occurred to me – I met sometimes with new deference, with augmented kindness – old schoolfellows and old teachers too, greeted me with generous warmth – and again - ecclesiastical brows lowered thunder on me. When I confronted one or two large-made priests I longed for the battle to come on – I wish they would speak out plainly. You must not understand that my schoolfellows and teachers were of the Clergy Daughters' School – in fact I was never there but for one little year as a very little girl – I am certain I have long been forgotten – though for myself I remember all and everything clearly: early impressions are ineffaceable.

It was not just in Yorkshire that the publication of *Shirley* revived and increased speculation about the identity of 'Currer Bell'; the reviewers too seemed more interested in this – and in the question of the author's sex especially – than in the novel itself.

Review of Shirley *from the* Daily News, *31 October 1849*

There are few things more forbidding than the commencement of a novel by the author of *Jane Eyre*. Like people who put dwarfs and monsters to keep their gates, or ugly dogs to deter idle folk from entering, so doth this writer manage to have an opening chapter or two of the most deterring kind. What so disgusting as the family in the midst of whom Jane Eyre is first discovered? The three curates and their junketing, with whom *Shirley* commences, is quite as vulgar, as unnecessary, and as disgusting . . . But what is striking is the sentiment. *Shirley* is the anatomy of the female heart. By *Shirley* we mean the book, and not the personage; for the true heroine is the rector's niece, the history of whose heart is one of the most beautiful chronicles ever set down by a female pen. For that Currer Bell is petticoated will be as little doubted by the readers of her work as that Shirley Keeldar is breeched.

The merit of the work lies in the variety, beauty, and truth of its female character. Not one of its men are genuine. There are no such men. There are no *Mr Helstones*, *Mr Yorkes*, or *Mr Moores*. They are all as unreal as Madame Tussaud's waxworks.

Charlotte to William Smith Williams; Haworth, 1 November 1849

I have just received the 'Daily News.' Let me speak the truth – when I read it my heart sickened over it. It is not a good review – it is unutterably false. If 'Shirley' strikes all readers as it has struck that one – but – I shall not say what follows.

On the whole I am glad a decidedly bad notice has come first – a notice whose inexpressible ignorance first stuns and then stirs me. Are there no such men as the Helstones and Yorkes?

Yes there are

Is the first chapter disgusting or vulgar?

It is not: it is real.

As for the praise of such a critic – I find it silly and nauseous – and I scorn it.

Were my Sisters now alive they and I would laugh over this notice

– but they sleep – they will wake no more for me – and I am a fool
to be so moved by what is not worth a sigh –

Believe me
Yours sincerely
C B–

You must excuse me if I seem hasty – I fear I really am not as firm
as I used to be – nor so patient: whenever any shock comes, I feel
that almost all supports have been withdrawn.

Charlotte to G. H. Lewes; Haworth, 1 November 1849

It is about a year and a half since you wrote to me but it seems a
longer period, because since then it has been my lot to pass some
black milestones in the journey of life: since then there have been
intervals when I have ceased to care about literature and critics and
fame – when I have lost sight of whatever was prominent in my
thoughts at the first publication of 'Jane Eyre' – but now I want
these things to come back – vividly – if possible – consequently it
was a pleasure to receive your note. I wish you did not think me a
woman: I wish all reviewers believed 'Currer Bell' to be a man –
they would be more just to him. You will – I know – keep measuring
me by some standard of what you deem becoming to my sex –
where I am not what you consider graceful – you will condemn
me. All mouths will be open against that first chapter – and that first
chapter is true as the Bible – nor is it exceptional

come what will – I cannot when I write think always of myself
– and of what is elegant and charming in femininity – it is not on
those terms or with such ideas I ever took pen in hand; and if it is
only on such terms my writing will be tolerated – I shall pass away
from the public and trouble it no more. Out of obscurity I came –
to obscurity I can easily return –

Review of Shirley *from the* Atlas, *3 November 1849*

The first chapter of *Shirley* is enough to deter many a reader from
advancing a step further than the threshold. It required all the

remembered fascinations of *Jane Eyre* to keep down the feelings of dissatisfaction (we had nearly written another word with the same commencement) which the first chapter of *Shirley* raised up within us. All this is very coarse – very irreverential. And there is besides, discernible in other parts, an unseemly mode of allusion to solemn topics, a jesting with scriptural names, and a light usage of scriptural expressions, which will grate painfully upon the feelings of a considerable number of Currer Bell's many-minded readers.

★*Charlotte to James Taylor; Haworth, 6 November 1849*

I am afraid Mr Williams told you I was sadly 'put out' about 'the Daily News', and I believe it is to that circumstance I owe your letters. But I have now made good resolutions which were tried this morning by another notice in the same style in the 'Observer'. The praise of such critics mortifies more than their blame: an author who becomes the object of it cannot help momentarily wishing he had never written – and, speaking for myself alone, I <u>do</u> wish these hirelings of the Press were still ignorant of my being a woman. Why can they not be content to take Currer Bell for a man?

I imagined – mistakenly it now appears – that 'Shirley' bore fewer traces of a female hand than 'Jane Eyre': that I have misjudged disappoints me a little – though I cannot exactly see where the error lies.

You keep to your point about the Curates; since you think me to blame, you do right to tell me so. I rather fancy I shall be left in a minority of one on that subject.

Charlotte to Ellen; Haworth, 16 November 1849

You are not to suppose any of the characters in Shirley intended as literal portraits – it would not suit the rules of Art – nor my own feelings to write in that style – we only suffer reality to <u>suggest</u> – never to <u>dictate</u> – the heroines are abstractions and the hero[e]s also – qualities I have seen, loved and admired are here and there put in as decorative gems to be preserved in that setting. Since you say you could recognize the originals of all except the heroines – pray whom did you suppose the two Moores to represent?

Charlotte was amused by Ellen's naivety in assuming that she could identify among her acquaintances the originals of Charlotte's fictitious characters, but other letters she received at this time provoked more complex emotions. One of them, from Mrs Elizabeth Gaskell, who would later become Charlotte's friend and biographer, touched her so deeply that she felt compelled to reply. It was a measure of how much she had been impressed by Mrs Gaskell's delicate tact that, though she still refused to reveal her true identity, Charlotte admitted her to the secret of her sex.

Charlotte to Mrs Gaskell; Haworth, 17 November 1849

Currer Bell <u>must</u> answer Mrs Gaskell's letter – whether forbidden to do so or not – and She must acknowledge its kind, generous sympathy with all her heart.

Yet Mrs Gaskell must not pity Currer Bell too much: there are thousands who suffer more than she: dark days she has known; the worst, perhaps, were days of bereavement, but though C.B. is the survivor of most that were dear to her, she has one near relative still left, and therefore cannot be said to be quite alone.

Currer Bell will avow to Mrs Gaskell that her chief reason for maintaining an incognito is the fear that if she relinquished it, strength and courage would leave her, and she should ever after shrink – from writing the plain truth.

> Mrs Gaskell
> Novbr 17th/49

Mrs Gaskell to Catherine Winkworth; Manchester, November 1849

Currer Bell (aha! what will you give me for a secret?)   She's a she – that I will tell you – who has sent me 'Shirley'.

Despite her anxiety to maintain her anonymity, Charlotte could not resist an invitation to spend some time in London on a private visit to the family home of her publisher, George Smith. It was decided that she would travel down on the train at the end of November and spend a couple of weeks with the Smiths at Westbourne Place. Inevitably, as the anniversary of Emily's death approached, Charlotte could not help thinking of how her circumstances had changed since her last visit to London.

Charlotte to William Smith Williams; Haworth, 19 November 1849

Now that I have almost formed the resolution of coming to London – the thought begins to present itself to me under a pleasant aspect; at first it was sad; it recalled the last time I went and with whom, and to whom I came home, and in what dear companionship I again and again narrated all that had been seen, heard and uttered in that visit. Emily would never go into any sort of society herself, but whenever I went, I could on my return, communicate to her a pleasure that suited her by giving the distinct, faithful impression of each scene I had witnessed. When pressed to go, she would sometimes say 'What is the use? Charlotte will bring it all home to me.' And indeed I delighted to please her thus. My occupation is gone now.

Charlotte to Ellen; Westbourne Place, Bishop's Road, London, 4 December 1849

I came to this big Babylon last Thursday, and have been in what seems to me a sort of whirl ever since, for changes, scenes and stimulus which would be a trifle to others, are much to me . . . Mrs Smith received me at first like one who has had the strictest orders to be scrupulously attentive – I had fire in my bedroom evening and morning – two wax candles – &c. &c. and Mrs S & her daughters seemed to look on me with a mixture of respect and alarm – but all this is changed – that is to say the attention and politeness continue as great as ever – but the alarm and estrangement are quite gone – she treats me as if she liked me and I begin to like her much – kindness is a potent heart winner. I had not judged too favourably of her son on a first impression – he pleases me much: I like him better even as a son and brother than as a man of business. Mr Williams too is really most gentlemanly and well-informed – his weak points he certainly has – but these are not seen in society. Mr Taylor – the little man – has again shewn his parts. of him I have not yet come to a clear decision: abilities he has – for he rules the Firm (which Dr Wheelwright told me the other day is considerably the largest publishing concern in London) he keeps 40 young men under strict control by his iron will – his young Superior likes him which – to speak truth – is more than I do at present – in fact – I suspect he is of the Helstone order of men – rigid, despotic, and self-willed – He tries to be very kind and even to express sympathy sometimes – and he does not manage it – he has a determined, dreadful nose in the middle of his face which when poked into my countenance cuts into my soul like iron – Still he is horribly intelligent, quick, searching, sagacious – and with a memory of relentless tenacity: to turn to Williams after him or to Smith himself is to turn from granite to easy down or warm fur.

I have seen Thackeray.

No more at present from yours &c.,

C Brontë

Charlotte to Patrick; London, 5 December 1849

Dear Papa

I must write another line to you to tell you how I am getting on. I have seen a great many things since I left home about which I hope to talk to you at future tea times at home. I have been to the theatre and seen Macready in 'Macbeth,' I have seen the pictures in the National Gallery. I have seen a beautiful exhibition of Turner's paintings, and yesterday I saw Mr Thackeray. He dined here with some other gentlemen. He is a very tall man – above six feet high, with a peculiar face – not handsome – very ugly indeed – generally somewhat satirical and stern in expression, but capable also of a kind look. He was not told who I was – he was not introduced to me – but I soon saw him looking at me through his spectacles and when we all rose to go down to dinner – he just stept quietly up and said 'Shake hands' so I shook hands – He spoke very few words to me – but when he went away he shook hands again in a very kind way. It is better – I should think to have him for a friend than an enemy – for he is a most formidable looking personage. I listened to him as he conversed with the other gentlemen – all he says is most simple, but often cynical, harsh, and contradictory. I get on quietly – most people know me I think, but they are far too well-bred to shew that they know me – so that there is none of that bustle or that sense of publicity I dislike.

Review of Shirley from The Times, 7 December 1849

. . . a very simple story, which it has taken a thousand octavo pages to tell, and to tell most cumbrously and artificially . . . Indeed, the whole structure seems erected for the simple purpose of enabling these creatures of the author's brain – certainly not of our every-day world – to do nothing, but talk after the manner of such purely intellectual companions.

And it would be unjust to the fair authoress – for lady she is, let who will say to the contrary – if we did not allow that at times the talk is worthy of her genius and that gems of rare thought and glorious passion shine here and there throughout her volumes. But the infrequent brilliancy seems but to make more evident and unsightly the surrounding gloom. *Shirley* is not a picture of real life; it is not a work that contains the elements of popularity, that will grapple with the heart of mankind and compel its homage. It is a mental exercise that can bring its author no profit, and will not extend by the measure of an inch her previous well-deserved success. Millions understood her before – she may count by units those who will appreciate her now. *Jane Eyre* was not a pure romance, *Shirley* is at once the most high flown and the stalest of fictions.

Mrs Gaskell, Life of Charlotte Brontë (Smith, Elder & Co., 1857)

Her hosts took pleasure in showing her the sights of London. On one of the days which had been set apart for some of these pleasant excursions, a severe review of *Shirley* was published in the *Times*. She had heard that her book would be noticed by it, and guessed that there was some particular reason for the care with which her hosts mislaid it on that particular morning. She told them that she was aware why she might not see the paper. Mrs Smith at once admitted that her conjecture was right, and said that they had wished her to go to the day's engagement before reading it. But she quietly persisted in her request to be allowed to have the paper. Mrs Smith took her work, and tried not to observe the countenance, which the other tried to hide between the large sheets; but she could not help becoming aware of tears stealing down the face and dropping on the lap. The first remark Miss Brontë made was to express her fear lest so severe a notice should check the sale of the book, and injuriously affect her publishers. Wounded as she was, her first thought was for others.

Charlotte to Ellen; London, 9 December 1849

I am only going to pen a very hasty reply now, as there are several people in the room and I cannot write in company. You seem to suppose I must be very happy, dear Nell, and I see you have twenty romantic notions in your head about me. These last you may dismiss at once. As to being happy, I am under scenes and circumstances of excitement; but I suffer acute pain sometimes, mental pain, I mean. At the moment Mr Thackeray presented himself, I was thoroughly faint from inanition, having eaten nothing since a very slight breakfast, and it was then <u>seven</u> o'clock in the evening. Excitement and exhaustion together made savage work of me that evening. What he thought of me I cannot tell. This evening I am going to meet Miss Martineau. She has written to me most kindly. She knows me only as Currer Bell. I am going alone in the carriage; how I shall get on I do not know.

Charlotte had long admired Harriet Martineau, the essayist and novelist, who had overcome the handicap of deafness to become a prolific and acclaimed writer. Learning that Miss Martineau was also on a visit to London and staying close at hand with relatives, Charlotte seized the opportunity to seek an introduction. Lucy, Harriet's cousin by marriage and hostess to the meeting, could hardly contain her glee as she recounted the tale to her son.

Lucy Martineau to her son, Jack; London, 10 December 1849

You know Harriet Martineau was here for 2 or 3 days. Well, on Saturday she rec[eived] a note from 'Currer Bell', (the assumed name of the Author of Jane Eyre) expressing the greatest admiration of her, & her 'Deerbrook', & begging to be allowed to call on her, as   he anxiously desired an interview for other reasons than mere curiosity. So as 'Currer Bell's' note was dated f[ro]m a house very near us, H[arrie]tt wrote in answer that we her friends with whom she was staying, hoped he w[oul]d join our early tea next day at six o'clock – now the fun was, how to direct the note, for no one has ever yet decided whether Currer Bell is a man or a woman – a previous note H[arrie]tt had directed to Currer Bell Esqre, but had begun her note, Madam – being of opinion that Jane Eyre is written by a woman. This 2nd note however she directed, quaker fashion, to Currer Bell, alone – & Joseph who took it, brought an answer of joyful acceptance, adding 'I will try to be patient till 6 o'clock' – So all day long as H[arrie]tt tells the story we were wondering what sort of a being this same Currer Bell w[oul]d turn out to be: whether a tall moustached man six feet high, or an aged female, or a girl, or – altogether a ghost, a hoax or a swindler! If not a hoax we decided that he or she must in decent manners let itself be announced by its true name – & H[arrie]tt who w[oul]d not be able to hear Yelland announce it, told us that we really must shout it distinctly to her thro' her trumpet otherwise the mystery w[oul]d at last be only half solved to her. So when 6 oclock came, I lighted plenty of candles that we might see what manner of man or womankind it was, & we sat in wondering expectation – Lina as much entertained as any of us. The hand pointed to 5 minutes past six, & we said it is a hoax after all! When lo! a carriage stopped at the door, the bell rung, and Yelland flung open the door announcing ------- ---------! & in came a neat little woman, a very little sprite of a creature nicely dressed; & with nice tidy bright hair – Tho' the cat was out of the bag here, we are bound not to tell her name, for she does not wish it to be made generally known, sooner than it of necessity will be – & that will not be long I expect. Her voice and way of speaking, somehow in the upper part of her nose, is extremely like the Miss

255

Mitchells . . . It was a very interesting evening indeed. We left the 2 Authoresses together for part of it, but they soon joined us again, & she was so pleasant & so naive, that is to say so innocent and un Londony that we were quite charmed with her.

Harriet Martineau, Autobiography *(Smith, Elder & Co., 1877)*

Precisely as the time-piece struck six, a carriage stopped at the door; and after a minute of suspense, the footman announced 'Miss Brogden;' whereupon, my cousin informed me that it was Miss Brontë; for we had heard the name before, among others, in the way of conjecture. – I thought her the smallest creature I had ever seen (except at a fair) and her eyes blazed, as it seemed to me. She glanced quickly round; and my trumpet pointing me out, she held out her hand frankly and pleasantly. I introduced her, of course, to the family; and then came a moment which I had not anticipated. When she was seated by me on the sofa, she cast up at me such a look, – so loving, so appealing, – that, in connexion with her deep mourning dress, and the knowledge that she was the sole survivor of her family, I could with the utmost difficulty return her smile, or keep my composure. I should have been heartily glad to cry. We soon got on very well; and she appeared more at her ease that evening than I ever saw her afterwards, except when we were alone. My hostess was so considerate as to leave us together after tea, in case of C.B. desiring to have private conversation with me. She was glad of the opportunity to consult me about certain strictures of the reviewers which she did not understand, and had every desire to profit by. I did not approve the spirit of those strictures; but I thought them not entirely groundless. She besought me then, and repeatedly afterwards, to tell her, at whatever cost of pain to herself, if I saw her afford any justification of them.

★*Charlotte to George Smith; Haworth, 17 December 1849*

Decbr 17th 1849

My dear Sir
    I should not feel content if I omitted writing to you as well as to

17. Charlotte's letter of 8 January 1845 (see pp. 124–5) to Monsieur Heger, her Belgian professor at the Pensionnat Heger, describing her sufferings in being parted from him. In exasperation, or perhaps wishing to protect Charlotte from herself, Monsieur Heger tore up the letter and threw it away. It was found in his wastebin by Madame Heger who, suspicious about Charlotte's relationship with her husband, carefully stitched it back together again and preserved it for future use.

18. The Heger family, painted in 1848 by Ange François. From left to right, Monsieur Heger, whose portrait bears out Charlotte's description of him a few years earlier, Victorine, Prosper, Madame Heger, Louise (behind her mother, wearing a hat), the baby Paul, Marie and Claire.

19. A pine tree, drawn from a copy book by Emily in 1842 and presented by her to a fellow pupil at the Pensionnat Heger, Louise de Bassompierre.

20. Charlotte's study of a watermill, copied from an engraving or copy book while she was at Brussels. Though undated, the drawing was probably done in 1842, before Charlotte's obvious passion for Monsieur Heger soured her relationship with his wife. Ironically, in view of her later opinion of Madame Heger, it is inscribed 'A token of affection and respect to Madame Heger from one of her pupils.'

21. A pencil drawing by Anne of the church at Little Ouseburn which she attended with the Robinson family when she was a governess at Thorp Green (1840–45).

22. Unlike Anne, Branwell was not required to 'live in' with the Robinson family at Thorp Green, but was allowed the relative independence of lodgings at the former 'Monk's House' in the grounds of the Hall. Branwell drew this sketch on 25 August 1844, writing beneath it: 'This is only a rough pen and ink sketch of the back of my lodgings – the "<u>old</u> Hall," built about 1680 – or 85.'

23. An early photograph, probably taken about 1860, of St Nicholas' Cliff, Scarborough. Anne visited Scarborough several times with the Robinson family of Thorp Green and, at her express wish, returned there with Charlotte and Ellen in May 1849 when she was dying. During this last visit, the three women paid the entrance fee to walk over the toll-bridge (seen in the foreground), from which there were spectacular views. Anne died on 28 May at no. 2, The Cliff, which was part of the tall block of buildings just above the bridge in the photograph. Woods' Lodgings, as these were known, were demolished in the nineteenth century to make way for the Grand Hotel.

24. (Above) The interior of Haworth Old Church, which, with its three-decker pulpit and box pews, was demolished in 1879. The plaque on the far wall between the windows is a memorial to the Brontë family, whose vault lies nearby under the church floor. Aunt Branwell and all the Brontës, except Anne, who was interred in St Mary's churchyard at Scarborough, were buried here.

25 and 26. (Right) Emily's and Branwell's funeral cards, which were given out to mourners at their funerals and sent to inform absent relatives and friends of their deaths. Emily's was evidently printed by Joseph Fox, the confectioner who must have supplied her funeral tea. In the days before photography became commonplace, these cards were often preserved as memorials of the deceased. As there are none for Anne, it would appear that her death and burial in Scarborough precluded the printing of such cards: only Charlotte, Ellen, Margaret Wooler and the doctor who attended her deathbed were present at her funeral.

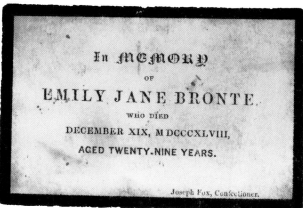

27. George Smith (1824–1901), head of the firm of Smith, Elder & Co., which published Charlotte's novels. Smith became a personal friend and regular correspondent of Charlotte's and may even have proposed marriage to her.

28. A previously unpublished photograph of William Smith Williams (1800–1875), reader at Smith, Elder & Co., whose friendship, encouragement and literary advice were highly valued by Charlotte.

29. Colnaghi's photograph of William Makepeace Thackeray (1811–63), 'the intellectual boa constrictor' who alternately enthralled and infuriated Charlotte. They met several times, with not entirely happy consequences for either party.

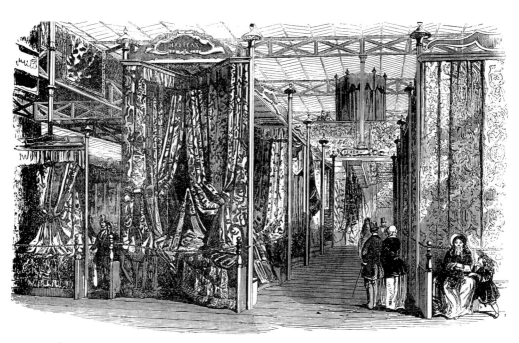

30. An engraving in the *Illustrated London News* of 5 July 1851, depicting the Halifax Court at the Great Exhibition. Though dismissed by the paper as 'an indifferent display', the magnificence of the draped hangings of locally produced cloth justifies Charlotte's description of the Exhibition as 'a mighty Vanity Fair'.

31. Arthur Bell Nicholls (1819–1906), curate of Haworth from 1845, who married Charlotte in 1854. After her death the following year, he remained at Haworth for the next six years, devoting himself to her father and his parish. When Patrick died in 1861, Arthur returned to live permanently in his native Ireland.

32. The Reverend Patrick Brontë (1777–1861), a photograph taken after he had outlived all his family, probably in about 1860. His neckcloth, which had once, when fashionable, been modest in size, was now of vast proportions due to his belief that it protected him from bronchial complaints. Note also his spectacles: though frequently believed to be blind by his visitors, Patrick never completely lost his sight, but his eyes were weak and liable to cataract.

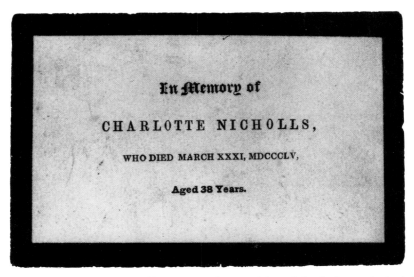

In Memory of

CHARLOTTE NICHOLLS,

WHO DIED MARCH XXXI, MDCCCLV,

Aged 38 Years.

33. Charlotte's funeral card, like that of her sister Emily, was plain and simple. Interestingly, it is also a graphic example of her widower's dislike of the prurient popular interest in his wife because of her literary fame. Though Charlotte always signed herself 'Charlotte Brontë Nicholls' after her marriage, Arthur preferred the simpler – and anonymous – 'Charlotte Nicholls' for her memorial card.

34. Haworth churchyard, seen from the Sunday school. The trees were not there in the Brontës' day (they were planted in the 1870s), but the characteristic box tombs still fill the churchyard as they did then. Half obscured by the base of the large tree on the right is the tilted gravestone of Tabby Aykroyd (d. 1855), the Brontës' servant for thirty years. Behind the tree can also be seen a corner of the Parsonage garden wall.

your Mother, for I must tell you as well as her how much the pleasure of my late visit was enhanced by her most considerate attention and goodness. As to yourself – what can I say? Nothing. And it is as well: words are not at all needed: very easy is it to discover that with you to gratify others is to gratify yourself; to serve others is to afford yourself a pleasure. I hope this may long be the case, and I wish the Leigh Hunts and the Jameses may never spoil your nature. I suppose you will experience your share of ingratitude and encroachment – but do not let them alter you. Happily they are the less likely to do this because you are half a Scotchman and therefore must have inherited a fair share of prudence to qualify your generosity, and of caution to protect your benevolence. Currer Bell bids you farewell for the present

CB –

G Smith Esq.

Charlotte to William Smith Williams; Haworth, 19 December 1849

Brief as my visit to London was – it must for me be memorable. I sometimes fancied myself in a dream: I could scarcely credit the reality of what passed: for instance when I walked into the room and put my hand into Miss Martineau's the action of saluting her and the fact of her presence seemed visionary. Again when Mr Thackeray was announced and I saw him enter, looked up at his tall figure, heard his voice the whole incident was truly dream-like – I was only certain it was true because I became miserably destitute of self-possession. Amour propre suffers terribly under such circumstances woe to him that thinks of himself in the presence of intellectual greatness! Had I not been obliged to speak, I could have managed well, but it behoved me to answer when addressed and the effort was torture – I spoke stupidly.

★*Charlotte to Ellen; Haworth, 19 December 1849*

Here I am at Haworth once more. I feel as if I had come out of an exciting whirl – Not that the hurry or stimulus would have seemed

257

much to one accustomed to society and change – but to me they were very marked. My strength and spirits too often proved quite insufficient for the demand on their exertion – I used to bear up as well and as long as I possibly could – for whenever I flagged I could see Mr Smith became disturbed – he always thought something had been said or done to annoy me – which never once happened – for I met with perfect good-breeding even from antagonists – men who had done their best or worst to write me down. I explained to him over and over again that my occasional silence was only failure of the power to talk – never of the will – but still he always seemed to fear there was another cause underneath.

Mrs Smith is rather a stern woman – but she has sense and discrimination – she watched me very narrowly – when I was surrounded by gentlemen – she never took her eye from me – I liked the surveillance – both when it kept guard over me amongst many or only with her cherished and valued Son – She soon – I am convinced – saw in what light I viewed both her George and all the rest – Thackeray included. Her George is a very fine specimen of a young English Man of business – so I regard him and I am proud to be one of his props.

A couple of days after Christmas, Ellen Nussey arrived at the Parsonage on a visit that was to last three weeks. For the first time, Charlotte was able to tell her friend all about her other life as an authoress and describe to her the impressions she had gained of London and its literary circles.

Charlotte to William Smith Williams; Haworth, 3 January 1850

I have to acknowledge the receipt of the 'Morning Chronicle' with a good review – and of the 'Church of Engl[an]d Quarterly' and the 'Westminster' with bad ones: I have also to thank you for your letter which would have been answered sooner had I been alone, but just now I am enjoying the treat of my friend Ellen's society and she makes me indolent and negligent – I am too busy talking to her all day to do anything else. You allude to the subject of female-friendships and express wonder at the infrequency of sincere attachments amongst women – As to married women, I can well understand that they should be absorbed in their husbands and children – but single women often like each other much and derive great solace from their mutual regard –. Friendship however is a plant which cannot be forced – true friendship is no gourd springing up in a night and withering in a day. When I first saw Ellen I did not care for her – we were schoolfellows – in the course of time we learnt each others faults and good points – we were contrasts – still we suited – affection was first a germ, then a sapling – then a strong tree: now – no new friend, however lofty or profound in intellect – not even Miss Martineau herself – could be to me what Ellen is, yet she is no more than a conscientious, observant, calm, well-bred Yorkshire girl. She is without romance – if she attempts to read poetry – or poetic prose aloud – I am irritated and deprive her of the book – if she talks of it I stop my ears – but she is good – she is true – she is faithful and I love her.

Canon William Margetson Heald, vicar of Birstall, to Ellen; Birstall, 8 January 1850

Dear Ellen,

Fame says you are on a visit with the renowned Currer Bell, the 'great-unknown' of the present day. The celebrated 'Shirley' has just found its way hither – and as one always reads a book with more interest when one has a correct insight into the writer's designs, I write to ask a favour, which I ought not to be regarded as presumptuous in saying that I think I have a species of claim to ask – on the ground of a sort of 'poetical justice.' The interpretation of this enigma is – that the story goes that either I or my father, I do not exactly know which, are part of 'Currer Bell's' stock in trade under the title of Mr Hall – In that Mr Hall is represented as black, bilious & of dismal aspect, stooping a trifle & indulging a little now & then in the indigenous dialect – this seems to sit very well on your humble servant – other traits do better for my good father than myself – However – though I had no idea that I should ever be made a means to amuse the public, Currer Bell is perfectly welcome to what she can make of so unpromising a subject – But I think I have a fair claim in return to be let into the secret of the company I have got into – Some of them are good enough to tell & need no Oedipus to solve the riddle – I can tabulate for instance The Yorke family for the Taylors, Mr Moore – Mr Cartwright & Mr Helstone is clearly meant for Mr Roberson – tho the authoress has evidently got her idea of his character thro an unfavourable medium & does not understand the full value of one of the most admirable characters I ever knew or expect to know – Mary thinks she descries Cecilia Crowther & Miss Johnson (afterwards Mrs Westerman) in two old maids –

Now pray get us a full light on all other names & localities that are adumbrated in this said 'Shirley.' When some of the prominent characters will be recognised by every one who knows our quarters, there can be no harm in letting one know who may be intended by the rest – &, if necessary, I will bear Currer Bell harmless & not let the world know that I have my intelligence from head quarters –

In January 1850, one of Charlotte's correspondents, the critic G. H. Lewes, published an anonymous review of *Shirley* which mortified her. Inexcusably, after Charlotte had made her views on the question of her sex quite clear, Lewes not only castigated *Shirley* on the grounds of its author's femininity but also made public the knowledge he had acquired from her in their private correspondence.

G. H. Lewes, review of Shirley *in the* Edinburgh Review, *January 1850*

We take Currer Bell to be one of the most remarkable of *female* writers; and believe it is now scarcely a secret that Currer Bell is the pseudonyme of a woman. An eminent contemporary, indeed, has employed the sharp vivacity of a female pen to prove 'upon irresistible evidence' that 'Jane Eyre' *must be* the work of a man! But all that 'irresistible evidence' is set aside by the simple fact that Currer Bell *is* a woman. We never, for our own parts, had a moment's doubt on the subject . . . The fair and ingenious critic was misled by her own acuteness in the perception of details; and misled also in some other way, and more uncharitably, in concluding that the *author* of 'Jane Eyre' was a heathen educated among heathens, – the *fact* being, that the *authoress* is the daughter of a clergyman!

Faults enough [*Jane Eyre*] has undoubtedly: faults of conception, faults of taste, faults of ignorance, but in spite of all, it remains a book of singular fascination. A more masculine book, in the sense of vigour, was never written. Indeed that vigour often amounts to coarseness, – and is certainly the very antipode to 'lady-like.'

This same over-masculine vigour is even more prominent in 'Shirley,' and does not increase the pleasantness of the book. A pleasant book, indeed, we are not sure that we can style it. Power it has unquestionably, and interest too, of a peculiar sort; but not the agreeableness of a work of art . . . 'Shirley' is inferior to 'Jane Eyre' in several important points. It is not quite so true; and it is not so fascinating. It does not so rivet the reader's attention, nor hurry him through all obstacles of improbability, with so keen a sympathy in its reality. It is even coarser in texture, too, and not unfrequently flippant; while the characters are almost all disagreeable, and exhibit intolerable rudeness of manner . . . Again we say that 'Shirley' cannot be received as a work of art. It is not a picture; but a portfolio of random sketches for one or more pictures . . . Power is stamped on various parts of it; power unmistakeable, but often misapplied. Currer Bell has much yet to learn, – and, especially, the discipline of her own tumultuous energies. She must learn also to sacrifice a little of her Yorkshire roughness to the demands of good taste: neither saturating her writings with such rudeness and offensive harshness, nor suffering her style to wander into such vulgarities as would be inexcusable – even in a man.

Charlotte to William Smith Williams; Haworth, 10 January 1850

I have received and perused the 'Edinburgh Review' – it is very brutal and savage. I am not angry with Lewes – but I wish in future he would let me alone – and not write again what makes me feel so cold and sick as I am feeling just now –

Charlotte to G. H. Lewes; Haworth, January 1850

I can be on my guard against my enemies, but God deliver me from my friends!

Currer Bell

G H Lewes Esqr

Charlotte to G. H. Lewes; Haworth, 19 January 1850

My dear Sir

I will tell you why I was so hurt by that review in the Edinburgh; not because its criticism was keen or its blame sometimes severe; not because its praise was stinted (for indeed I think you give me quite as much praise as I deserve) but because, after I had said earnestly that I wished critics would judge me as an <u>author</u> not as a woman, you so roughly – I even thought – so cruelly handled the question of sex. I daresay you meant no harm, and perhaps you will not now be able to understand why I was so grieved at, what you will probably deem such a trifle; but grieved I was, and indignant too.

There was a passage or two which you did quite wrong to write.

However I will not bear malice against you for it: I know what your nature is; it is not a bad or an unkind one, though you would often jar terribly on some feelings with whose recoil and quiver you could not possibly sympathize. I imagine you are both enthusiastic and implacable, as you are at once sagacious and careless. You know much and discover much, but you are in such a hurry to tell it all, you never give yourself time to think how your reckless eloquence may affect others, and, what is more, if you knew how it did affect them you would not much care.

However I shake hands with you: You have some excellent points; you can be generous: I still feel angry and think I do well to be angry, but it is the anger one experiences for rough play rather than for foul play.

I am yours with a certain respect and more chagrin
Currer Bell

Charlotte could no longer maintain her anonymity, even at home, where her secret was fast becoming an open one. Now she had to contend with the fact that people she knew were reading her books – and were unable to dissociate Charlotte Brontë from Currer Bell. Even the Reverend Arthur Bell Nicholls, Patrick's curate since 1845, who was himself depicted in *Shirley*, could not resist the temptation.

Charlotte to Ellen; Haworth, 19 January 1850

All you tell me about the notoriety of 'Shirley' in Dewsbury &c. is almost as good as an emetic to me – I should really 'go off at side' if I thought too much about it. Mr Nicholls having finished 'Jane Eyre' is now crying out for the 'other book' – he is to have it next week – much good may it do him.

Charlotte to Ellen; Haworth, 28 January 1850

Mr Nicholls has finished reading 'Shirley'   he is delighted with it – John Brown's wife seriously thought he had gone wrong in the head as she heard him giving vent to roars of laughter as he sat alone – clapping his hands and stamping on the floor. He would read all the scenes about the curates aloud to papa – he triumphed in his own character.

What Mr Grant will say is another question. No matter.

Charlotte to Ellen; Haworth, 5 February 1850

Martha came in yesterday – puffing and blowing and much excited – 'I've heard sich news' she began – 'What about?' 'Please ma'am you've been and written two books – the grandest books that ever was seen – My Father has heard it at Halifax and Mr George Taylor and Mr Greenwood and Mr Merrall at Bradford – and they are going to have a meeting at the Mechanics' Institute and to settle about ordering them.' 'Hold your tongue, Martha, and be off.' I fell into a cold sweat. 'Jane Eyre' will be read by John Brown by Mrs Taylor and Betty – God help keep & deliver me!

★★*Charlotte to Mr Lovejoy, a librarian; Haworth, 5 February 1850*

It is respectfully suggested to Mr Lovejoy that as 'Currer Bell' is the only name which has been acknowledged in connection with the authorship of 'Jane Eyre' and 'Shirley' that name alone can with propriety be printed in a Library Catalogue. Rumour must at all times be regarded as an unsafe guide.

Charlotte to Margaret Wooler; Haworth, 14 February 1850

As to 'Jane Eyre' and 'Shirley', the books are taking their chance in the world, getting abused here, praised there, knocked about everywhere. Currer Bell does not break his heart about the opinion of a discriminating public; if his friends object to the works he is sorry – but he could change nothing; what is written, is written, and in his conscience he is very quiet.

I am sorry the Clergy do not like the doctrine of Universal Salvation; I think it a great pity for their sakes, but surely they are not so unreasonable as to expect me to deny or suppress what I believe the truth!

Some of the clergy will not like 'Shirley'; I confess the work has one prevailing fault – that of too tenderly and partially veiling the errors of 'the Curates.' Had Currer Bell written all he has seen and knows concerning those worthies – a singular work would have been the result.

I need not thank you for the sincerity and frankness with which you have spoken to me about 'Jane Eyre.' Of course, knowing you as I do, I was certain that whenever you did speak, you would speak sincerely. You seem to think that I had feared some loss in your esteem owing to my being the reputed Author of this book – such a fear – one so unjust to both you and myself, never crossed my mind. When I was in London – a woman whose celebrity is not wider than her moral standing is elevated – and in each point she has no living superior – said to me 'I have ever observed that it is to the coarse-minded alone – "Jane Eyre" is coarse.' This remark tallied with what I had myself noticed; I felt its truth; And, feeling it, be assured my dear Miss Wooler – I was at ease on the secret opinion of <u>your</u> heart – You may and do object to certain phrases, exclamations &c. phrases and exclamations however, which, viewing them from an artistic point of view, my judgement ratifies as consistent and characteristic – but I have not hitherto fancied that you have withdrawn from me your esteem.

I own when I hear any one making an exaggerated outcry against 'Jane Eyre' immediately in my own mind I come to no very complimentary conclusion respecting the natural quality of that persons taste and propensities.

Charlotte to Ellen; Haworth, 16 February 1850

The Haworth People have been making great fools of themselves about 'Shirley' – they take it in an enthusiastic light – when they got the vols. at the Mech[anics'] Instit[utio]n all the members wanted them – they cast lots for the whole three – and whoever got a vol. was only allowed to keep it two days and to be fined a shilling per diem for longer detention – It would be mere nonsense and vanity to tell you what they say . . . I had rather a foolish letter from Miss Wooler the other day – some things in it nettled me – especially an unnecessarily earnest assurance that in spite of all I had gone and done in the writing line – I still retained a place in her esteem. My answer took strong and high ground at once I said I had been troubled by no doubts on the subject – that I neither did myself nor her the injustice to suppose there was anything in what I had written to incur the just forfeiture of esteem. I was aware – I intimated – that some persons thought proper to take exceptions at 'Jane Eyre' – and that for their own sakes I was sorry as I invariably found them individuals in whom the animal largely predominated over the intellectual – persons by nature coarse, by inclination sensual, whatever they might be by education and principle.

Chapter Twelve

1850

Charlotte to Ellen; Haworth, 16 February 1850

Dear Nell

I believe I should have written to you before but I don't know what heaviness of spirit has beset me of late, made my faculties dull, made rest weariness and occupation burdensome. Now and then the silence of the house – the solitude of the room has pressed on me with a weight I found it difficult to bear – and Recollection has not failed to be as alert, poignant, obtrusive as other feelings were languid. I attribute this state of things partly to the weather – Quicksilver invariably falls low in storms and high winds – and I have ere this been warned of approaching disturbance in the atmosphere by a sense of bodily weakness and deep, heavy mental sadness – such as some would call <u>presentiment</u> – presentiment indeed it is – but not at all supernatural . . . I have had no letters from London for a long time – and am very much ashamed of myself to find – now when that stimulus is withdrawn – how dependent upon it I had become – I cannot help feeling something of the excitement of expectation till post-hour comes and when day after day it brings nothing – I get low. This is a stupid, disgraceful, unmeaning State of things – I feel bitterly enraged at my own dependence and folly – It is so bad for the mind to be quite alone – to have none with whom to talk over little crosses and disappointments and laugh them away. If I could write I daresay I should be better but I cannot write a line. However (D.V.) I shall contend against the idiocy . . . A few days since a little incident happened which curiously touched me. Papa put into my hands a little packet of letters and papers – telling me that they were Mamma's and that I might read them – I did read them in a frame of mind I cannot describe – the papers were yellow with time all having been written before I was born – it was strange to peruse now for the first time the records of a mind whence my own sprang – and most strange – and at once sad and sweet to find that mind of a truly fine, pure and elevated order. They were written to papa before they were married – there is a rectitude, a refinement, a constancy, a modesty, a sense – a gentleness about them indescribable. I wished She had lived and that I had known her.

Maria Branwell's letters to Patrick were all written in the five months between their engagement and marriage on 29 December 1812. The affianced couple had only met for the first time earlier in that year when Maria, an orphan from Penzance, came to stay with her uncle, John Fennell, headmaster of Woodhouse Grove School, near Bradford. Despite the delicacy of her situation, Maria handled it with tact and discretion.

Maria Branwell to Patrick; Woodhouse Grove, Rawdon, 26 August 1812

My dear friend,

This address is sufficient to convince you that I not only permit, but approve of yours to me – I do indeed consider you as my *friend*; yet, when I consider how short a time I have had the pleasure of knowing you, I start at my own rashness, my heart fails, and did I not think that you would be disappointed and grieved at it, I believe I should be ready to spare myself the task of writing. Do not think that I am so wavering as to repent of what I have already said. No, believe me, this will never be the case, unless you give me cause for it. You need not fear that you have been mistaken in my character. If I know anything of myself, I am incapable of making an ungenerous return to the smallest degree of kindness, much less to you whose attentions and conduct have been so particularly obliging. I will frankly confess that your behaviour and what I have seen and heard of your character has excited my warmest esteem and regard, and be assured you shall never have cause to repent of any confidence you may think proper to place in me, and that it will always be my endeavour to deserve the good opinion which you have formed, although human weakness may in some instances cause me to fall short. In giving you these assurances I do not depend upon my own strength, but I look to Him who has been my unerring guide through life, and in whose continued protection and assistance I confidently trust . . . I will now candidly answer your questions. The <u>politeness of others</u> can never make me forget your kind attentions, neither can I <u>walk our accustomed rounds</u> without thinking on you, and, why should I be ashamed to add, wishing for your presence. If you knew what were my feelings whilst writing this you would pity me. I wish to write the truth and give you satisfaction, yet fear to go too far, and exceed the bounds of propriety. But whatever I may say or write I will <u>never deceive</u> you, or <u>exceed the truth</u>.

Maria Branwell to Patrick; Woodhouse Grove, Rawdon,
18 September 1812

How readily do I comply with my dear Mr B's request! You see, you have only to express your wishes, and as far as my power extends I hesitate not to fulfil them. My heart tells me that it will always be my pride and pleasure to contribute to your happiness, nor do I fear that this will ever be inconsistent with my duty as a Christian. My esteem for you and my confidence in you is so great, that I firmly believe you will never exact anything from me which I could not conscientiously perform. I shall in future look to you for assistance and instruction whenever I may need them, and hope you will never withhold from me any advice or caution you may see necessary.

For some years I have been perfectly my own mistress, subject to no <u>control</u> whatever – so far from it, that my sisters who are many years older than myself, and even my dear mother, used to consult me in every case of importance, and scarcely ever doubted the propriety of my opinions and actions. Perhaps you will be ready to accuse me of vanity in mentioning this, but you must consider that I do not <u>boast</u> of it, I have many times felt it a disadvantage; and although, I thank God, it never led me into error, yet, in circumstances of perplexity and doubt, I have deeply felt the want of a guide and instructor.

At such times I have seen and felt the necessity of supernatural aid, and by fervent applications to a throne of grace I have experienced that my heavenly Father is able and willing to supply the place of every earthly friend. I shall now no longer feel this want, this sense of helpless weakness, for I believe a kind Providence has intended that I shall find in you every earthly friend united; nor do I fear to trust myself under your protection, or shrink from your control. It is pleasant to be subject to those we love, especially when they never exert their authority but for the good of the subject. How few would write in this way! But I do not fear that <u>you</u> will make a bad use of it. You tell me to write my thoughts, and thus as they occur I freely let my pen run away with them.

Maria Branwell to Patrick; Woodhouse Grove, Rawdon,
23 September 1812

I already feel a kind of participation in all that concerns you. All praises and censures bestowed on you must equally affect me. Your joys and sorrows must be mine. Thus shall the one be increased and the other diminished. While this is the case we shall, I hope, always find 'life's cares' to be 'comforts.' And may we feel every trial and distress, for such must be our lot at times, bind us nearer to God and to each other! My heart earnestly joins in your comprehensive prayers. I trust they will unitedly ascend to a throne of grace, and through the Redeemer's merits procure for us peace and happiness here and a life of eternal felicity hereafter. Oh, what sacred pleasure there is in the idea of spending an eternity together in perfect and uninterrupted bliss!

Maria Branwell to Patrick; Woodhouse Grove, Rawdon, 3 October 1812

Two months ago I could not possibly have believed that you would ever engross so much of my thoughts and affections, and far less could I have thought that I should be so forward as to tell you so. I believe I must forbid you to come here again unless you can assure me that you will not steal any more of my regard.

Maria Branwell to Patrick; Woodhouse Grove, Rawdon,
21 October 1812

With the sincerest pleasure do I retire from company to converse with him whom I love beyond all others. Could my beloved friend see my heart he would then be convinced that the affection I bear him is not at all inferior to that which he feels for me – indeed I sometimes think that in truth and constancy it excels. But do not think from this that I entertain any suspicions of your sincerity – no, I firmly believe you to be sincere and generous, and doubt not in the least that you feel all you express. In return, I entreat that you will do me the justice to believe that you have not only a very large portion of my affection and esteem, but all that I am capable of feeling, and from henceforth measure my feelings by your own. Unless my love for you were very great how could I so contentedly give up my home and all my friends – a home I loved so much that I have often thought nothing could bribe me to renounce it for any great length of time together, and friends with whom I have been so long accustomed to share all the vicissitudes of joy and sorrow? Yet these have lost their weight, and though I cannot always think of them without a sigh, yet the anticipation of sharing with you all the pleasures and pains, the cares and anxieties of life, of contributing to your comfort and becoming the companion of your pilgrimage, is more delightful to me than any other prospect which this world can possibly present.

Maria Branwell to Patrick; Woodhouse Grove, Rawdon,
18 November 1812

My dear saucy Pat, . . . I suppose you never expected to be much the richer for me but I am sorry to inform you that I am still poorer than I thought myself. – I mentioned having sent for my books clothes, &c. On Saturday ev[enin]g about the time when you were writing the description of your imaginary shipwreck, I was reading & feeling the effects of a real one, having then received a letter from my sister giving me an account of the vessel in which she had sent my box, being stranded on the coast of Devonshire, in consequence of which the box was dashed to pieces with the violence of the sea & all my little property, with the exception of a very few articles, swallowed up in the mighty deep – If this should not prove the prelude to something worse, I shall think little of it, as it is the first disastrous circumstance which has occurred since I left my home, & having been so highly favored it would be highly ungrateful in me were I to suffer this to dwell much on my mind . . . Both the Dr and his lady very much wish to know what kind of address we make use of in our letters to each other – I think they would scarcely hit on this!!

Reading her long-dead mother's cheerful, chatty letters, so full of optimism and anticipation, can have done little to lift Charlotte's low spirits. Her sense of isolation had become overpowering and, because she had no work on hand, she could not take refuge in her writing. It was therefore with mixed feelings that she had her first encounter with Sir James Kay Shuttleworth, a former secretary to the Committee of the Council on Education, who lived just over the border in Lancashire and was determined to patronize the author so fortuitously discovered on his doorstep.

Charlotte to Ellen; Haworth, 5 March 1850

Various folks are beginning to come boring to Haworth, on the wise errand of seeing the scenery described in 'Jane Eyre' and 'Shirley'; amongst others, Sir J K Shuttleworth and Lady Shuttleworth have persisted in coming; they were here on Friday. The baronet looks in vigorous health, he scarcely appears more than thirty-five, but he says he is forty-four; Lady Shuttleworth is rather handsome and still young. They were both quite unpretending, etc. When here they again urged me to visit them. Papa took their side at once, would not hear of my refusing; I must go, – this left me without plea or defence. I consented to go for three days, they wanted me to return with them in the carriage, but I pleaded off till to-morrow. I wish it was well over.

Charlotte to William Smith Williams; Haworth, 16 March 1850

I mentioned – I think – that we had had one or two visitors at Haworth lately – amongst them were Sir James Kaye Shuttleworth and his Lady – before departing they exacted a promise that I would visit them at Gawthorpe Hall their residence on the borders of East Lancashire. I went reluctantly for it is always a difficult and painful thing to me to meet the advances of people whose kindness I am in no position to repay. Sir James is a man of polished manners with clear intellect and highly cultivated mind. On the whole I got on very well with him; his health is just now somewhat broken by his severe official labours, and the quiet drives to old ruins and old halls situated amongst older hills and woods, the dialogues (perhaps I should rather say monologues for I listened far more than I talked) by the fireside in his antique oak-panelled drawing-room, while they suited him, did not too much oppress and exhaust me – The house too is very much to my taste – near three centuries old, grey, stately and picturesque; on the whole – now that the visit is over, I do not regret having paid it – The worst of it is that there is now some menace hanging over my head of an invitation to go to them in London during the season – this, which would doubtless be a great enjoyment to some people, is a perfect terror to me.

Charlotte to George Smith; Haworth, 16 March 1850

I return Mr Thornton Hunt's note after reading it carefully. I tried very hard to understand all he says about 'Art', but, to speak truth, my efforts were crowned with incomplete success. There is a certain jargon in use amongst critics on this point, through which it is physically and morally impossible for me to see daylight – One thing however I see plainly enough, and that is Mr Currer Bell needs improvement and ought to strive after it – and this (D.V.) he honestly intends to do – taking his time, however – and following as his guides Nature and Truth; if these lead to what the Critics call 'Art' it is all very well – but if not that grand desideratum has no chance of being run after or caught. The puzzle is that while the people in the South object to my delineation of Northern life and manners, the people of Yorkshire and Lancashire approve: they say it is precisely that contrast of rough nature with highly artificial cultivation which forms one of their main characteristics; Such or something very similar has been the observation made to me lately whilst I have been from home by members of some of the ancient East Lancashire families whose mansions lie on the hilly borderland between the two counties – the question arises whether do the London Critics or the old Northern Squires understand the matter best?

Charlotte to Ellen; Haworth, 19 March 1850

The brief absence from home – though in some respects trying and painful in itself – has I think given a better tone to my spirits – All through the month of Feb[ruar]y – I had a crushing time of it – I could not escape from or rise above certain most mournful recollections – the last days – the sufferings – the remembered words – most sorrowful to me – of those who – Faith assures me – are now happy. At evening – and bedtime such thoughts would haunt me – bringing a weary heartache.

J. Berry, of Spencer, Massachusetts, to the Editor of the Boston Weekly Museum; *2 March 1850*

I wish to say a word about the author of 'Jane Eyre' . . . I think I was 'born and bred' within a stone's throw of her early home and her father's residence. Her father is Rector of Haworth, (the Brierfield of Shirley), a village ten miles west of Bradford Yorks. He has been minister of that parish for about thirty years, (he christened me), and has been much respected by church-going folks. I have heard him preach often. During the last few years he has not preached much, his eyesight having failed him, which he nearly lost for a while. He had it restored, however, after resorting to an eye-imfirmary. [*sic*] He has a large head and strongly marked features; but he is now old, and his hair is white.

As my days were passed mostly in the mill, I have no very particular recollection of his children. I know of only three, two daughters and a son. The son came home a year or two ago, having just finished his education. He was thought to be an able artist.

The two sisters have lived in Bradford for a number of years, although they have made the tour of Europe. When at home, they might often be seen together, taking their daily walk on the Fieldhead foot-path, with their favourite dog. The Rectory stands just on top of the churchyard, as described in 'Shirley.' The descriptions, in the locality, are true to nature; and her names are real. I know some of the characters in 'Shirley' as well as I know my own father.

I would like to tell you much about that neighborhood; but I am a factory boy, and must not attempt it. The authoress is young, about 28; and, as Airedale is as full of romantic incident as Tweedale, the public may expect much more from her.

Charlotte to Ellen; Haworth, 30 March 1850

I enclose a slip of newspaper for your amusement – me it both amused and touched – for it alludes to some who are in this world no longer. It is an extract from an American Paper – and is written by an emigrant from Haworth – you will find it a curious mixture of truth and inaccuracy, return it when you write again. I also send you for perusal an opinion of 'Jane Eyre' written by a <u>working man</u> in this village; rather I should say a record of the feelings the book excited in the poor fellow's mind; it was not written for my inspection nor does the writer now know that his little document has by intricate ways – come into my possession – and I have forced those who gave it, to promise that they will never inform him of this circumstance. He is a modest, thoughtful, feeling, reading being – to whom I have spoken perhaps about three times in the course of my life – his delicate health renders him incapable of hard or close labour, he and his family are often under the pressure of want. He feared that if 'Miss Brontë saw what he had written she would laugh it to scorn' but Miss Brontë considers it one of the highest, because one of the most truthful and artless tributes her work has yet received, you must return this likewise; I do you great honour in shewing it to you.

Charlotte to Amelia Ringrose, fiancée of Joe Taylor; Haworth,
31 March 1850

Experience has taught me to enter fully into all you say respecting your poor Mamma's last illness and death. It is indeed difficult under such circumstances for near relatives to realize the actual parting of soul from body. The longer we have watched the gradual attentuation of the thread of life, the more its final severance seems to take us by surprise. And then too, most truly do you describe the oblivion of faults which succeeds to Death. No sooner are the eyes grown dim, no sooner is the pulse stilled than we forget what anxiety, what anguish, what shame the frailties and vices of that poor unconscious mould of clay once caused us; yearning love and bitter pity are the only sentiments the heart admits, but with these, for a time, it is sorely oppressed. Sometimes, in thinking over this, I have said to myself: If man can so forgive his fellow, how much more shall God pardon his creature?

The bustle with which you are now surrounded is painful in one sense, but – in another – I hope it will be profitable. We should never shrink with cowardice from the contemplation of Death, but after a near view, an actual contact with that King of terrors it is not good to be left unoccupied and solitary to brood over his awful lineaments. Often when I am alone, I try with all my might to look beyond the grave, to follow my dear Sisters and my poor brother to that better world where – I trust – they are all now happy, but still, dear Amelia, I cannot help recalling all the details of the weeks of sickness, of the mortal conflict, of the last difficult agony: there are moments when I know not whither to turn or what to do, so sharp, so dark and distressing are these remembrances, so afflicted am I that beings so loved should have had to pass out of Time into Eternity – by a track so rough and painful. I ought not to write this, but you have a kind heart and will forgive me. Mention not a word of it to Ellen; it is a relief to write it down, but it would be great pain to talk it over.

Mary Taylor to Charlotte; Wellington, New Zealand, 5 April 1850

About a week since I received your last melancholy letter with the account of Ann's death and y[ou]r utter indifference to everything, even to the success of your last book. Though you do not say this it is pretty plain to be seen from the style of your letter. It seems to me hard indeed that you who would succeed better than anyone in making friends and keeping them should be condemned to solitude from you[r] poverty. To no one would money bring more happiness, for no one would use it better than you would. – For me with my headlong selfindulgent habits I am perhaps better without it, but I am convinced it would give you great and noble pleasures. Look out then for success in writing. You ought to care as much for that as you do for going to Heaven. Though the advantages of being employed appear to you now the best part of the business you will soon please God have other enjoyments from your success. Railway shares will rise, your books will sell and you will acquire influence and power and then most certainly you will find something to use it in which will interest you and make you exert yourself.

★*Charlotte to William Smith Williams; Haworth, 3 April 1850*

As to the 'Times,' as you say – the acrimony of its critique has proved, in some measure, its own antidote; to have been more effective – it should have been juster. I think it has had little weight here in the North; it may be that annoying remarks, if made, are not suffered to reach my ear, but certainly, while I have heard little condemnatory of 'Shirley' – more than once have I been deeply moved by manifestations of even enthusiastic approbation. I deem it unwise to dwell much on these matters, but for once I must permit myself to remark that the generous pride many of the Yorkshire people have taken in the matter has been such as to awake and claim my gratitude – especially since it has afforded a source of reviving pleasure to my Father in his old age. The very Curates – poor fellows! shew no resentment; each characteristically finds solace for his own wounds in crowing over his brethren. Mr Donne was – at first, a little disturbed; for a week or two He fidgetted about the neighbourhood in some disquietude – but he is now soothed down, only yesterday I had the pleasure of making him a comfortable cup of tea and seeing him sip it with revived complacency. It is a curious fact that since he read 'Shirley' he has come to the house oftener than ever and been remarkably meek and assiduous to please – Some people's natures are veritable enigmas – I quite expected to have one good scene at the least with him, but as yet nothing of the sort has occurred – and if the other curates do not tease him into irritation, he will remain quiet now.

Charlotte to William Smith Williams; Haworth, 12 April 1850

The perusal of Southey's Life has lately afforded me much pleasure; the autobiography with which it commences is deeply interesting and the letters which follow are scarcely less so, disclosing as they do a character most estimable in its integrity and a nature most amiable in its benevolence, as well as a mind admirable in its talent. Some people assert that Genius is inconsistent with domestic happiness, and yet Southey was happy at home and made his home happy; he not only loved his wife and children though he was a poet, but he loved them the better because he was a poet. He seems to have been without taint of worldliness; London, with its pomps and vanities, learned coteries with their dry pedantry rather scared than attracted him; he found his prime glory in his genius, and his chief felicity in home-affections. I like Southey.

I have likewise read one of Miss Austen's works 'Emma' – read it with interest and with just the degree of admiration which Miss Austen herself would have thought sensible and suitable – anything like warmth or enthusiasm; anything energetic, poignant, heart-felt, is utterly out of place in commending these works: all such demonstration the authoress would have met with a well-bred sneer, would have calmly scorned as outré and extravagant. She does her business of delineating the surface of the lives of genteel English people curiously well; there is a Chinese fidelity, a miniature delicacy in the painting: she ruffles her reader by nothing vehement, disturbs him by nothing profound: the Passions are perfectly unknown to her; she rejects even a speaking acquaintance with that stormy

Sisterhood; even to the Feelings she vouchsafes no more than an occasional graceful but distant recognition; too frequent converse with them would ruffle the smooth elegance of her progress. Her business is not half so much with the human heart as with the human eyes, mouth, hands and feet; what sees keenly, speaks aptly, moves flexibly, it suits her to study, but what throbs fast and full, though hidden, what the blood rushes through, what is the unseen Seat of Life and the sentient target of Death – this Miss Austen ignores; she no more, with her mind's eye, beholds the heart of her race than each man, with bodily vision sees the heart in his heaving breast. Jane Austen was a complete and most sensible lady, but a very incomplete, and rather insensible (not senseless) woman, if this is heresy – I cannot help it. If I said it to some people (Lewes for instance) they would directly accuse me of advocating exaggerated heroics, but I am not afraid of your falling into any such vulgar error.

Mary Taylor to Charlotte; Wellington, New Zealand, c. 29 April 1850

I have seen some extracts from 'Shirley' in which you talk of women working. And this first duty, this great necessity you seem to think that some women may indulge in – if they give up marriage & don't make themselves too disagreeable to the other sex. You are a coward & a traitor. A woman who works is by that alone better than one who does not & a woman who does not happen to be rich & who still earns no money & does not wish to do so, is guilty of a great fault – almost a crime – A dereliction of duty which leads rapidly and almost certainly to all manner of degradation. It is very wrong of you to plead for toleration for workers on the ground of their being in peculiar circumstances & few in number or singular in disposition. Work or degradation is the lot of all except the very small number born to wealth.

Charlotte had been planning another trip to London for some time. Her own preference was to stay with the Smith family again, but Sir James Kay Shuttleworth was insistent that she should travel there under his wing and, through him, be introduced to London society.

★*Charlotte to Ellen; Haworth, 11 May 1850*

Last Friday was the day appointed for me to go to Lancashire, but I did not think Papa well enough to be left and accordingly begged Sir James & his lady to return to Town without me. It was arranged that we were to stay at several of their friends' and relations' houses on the way – a week or more would have been taken up in the journey – I cannot say that I regret having missed this ordeal, I would as lief have walked amongst red-hot ploughshares, but I do regret one great treat which I shall now miss. Next Wednesday is the Anniversary dinner of the Royal Literary Fund Society held in Freemasons' Hall – Octavian Blewitt – the Secretary – offered me a Ticket for the Ladies Gallery – I should have seen all the great Literati and Artists gathered in the Hall below and heard them speak – Thackeray and Dickens are always present among the rest – this cannot now be – I don't think all London can afford another sight to me so interesting.

Charlotte to Lady Kay Shuttleworth; Haworth, 18 May 1850

I am glad to say that Papa is now so much better that I think I may, without misgiving, obey his wishes in no longer deferring my visit to Town. If all be well, I trust to have the real pleasure of seeing Yourself and Sir James next Thursday. Should any other day appear to you preferable to Thursday, you will I am sure, be kind enough to write and say so, and I will arrange accordingly.

As to any harassing doubts and fears I may still entertain, I shall not suffer myself to say a word about them; Sir James shewed me, how to regard the visit; strictly in the light of a lesson; to that view of the matter I mean to adhere.

Believe me, dear Lady Kay Shuttleworth
Yours sincerely & respectfully
C Brontë

I shall come by the train which reaches Euston-Square at 10 o'clock p.m. In case of missing this train by any chance, I shall take the express which arrives half an hour later.

Charlotte to Ellen; Haworth, 21 May 1850

My visit is again postponed. Sir James, I am sorry to say, is most seriously ill, two physicians are in attendance twice a day, and company and conversation, even with his own relatives, are prohibited as too exciting. Notwithstanding this, he has written two notes to me himself, claiming a promise that I will wait till he is better, and not allow any one else 'to introduce me,' as he says, 'into the Oceanic life of London.' Sincerely sorry as I was for him, I could not help smiling at this sentence. But I shall willingly promise. I know something of him, and like part at least of what I do know.

Charlotte to James Taylor; Haworth, 22 May 1850

. . . my journey to London is again postponed – and this time indefinitely . . . Once more then I settle myself down in the quietude of Haworth Parsonage, with books for my household companions and an occasional letter for a visitor – a mute society but neither quarrelsome, nor vulgarizing nor unimproving . . . I have just received yours of this morning; thank you for the enclosed note. The longings for liberty & leisure which May sunshine wakens in you, stir my sympathy – I am afraid Cornhill is little better than a prison for its inmates, on warm Spring or Summer days – It is a pity to think of you all toiling at your desks in such genial weather as this. For my part I am free to walk on the moors – but when I go out there alone – everything reminds me of the times when others were with me and then the moors seem a wilderness, featureless, solitary, saddening – My sister Emily had a particular love for them, and there is not a knoll of heather, not a branch of fern, not a young bilberry leaf not a fluttering lark or linnet but reminds me of her. The distant prospects were Anne's delight, and when I look round, she is in the blue tints, the pale mists, the waves and shadows of the horizon. In the hill-country silence their poetry comes by lines and stanzas into my mind: once I loved it – now I dare not read it – and am driven often to wish I could taste one draught of oblivion and forget much that, while mind remains, I never shall forget.

Charlotte to Mrs Smith, George Smith's mother; Haworth, 25 May 1850

I consider it however very doubtful whether [Sir James Kay Shuttle-worth] will be well enough to render my visit advisable; and even should I go – still – my conviction is that a brief stay will seem to me the best. In that case, after a few days with my 'fashionable friends' (as you call them) I believe I should be excessively disposed, and probably profoundly thankful to subside into any quiet corner of your drawing-room, where I might find a chair of suitable height.

I am sorry you have changed your residence as I shall now again lose my way in going up and down stairs, and stand in great tribulation, contemplating several doors, and not knowing which to open.

★Charlotte to Ellen; 76 Gloucester Terrace, Hyde Park Gardens, London, 3 June 1850

I came to London last Thursday – I am staying at Mrs Smith's who has changed her residence as the address will shew. A good deal of writing backwards and forwards persuasion &c., took place before this step was resolved on, but at last I explained to Sir James that I had some little matters of business to transact (which is, in fact, the case) and that I should stay quietly at my publisher's – He has called twice – and Lady S- once: each of them alone – he is in a fearfully nervous state as I gathered from his appearance, from what his wife said and from what he said himself. To my great horror he talks of my going with them to Hampton Court, Windsor &c. God knows how I shall get on – I perfectly dread it.

Charlotte to Patrick; London, 4 June 1850

Since I wrote I have been to the Opera; to the Exhibition of the Royal Academy, where there were some fine paintings, especially a large one by Landseer of the Duke of Wellington on the field of Waterloo, and a grand, wonderful picture of Martin's from Campbell's poem of the 'Last Man,' showing the red sun fading out of the sky, and all the soil of the foreground made up of bones and skulls.

The secretary of the Zoological Society also sent me an honorary ticket of admission to their gardens, which I wish you could see. There are animals from all parts of the world enclosed in great cages in the open air amongst trees and shrubs – lions, tigers, leopards, elephants, numberless monkeys, camels, five or six camelopards, a young hippopotamus with an Egyptian for its keeper; birds of all kind – eagles, ostriches, a pair of great condors from the Andes, strange ducks and waterfowl which seem very happy and comfortable, and build their nests among the reeds and edges of the lakes where they are kept. Some of the American birds make inexpressible noises.

There are also all sorts of living snakes and lizards in cages, some great Ceylon toads not much smaller than Flossy, some large foreign rats nearly as large and fierce as little bull-dogs. The most ferocious and deadly-looking things in the place were these rats, a laughing hyena (which every now and then uttered a hideous peal of laughter such as a score of maniacs might produce) and a cobra di capello snake. I think this snake was the worst of all: it had the eyes and face of a fiend, and darted out its barbed tongue sharply and incessantly.

Charlotte to Ellen; London, 12 June 1850

Of course I cannot in a letter give you a regular chronicle of how my time has been spent – I can only just notify what I deem three of the chief incidents – A sight of the Duke of Wellington at the Chapel Royal – (he is a real grand old man) a visit to the House of Commons (which I hope to describe to you some day when I see you) and – last not least – an interview with Mr Thackeray. He made a morning-call and sat above two hours – Mr Smith only was in the room the whole time. He described it afterwards as a queer scene; and I suppose it was. The giant sat before me – I was moved to speak to him of some of his shortcomings (literary of course) one by one the faults came into my mind and one by one I brought them out and sought some explanation or defence – He did defend himself like a great Turk and heathen – that is to say, the excuses were often worse than the crime itself. The matter ended in decent amity – if all be well I am to dine at his house this evening.

William Makepeace Thackeray's daughter, Anne Thackeray Ritchie, from her Chapters from Some Memoirs *(London, Macmillan & Co., 1894)*

One of the most notable persons who ever came into our bow-windowed drawing-room in Young Street is a guest never to be forgotten by me – a tiny, delicate, little person, whose small hand nevertheless grasped a mighty lever which set all the literary world of that day vibrating. I can still see the scene quite plainly – the hot summer evening, the open windows, the carriage driving to the door as we all sat silent and expectant; my father, who rarely waited, waiting with us; our governess and my sister and I all in a row, and prepared for the great event. We saw the carriage stop, and out of it sprang the active, well-knit figure of Mr George Smith, who was bringing Miss Brontë to see our father. My father, who had been walking up and down the room, goes out into the hall to meet his guests, and then, after a moment's delay, the door opens wide, and the two gentlemen come in, leading a tiny, delicate, serious, little lady, pale, with fair straight hair, and steady eyes. She may be a little over thirty; she is dressed in a little barège dress, with a pattern of faint green moss. She enters in mittens, in silence, in seriousness; our hearts are beating with wild excitement. This, then, is the authoress, the unknown power whose books have set all London talking, reading, speculating . . . The moment is so breathless that dinner comes as a relief to the solemnity of the occasion, and we all smile as my father stoops to offer his arm; for, though genius she may be, Miss Brontë can barely reach his elbow. My own personal impressions are that she is somewhat grave and stern, especially to forward little girls who wish to chatter. Mr George Smith has since told me how she afterwards remarked upon my father's wonderful forbearance and gentleness with our uncalled-for incursions into the conversation. She sat gazing at him with kindling eyes of interest, lighting up with a sort of illumination every now and then as she answered him. I can see her bending forward over the table, not eating, but listening to what he said as he carved the dish before him . . . It was a gloomy and silent evening. Every one waited for the brilliant conversation which never began at all. Miss

Brontë retired to the sofa in the study and murmured a low word now and then to our kind governess, Miss Truelock. The room looked very dark, the lamp began to smoke a little, the conversation grew dimmer and more dim, the ladies sat round still expectant, my father was too much perturbed by the gloom and silence to be able to cope with it at all. Mrs Brookfield, who was in the doorway by the study, near the corner in which Miss Brontë was sitting, leant forward with a little commonplace, since brilliance was not to be the order of the evening. 'Do you like London, Miss Brontë?' she said; another silence, a pause, then Miss Brontë answers, 'Yes and No,' very gravely.

★*Charlotte to Ellen; London, 21 June 1850*

My London visit has much surpassed my expectations this time; I have suffered less and enjoyed more than before – rather a trying termination yet remains to me. Mrs Smith's youngest son is at school in Scotland, and George – her eldest – is going to fetch him home for the vacation: the other evening he announced his intention of taking one of his sisters with him – and the evening afterwards he further proposed that Miss Brontë should go down to Edinburgh and join them there and see that city and its suburbs – I concluded he was joking – laughed and declined – however it seems he was in earnest; being always accustomed to have his will, he brooks op-position ill. The thing appearing to me perfectly out of the question – I still refused – Mrs Smith did not at all favour it – you may easily fancy how she helped me to sustain my opposition – but her worthy son only waxed more determined – his mother is master of the house – but he is master of his mother – this morning she came and entreated me to go – 'George wished it so much; he had begged her to use her influence' – &c.&c- Now I believe that George and I understand each other very well – and respect each other very sincerely – we both know the wide breach time has made between us – we do not embarrass each other, or very rarely – my six or eight years of seniority, to say nothing of lack of all pretension to beauty &c. are a perfect safeguard – I should not in the least fear to go with him to China – I like to see him pleased – I greatly <u>dislike</u>

to ruffle and disappoint him – so he shall have his mind – and, if all be well – I mean to join him in Edinburgh after I shall have spent a few days with you. With his buoyant animal spirits and youthful vigour he will make severe demands on my muscles and nerves – but I daresay I shall get through somehow – and then perhaps come back to rest a few days with you before I go home.

George Smith may have been able to persuade his mother to drop her objections to the trip, but Charlotte's friends were horrified at the impropriety of a young, unmarried man and woman travelling alone together in the wilds of Scotland, especially as that man and woman clearly had a strong liking for each other. Ellen brought all her influence to bear and finally won a concession: Charlotte would go as far as Edinburgh with George Smith, but would not venture on into the Highlands. This was perhaps wise, for the strain of even this trip proved too much for Charlotte and she returned to Brookroyd, Ellen's home, in a state of nervous collapse. Though it was claimed that this was due to the excitement of the journey, both Ellen and Patrick suspected that it was really because George Smith had proposed marriage to Charlotte.

Patrick to Ellen; 12 July 1850

My dear Miss Nussey,

Notwithstanding your kind letter, is cautiously worded, it gives me considerable uneasiness – One thing comforts me, that in you, she will have the kindest and best nurse. It may be that she is labouring under one of her usual bilious attacks, and if so, she will I trust, through a merciful providence, speedily recover – Should you see any feverish symptoms, call in the ablest Medical advice, for the expenses of which, I will be answerable – And lose no time – And write to me, soon, as soon as you can – Charlotte well knows, that I am rather prone to look at the dark side of things, and cunningly to search out for it, and find it, if it has any existence – . . . Tell Charlotte to keep up her spirits – When, once more, she breathes the free exhilarating air of Haworth, it will blow the dust and smoke, and impure malaria of London, out of her head, and heart –

Charlotte to Ellen; Haworth, 15 July 1850

I got home very well – and full glad was I that no insuperable obstacle has deferred my return one single day longer. Just at the foot of Bridgehouse hill I met John Greenwood – staff in hand – he fortunately saw me in the cab – stopped and informed me he was setting off to Brookroyd by Mr Brontë's orders to see how I was – for that he had been quite miserable ever since he got Miss Nussey's letter – I found on my arrival that papa had worked himself up to a sad pitch of nervous excitement and alarm – in which Martha and Tabby were but too obviously joining him – I can't deny but I was annoyed; there really being small cause for it all . . . I have recently found that Papa's great discomposure had its origin in two sources – the vague fear of my being somehow about to be married to somebody – having 'received some overtures' as he expressed himself – as well as in apprehension of illness – I have distinctly cleared away the first cause of uneasiness –

Charlotte to Ellen; Haworth, 18 July 1850

I am beginning to get settled at home – but the solitude seems heavy as yet – it is a great change, but in looking forward – I try to hope for the best. So little faith have I in the power of any temporary excitement to do real good – that I put off day by day writing to London to tell them I am come home – and till then it was agreed I should not hear from them. It is painful to be dependent on the small stimulus letters give – I sometimes think I will renounce it altogether, close all correspondence on some quiet pretext, and cease to look forward at post-time for any letters but yours.

Charlotte to William Smith Williams; Haworth, 20 July 1850

The six weeks of change and enjoyment are past but they are not lost; Memory took a sketch of each as it went by and, especially, a distinct daguerreotype of the two days I spent in Scotland. Those were two very pleasant days. I always liked Scotland as an idea, but now, as a reality, I like it far better; it furnished me with some hours as happy almost as any I ever spent. Do not fear however that I am going to bore you with description; you will, before now, have received a pithy and pleasant report of all things, to which any addition of mine would be superfluous.

My present endeavours are directed towards recalling my thoughts, cropping their wings drilling them into correct discipline and forcing them to settle to some useful work: they are idle and keep taking the train down to London or making a foray over the Border, especially are they prone to perpetrate that last excursion – and who indeed that has once seen Edinburgh, with its couchant crag-lion, but must see it again in dreams waking or sleeping? My dear Sir, do not think I blaspheme when I tell you that your Great London as compared to Dun-Edin 'mine own romantic town' is as prose compared to poetry, or as a great rumbling, rambling, heavy Epic – compared to a lyric brief, bright, clear and vital as a flash of lightning. You have nothing like Scott's Monument, or, if you had that and all the glories of architecture assembled together, you have nothing like Arthur's Seat, and above all you have not the Scotch National Character – and it is that grand character after all which gives the land its true charm, its true greatness.

Charlotte to George Smith; Haworth, 27 July 1850

Papa will write and thank you himself for the portrait when it arrives. As for me, you know, a standing interdict seals my lips . . . Were you still in Glencoe, or even in Edinburgh, I might write you a longer and more discursive letter, but mindful of the 'fitness of things' and of the effect of locality, reverent too of the claims of business, I will detain your attention no longer.

Charlotte to her friend from Brussels, Laetitia Wheelwright; Haworth, 30 July 1850

My stay in Scotland was short, and what I saw was chiefly comprised in Edinburgh and the neighbourhood, in Abbotsford and in Melrose, for I was obliged to relinquish my first intention of going from Glasgow to Oban and thence through a portion of the Highlands –

but – though the time was brief, and the view of objects limited, I found such a charm of situation, association and circumstance that I think the enjoyment experienced in that little space equalled in degree and excelled in kind all which London yielded during a month's sojourn. Edinburgh compared to London is like a vivid page of history compared to a huge dull treatise on Political Economy – and as to Melrose and Abbotsford the very names possess music and magic.

While Charlotte was in London, George Smith had taken her to have her portrait taken by the society painter, George Richmond. This he now sent to Haworth, together with an engraving of a portrait of the Duke of Wellington for Patrick.

Charlotte to Ellen; Haworth, 1 August 1850

My portrait is come from London – and the Duke of Wellington's and kind letters enough – Papa thinks the portrait looks older than I do – he says the features are far from flattered, but acknowledges that the expression is wonderfully good and life-like.

Charlotte to George Smith; Haworth, 1 August 1850

Papa seems much pleased with the portrait, as do the few other persons who have seen it, with one notable exception, viz. our old servant, who tenaciously maintains that it is not like – that it is too old-looking – but, as she, with equal tenacity, asserts that the Duke of Wellington's picture is a portrait of 'the Master' (meaning papa), I am afraid not much weight is to be ascribed to her opinion; doubtless she confuses her recollections of me as I was in childhood with present impressions.

Patrick to George Smith; Haworth, 2 August 1850

The two portraits, have, at length, safely arrived, and have been as safely hung up, in the best light, and most favourable position. Without flattery, the Artist, in the portrait of my daughter, has fully proved, that the fame which he has acquired, has been fairly earn'd. Without ostentatious display, with admirable tact and delicacy, he has produced a correct, likeness, and succeeded, in a graphic representation of mind, as well as matter, and with only black and white, has given prominence, and seeming, life, and speech, and motion – I may be partial, and perhaps, somewhat enthusiastic, in this case, but in looking on the picture, which improves upon acquaintance, as all real works of art do – I fancy I see strong indications, of the Genius, of the Author, of 'Shirley', and 'Jane Eyre' –

The portrait of the Duke of Wellington – of all – which I have seen, comes the nearest to my preconceived idea of that great man, to whom Europe, and the other portions of the civilized world, in the most dangerous crisis of their affairs, intrusted their cause – and in whom, under providence, they did not trust in vain. It now remains for me only to thank you, which I do, most sincerely – For the sake of the Giver, as well as the gift, I will lay the portraits up, for life, amongst my most highly valued treasures; and have only to regret, that some are missing, who, with better taste and skill, than I have, would have fully partaken of my joy –

I beg leave to remain,
with much respect,
My Dear Sir,
Yours, faithfully,
P. Brontë

Please to give my kindest and most respectful regards, to Mr Williams, whom I have often heard of but never seen – and to, Mr Taylor, whom I had the pleasure of seeing, when he ventured into this wild region.

Charlotte to George Smith; Haworth, 5 August 1850

The peculating Post-Office Clerk – evidently holding a Publisher's principles respecting the value of poetry – has not paid Wordsworth's book the compliment of detaining it: it arrived safely and promptly.

May I tell you how your morning reveries respecting Glencoe and Loch Katrine will probably end? The thought has just come into my head and must be written down. Some day – you will be even later than usual in making your appearance at breakfast; your anxious Mother, on going up to make inquiries, will find you, deep in undeniable inspiration, on the point of completing the 12th canto of 'The Highlands: A grand descriptive, romantic and sentimental Poem,' by George Smith Esq

Mary Taylor to Charlotte; New Zealand, 13 August 1850

On Wednesday I began Shirley and continued in a curious confusion of mind till now principally ab[ou]t the handsome foreigner who was nursed in our house when I was a little girl. – By the way you've put him in the servant's bedroom. You make us all talk much as I think we sh[oul]d have done if we'd ventured to speak at all – What a little lump of perfection you've made me! There is a strange feeling in reading it of hearing us all talking. I have not seen the matted hall and painted parlour windows so plain these 5 years. But my Father is not like. He hates well enough and perhaps loves too but he is not honest enough. It was from my father I learnt not to marry for money nor to tolerate any one who did and he never w[oul]d advise any one to do so or fail to speak with contempt of those who did.

Charlotte to Ellen; Haworth, 16 August 1850

I am going on Monday (D.V.) a journey. whereof the prospect cheers me not at all – to Windermere in Westmoreland to spend a few days with Sir J K Shuttleworth who has taken a house there for the Autumn and Winter – I consented to go with reluctance – chiefly to please Papa whom a refusal on my part would much have annoyed – but I dislike to leave him – I think he is not worse – but his complaint is still weakness – weakness – It is not right to anticipate evil, and to be always looking forward with an apprehensive spirit – but I think   grief is a two-edged sword – it cuts both ways – the memory of one loss is the anticipation of another.

Charlotte to Patrick; Briery Close, Windermere, 20 August 1850

I reached this place yesterday evening at 8 o'clock after a safe though rather tedious journey. I had to change carriages three times and to wait an hour and a half at Lancaster. Sir James came to meet me at the Station – both he and Lady Shuttleworth gave me a very kind reception – This place is exquisitely beautiful though the weather is cloudy misty and stormy – but the sun bursts out occasionally and shews the hills and the lake. Mrs Gaskell is coming here this evening and one or two other people.

Mrs Gaskell to Katie Winkworth; Plymouth Grove, Manchester, 25 August 1850

Dark when I got to Windermere station; a drive along the level road to Low-wood, then a regular clamber up a steep lane; then a stoppage at a pretty house, and then a pretty drawing-room much like the South End one, in which were Sir James and Lady K. S., and a little lady in black silk gown, whom I could not see at first for the dazzle in the room; she came up & shook hands with me at once – I went up to unbonnet &c, came down to tea. The little lady worked away and hardly spoke, but I had time for a good look at her. She is, (as she calls herself) <u>undeveloped</u>; thin and more than ½ a head shorter than I, soft brown hair not so dark as mine; eyes (very good and expressive looking straight & open at you) of the same colour, a reddish face; large mouth & many teeth gone; altogether <u>plain</u>; the forehead square, broad, and <u>rather</u> overhanging. She has a very sweet voice, rather hesitates in choosing her expressions, but when chosen they seem without an effort, <u>admirable</u> and <u>just</u> befitting the occasion. There is nothing overstrained but perfectly simple . . . She is more like Miss Fox in character & ways than anyone, if you can fancy Miss Fox to have gone through suffering enough to have taken out every spark of merriment, and <u>shy</u> & silent from the habit of extreme intense solitude.

Charlotte to Ellen; Haworth, 26 August 1850

My visit passed off very well – now that it is over I am glad I went – The scenery is of course grand, could I have wandered about amongst those hills <u>alone</u> – I could have drank in all their beauty – even in a carriage – with company, it was very well. Sir James was all the while as kind and friendly as he could be – he is in much better health – Lady Shuttleworth never got out – being confined to the house with a cold – but fortunately there was Mrs Gaskell (the authoress of 'Mary Barton') who came to the Briery the day after me – I was truly glad of her companionship She is a woman of the most genuine talent – of cheerful, pleasing and cordial manners and – I believe – of a kind and good heart. Miss Martineau was from home – she always leaves her house at Ambleside during the Lake Season to avoid the constant influx of visitors to which she would otherwise be subject . . . My previous opinions both of Sir James and Lady Shuttleworth are confirmed – I honour his intellect – with his heart – I believe I shall never have sympathy – He behaves to me with marked kindness – Mrs Gaskell said she believed he had for me a sincere and strong friendship – I am grateful for this – yet I scarcely desire a continuation of the interest he professes in me – were he to forget me – I could not feel regret – In observing his behaviour to others – I find that when once offended his forgiveness is not to be again purchased except perhaps by servile submission. The substratum of his character is hard as flint To Authors as a class (the imaginative portion of them) he has a natural antipathy, their virtues give him no pleasure – their faults are wormwood and gall in his soul: he perpetually threatens a visit to Haworth – may this be averted!

Mrs Gaskell to Eliza Fox; Manchester, 27 August 1850

Miss Brontë <u>is</u> a nice person. Like you, Tottie, without your merriment: poor thing she can hardly smile she has led such a hard cruel (if one may dare to say so,) life. She is quiet sensible unaffected with high noble aims. Lady K S was confined to one room so she and I had much of our day to ourselves (with the exception of some lectures on art, and 'bringing ourselves down to a lower level,' and 'the beauty of expediency,' from that eminently practical man Sir James, who has never indulged in the exercise of any talent which could not bring him a tangible and speedy return. However he was very kind; and really took trouble in giving us, Miss Brontë especially, good advice; which she received with calm resignation.) She is sterling and true; and if she is a little bitter she checks herself, and speaks kindly and hopefully of things and people directly; the wonder to me is how she can have kept heart and power alive in her life of desolation.

Charlotte to Mrs Gaskell; Haworth, 27 August 1850

. . . Papa and I have just had tea; he is sitting quietly in his room, and I in mine; 'storms of rain' are sweeping over the garden and churchyard: as to the moors, they are hidden in thick fog. Though alone I am not unhappy; I have a thousand things to be thankful for, and, amongst the rest, that this morning I received a letter from you, and that this evening I have the privilege of answering it.

The September issue of the *Palladium* carried an unsigned article by Sydney Dobell, a young poet, who wrote in terms of the highest praise of *Wuthering Heights*. Despite Charlotte's denial in the preface to *Shirley*, Dobell remained convinced that Currer, Ellis and Acton Bell were all one and the same person and that *Wuthering Heights* was a juvenile production of the author.

Sydney Dobell, review from the Palladium, *September 1850*

Not a subordinate place or person in this novel, but bears more or less the stamp of high genius . . . one looks back at the whole story as to a world of brilliant figures in an atmosphere of mist; shapes that come out upon the eye, and burn their colours into the brain, and depart into the enveloping fog. It is the unformed writing of a giant's hand; the 'large utterance' of a baby god . . . In the early efforts of unusual genius, there are not seldom unconscious felicities which maturer years may look back upon with envy. The child's hand wanders over the strings. It cannot combine them in the chords and melodies of manhood; but its separate notes are perfect in themselves, and perhaps sound all the sweeter for the Aeolian discords from which they come.

We repeat, that there are passages in this book of *Wuthering Heights* of which any novelist, past or present, might be proud. Open the first volume at the fourteenth page, and read to the sixty-first. There are few things in modern prose to surpass these pages for native power . . . The thinking-out of some of these pages . . . is the masterpiece of a poet, rather than the hybrid creation of the novelist . . . We are at a loss to find anywhere in modern prose . . . in the same space, such wealth and such economy, such apparent ease, such instinctive art.

Charlotte to James Taylor; Haworth, 5 September 1850

The article in the 'Palladium' is one of those notices over which an author rejoices with trembling. He rejoices to find his work finely, fully, fervently appreciated – and trembles under the responsibility such appreciation seems to devolve upon him. I am counselled to wait and watch. D.V. I will do so. Yet it is harder work to wait with the hands bound and the observant and reflective faculties at their silent unseen work, than to labour mechanically.

I need not say how I felt the remarks on 'Wuthering Heights'; they woke the saddest yet most grateful feelings; they are true, they are discriminating; they are full of late justice – but it is very late – alas! in one sense – too late. Of this, however, and of the pang of regret for a light prematurely extinguished – it is not wise to speak much. Whoever the author of this article may be, I remain his Debtor.

Yet – you see – even here – 'Shirley' is disparaged in comparison with 'Jane Eyre' and yet I took great pains with 'Shirley.' I did not hurry; I tried to do my best, and my own impression was that – it was not inferior to the former work; indeed I had bestowed on it more time, thought and anxiety – but great part of it was written under the shadow of impending calamity – and the last volume – I cannot deny was composed in the eager, restless endeavour to combat mental sufferings that were scarcely tolerable.

Chapter Thirteen

1850–51

When Smith, Elder & Co. approached Charlotte with the idea of republishing her sisters' novels under their own imprint she welcomed the idea, not least because it would give her the chance to make clear, once and for all, that Currer, Ellis and Acton Bell were indeed three separate and individual writers. It would also give her occupation at a time when the winter months were stretching emptily before her, with all the added poignancy of the anniversaries of her brother's and sisters' deaths to face. There was, too, a certain satisfaction in securing the books from the unreliable Thomas Newby and bringing them within the fold of her own publisher.

Charlotte to William Smith Williams; Haworth, 5 September 1850

I should much like to carry out your suggestion respecting a reprint of 'Wuthering Heights' and 'Agnes Grey' in I vol. with a prefatory and explanatory notice of the authors – but the question occurs – would Newby claim it? I could not bear to commit it to any other hands than those of Mr Smith. 'Wildfell Hall' it hardly appears to me desirable to preserve. The choice of subject in that work is a mistake – it was too little consonant with the character – tastes and ideas of the gentle, retiring, inexperienced writer. She wrote it under a strange, conscientious, half-ascetic notion of accomplishing a painful penance and a severe duty. Blameless in deed and almost in thought – there was from her very childhood a tinge of religious melancholy in her mind – this I ever suspected – and I have found amongst her papers, mournful proofs that such was the case. As to additional compositions, I think there would be none – as I would not offer a line to the publication of which my sisters themselves would have objected.

Charlotte to William Smith Williams; Haworth, 13 September 1850

Mr Newby undertook first to print 350 copies of 'Wuthering Heights', but he afterwards declared he had only printed 250. I doubt whether he could be induced to return the £50 without a good deal of trouble – much more than I should feel justified in delegating to Mr Smith. For my own part, the conclusion I drew from the whole of Mr Newby's conduct to my Sisters – was that he is a man with whom it is desirable to have little to do; I think he must be needy as well as tricky – and if he is, one would not distress him, even for one's rights.

If Mr Smith thinks proper to reprint 'Wuthering Heights & Agnes Grey', I would prepare a Preface comprising a brief and simple notice of the authors – such as might set at rest all erroneous conjectures respecting their identity – and adding a few poetical remains of each.

In case this arrangement is approved – you will kindly let me know – and I will commence the task – (a sad but, I believe – a necessary one) – and send it when finished.

Charlotte to Ellen; Haworth, 14 September 1850

I wish – dear Ellen – you would tell me what is the 'twaddle about my marrying, &c.' which you hear – If I knew the details I should have a better chance of guessing the quarter from which such gossip comes – as it is, I am quite at a loss. Whom am I to marry? I think I have scarcely seen a single man with whom such a union would be possible since I left London – Doubtless there are men whom if I chose to encourage I might marry – but no matrimonial lot is even remotely offered me which seems to me truly desirable: and even if that were the case – there would be many obstacles – the least allusion to such a thing is most offensive to Papa.

An article entitled 'Currer Bell' has lately appeared in the 'Palladium' a new periodical published in Edinburgh. It is an eloquent production and one of such warm sympathy and high appreciation as I had never expected to see – it makes mistakes about authorship &c. but these I hope one day to set right.

Charlotte to George Smith; Haworth, 18 September 1850

You should be very thankful that books cannot 'talk to each other as well as to their readers'. Conceive the state of your warehouse if such were the case. The Confusion of Tongues at Babel, or a congregation of Irvingites in full exercise of their miraculous gift – would offer but a feeble type of it. Terrible too would be the quarrelling. Yourself and Mr Taylor and Mr Williams would all have to go in several times in the day to part or silence the disputants. Dr Knox alone, with his 'Race, a Fragment' (a book which I read with combined interest, amusement and edification) would deliver the voice of a Stentor if any other book ventured to call in question his favourite dogmas.

Still I like the notion of a mystic whispering amongst the lettered leaves – and perhaps at night when London is asleep and Cornhill desert, when all your clerks and men are away and the warehouse is shut up – such a whispering may be heard – by those who have ears to hear.

Charlotte to George Smith; Haworth, September 1850

'Wuthering Heights & Agnes Grey' were published by Mr Newby on the condition that my Sisters should share the risk. Accordingly they advanced 50£, Mr Newby engaging to repay it as soon as the work should have sold a sufficient number of copies to defray expenses – and Mr Newby mentions in his letter to my sister on the subject that 'the sale of 250 copies would leave a <u>surplus</u> of 100£ to be divided' No portion of the sum advanced has yet been returned and, as it appears that the work is now entirely out of print – I should feel greatly obliged if you would call upon Mr Newby and inquire whether it be convenient to him to refund the amount received.

For 'The Tenant of Wildfell Hall', my Sister Anne was to receive 25£ on the day of publication – A second 25£ on the sale reaching 250 copies, 50£ more on its extending to 400 copies, and another 50£ on 500 being sold.

Two instalments of 25£ each were paid to my Sister. I should be glad if you could learn how many copies of the work have been sold on the whole – and whether any further sum is now due. Trusting you will excuse the trouble I give you

I am, my dear Sir
Yours very sincerely
C Brontë

Charlotte, Biographical Notice of Ellis and Acton Bell*; Haworth, 19 September 1850*

In externals, they were two unobtrusive women; a perfectly secluded life gave them retiring manners and habits. In Emily's nature the extremes of vigour and simplicity seemed to meet. Under an unsophisticated culture, inartificial tastes, and an unpretending outside, lay a secret power and fire that might have informed the brain and kindled the veins of a hero; but she had no worldly wisdom; her powers were unadapted to the practical business of life; she would fail to defend her most manifest rights, to consult her most legitimate advantage. An interpreter ought always to have stood between her and the world. Her will was not very flexible, and it generally opposed her interest. Her temper was magnanimous, but warm and sudden; her spirit altogether unbending.

Anne's character was milder and more subdued; she wanted the power, the fire, the originality of her sister, but she was well-endowed with quiet virtues of her own. Long-suffering, self-denying, reflective, and intelligent, a constitutional reserve and taciturnity placed and kept her in the shade, and covered her mind, and especially her feelings, with a sort of nun-like veil, which was rarely lifted. Neither Emily nor Anne was learned; they had no thought of filling their pitchers at the well-spring of other minds; they always wrote from the impulse of nature, the dictates of intuition, and from such stores of observation as their limited experience had enabled them to amass. I may sum up all by saying, that for strangers they were nothing, for superficial observers less than nothing; but for those who had known them all their lives in the intimacy of close relationship, they were genuinely good and truly great.

This notice has been written, because I felt it a sacred duty to wipe the dust off their gravestones, and leave their dear names free from soil.

Currer Bell

Charlotte to William Smith Williams; Haworth, 20 September 1850

I herewith send you a very roughly written copy of what I have to say about my Sisters. When you have read it, you can better judge whether the word 'Notice' or 'Memoir' is the most appropriate. I think – the former. Memoir seems to me to express a more circumstantial and different sort of account. My aim is to give a just idea of their identity, not to write any narrative of their simple, uneventful lives. I depend on you for faithfully pointing out whatever may strike you as faulty. I could not write it in the conventional form – that I found impossible.

Charlotte to Mrs Gaskell; Haworth, 26 September 1850

The little book of Rhymes [*Poems* by Currer, Ellis & Acton Bell] was sent by way of fulfilling a rashly made promise; and the promise was made to prevent you from throwing away four shillings in an injudicious purchase: I do not like my own share of the work, nor care that it should be read: Ellis Bell's poems I think good and vigorous, and Acton's have the merit of truth and simplicity. Mine are chiefly juvenile productions; the restless effervescence of a mind that would not be still. In those days, the sea too often 'wrought and was tempestuous' and weed, sand, shingle – all turned up in the tumult. This image is much too magniloquent for the subject, but you will pardon it.

Charlotte to Margaret Wooler; Haworth, 27 September 1850

My dear Miss Wooler

When I tell you that I have already been to the Lakes this season, and that it is scarcely more than a month since I returned, you will

299

understand that it is no longer within my option to accept your kind invitation.

I wish I could have gone to you: I wish your invitation had come first; to speak the truth it would have suited me better than the one by which I profited; it would have been pleasant – soothing – in many ways beneficial, to have spent two weeks with you in your cottage-lodgings – but these reflections are vain; I have already had my excursion, and there is and [*sic*] end of it.

Sir James Kay Shuttleworth is residing near Windermere at a house called 'The Briery' – and it was there I was staying for a little time in August. He very kindly shewed me the scenery – <u>as it can be seen from a carriage</u> and I discerned that the 'Lake Country' is a glorious region – of which I had only seen the similitude in dreams – waking or sleeping – but – my dear Miss Wooler – I only half enjoyed it – because I was only half at my ease.

Decidedly, I find it does not agree with me to prosecute the search of the picturesque in a carriage. A waggon, a spring-cart, even a post-chaise might do – but the carriage upsets everything. I longed to slip out unseen, and to run away by myself in amongst the hills and dales. Erratic and vagrant instincts tormented me, and these I was obliged to control, or rather, suppress – for fear of growing in any degree enthusiastic, and thus drawing attention to 'the lioness' the authoress – the She-Artist. Sir James is a man of ability – even of intellect – but not a man in whose presence one willingly unbends.

Charlotte to William Smith Williams; Haworth, 28 September 1850

It is my intention to write a few lines of remark on 'W.Heights' which however I propose to place apart as a brief preface before the tale – I am likewise compelling myself to read it over – for the first time of opening the book since my sister's death. Its power fills me with renewed admiration – but yet I am oppressed – the reader is scarcely ever permitted a taste of unalloyed pleasure – every beam of sunshine is poured down through black bars of threatening cloud – every page is surcharged with a sort of moral electricity; and the writer was unconscious of all this – nothing could make her conscious of it.

And this makes me reflect – perhaps I am too incapable of perceiving the faults and peculiarities of my own style.

I should wish to revise the proofs, if it be not too great an inconvenience to send them. It seems to me advisable to modify the orthography of the old servant Joseph's speeches – for though – as it stands – it exactly renders the Yorkshire accent to a Yorkshire ear – yet I am sure Southerns must find it unintelligible – and thus one of the most graphic characters in the book is lost on them.

Charlotte to Ellen; Haworth, September 1850

There is nothing wrong, and I write you a line as you desire, merely to say that I am busy just now – Mr Smith wishes to reprint some of Emily's and Anne's works – with a few little additions from the papers they have left – and I have been closely engaged in revising, transcribing – preparing a Preface – Notice &c. as the time for doing this is limited I am obliged to be industrious – I found the task at first exquisitely painful & depressing – but regarding it in the light of a sacred duty – I went on – and now can bear it better – It is work however that I cannot do in the evening – for if I did, I should have no sleep at night.

While Charlotte was at work on her melancholy task of going through her sisters' papers, she had two visitors. John Stores Smith, who came from Halifax, was an aspiring writer who had sent copies of his books to Charlotte and now sought an interview. He was followed by William Forster and his wife, Jane, a daughter of Thomas Arnold.

John Stores Smith, A Day with Charlotte Brontë, *from the* Free Lance, *14 March 1868*

I was shown across the lobby into the parlour to the left, and there I found Miss Brontë, standing in the full light of the window, and I had ample opportunity of fixing her upon my memory, where her image is vividly present to this hour. She was diminutive in height, and extremely fragile in figure. Her hand was one of the smallest I have ever grasped. She had no pretensions to being considered beautiful, and was as far removed from being plain. She had rather light brown hair, somewhat thin, and drawn plainly over her brow. Her complexion had no trace of colour in it, and her lips were pallid also; but she had a most sweet smile, with a touch of tender melancholy in it. Altogether she was as unpretending, undemonstrative, quiet a little lady as you could well meet. Her age I took to be about five-and-thirty. But when you saw and felt her eyes, the spirit that created *Jane Eyre* was revealed at once to you. They were rather small, but of a very peculiar colour, and had a strange lustre and intensity. They were chameleon-like, a blending of various brown and olive tints. But they looked you through and through – and you felt they were forming an opinion of you, not by mere acute noting of Lavaterish physiognomical peculiarities, but by a subtle penetration into the very marrow of your mind, and the innermost core of your soul. Taking my hand again she apologised for her enforced absence, and, as she did so, she looked right through me. There was no boldness in the gaze, but an intense, direct, searching look, as of one who had the gift to read hidden mysteries, and the right to read them. I had a feeling that I never experienced before or since, as though I was being mesmerised. It was almost a relief when the look was removed, and we sat down together to table. During dinner I had always a feeling that those eyes were on me, when I was looking down myself, and when I looked at her, and her gaze was on her plate, I still could not divest myself of the sensation that those eyes could see one through their lids. We did not converse much while the simple meal was being dispatched, but afterwards we had a ceaseless talk extending over fully two hours. I have not one single phrase of her conversation to chronicle. There was neither wit, nor fancy, nor brilliance in her remarks. Her talk was remarkable for strong, shrewd, homely sense; tersely, briefly, directly and vigorously expressed. There was not a trace of the literary woman about her. No attempt at effect, no tours de phrase. The merit of her remarks lay altogether in the matter and not the least in the manner. About herself and sisters, and family generally, she was reticent, and seemed to put the subject markedly away from her. She confined her observations to myself, my designs and prospects, and to the expression of her views of London literary men and their lives and characters.

Jane Forster to Mrs Gaskell; 3 October 1850

Miss Brontë put me so in mind of her own 'Jane Eyre.' She looked smaller than ever, and moved about so quietly, and noiselessly, just like a little bird, as Rochester called her, barring that all birds are joyous, and that joy can never have entered that house since it was first built; and yet, perhaps, when that old man married, and took home his bride, and children's voices and feet were heard about the house, even that desolate crowded graveyard and biting blast could not quench cheerfulness and hope. Now there is something touching in the sight of that little creature entombed in such a place, and moving about herself like a spirit, especially when you think that the slight still frame encloses a force of strong fiery life, which nothing has been able to freeze or extinguish.

Neither of Charlotte's visitors realized how deeply their hostess had been affected by reading through her sisters' papers and preparing them for publication. The task had, in fact, revived acutely all the feelings of bitterness and depression which had followed her brother's and sisters' deaths.

Charlotte to William Smith Williams; Haworth, 2 October 1850

Miss Martineau has several times lately asked me to go and see her – and though this is a dreary season for travelling northward – I think if Papa continues pretty well – I shall go in a week or two. I feel to my deep sorrow – to my humiliation – that it is not in my power to bear the canker of constant solitude – I had calculated that when shut out from every enjoyment – from every stimulus but what could be derived from intellectual exertion, my mind would rouse itself perforce – It is not so: even intellect – even imagination will not dispense with the ray of domestic cheerfulness – with the gentle spur of family discussion – Late in the evenings and all through the nights – I fall into a condition of mind which turns entirely to the Past – to memory, and memory is both sad and relentless. This will never do – and will produce no good – I tell you this that you may check false anticipations. You cannot help me – and must not trouble yourself in any shape to sympathize with me. It is my cup – I must drink it as others drink theirs – Yours sincerely

CB.

Charlotte to Ellen; Haworth, 23 October 1850

I trust you are well – dear Ellen – I am very decent indeed in bodily health and am both angry and surprised at myself for not being better in spirits – for not growing accustomed or at least resigned to the solitude and isolation of my lot – But my late occupation left a result for some days and indeed still, very painful. The reading over of papers, the renewal of remembrances brought back the pang of bereavement and occasioned a depression of spirits well nigh intolerable – for one or two nights I scarcely knew how to get on till morning – and when morning came I was still haunted with a sense of sickening distress – I tell you these things – because it is absolutely necessary to me to have some relief – You will forgive me – and not to trouble yourself – or imagine that I am one whit worse than I say – it is quite a mental ailment – and I believe and hope is better now – I think so because I can speak about it which I never can when grief is at its worst.

I thought to find occupation and interest in writing when alone at home – but hitherto my efforts have been very vain – the deficiency of every stimulus is so complete.

You will recommend me I daresay to go from home – but that does no good – even could I again leave Papa with an easy mind (thank God! he is still better) I cannot describe what a time of it I had after my return from London – Scotland &c. there was a reaction that sunk me to the earth – the deadly silence solitude, desolation were awful – the craving for companionship – the hopelessness of relief – were what I should dread to feel again.

Charlotte to James Taylor; Haworth, 6 November 1850

I have just finished reading the Life of Dr Arnold, but now when I wish – in accordance with your request – to express what I think of it – I do not find the task very easy – proper terms seem wanting . . . I was struck by the almost unbroken happiness of his life; a happiness resulting chiefly no doubt from the right use to which he put that health and strength which God had given him, but also owing partly to a singular exemption from those deep and bitter griefs which most human beings are called on to endure. His wife was what he wished; his children were healthy and promising; his own health was excellent, his undertakings were crowned with success; even Death was kind – for however sharp the pains of his last hour – they were but brief – God's blessing seems to have accompanied him from the cradle to the grave. One feels thankful to know that it has been permitted to any man to live such a life.

When I was in Westmoreland last August – I spent an evening at Fox How where Mrs Arnold and her daughters still reside. It was twilight as I drove to the place and almost dark ere I reached it; still I could perceive that the situation was exquisitely lovely: the house looked like a nest half-buried in flowers and creepers – and, dusk as it was, I could <u>feel</u> that the valley and the hills round were beautiful as imagination could dream. Mrs Arnold seemed an amiable and must once have been a very pretty woman; her daughters I liked much . . . I had not then read Dr Arnold's Life; otherwise the visit would have interested me even more than it actually did.

Smith, Elder & Co's edition of *Wuthering Heights & Agnes Grey*, with Charlotte's Biographical Notice of her sisters and Prefaces to Emily's novel and a selection of her poems, was published on 10 December 1850. Newby had proved elusive and difficult to the last.

Charlotte to George Smith; Haworth, 3 December 1850

As to Mr Newby – he charms me. First – there is the fascinating coyness with which he shuns your pursuit. For a month, or nearly two months, you have been fondly hoping to win from him an interview, while he has been making himself scarce as violets at Christmas, aristocratically absenting himself from Town, evading your grasp like a Publisher metamorphosed into a Rainbow. Then, when you come upon him in that fatal way in Regent Street, pin him down and hunt him home with more promptitude than politeness, and with a want of delicate consideration for your victim's fine feelings calculated to awaken emotions of regret – that victim is still ready for the emergency. Scorning to stand on the defensive, he at once assumes the offensive. Not only has he realised no profit, he has sustained actual loss! And – to account for this – adds with a sublime boldness of invention – that the author 'wished him to spend all possible profits in advertisements'!

Equally well acted too is the artless simplicity of his surprise at the news you communicate; and his pretty little menace of a 'chancery-injunction' consummates the picture and makes it perfect . . . On referring to Mr Newby's letters, I find in one of them, a boast that he is 'advertising vigorously.' I remember that this flourish caused us to look out carefully for the results of his vast exertions – but though we everywhere encountered 'Jane Eyre' – it was as rare a thing to find an advertisement of 'Wuthering Heights' as it appears to be to meet Mr Newby in Town at an unfashionable season of the year . . . I would say something about regret for the trouble you have had in your chase of this ethereal and evanescent ornament of 'the Trade' but I fear apologies would be even worse than thanks – Both these shall be left out – and you shall only be requested to

> Believe me
> Yours sincerely
> C Brontë

Charlotte to Sydney Dobell; Haworth, 8 December 1850

To Mr Dobell.

I offer this little book to my critic in the 'Palladium,' and he must believe it accompanied by a tribute of the sincerest gratitude, not so much for anything he has said of myself, as for the noble justice he has rendered to one dear to me as myself – perhaps dearer, and perhaps one kind word spoken for her awakens a deeper, tenderer sentiment of thankfulness than eulogies heaped on my own head.

As you will see when you have read the biographical notice, my sister cannot thank you herself; she is gone out of your sphere and mine, and human blame and praise are nothing to her now; but to me – for her sake – they are something still; it revived me for many a day to find that – dead as she was – the work of her genius had at last met with worthy appreciation.

The looming anniversary of Emily's death finally drove Charlotte from home; she could not face that day alone. Instead, she sought sanctuary and stimulation at Ambleside, in the company of Harriet Martineau.

Charlotte to Ellen; The Knoll, Ambleside, 18 December 1850

I can write to you now for I am away from home and relieved, temporarily at least, by change of air and scene from the heavy burden of depression which I confess has for nearly 3 months been sinking me to the earth. I never shall forget last Autumn. Some days and nights have been cruel – but now – having once told you this – I need say no more on the subject. My loathing of Solitude grew extreme; my recollection of my Sisters intolerably poignant; I am better now.

I am at Miss Martineau's for a week – her house is very pleasant both within and without – arranged at all points with admirable neatness and comfort – Her visitors enjoy the most perfect liberty; what she claims for herself she allows them. I rise at my own hour, breakfast alone – (she is up at five, takes a cold bath and a walk by starlight and has finished breakfast and got to work by 7 o'clock) I pass the morning in the drawing-room – she in her study. At 2 o'clock we meet, work, talk and walk together till 5 – her dinner hour – spend the evening together – when she converses fluently, abundantly and with the most complete frankness – I go to my own room soon after ten – she sits up writing letters till twelve. She appears exhaustless in strength and spirits, and indefatigable in the faculty of labour. She is a great and a good woman; of course not without peculiarities but I have seen none as yet that annoy me. She is both hard and warm-hearted, abrupt and affectionate – liberal and despotic. I believe she is not at all conscious of her own absolutism. When I tell her of it, she denys the charge warmly – then I laugh at her. I believe she almost rules Ambleside. Some of the gentry dislike her, but the lower orders have a great regard for her. I will not stay more than a week because about Christmas relations and other guests will come. Sir J and Lady Shuttleworth are coming here to dine on Thursday – I mean to get off going there if I possibly can without giving downright offence.

Matthew Arnold to Miss Wightman; Fox How, Ambleside, 21 December 1850

At seven came Miss Martineau and Miss Brontë (Jane Eyre); talked to Miss M (who blasphemes frightfully) about the prospects of the Church of England, and, wretched man that I am, promised to go and see her cow-keeping miracles tomorrow – I, who hardly know a cow from a sheep. I talked to Miss Brontë (past thirty and plain, with expressive gray eyes though) of her curates, of French novels, and her education in a school at Brussels, and saw the lions roaring to their dens at half past nine, and came to talk to you.

Charlotte to William Smith Williams; Haworth, 1 January 1851

I trust to have obtained benefit from my visit to Miss Martineau – a visit more interesting I certainly never paid: if self-sustaining strength can be acquired by example, I ought to have got good – but my nature is not hers – I could not make it so though I were to submit it seventy times seven to the furnace of affliction and discipline it for an age under the hammer and anvil of toil and self-sacrifice. Perhaps if I were like her I should not admire her as much as I do. She is somewhat absolute – though quite unconsciously so – but she is likewise kind with an affection at once abrupt and constant whose sincerity you cannot doubt. It was delightful to sit near her in the evening and hear her converse – myself mute. She speaks with what seems to me a wonderful fluency and eloquence. Her animal spirits are as unflagging as her intellectual powers – I was glad to find her health excellent. I believe neither Solitude nor loss of friends would break her down – I saw some faults in her but some how I liked them for the sake of her good points. It gave me no pain to feel insignificant mentally and corporeally in comparison with her.

Charlotte to James Taylor; Haworth, 15 January 1851

My visit to Westmoreland has certainly done me good. Physically – I was not ill before I went there – but my mind had undergone some painful laceration in the course of looking over my Sisters' papers, mementos and memoranda that would have been nothing to others, conveyed for me so keen a sting. Near at hand there was no lightning or effacing the sad impression by refreshing intercourse, from my Father, of course, my sole care was to conceal it – age demanding the same forbearance as infancy – in the communication of grief – Continuous solitude grew more than I could bear and – to speak truth – I was glad of a change – You will say that we ought to have power in ourselves either to bear circumstances or to bend them. True – we should do our best to this end – but sometimes our best is unavailing. However – I am better now, and most thankful for the respite.

Charlotte had been in regular correspondence with James Taylor, the 'little man' as she referred to him, and George Smith, since her visit to London the previous summer. Their letters were sent on to Ellen, who, despite Charlotte's protestations, quickly perceived that there was more to them than met the eye. When George Smith casually mentioned that Charlotte might like to accompany him on a trip down the Rhine, Ellen immediately heard wedding bells ringing.

Charlotte to Ellen; Haworth, 20 January 1851

Dear Nell – your last letter but one made me smile. I think you draw great conclusions from small inferences. I think those 'fixed intentions' you fancy – are imaginary – I think the 'undercurrent' amounts simply to this – a kind of natural liking and sense of something congenial. Were there no vast barrier of age, fortune &c.

there is perhaps enough personal regard to make things possible which now are impossible. If men and women married because they like each others' temper, look, conversation, nature and so on – and if besides, years were more nearly equal – the chance you allude to might be admitted as a chance – but other reasons regulate matrimony – reasons of convenience, of connection, of money. Meantime I am content to have him as a friend and pray God to continue to me the commonsense to look on one so young so rising and so hopeful in no other light. That hint about the Rhine disturbs me; I am not made of stone – and what is mere excitement to him – is fever to me. However it is a matter for the Future and long to look forward to – As I see it now, the journey is out of the question – for many reasons – I rather wonder he should think of it – I cannot conceive either his mother or his sisters relishing it, and all London would gabble like a countless host of geese –

Charlotte to Ellen; Haworth, 30 January 1851

you are to say no more about 'Jupiter' and 'Venus' – what do you mean by such heathen trash? The fact is no fallacy can be wilder and I won't have it hinted at even in jest, because my common sense laughs it to scorn – The idea of the 'little man' [James Taylor] shocks me less – it would be a more likely match – if 'matches' were at all in question, which they are not. He still sends his little newspaper – and the other day there came a letter of a bulk, volume, pith, judgement and knowledge, worthy to have been the product of a giant. You may laugh as much and as wickedly as you please – but the fact is there is a quiet constancy about this, my diminutive and red-haired friend, which adds a foot to his stature – turns his sandy locks, dark and altogether dignifies him a good deal in my estimation – However I am not bothered by much vehement ardour – there is the nicest distance and respect preserved now – which makes matters very comfortable –

This is all nonsense – Nell – and so you will understand it

Preparing her sisters' works for publication by Smith, Elder & Co. had partially assuaged Charlotte's guilt about her failure to follow *Shirley* with another novel of her own. Acutely aware that everyone was anxiously waiting for her to set to work, she still found herself completely lacking in inspiration. Once again, she resorted to offering to revise *The Professor* for publication – and once again her offer was refused.

Charlotte to George Smith; Haworth, 5 February 1851

'The Professor' has now had the honour of being rejected nine times by the 'Tr–de' (three rejections go to your own share); you may affirm that you accepted it this last time, but that cannot be admitted; if it were only for the sake of symmetry and effect, I must regard this martyrised M.S. as repulsed or at any rate – withdrawn for the ninth time! Few – I flatter myself – have earned an equal distinction, and of course my feelings towards it can only be paralleled by those of a doting parent towards an idiot child. Its merits – I plainly perceive – will never be owned by anybody but Mr Williams and me; very particular and unique must be our penetration, and I think highly of us both accordingly. You may allege that that merit is not visible to the naked eye. Granted; but the smaller the commodity – the more inestimable its value.

You kindly propose to take 'The Professor' into custody. Ah – No! His modest merit shrinks at the thought of going alone and unbefriended to a spirited Publisher. Perhaps with slips of him you might light an occasional cigar – or you might remember to lose him some day – and a Cornhill functionary would gather him up and consign him to the repositories of waste paper, and thus he would prematurely find his way to the 'buttermen' and trunkmakers. No – I have put him by and locked him up – not indeed in my desk, where I could not tolerate the monotony of his demure quaker countenance, but in a cupboard by himself.

Something you say about going to London – but the words are dreamy, and fortunately I am not obliged at present to hear or answer them. London and Summer are many months away; our moors are all white with snow just now and little redbreasts come every morning to the window for crumbs: one can lay no plans three or four months beforehand. Besides – I don't deserve to go to London; nobody merits a treat or a change less. I secretly think, on the contrary, I ought to be put in prison and kept on bread and water in solitary confinement without even a letter from Cornhill – till I had written a book. One of the two things would certainly result from such a mode of treatment pursued for twelve months; either I should come out, at the end of that time, with a 3 vol. M.S. in my hand, or else with a condition of intellect that would exempt me ever after from literary efforts and expectations.

Charlotte to James Taylor; 11 February 1851

Have you yet read Miss Martineau's and Mr Atkinson's new work 'Letters on the Nature and Development of Man?'. If you have not – it would be worth your while to do so.

Of the impression this book has made on me – I will not now say much. It is the first exposition of avowed Atheism and Materialism I have ever read; the first unequivocal declaration of disbelief in the existence of a God or a Future Life – I have ever seen. In judging of such exposition and declaration – one would wish entirely to put aside the sort of instinctive horror they awaken and to consider them in an impartial spirit and collected mood. This I find it difficult to do. The strangest thing is that we are called on to rejoice over this hopeless blank – to receive this bitter bereavement as great gain – to welcome this unutterable desolation as a state of pleasant freedom. Who <u>could</u> do this if he would? Who <u>would</u> do it if he could?

Sincerely – for my own part – do I wish to find and know the Truth – but if <u>this</u> be Truth – well may she guard herself with mysteries and cover herself with a veil. If this be Truth – Man or Woman who beholds her can but curse the day he or she was born.

Charlotte had discussed the problem of finding a suitable subject for her next novel with George Smith. Perhaps jokingly, he suggested that there was plenty of material for her at Cornhill in her publisher's offices. Despite the tenor of her response, Charlotte would indeed draw upon some of her London friends for characters in *Villette*, George Smith himself and his mother amongst the number.

Charlotte to George Smith; Haworth, 8 March 1851

Do you know that the first part of your note is most dangerously suggestive? What a rich field of subject you point out in your allusions to Cornhill &c. – a field at which I myself should only have ventured to glance like the Serpent at Paradise; but when Adam himself opens the gates and shews the way in what can the honest Snake do but bend its crest in token of gratitude and glide rejoicingly through the aperture?

But – no: don't be alarmed. You are all safe from Currer Bell – safe from his satire – safer from his eulogium. We cannot (or at least I cannot) write of our acquaintance with the consciousness that others will recognise their portraits, or that they themselves will know the hand which has sketched them. Under such circumstances the pencil would falter in the fingers and shrink alike from the indication of bold shades and brilliant lights (especially the last because it would look like flattery;) plain speaking would seem audacious – praise – obtrusive.

Were it possible that I could take you all fearlessly, like so many abstractions, or historical characters that had been dust a hundred years – could handle, analyse – delineate you, without danger of the picture being recognised either by yourselves or others – I should think my material abundant and rich. This however is no more possible than that the Nurse should give the child the moon out of the sky. So – I repeat it – you are <u>very</u> safe.

Major changes were about to take place at Smith, Elder & Co., changes which would have a profound effect on Charlotte personally. George Smith was increasingly absorbed in trying to extricate the firm from financial problems, caused by one of his partners, and James Taylor, 'the little man', was about to be sent to India to take over the management of Smith, Elder & Co.'s affairs there. His imminent departure brought him to a resolution. He asked permission to call on Charlotte in Haworth before he left and then made her a proposal of marriage. Though not unexpected, it was not welcome.

Charlotte to George Smith; Haworth, 31 March 1851

What you say about relinquishing your proposed Continental trip stirs in me a feeble spirit of emulation. By way of imitation on a small scale – I would fain give up all thoughts of going to London or elsewhere this Spring or Summer. Were I but as sure as you are of being able to work to some purpose – gladly – gladly would I make the sacrifice – indeed it would be no sacrifice – I have before this found in absorbing work – a curative and comforting power not to be yielded by relaxation . . . With inly-felt wishes for your success – and renewed and earnest injunctions that you will <u>never</u> permit the task of writing to Currer Bell to add however slightly to your burdens – (for – whether you think so or not – he is a disciplined person who can endure long fastings and exist on very little food – just what Fate chooses to give – and indeed can do without)

Charlotte to Ellen; Haworth, 4 April 1851

Mr Taylor has been and is gone; things are just as they were. I only know in addition to the slight information I possessed before that this Indian undertaking is necessary to the continued prosperity of the Firm of Smith Elder & Co. and that he – Taylor – alone was pronounced to possess the power and means to carry it out successfully – that mercantile honour combined with his own sense of duty obliged him to accept the post of honour and of danger to which he has been appointed that he goes with great personal reluctance and that he contemplates an absence of five years.

He looked much thinner and older – I saw him very near and once through my glass – the resemblance to Branwell struck me forcibly – it is marked. He is not ugly – but very peculiar; the lines in his face show an inflexibility and – I must add – a hardness of character which do not attract. As he stood near me – as he looked at me in his keen way, it was all I could do to stand my ground tranquilly and steadily and not to recoil as before. It is no use saying anything if I am not candid – I avow then that on this occasion – predisposed as I was to regard him very favourably – his manners and his personal presence scarcely pleased me more than at the first interview. He gave me a book at parting requesting in his brief way that I would keep it for his sake and adding hastily 'I shall hope to hear from you in India – your letters <u>have</u> been and <u>will</u> be a greater refreshment than you can think or I can tell.'

And so he is gone, and stern and abrupt little man as he is – too often jarring as are his manners – his absence and the exclusion of his idea from my mind – leave me certainly with less support and in deeper solitude than before.

Charlotte to Ellen; Haworth, 9 April 1851

Certainly I shall not soon forget last Friday – and <u>never</u>, I think, the evening and night succeeding that morning and afternoon – evils seldom come singly – and soon after Mr T- was gone – papa who had been better grew much worse; he went to bed early and was very sick and ill for an hour and when at last he began to doze and I left him – I came down to the dining-room with a sense of weight, fear and desolation hard to express and harder to endure. A wish that you were with me <u>did</u> cross my mind but I repulsed it as a most selfish wish – indeed it was only short-lived – my natural tendency in moments of this sort is to get through the struggle alone – to think that one is burdening and racking others – makes all worse.

You speak to me in soft consolatory accents, but I hold far sterner language to myself, dear Nell. An absence of five years – a dividing expanse of three oceans – the wide difference between a man's active career and a woman's passive existence – these things are almost equivalent to an eternal separation – But there is another thing which forms a barrier more difficult to pass than any of these. Would Mr T- and I ever suit –? could I ever feel for him enough love to accept of him as a husband? Friendship – gratitude – esteem I have – but each moment he came near me – and that I could see his eyes fastened on me – my veins ran ice. Now that he is away I feel far more gently towards him – it is only close by that I grow rigid – stiffening with a strange mixture of apprehension and anger – which nothing softens but his retreat and a perfect subduing of his manner. I did not want to be proud nor intend to be proud – but I was forced to be so.

Charlotte to Mrs Smith, George Smith's mother; Haworth,
17 April 1851

Before I received your note, I was nursing a comfortable and complacent conviction that I had quite made up my mind not to go to London this year: the Great Exhibition was nothing – only a series of bazaars under a magnified hot-house – and I myself was in a pharisaical state of superiority to temptation. But Pride has its fall. I read your invitation and immediately felt a great wish to descend from my stilts. Not to conceal the truth – I should like to come and see you extremely well.

Charlotte to George Smith; Haworth, 19 April 1851

My scheme of emulation appears to have terminated in a somewhat egregarious failure, as perhaps your Mother may have told you. One can't help it. One does not profess to be made out of granite.

Your project, depend on it, has been quite providentially put a stop to. And do you really think I would have gone to the Rhine this summer? Do you think I would have partaken in all that unearned pleasure?

Now – listen to a serious word. You might <u>possibly</u> have persuaded me to go; (I do not <u>think</u> that you would – but it does not become me to be very positive on that point – seeing that proofs of inflexibility do not abound) yet had I gone – I should not have been truly happy; self-reproach would have gnawed at the root of enjoyment; it is only drones and wasps who willingly eat honey they have not hived, and I protest against being classed with either of these insects. Ergo; though I am sorry for your own and your Sister's sake that your Castle on the Rhine has turned out a Castle in the Air – I am not at all sorry for mine.

Charlotte to Ellen; Haworth, 23 April 1851

I have heard from Mr Taylor to-day – a quiet little note – he returned to London a week since on Saturday – he has since kindly chosen and sent me a parcel of books – He leaves England May 20th   his note concludes with asking whether he has any chance of seeing me in London before that time. I must tell him that I have already fixed June for my visit and therefore in all human probability we shall see each other no more.

There is still a want of plain mutual understanding in this business – and there is sadness and pain in more ways than one. My conscience – I can truly say – does not <u>now</u> accuse me of having treated Mr Taylor with injustice or unkindness – What I once did wrong in this way, I have endeavoured to remedy both to himself and in speaking of him to others – Mr Smith to wit – though I more than doubt that last opinion will ever reach him; I am sure he has estimable and sterling qualities – but with every disposition & with every wish – with every intention even to look on him in the most favourable point of view at his last visit – it was impossible to me in my inmost heart to think of him as one that might one day be acceptable as a husband. It would sound harsh were I to tell even <u>you</u> the estimate I felt compelled to form respecting him; dear Nell – I looked for something of the gentleman – something I mean of the <u>natural</u> gentleman – you know I can dispense with acquired polish – and for looks – I know myself too well to think that I have any right to be exacting on that point – I could not find one gleam – I could not see one passing glimpse of true good-breeding – it is hard to say – but it is <u>true</u>. In mind too; – though clever, – he is second-rate; – thoroughly second-rate. One does not like to say these things – but one had better be honest – Were I to marry him – my heart would bleed – in pain and humiliation – I could not – <u>could</u> not look up to him – No – if Mr T be the only husband Fate offers to me – single I must always remain. But yet – at times I grieve for him – and perhaps it is superfluous -- for I cannot think he will suffer much – a hard nature – occupation – change of scene will befriend him.

Charlotte to Ellen; Haworth, 5 May 1851

I discover with some surprise that Papa has taken a decided liking to Mr Taylor. The marked kindness of his manner to the little man when he bid him good bye – exhorting him to be 'true to himself his Country and his God' and wishing him all good wishes – struck me with some astonishment at the time – and whenever he has alluded to him since it has been with significant eulogy. When I alleged that he was 'no gentleman' – he seemed out of patience with me for the objection – You say Papa has penetration – on this subject I believe he has indeed. I have told him nothing – yet he seems to be au fait to the whole business – I could think at some moments – his guesses go farther than mine. I believe he thinks a prospective union, deferred for 5 years, with such a decorous reliable personage would be a very proper and advisable affair – However I ask no questions and he asks me none, and if he did, I should have nothing to tell him – nor he me for he & Mr T- were never long enough alone together to have had any communication on the matter – . . . I enclose a letter of Mr Morgan's to Papa – written just after he had read 'Shirley.' It is curious to see the latent feeling roused in the old gentleman – I was especially struck by his remark about the chap. entitled 'The Valley of the Shadow &c.' he must have a true sense of what he read or he could not have made it.

Charlotte now began to make preparations for her forthcoming visit to London where she was again to stay with George Smith and his mother. Her excitement betrayed itself in her letters and in her arrangements for the purchase of new clothes – for this would be the first time since her sisters' deaths that George Smith would see her in anything other than mourning.

Charlotte to Ellen; Haworth, 10 May 1851

Do you know that I was in Leeds on the very same day with you – last Wednesday? I had thought of telling you when I was going – and having your help and company in buying a bonnet, &c. but then I reflected this would be merely making a selfish use of you – so I determined to manage or mismanage the matter alone – I went to Hunt & Hall's for the bonnet – and got one which seemed grave and quiet there amongst all the splendours – but now it looks infinitely too gay with its pink lining – I saw some beautiful silks of pale sweet colours but had not the spirit or the means to launch out at the rate of 5s. per y[ar]d and went and bought a black silk at 3s.

after all – I rather regret this – because Papa says he would have lent me a sovereign if he had known. I believe if you had been there you would have forced me to get into debt.

Charlotte to George Smith; Haworth, 12 May 1851

Of course I am not in the least looking forwards to going to London – nor reckoning on it – nor allowing the matter to take any particular place in my thoughts: no: I am very sedulously cool and nonchalant. Moreover – I am not going to be glad to see anybody there: <u>gladness</u> is an exaggeration of sentiment one does not permit oneself: to be <u>pleased</u> is quite enough – and not too well pleased either – only with pleasure of a faint tepid kind – and to a stinted penurious amount. Perhaps – when I see your Mother and Mr Williams again – I shall just be able to get up a weak flicker of gratification – but that will be all. From even this effort – I shall be exempt on seeing <u>you</u>. Authors and Publishers are never expected to meet with any other than hostile feelings and on shy and distant terms. They never ought to have to shake hands: they should just bow to each other and pass by on opposite sides – keeping several yards distance between them. And besides – if obliged to communicate by Post – they should limit what they have to say to concise notes of about 3 lines apiece – which reminds me that this is too long and that it is time I thanked you for sending the Dividend – and begged with proper form to be permitted to subscribe myself –

respectfully Yours,
C Brontë

Charlotte to Ellen; Haworth, 21 May 1851

Your poor Mother is like Tabby – Martha and Papa – all these fancy I am somehow – by some mysterious process to be married in London – or to engage myself to matrimony – How I smile internally! How groundless and impossible is the idea! Papa seriously told me yesterday that if I married and left him – he should give up housekeeping and go into lodgings!!!

Charlotte to Sydney Dobell, author of the article in the Palladium; *Haworth, 24 May 1851*

I know nothing of such an orchard country as you describe. I have never seen such a region. Our hills only confess the coming of summer by growing green with young fern and moss, in secret little hollows. Their bloom is reserved for autumn; then they burn with a kind of dark glow, different, doubtless, from the blush of garden blossoms. About the close of next week I expect to go to London, to pay a brief and quiet visit. I fear chance will not be so propitious as to bring you to town while I am there; otherwise how glad I should be if you would call!

Chapter Fourteen

1851–2

Charlotte arrived in London at the end of May. Though she had intended to pay her usual brief and quiet visit, it soon turned into the busiest, most public and, at six weeks' duration, the lengthiest of her career. However insignificant her appearance, she was unable to escape attention; everyone wanted to meet the author of *Jane Eyre*, as she discovered when she attended one of Thackeray's lectures. A rather different slant to this particular story was later given by George Smith, who had taken Charlotte to hear her hero speak.

Charlotte to Patrick; 76 Gloucester Terrace, Hyde Park Gardens, London, 30 May 1851

Dear Papa

I have now heard one of Mr Thackeray's lectures and seen the Great Exhibition. On Thursday afternoon I went to hear the Lecture. It was delivered in a large and splendid kind of saloon – that in which the Great Balls of Almack's are given – the walls were all painted and gilded the benches were sofas stuffed and cushioned and covered with blue damask, the audience was composed of the very elite of London Society – Duchesses were there by the score – and amongst them the great and beautiful Duchess of Sutherland – the Queen's Mistress of the Robes. Amidst all this Thackeray just got up and spoke with as much simplicity and ease as if he had been speaking to a few friends by his own fireside – The Lecture was truly good: he has taken pains with the composition, it was finished without being in the least studied – a quiet humour and graphic force enlivened it throughout. He saw me as I entered the room and came straight up and spoke very kindly – he then took me to his Mother – a fine handsome old lady and introduced me to her. After the lecture somebody came behind me, leaned over the bench and said 'Will you permit me, as a Yorkshireman to introduce myself to you?' I turned round – was puzzled at first by the strange face I met – but in a minute I recognised the features. 'You are the Earl of Carlisle' I said   he smiled and assented – he went on to talk for sometime in a courteous kind fashion – he asked after you – recalled the platform electioneering scene at Haworth and begged to be remembered to you. Dr Forbes came up afterwards – and Mr Monckton Milnes – a Yorkshire Member of Parliament, who intro-duced himself on the same plea as Lord Carlisle.

Yesterday we went to the Crystal Palace – the exterior has a strange and elegant but somewhat unsubstantial effect – The interior is like a mighty Vanity Fair – the brightest colours blaze on all sides – and ware of all kinds – from diamonds to spinning jennies and Printing Presses, are there to be seen – It was very fine – gorgeous – animated – bewildering – but I liked Thackeray's lecture better.

I hope dear Papa that you are keeping well – with kind regards to Tabby and Martha and hopes that they are well too – I am

Your affectionate daughter
C Brontë

George Smith, A Memoir with Some Pages of Autobiography *(London, privately printed, 1902)*

On another occasion Thackeray roused the hidden fire in Charlotte Brontë's soul, and was badly scorched himself as the result. My mother and I had taken her to one of Thackeray's lectures on 'The English Humourists.' After the lecture Thackeray came down from the platform and shook hands with many of the audience, receiving their congratulations and compliments. He was in high spirits, and rather thoughtlessly said to his mother – Mrs Carmichael Smyth – 'Mother, you must allow me to introduce you to Jane Eyre.' This was uttered in a loud voice, audible over half the room. Everybody near turned round and stared at the disconcerted little lady, who grew confused and angry when she realised that every eye was fixed upon her. My mother got her away as quickly as possible.

On the next afternoon Thackeray called. I arrived at home shortly afterwards, and when I entered the drawing-room found a scene in full progress. Only these two were in the room. Thackeray was standing on the hearthrug, looking anything but happy. Charlotte Brontë stood close to him, with head thrown back and face white with anger. The first words I heard were, 'No, Sir! If _you_ had come to our part of the country in Yorkshire, what would you have thought of me if I had introduced you to my father, before a mixed company of strangers, as "Mr Warrington"?' Thackeray replied, 'No, you mean "Arthur Pendennis."' 'No, I _don't_ mean Arthur Pendennis!' retorted Miss Brontë; 'I mean Mr Warrington, and Mr Warrington would not have behaved as you behaved to me yesterday.' The spectacle of this little woman, hardly reaching to Thackeray's elbow, but, somehow, looking stronger and fiercer than himself, and casting her incisive words at his head, resembled the dropping of shells into a fortress.

By this time I had recovered my presence of mind, and hastened to interpose. Thackeray made the necessary and half-humorous apologies, and the parting was a friendly one.

Charlotte to Ellen; London, 2 June 1851

On Saturday I saw the Exhibition at Somerset House – about half a dozen of the pictures are good and interesting – the rest of little worth. Sunday – yesterday – was a day to be marked with a white stone – through most of the day I was very happy without being tired or over-excited – in the Afternoon – I went to hear D'Aubigny – the great Protestant French Preacher – it was pleasant – half sweet – half sad – and strangely suggestive to hear the French language once more. For health – I have so far got on very fairly considering that I came here far from well – Mr Taylor is gone some weeks since – I hear more open complaints now about his temper – than I did so long as he was in London – I am told it is unfortunately irritable – Of Mr Williams' society I have enjoyed one evening's allowance and liked it and him as usual – on such occasions his good qualities – of ease kindliness and intelligence are seen and his little faults and foibles hidden. Mr S. is somewhat changed in appearance – he looks a little older, darker and more care-worn – his ordinary manner is graver – but in the evening his spirits flow back to him – Things and circumstances seem here to be as usual – but I fancy there has been some crisis in which his energy and filial affection have sustained them all – this I judge from seeing that Mother and Sisters are more peculiarly bound to him than ever and that his slightest wish is an unquestioned law.

Charlotte to Patrick; London, 7 June 1851

Yesterday I went for the second time to the Crystal Palace – we remained in it about three hours – and I must say I was more struck with it on this occasion that [*sic*] at my first visit. It is a wonderful place – vast – strange new and impossible to describe. Its grandeur does not consist in <u>one</u> thing but in the unique assemblage of <u>all</u> things – Whatever human industry has created – you find there – from the great compartments filled with Railway Engines and boilers, with Mill-Machinery in full work – with splendid carriages of all kinds – with harness of every description – to the glass-covered and velvet spread stands loaded with the most gorgeous work of the goldsmith and silversmith – and the carefully guarded caskets full of real diamonds and pearls worth hundreds of thousands of pounds. It may be called a Bazaar or a Fair – but it is such a Bazaar or Fair as eastern Genii might have created. It seems as if magic only could have gathered this mass of wealth from all the ends of the Earth – as if none but supernatural hands could have arranged it thus – with such a blaze and contrast of colours and marvellous power of effect. The multitude filling the great aisles seems ruled and subdued by some invisible influence – Amongst the thirty thousand souls that peopled it the day I was there, not one loud noise was to be heard – not one irregular movement seen – the living tide rolls on quietly – with a deep hum like the sea heard from a distance.

Mr Thackeray is in high spirits about the success of his lectures – it is likely to add largely both to his fame and purse; he has however deferred this week's lecture till next Thursday at the earnest petition of the Duchesses and Marchionesses – who on the day it should have been delivered were necessitated to go down with the Queen and Court to Ascot Races. I told him I thought he did wrong to put it off on their account – and I think so still.

Charlotte to Mrs Joe Taylor; London, 7 June 1851

I have been rather more than a week in London – on the whole I am very quiet – for neither mentally or physically can I do with bustle – The Crystal Palace – you may believe is a famous and wonderful sight – I have been to it twice – and thought more of it the second time than the first – I think it requires a little consideration duly to get into the might – magic and mystery of the thing – it is hard work – going over it – after some three or four hours' peregrination – you come out very sufficiently bleached and broken in bits – when you come home you drop into a chair – or better – on to a bed, and don't rise for any invitation or menace or clamorous dinner-bell – till you have had a space of rest . . . To-night – (if all be well) I expect to hear and see Rachel – at the French Theatre. I wonder whether she will fulfil reasonable expectation – as yet it has not been my lot to set eyes on any serious acting for which I cared a fig –

Charlotte to Mrs Joe Taylor; London, 11 June 1851

I have seen Rachel – her acting was something apart from any other acting it has come in my way to witness – her soul was in it – and a strange soul she has – I shall not discuss it – it is my hope to see her again – She and Thackeray are the two living things that have a spell for me in this great London – and one of these is sold to the Great Ladies – and the other – I fear – to Beelzebub.

Charlotte to Ellen; London, 11 June 1851

I sit down to write you this morning in an inexpressibly flat state having spent the whole of yesterday and the day before in a gradually increasing headache which grew at last rampant and violent – ended with excessive sickness – and this morning I am better but quite weak and washy. I hoped to leave my headaches behind me at Haworth – but it seems I brought them carefully packed in my trunk and very much have they been in my way since I came.

Charlotte to Patrick; London, 14 June 1851

All other sights seem to give way to the Great Exhibition – into which thousands and tens of thousands continue to pour every day – I was in it again yesterday afternoon and saw the ex-royal family of France – the old Queen – the Duchess of Orleans and her two sons, &c. pass down the transept. I almost wonder the Londoners don't tire a little of this vast Vanity Fair – and indeed a new toy has somewhat diverted the attention of the grandees lately – viz. a Fancy Ball given last night by the Queen – the great lords and ladies have been quite wrapt up in preparations for this momentous event – their pet and darling – Mr Thackeray – of course sympathizes with them – he was here yesterday to dinner – and left very early in the evening in order that he might visit respectively the Duchess of Norfolk – the Marchioness of Londonderry – Ladies Chesterfield and Clanricarde – and see them all in their fancy costumes of the reign of Charles 2nd – before they set out for the Palace!

One of Charlotte's more unconventional outings during this London trip was to attend a Catholic meeting where, for the first time, she saw the *bête noire* of English Protestants, Nicholas Wiseman. As she reveals in this emotive account to her father, Charlotte shared fully in the anti-Catholic hysteria which had swept the country on Wiseman's recent elevation to the newly recreated archbishopric of Westminster and to a Cardinal's hat.

Charlotte to Patrick; London, 17 June 1851

Yesterday I saw Cardinal Wiseman and heard him speak. It was at a meeting for the Roman Catholic Society of St Vincent de Paul; the Cardinal presided. He is a big portly man something of the shape of Mr Morgan; he has not merely a double but a treble and quadruple chin; he has a very large mouth with oily lips, and looks as if he would relish a good dinner with a bottle of wine after it. He came swimming into the room smiling, simpering, and bowing like a fat old lady, and sat down very demure in his chair, and looked the picture of a sleek hypocrite. He was dressed in black like a bishop or dean in plain clothes, but wore scarlet gloves and a brilliant scarlet waistcoat. A bevy of inferior priests surrounded him, many of them very dark-looking and sinister men. The Cardinal spoke in a smooth whining manner, just like a canting Methodist preacher. The audience seemed to look up to him as to a god. A spirit of the hottest zeal pervaded the whole meeting. I was told afterwards that except myself and the person who accompanied me there was not a single Protestant present. All the speeches turned on the necessity of straining every nerve to make converts to popery. It is in such a scene that one feels what the Catholics are doing. Most persevering and enthusiastic are they in their work! Let Protestants look to it.

Charlotte to Ellen; London, 19 June 1851

I cannot boast that London has agreed with me well this time – the oppression of frequent head-ache – sickness and a low tone of spirits has poisoned many moments which might otherwise have been pleasant – Sometimes I have felt this hard and been tempted to murmur at Fate which condemns me to comparative silence and solitude for eleven months in the year – and in the twelveth while offering social enjoyment takes away the vigour and cheerfulness which should turn it to account. But circumstances are ordered for us, and we must submit –

Charlotte's fascination with the French actress, 'Rachel' (Elisa Felix), whom she would later depict as 'Vashti' in *Villette*, led her to pay a second, even more memorable visit to the theatre. This time, she saw Rachel in the part of Camilla, the tragic heroine of Corneille's classic play, *Horace*, a role which she played with such extraordinary passion that Charlotte was as much horrified and repelled as impressed.

Charlotte to Ellen; London, 24 June 1851

On Saturday I went to hear & see Rachel – a wonderful sight – terrible as if the earth had cracked deep at your feet and revealed a glimpse of hell – I shall never forget it – she made me shudder to the marrow of my bones: in her some fiend has certainly taken up an incarnate home. She is not a woman – she is a snake – she is the ---.

Charlotte to Sydney Dobell; written from Plymouth Grove, Manchester, where Charlotte stayed with Mrs Gaskell for two days on her return from London; 28 June 1851

Thackeray and Rachel have been the two points of attraction for me in town: the one, being a human creature, great, interesting, and <u>sometimes</u> good and kind; the other, I know not what, I think a demon. I saw her in Adrienne Lecouvreur and in Camilla – in the last character I shall <u>never</u> forget her – she will come to me in sleepless nights again and yet again. Fiends can hate, scorn, rave, wreathe, and <u>agonize</u> as she does, not mere men and women. I neither love, esteem, nor admire this strange being, but (if I could bear the high mental stimulus so long), I would go every night for three months to watch and study its manifestations.

Charlotte to Mrs Smith; Haworth, 1 July 1851

My dear Mrs Smith

Once more I am at home where – I am thankful to say – I found my Father very well. The journey to Manchester was a little hot and dusty – but otherwise pleasant enough. The two stout gentlemen who filled a portion of the carriage when I got in – quitted it at Rugby – and two other ladies and myself had it to ourselves the rest of the way.

The visit to Mrs Gaskell formed a cheering break in the journey – She is a woman of many fine qualities and deserves the epithet which I find is generally applied to her – charming. Her family consists of four little girls – all more or less pretty and intelligent – these scattered through the rooms of a somewhat spacious house –

seem to fill it with liveliness and gaiety. Haworth Parsonage is rather a contrast – yet even Haworth Parsonage does not look gloomy in this bright summer weather: it is somewhat still – but with the windows open – I can hear a bird or two singing on certain thorn-trees in the garden. My Father and the Servants think me looking better than when I left home, and I certainly feel better myself for the change.

You are too much like your Son to render it advisable that I should say much about your kindness during my visit. However, one cannot help (like Captain Cuttle) making a note of these matters. Papa says I am to thank you in his name and to offer you his respects which I do accordingly. With truest regards to all your circle

Believe me very sincerely
Yours –
C Brontë.

Charlotte to George Smith; Haworth, 1 July 1851

After a month's voyaging I have cast anchor once more – in a rocky and lonely little cove, no doubt, but still – safe enough. The visit to Mrs Gaskell on my way home – let me down easily – though I only spent two days with her – they were very pleasant. She lives in a large – cheerful, airy house, quite out of Manchester Smoke – a garden surrounds it, and as in this hot weather, the windows were kept open – a whispering of leaves and perfume of flowers always pervaded the rooms. Mrs Gaskell herself is a woman of whose conversation and company I should not soon tire – She seems to me kind, clever, animated and unaffected – her husband is a good and kind man too.

I went to Church by myself on Sunday Morning (they are Unitarians) On my return shortly before the family came home from Chapel – the servant said there was a letter for me. I wondered from whom – not expecting my Father to write and not having given the address elsewhere. Of course I was not at all pleased when the small problem was solved by the letter being brought – I never care for hearing from you the least in the world. Comment on the purport of your letter is unnecessary. I am glad – yet hardly dare permit myself to congratulate till the M.S. is fairly created and found to be worthy of the hand – pen and mind whence it is to emanate. This promise to go down into the country is all very well – yet secretly I cannot but wish that a sort of 'Chamber in the Wall' might be prepared at Cornhill – furnished (besides the bed, table, stool and candlestick which the Shunamite 'set' for Elisha) with a desk, pens, ink and paper. There the Prophet might be received and lodged; subjected to a system kind (perhaps) yet firm; roused each morning at six punctually – by the contrivance of that virtuous self-acting couch which casts from it its too fondly clinging inmate; served, on being duly arrayed, with a <u>slight</u> Breakfast of tea and toast: then – with the exception of a crust at one – no further gastronomic interruption to be allowed till 7.p.m. at which time – the greatest and most industrious of modern authors – should be summoned by the most spirited and vigilant of modern publishers to a meal comfortable and comforting – in short a good dinner – elegant, copious, convivial (in moderation) of which they should partake together in the finest spirit of geniality and fraternity – part at half-past nine – and at that salutary hour – withdraw each to recreating repose. Grand – would be the result of such a system pursued for six months.

The visit to London had not only refreshed Charlotte's spirits and instilled her with new enthusiasm for writing her next book, it had also renewed and increased the mutual liking between author and publisher. Though her letters to him were often tongue-in-cheek, they became increasingly flirtatious – though propriety was maintained by referring to herself as 'Currer Bell', rather than 'Charlotte Brontë'. Occasionally, but even then under the guise of giving advice, she allowed herself to express her admiration of him quite openly.

★*Charlotte to George Smith; Haworth, 8 July 1851*

If I had a right to whisper a word of counsel – it should be merely this. Whatever your present self may be – resolve with all your strength of resolution – never to degenerate thence – Be jealous of a shadow of falling off. Determine rather to look above that standard and strive beyond it. Everybody appreciates social properties – and likes his neighbour for possessing them – but perhaps few dwell on a friend's capacity for the intellectual or care how this might expand, if there were but facilities allowed for cultivation and space given for growth.

It seems to me that – even should such space and facilities be denied by stringent circumstances and a rigid Fate – still it should do you good fully to know and tenaciously to remember that you have such a capacity. When other people overwhelm you with acquired Knowledge – such as you have not had opportunity – perhaps – not application – to gain – derive not pride – but support from this thought. 'If no books had ever been written – some of these minds would themselves have remained blank pages – they only take an impression – they were not born with a record of thought on the brain, or an instinct of sensation on the heart. If I had never seen a printed volume, Nature would have offered my perceptions a varying picture and a continuous narrative which, without any other teacher than herself, would have schooled me to knowledge unsophisticated but genuine.' . . . Before I received your last – I had made up my mind to tell you that I should expect no letter from Cornhill for three months to come (intending afterwards to extend this abstinence to six months for I am jealous of becoming dependent on this indulgence – you – doubtless cannot see why, because you do not live my life) Nor shall I now <u>expect</u> a letter – but since you say that you would like to write now and then – I cannot say <u>never write</u> without imposing on my real wishes a falsehood which they reject – and doing to them a violence to which they entirely refuse to submit; I can only observe that when it pleases you to write whether seriously or for a little amusement – your notes – if they come to me – will come where they are welcome.

It was not just letters that Charlotte craved, but companionship, and after the bustle of her London visit, Haworth was unbearably quiet. She therefore wrote to two of her oldest friends, Ellen Nussey and Margaret Wooler, inviting them both to stay. Ellen accepted but Miss Wooler was forced to decline.

Charlotte to Margaret Wooler; Haworth, 14 July 1851

My first feeling on receiving your note was one of disappointment, but a little consideration sufficed to shew me that 'all was for the best.' In truth it was a great piece of extravagance on my part to ask you and Ellen Nussey together; it is much better to divide such good things. To have your visit in <u>prospect</u> will console me when hers is in <u>retrospect</u>. Not that I mean to yield to the weakness of clinging dependently to the society of friends – however dear – but still as an occasional treat I must value and even seek – such society as a necessary of life . . . The pleasures of society – I cannot offer you, nor those of fine scenery, but I place very much at your command the moors – some books – a series of quiet 'curling-hair times' – and an old pupil into the bargain.

The restorative effects of London and Ellen's visit did not last long; indeed, the contrast between those cheerful, sociable times and the monotony and loneliness of life at Haworth only increased Charlotte's depression. Letters were her only comfort and relief.

Charlotte to Ellen; Haworth, 1 September 1851

It is useless to tell you how I live – I endure life – but whether I enjoy it or not is another question – However I get on – The weather I think has not been good lately – or else the beneficial effects of change of air and scene are evaporating – in spite of regular exercise – the old head-aches – and starting wakeful nights are coming upon me again – But I <u>do</u> get on – and have neither wish nor right to complain.

★Charlotte to George Smith; Haworth, 8 September 1851

I ought not to forget – and indeed have not forgotten that your last propounds to this same Currer Bell a question about a 'Serial'. My dear Sir – give Currer Bell the experience of a Thackeray or the animal spirit of a Dickens, and then repeat the question. Even <u>then</u> he would answer, 'I will publish no Serial of which the last number is not written before the first comes out.' At present he would merely say that it is not worth your while to think of him.

I am glad you like the 'Early Rising on Cold Water System' as prescribed by Miss Martineau. You must be sure and try it, first on yourself – and then you must coax Mr Thackeray as one of the 'authors with whom you have influence' to adopt it. Nothing can be better suited to the 'Portly Classes,' like 'the Trade;' nor perhaps to the Anakim of Intellect such as Miss Martineau and Mr Thackeray – but never mind the small fry – the wretched – thin – under-sized scribblers; that Winter-Morning Walk by frosty star-light – that ice-cold bath and 3 tumblers of cold water would extinguish us altogether – and 'Small loss' – you would remark – Well – I incline to think so too. Meantime – I believe one of them to be

Sincerely yours
C Brontë

Charlotte to George Smith; Haworth, 15 September 1851

People say it is wrong to write speak or act on the spur of the moment or from first impulses – but I must do so for once. Your note of this morning is <u>so</u> like yourself – and – I must add – the best part of yourself – the <u>best</u> because the most individual – the least like ordinary-minded, ordinary feeling people who hardly ever doubt themselves – or think that what <u>they</u> have done can be in fault: but how far astray you are! How widely mistaken! <u>No</u> indeed your letter did not displease me – how could it? And you shall not find fault with what I like – for I <u>did</u> like the letter – nor shall you imagine me such a paltry-minded, porcupine-souled person as to fancy offence in what is genial, life-like and full of pleasant spirit . . . You mention the words 'flippancy and impertinent license'. Allow me to say that you never need to mention these words because (it seems to me) that your nature has nothing to do with the qualities they represent – nothing in this world. I do not believe that except perhaps to people who had themselves a good deal of effrontery and hardness – you could be otherwise than kindly and considerate – you are always so to Currer Bell – and always have been, which is one chief reason why he has a friendship for you: You must leave a contrary line of conduct to people of another species – of the Mr Lewes-order for instance. You are not like Mr Lewes – are you? If you are one atom like Mr Lewes – I will never trust my own instinct again – for I felt what he was through the very first letter he sent me – and had no wish ever to hear from – or write to him again – You appear to me something very different – <u>not</u> hard – <u>not</u> insolent – <u>not</u> coarse – <u>not</u> to be distrusted – all the contrary.

★*Charlotte to Mrs Gaskell, on an article in the* Westminster Review *by Mrs John Taylor, future wife of John Stuart Mill, whom Charlotte mistakenly believed to be the author; Haworth, 20 September 1851*

Of all the articles respecting which you question me – I have seen none except that notable one in the 'Westminster' on the Emancipation of Women. But why are you and I to think (perhaps I should rather say to <u>feel</u>) so exactly alike on some points that there can be no discussion between us? Your words on this paper express my thoughts. Well-argued it is – clear – logical – but – vast is the hiatus of omission – harsh the consequent jar on every finer chord of the soul.

What is this hiatus? I think I know and – knowing – I will venture to say; I think the writer forgets that there is such a thing as self-sacrificing love and disinterested devotion. When I first read the paper – I thought it was the work of a powerful-minded – clear-headed woman who had a hard jealous heart muscles of iron and nerves of bend leather; of a woman who longed for power and had never felt affection. To many women – affection is sweet – and power conquered – indifferent – though we all like influence won. I believe J S Mills would make a hard – dry dismal world of it – and yet he speaks admirable sense through a great portion of his article – especially when he says that if there be a natural unfitness in women for men's employment – there is no need to make laws on the subject – leave all careers open – let them try – those who ought to succeed will succeed or at least will have a fair chance – the incapable will fall back into their right place. He likewise disposes of the 'Maternity' argument very neatly. In short J S Mills' head is, I daresay – very good – but I feel disposed to scorn his heart – You are right when you say that there is a large margin in human nature over which the logicians have no dominion – glad am I that it is so.

Charlotte to George Smith; Haworth, 22 September 1851

Can I help wishing you well when I owe you directly or indirectly most of the good moments I now enjoy? Or can I avoid feeling grieved – mortified when the chance of aiding to give effect to my own wishes offers itself and – for want of strength – vitality – animal spirits – I know not what in men – passes by unimproved? Oh that Serial! It is of no use telling you what a storm in a tea-cup the mention of it stirred in Currer Bell's mind – what a fight he had with himself about it. You do not know – you cannot know how strongly his nature inclines him to adopt suggestions coming from so friendly a quarter; how he would like to take them up – cherish them – give them form – conduct them to a successful issue; and how sorrowfully he turns away feeling in his inmost heart that this work – this pleasure is not for him.

But though Currer Bell cannot do this – you are still to think him your friend – and you are still to be his friend. You are to keep a fraction of yourself – if it be only the end of your little finger – for him, and that fraction he will neither let gentleman or lady – author or artist – not even Miss McCrowdie (the Scotch Gentlewoman whose portrait you so graphically depict) take possession of – or so much as meddle with. He reduces his claim to a minute point – and that point he monopolizes.

At the end of September, Margaret Wooler paid her long-awaited visit to Haworth. Though her relationship with Charlotte had sometimes been prickly in the past, the two women now discovered a genuine admiration and affection for each other. Miss Wooler's serene acceptance of her spinsterhood and her quiet independence were both a comfort and an inspiration to Charlotte, whose greatest fear was that her own single state would turn her into a lonely and bitter old woman.

Charlotte to Ellen; Haworth, 3 October 1851

Do not think I have forgotten you because I have not written since your last . . . I have been busy – first with a somewhat unexpected visitor, a Cousin from Cornwall who has been spending a few days with us and now with Miss Wooler who came on Monday. The former personage we can discuss any time when we meet – Miss Wooler is and has been very pleasant. She is like good wine; I think time improves her – and really – whatever she may be in person – in mind she is younger than when at Roe-Head. Papa and She get on extremely well. I have just heard Papa walk into the dining-room and pay her a round compliment on her good sense. I think so far she has been pretty comfortable and likes Haworth – but as she only brought a small hand-basket of luggage with her she cannot stay long.

Charlotte to Margaret Wooler; Haworth, 21 October 1851

You very kindly refer with pleasure to your brief stay with us. My dear Miss Wooler – the visit was an enjoyment to me too – a <u>true</u> enjoyment; your society raised my spirits in a way that surprised myself – and which you could only appreciate by seeing me as I am alone – a spectacle happily not likely to come in your way. You speak of attentions rendered: I was not sensible of having made any exertion: to make you comfortable would be to make myself happy – but you would hardly permit me the opportunity of trying to do so . . . Papa enjoins me to give you his best respects and to say he hopes erelong to see you at Haworth again. He would not say this unless he meant it. Tabby and Martha have each with simple sincerity expressed the same wish; in short (D.V.) you will be <u>obliged</u> to visit us again some time –

Charlotte now decided that she simply had to get on with her next book. She was acutely conscious that it was nearly two years since the publication of *Shirley* and that her publishers had been remarkably forbearing in not pushing for its successor. In a new mood of self-discipline and resolve, she refused all invitations and settled down to write *Villette*.

Charlotte to Mrs Gaskell; Haworth, 6 November 1851

If anybody would tempt me from home <u>you</u> would, but – just now – from home I must not – will not go. I feel greatly better at present than I did three weeks ago. For a month or six weeks about the Equinox (autumnal and vernal) is a period of the year which, I have noticed, strangely tries me. Sometimes the strain falls on the mental – sometimes on the physical part of me – I am ill with neuralgic headache – or I am ground to the dust with deep dejection of spirits (not however such dejection but I can keep to myself). That weary time has – I think and trust – got over for this year. It was the anniversary of my poor brother's death and of my Sisters' failing health. I need say no more.

As to running away from home every time I have a battle of this sort to fight – it would not do. Besides the 'weird' would follow. As to shaking it off – that cannot be. I have declined to go to Mrs Fosters (Jane Arnold) to Miss Martineau – and now – I decline to go to you. But – listen! Do not think that I throw your kindness away or that it fails of doing the good you desire. On the contrary – the feeling expressed in your letter – proved by your invitation goes <u>right home</u> where you would wish it to go and heals as you would wish it to heal.

Charlotte to Ellen; Haworth, 19 November 1851

The only events of my life consist in that little change occasional letters bring. I have had two from Miss Wooler since she left Haworth which touched me much – She seems to think so much of a little congenial company – a little attention and kindness – that I am afraid these things are rare to her – she says she has not for many days known such enjoyment as she experienced during the ten days she stayed here – Yet you know what Haworth is – dull enough.

Charlotte to George Smith; Haworth, 20 November 1851

I have been able to work a little lately but I have quite made up my mind not to publish till Mr Thackeray's and Miss Martineau's books have had full career – so you will not think of me till next Autumn or thereabouts – is not this for the best? Meantime it is perhaps premature in me even to allude to the subject – but I do it partly to explain one of my motives for remaining at home this Winter. Winter is a better time for working than Summer – less liable to interruption. If I could always work – time would not be long – nor hours sad to me – but blank and heavy intervals still occur – when power and will are at variance. This however is talking Greek to an eminent and spirited Publisher. He does not believe in such things.

Charlotte to George Smith; Haworth, 28 November 1851

It is not at all likely that my book will be ready at the time you mention. If my health is spared I shall get on with it as fast as is consistent with its being done – if not <u>well</u> – yet as well as I can do it: <u>Not one whit faster</u>. When the mood leaves me (it has left me now – without vouch-safing so much as a word of a message when it will return) I put by the M.S. and wait till it comes back again; and God knows, I sometimes have to wait long – <u>very</u> long it seems to me.

Meantime – if I might make a request to you it would be this. Please to say nothing about my book till it is written and in your hands. You may not like it. I am not myself elated with it as far as it is gone – and authors – you need not be told – are always tenderly indulgent – even blindly partial to their own – even if it should turn out reasonably well – still – I regard it as ruin to the prosperity of an ephemeral book like a novel to be much talked about beforehand as if it were something great. People are apt to conceive – or at least to profess exaggerated expectations such as no performance can realise – then ensue disappointment and the due revenge – detraction and failure. If – when I write – I were to think of the critics who – I know – are waiting for Currer Bell, ready 'to break all his bones or ever he comes to the bottom of the den' – my hand would fall paralyzed on my desk. However I can but do my best – and then muffle my head in the mantle of Patience and sit down at her feet and wait.

The mood for writing had indeed left Charlotte, driven away by the unbearable misery consequent on the approaching second anniversary of Emily's death. As she did so often, Charlotte succumbed physically as well as mentally. Her illness was exacerbated by the understandable fear that she too was falling victim to the tuberculosis which had taken her brother and all her sisters. The death of Keeper, Emily's dog, could not have occurred at a worse moment, severing yet one more link with Charlotte's beloved sister.

Charlotte to Ellen; Haworth, 8 December 1851

Poor old Keeper died last Monday Morning – after being ill one night – he went gently to sleep – we laid his old faithful head in the garden. Flossy is dull and misses him. There was something very sad in losing the old dog; yet I am glad he met a natural fate – people kept hinting that he ought to be put away which neither Papa nor I liked to think of.

Charlotte to Ellen; Haworth, 17 December 1851

I cannot at present go to see you but I should be grateful if you could come and see me – were it only for a few days. To speak truth I have put on but a poor time of it during this month past – I kept hoping to be better – but was at last obliged to have recourse to medical advice – Sometimes I have felt very weak and low and longed much for society – but could not persuade myself to commit the selfish act of asking you merely for my own relief. The doctor speaks encouragingly, but as yet I don't get better. As the illness has been coming on for a long time – it cannot – I suppose – be expected to disappear all at once. I am not confined to bed but I am weak – have had no appetite for about three weeks – and my nights are very bad. I am well aware myself that extreme and continuous depression of spirits has had much to do with the origin of the illness – and I know a little cheerful society would do me more good than gallons of medicine.

Charlotte to Ellen; Haworth, 31 December 1851

Mr Ruddock came yesterday: unfortunately I was by no means so well as I had been last week – my head continued to ache all Monday – and yesterday the white tongue – parched mouth and loss of appetite were returned – accordingly I am to take more medicine. Mr R– however repeated that there was no organic disease – only a highly sensitive and irritable condition of the liver. It was Mr R– whom we saw in the gig on the moor that day we were walking out: he was going to a poor woman in labour. He saw us.

Charlotte to George Smith; Haworth, 31 December 1851

I am somewhat relieved about my health – being assured that notwithstanding some harassing symptoms – there is no organic unsoundness whatever – and encouraged to hope for better days if I am careful. The nervous system suffers the most – but I cannot tell how to steel it – Going from home is no cure.

Charlotte to Ellen; Haworth, 14 January 1852

My dear Ellen

I have certainly been ill enough since I wrote to you – but do not be alarmed or uneasy – I believe my sufferings have been partly – perhaps in a great measure owing to the medicine – the pills given me – they were alterative and contained a mixture of Mercury – this did not suit me – I was brought to a sad state – Thank God – I believe I am better – but too weak now to tell you particulars – Poor Papa has been in grievous anxiety – on the point of sending for Mr Teale, I had hard work to restrain him – Mr Ruddock was sorely flustered when he found what he had done – but I don't much blame him. Can't write more at present. Goodbye dear Nell

Yours faithfully,
C.B.

Charlotte to Margaret Wooler; Haworth, 20 January 1852

Your last kind note would not have remained so long unanswered if I had been in better health. While Ellen Nussey was with me, I seemed to recover wonderfully – but began to grow worse again the day she left, and this falling off proved symptomatic of a relapse. My Doctor called the next day; he said the headache from which I was suffering arose from inertness in the liver – prescribed some alterative pills and promised to call again in a week. I took the pills duly and truly – hoping for benefit – but every day I grew worse before the week was over I was very ill – unable to swallow any nourishment except a few tea-spoonsful of liquid per diem, my mouth became sore, my teeth loose, my tongue swelled, raw and ulcerated while water welled continually into my mouth. I knew by this time that Mercury had formed an ingredient in the alterative pills and that I was suffering from its effects. When my Doctor came and found me in this condition he was much shocked and startled; a result had been produced which he had not intended, nor anticipated: according to him the dose of blue pill he had given was not sufficient to salivate a child – and he talked much about exceptional sensitiveness of constitution &c. Strong medicines were then administered to counteract this mistake – so that altogether I have been much reduced. Thank God – I now feel better – and very grateful am I for the improvement – grateful no less for my dear Father's sake, than for my own.

Charlotte to Ellen; Haworth, 24 January 1852

And now my dear physician with reference to putting myself into your hands you must take notice of this – I am to live on the <u>very plainest</u> fare – to take <u>no butter</u> – at present I do not take tea – only milk and water with a little sugar and dry bread – this with an occasional mutton chop is my diet – and I like it better than anything else – During the week you were at Haworth – I did myself harm by eating too indiscriminately – but I am resolved to be more careful now – and indeed have no alternative if I wish to be well: Mr Ruddock has made me take tonics which have stimulated the appetite – but I eat little at a time.

By the last week in January, 1852, Charlotte was at last strong enough to accept Ellen's invitation to Brookroyd. Unfortunately, in doing so, she deprived herself of the opportunity of welcoming no less a figure than George Smith to Haworth Parsonage. Drawn by the alarming accounts of Charlotte's health, he had called in on his way to Scotland in order to see how she was for himself.

Charlotte to George Smith; Brookroyd, Birstall, 29 January 1852

I have rallied very rapidly within the last week and, as the date of this letter will shew you – am now from home – staying with the friend I told you of. I do wish now I had delayed my departure from home a few days longer that I might have shared with my Father the true pleasure of receiving you at Haworth Parsonage. Such a pleasure your visit would have been as I have sometimes dimly imagined but never ventured to realize.

Charlotte to Mrs Smith; Brookroyd, Birstall, 29 January 1852

Your note and invitation are very truly kind – but as Mr Smith will have told you – I am already from home trying the effect of those remedies you recommend – change of air and scene. I am much better than I was – though I cannot expect to be well all at once.

When I bid you good-bye in Euston Square Station – I determined in my own mind that I would not again come to London except under conditions which are yet unfulfilled. A treat must be earned before it can be enjoyed and the treat which a visit to you affords me is yet unearned, and must so remain for a time – how long I do not know.

I will tell you about my illness and how it came on. I suffered exceedingly from depression of spirits in the Autumn. Then – at the commencement of Winter the weather set in very severe. One day when I was walking out – I felt a peculiar pain in my right side. I did not think much of it at first – but was not well from that time. Soon after I took cold – the cold struck in, inflammatory action ensued, I had high fever at nights, the pain in my side became very severe – there was a constant burning and aching in my chest – I lost my sleep and could eat nothing. My own conclusion was that my lungs were affected – but on consulting a medical man – my lungs and chest were pronounced perfectly sound, and it appeared that the inflammation had fallen on the liver. I have since varied – being better sometimes when the internal fever subsided, and again worse when it was increased by change of weather or any other exciting cause – but I am told that there is no danger as it is a case of functional derangement – not of organic disease. The solitude of my life I have certainly felt very keenly this winter – but every one has his own burden to bear – and where there is no available remedy – it is right to be patient and trust that Providence will in his own good time lighten the load.

Charlotte to Mrs Gaskell; Brookroyd, Birstall, 6 February 1852

Thank you – my dear Mrs Gaskell, for your letter and all the kindness it expresses. As the date of this letter will shew – I am now from home – and have already benefited greatly by the kind attentions and cheerful society of the friends with whom I am staying – friends who probably do not care for me a pin – as Currer Bell – but who have known me for years as C.Brontë – and by whom I need not fear that my invalid weaknesses (which indeed I am fast overcoming) will be felt as a burden.

Certainly the past Winter has been to me a strange time – had I the prospect before me of living it over again – my prayer must necessarily be – 'Let this cup pass from me.'

Charlotte to Ellen; Haworth, 16 February 1852

Mr Ruddock to my dismay – came blustering in on Saturday – I had not intended to let him know of my return till this week – but somebody had caught sight of me at Keighley Station and told him I was come home. He was actually cross that I had not immediately written – he began about the quinine directly – I told him I thought it did not suit me – but he would not listen to reason – says it is the only thing to do me permanent good &c. however I procured a respite of a week – and meantime I go on with the hop-tea which as far as I know, agrees quite well. I said nothing about it to him – but I mentioned the potass – and he laughed it to scorn – I wish I knew better what to think of this man's skill. He seems to stick like a leech: I thought I should have done with him when I came home.

Charlotte had had a very narrow escape – as had the unfortunate Haworth surgeon, Mr Ruddock, who had almost earned a place for himself in the Hall of Eternal Shame by murdering his most famous patient. Charlotte's recovery was slow but with returning health came the ability to write again, which was a relief in itself. *Villette* began to take shape.

Chapter Fifteen

1852–3

The kindnesses of Smith, Elder & Co. towards their ailing authoress continued unabated. One especial privilege granted her was that of reading the first volume of William Thackeray's new novel, *The History of Henry Esmond, Esquire*, in manuscript before its publication. As usual, it roused both her admiration and indignation.

★*Charlotte to George Smith; Haworth, 14 February 1852*

It has been a great delight to me to read Mr Thackeray's Manuscript and I so seldom now express any sense of kindness that for once you must permit me without rebuke, to thank you for a pleasure so rare and special.

Yet I am not going to praise either Mr Thackeray or his book. I have read, enjoyed – been interested and – after all feel full as much ire and sorrow as gratitude and admiration. And still – one can never lay down a book of his – without the last two feelings having their part – be the subject of treatment what it may.

In the first half of the work what chiefly struck me was the wonderful manner in which the author throws himself into the spirit and letter of the times whereof he treats; the allusions, the illustrations, the style all seem to me so masterly in their exact keeping, their harmonious consistency, their nice natural truth, their pure exemption from exaggeration. No second-rate imitator can write in this way; no coarse scene painter can charm us with an allusion so delicate and perfect. But what bitter satire – what relentless dissection of diseased subjects! Well – and this too is right – or would be right if the savage surgeon did not seem so fiercely pleased with his work.

Thackeray likes to discover an ulcer or an aneurism; he has pleasure in putting his cruel knife or probe into quivering, living flesh. Thackeray would not like all the world to be good; no great satirist would like Society to be perfect.

As usual – he is unjust to women – quite unjust: there is hardly any punishment he does not deserve for making Lady Castlewood peep through a key-hole, listen at a door and be jealous of a boy and a milkmaid.

Many other things I noticed that – for my part – grieved and exasperated me as I read – but then again came passages so true – so deeply thought – so tenderly felt – one could not help forgiving and admiring.

I wish there was any one whose word he cared for to bid him good speed – to tell him to go on courageously with the book; he may yet make it the best thing he has ever written.

Charlotte to George Smith; Haworth, 17 February 1852

I do not think my note would do Mr Thackeray much good, but as – (so far as I recollect) it contains nothing I can have any objection to his seeing – you are quite at liberty to use your own discretion in the matter. What is said in that note – I would if I had nerve – and could speak without hesitating and looking like an idiot – say to himself – face to face – prepared of course – for any amount of sarcasm in reply – prepared too for those misconstructions which are the least flattering to human pride – and which we see and take in and smile at quietly and put by sadly: little ingenuities in which – if I mistake not – Mr Thackeray – with all his greatness – excels.

Charlotte to Margaret Wooler; Haworth, 12 March 1852

Your kind note holds out a strong temptation, but one that <u>must be resisted</u>. From home I must not go unless health or some cause equally imperative render a change necessary. For nearly four months now (<u>i.e.</u> since I first became ill) I have not put pen to paper – my work has been lying untouched and my faculties have been rusting for want of exercise; further relaxation is out of the question and <u>I</u>

will not permit myself to think of it. My publisher groans over my long delays; I am sometimes provoked to check the expression of his impatience with short and crusty answers.

Charlotte to Ellen; Haworth, 23 March 1852

You say, dear Nell – that you often wish I would chat on paper as you do. How can I –? Where are my materials? – is my life fertile in subjects of chat –? What callers do I see – what visits do I pay? No – you must chat and I must listen and say yes and no and thank you for five minutes recreation.

If Charlotte could not 'chat' to Ellen, she could and did pour out her heart to Mary Taylor, far away in New Zealand. Mary responded with her usual bracing advice – and news that her cousin, Ellen, with whom she had set up house and shop in Wellington, had died.

Mary Taylor to Charlotte; Wellington, New Zealand, April 1852

Your life in London is a 'new country' to me which I cannot even picture to myself. You seem to like it – at least some things in it, and yet your late letters to Mrs J[oe] Taylor talk of low spirits and illness. 'What's the matter with you now?' as my mother used to say, as if it were the twentieth time in a fortnight. It is really melancholy that now, in the prime of life, in the flush of your hard-earned prosperity, you can't be well! Did not Miss Martineau improve you? If she did, why not try her and her plan again? But I suppose if you had hope and energy to try, you w[oul]d be well.

Charlotte to Ellen; Haworth, 4 May 1852

The news of E. Taylor's death came to me last week in a letter from Mary – a long letter – which wrung my heart so – in its simple strong, truthful emotion – I have only ventured to read it once. It ripped up half-scarred wounds with terrible force – the death-bed was just the same – breath failing &c.

She fears she shall now in her dreary solitude become 'a stern, harsh, selfish woman' – this fear struck home – again and again I have felt it for myself – and what is <u>my</u> position – to Mary's?

**★★*Charlotte to Mrs Gaskell; Haworth, 22 May 1852*

I return all the letters in two packets – because I could not with clear conscience keep them longer unless I had thought of soon visiting Manchester, and these thoughts I do not entertain. Yet I keep the visit in view – and refresh myself now and then with a distant doubtful prospect thereof. On such and such conditions – (I say to myself) you shall one day go and see Mrs Gaskell. I only wish the conditions were fulfilled – but such is not the case.

Whenever I see Florence & Julia again – I shall feel like a fond but bashful suitor who views at a distance the fair personage to whom – in his clownish awe – he does not risk a near approach. Such is the clearest idea I can give you of my feeling towards children I like but to whom I am a stranger – and to what children am I not a stranger? They seem to me little wonders – their talk – their ways are all matter of half-admiring – half-puzzled speculation

Despite her intention not to go from home till she had completed her book, at the beginning of June, 1852, Charlotte spent a few weeks alone at Filey on the East Yorkshire coast, staying in the lodging house where she and Ellen had resided after Anne's death.

Charlotte to Patrick; Cliff House, Filey, 2 June 1852

On the whole I get on very well here – but I have not bathed yet as I am told it is much too cold and too early in the season. The Sea is very grand. Yesterday it was a somewhat unusually high tide – and I stood about an hour on the cliffs yesterday afternoon – watching the tumbling in of great tawny turbid waves – that made the whole shore white with foam and filled the air with a sound hollower and deeper than thunder. There are so very few visitors at Filey yet – that I and a few sea-birds and fishing-boats have often the whole expanse of sea, shore and cliff to ourselves – When the tide is out – the sands are wide – long and smooth and very pleasant to walk on.

When the high tides are in – not a vestige of sand remains. I saw a great dog rush into the sea yesterday – and swim and bear up against the waves like a seal – I wonder what Flossy would say to that.

On Sunday afternoon I went to a church which I should like Mr Nicholls to see. It was certainly not more than thrice the length and breadth of our passage – floored with brick – the walls green with mould – the pews painted white but the paint almost all worn off with time and decay – at one end there is a little gallery for the singers – and when these personages stood up to perform – they all turned their backs upon the congregation – and the congregation turned <u>their</u> backs on the pulpit and parson – The effect of this manoeuvre was so ludicrous – I could hardly help laughing – had Mr Nicholls been there – he certainly would have laughed out.

Charlotte to Ellen; Cliff House, Filey, 6 June 1852

I am at Filey utterly alone. Do not be angry. The step is right. I considered it and resolved on it with due deliberation. Change of air was necessary; there were reasons why I should <u>not</u> go to the South and why I should come here. On Friday I went to Scarbro', visited the church-yard and stone – it must be refaced and re-lettered – there are 5 errors. I gave the necessary directions – <u>that</u> duty then is done – long has it lain heavy on my mind – and that was a pilgrimage I felt I could only make alone.

Charlotte to Margaret Wooler; Filey-Bay, 23 June 1852

The first week or ten days – I greatly feared the sea-side would not suit me – for I suffered almost constantly from head-ache and other harassing ailments; the weather too was dark, stormy and excessively – <u>bitterly</u> cold; my Solitude, under such circumstances, partook of the character of Desolation; I had some dreary evening-hours and night-vigils. However – that passed; I think I am now better and stronger for the change, and in a day or two – hope to return home.

E. Nussey told me that Mr Wm Wooler said – people with my tendency to congestion of the liver – should walk three or four hours every day; accordingly I have walked as much as I could since

I came here, and look almost as sunburnt and weather-beaten as a fisherman or a bathing-woman with being out in the open air.

As to my work – it has stood obstinately still for a long while: certainly a torpid liver makes torpid brains: no spirit moves me.

Charlotte to Ellen; Haworth, 26 July 1852

I should not have written to you to-day by choice – lately I have again been harrassed with head-ache – the heavy electric atmosphere oppresses me much – Yet I am less miserable just now than I was a little while ago – a severe shock came upon me about Papa. He was suddenly attacked with acute inflammation of the eye. Mr Ruddock was sent for and after he had examined him – he called me into another room, and said that Papa's pulse was bounding at 150 per minute, that there was a strong pressure of blood on the brain – that in short the symptoms were decidedly apoplectic –

Active measures were immediately taken – by the next day the pulse was reduced to 90. – Thank God he is now better – though not well – the eye is still a good deal inflamed – He does not know his state – to tell him he had been in danger of apoplexy would almost be to kill him at once - it would increase the rush to the brain and perhaps bring about rupture – He is kept very quiet.

Charlotte to Ellen; Haworth, 3 August 1852

I write a line to say that Papa is now considered quite out of danger – his progress to health is not without relapse – but I think he gains ground if slowly – surely. Mr Ruddock says the seizure was quite of an apoplectic character – there was partial paralysis for two days – but the mind remained clear – in spite of a high degree of nervous irritation. One eye still remains inflamed – and Papa is weak – but all the muscular affection is gone – and the pulse is accurate. One cannot be too thankful that Papa's sight is yet spared – it was the fear of losing that which chiefly distressed him.

Charlotte to Ellen; Haworth, 25 August 1852

I write to tell you about yourself rather under constraint and in the dark – for your letters – dear Nell – are most remarkably oracular – dropping nothing but hints – which tie my tongue a good deal. What for instance can I say to your last postscript? It is quite Sybilline. I can hardly guess what checks you in writing to me – There is certainly no one in this house or elsewhere to whom I should shew your notes – and I do not imagine they are in any peril in passing through the Post-Offices.

Perhaps you think that as I generally write with some reserve – you ought to do the same. My reserve, however, has its foundation not in design, but in necessity – I am silent because I have literally nothing to say. I might indeed repeat over and over again that my life is a pale blank and often a very weary burden – and that the Future sometimes appals me – but what end could be answered by such repetition except to weary you and enervate myself?

The evils that now and then wring a groan from my heart – lie in position – not that I am a single woman and likely to remain a single woman – but because I am a lonely woman and likely to be lonely. But it cannot be helped and therefore imperatively must be borne – and borne too with as few words about it as may be.

Charlotte's depression was not helped by the slow progress of *Villette* and the feeling that, in taking so long to complete it, she was letting down her friends at Smith, Elder & Co.

Charlotte to Ellen; 24 September 1852

But oh Nell! I don't get on – I feel fettered – incapable – sometimes very low – However – at present the subject must not be dwelt upon – it presses me too hardly – nearly and painfully.

Charlotte to Ellen; Haworth, 9 October 1852

Papa expresses so strong a wish that I should ask you to come and I feel some little refreshment so absolutely necessary myself that I really must beg you to come to Haworth for one single week. I thought I would persist in denying myself till I had done my work – but I find it won't do – the matter refuses to progress – and this excessive solitude presses too heavily – So let me see your dear face Nell just for one reviving week.

Charlotte to Margaret Wooler; Haworth, 21 October 1852

Ellen Nussey has only been my companion one little week – I would not have her any longer – for I am disgusted with myself and my delays – and consider it was a weak yielding to temptation in me to send for her at all – but in truth my spirits were getting low – prostrate sometimes and she has done me inexpressible good. I wonder when I shall see you at Haworth again; both my Father and the servants have again and again insinuated a distinct wish that you should be requested to come in the course of the Summer and Autumn, but I always turned rather a deaf ear; 'Not yet' was my thought 'I want first to be free' – work first – then pleasure.

Freedom was close at hand for, by the end of the month, two thirds of *Villette* had been written and fair copied for her publishers. She sent off the manuscript with more trepidation than she had felt for any of her previous works. It was not just that the new book had been written without the benefit of her sisters' advice and criticism: she feared that George Smith would recognize his own portrayal as its hero, Dr John Bretton, and therefore the significance of the relationship between him and Lucy Snowe.

Charlotte to William Smith Williams; Haworth, 26 October 1852

In sending a return-box of books to Cornhill – I take the opportunity of enclosing 2 Vols. of M.S. the third Vol. is now so near completion that I trust, if all be well, I may calculate on its being ready in the course of two or three weeks. My wish is that the book should be published without Author's name –

I shall feel obliged if you will intimate the safe arrival of the manuscript.

Charlotte to George Smith; Haworth, 30 October 1852

You must notify me honestly what you think of 'Villette' when you have read it. I can hardly tell you how much I hunger to have some opinion besides my own, and how I have sometimes desponded and almost despaired because there was no one to whom to read a line – or of whom to ask a counsel. 'Jane Eyre' was not written under such circumstances, nor were two-thirds of 'Shirley'. I got so miserable about it, I could bear no allusion to the book – it is not finished yet – but now – I hope.

As to the anonymous publication – I have this to say. If the with-holding of the author's name should tend materially to injure the publisher's interest – to interfere with the booksellers' orders, &c. I would not press the point; but if no such detriment is contingent – I should be most thankful for the sheltering shadow of an incognito. I seem to dread the advertisements – the large lettered 'Currer Bell's New Novel' or 'New Work by the Author of "Jane Eyre"'. These, however, I feel well enough are the transcendentalisms of a retired wretch – and must not be intruded in the way of solid considerations; so you must speak frankly . . . You will see that 'Villette' touches on no matter of public interest. I cannot write books handling the topics of the day – it is of no use trying. Nor can I write a book for its moral – Nor can I take up a philanthropic scheme though I honour Philanthropy – And voluntarily and sincerely veil my face before such a mighty subject as that handled in Mrs Beecher Stowe's work – 'Uncle Tom's Cabin.' To manage these great matters rightly they must be long and practically studied – their bearings known intimately and their evils felt genuinely – they must not be taken up as a business-matter and a trading-speculation. I doubt not Mrs Stowe had felt the iron of slavery enter into her heart from childhood upwards long before she ever thought of writing books. The feeling throughout her work is sincere and not got up.

Charlotte to George Smith; Haworth, 3 November 1852

I feel very grateful for your letter: it relieved me much for I was a good deal harassed by doubts as to how 'Villette' might appear in other eyes than my own . . . As for the publishing arrangements – I leave them to Cornhill. There is undoubtedly a certain force in what you say about the inexpediency of affecting a mystery which cannot be sustained – so you must act as you think is for the best. I submit also to the advertisements and large letters – but under protest, and with a kind of ostrich-longing for concealment.

Most of the 3rd vol. is given to the development of the 'crabbed Professor's' character. Lucy must not marry Dr John; he is far too youthful, handsome, bright-spirited and sweet-tempered; he is a 'curled darling' of Nature and of Fortune; he must draw a prize in Life's Lottery; his wife must be young, rich and pretty; he must be made very happy indeed. If Lucy marries anybody – it must be the Professor – a man in whom there is much to forgive – much to 'put up with.' But I am not leniently disposed towards Miss <u>Frost</u> – from the beginning I never intended to appoint her lines in pleasant places.

Charlotte to William Smith Williams; Haworth, 6 November 1852

I must not delay thanking you for your kind letter with its candid and able commentary on 'Villette.' With many of your strictures – I concur. The 3rd vol. may perhaps do away with some of the objections – others will remain in force. I do not think the interest of the story culminates anywhere to the degree you would wish. What climax there is – does not come on till near the conclusion – and even then – I doubt whether the regular novel-reader will consider 'the agony piled sufficiently high' – (as the Americans say) or the colours dashed on to the Canvass with the proper amount of daring. Still – I fear they must be satisfied with what is offered: my palette affords no brighter tints – were I to attempt to deepen the reds or burnish the yellows – I should but botch.

Unless I am mistaken – the emotion of the book will be found to be kept throughout in tolerable subjection. As to the name of the heroine – I can hardly express what subtility of thought made me decide upon giving her a cold name; but – at first – I called her 'Lucy Snowe' (spelt with an 'e') which 'Snowe' I afterwards changed to 'Frost.' Subsequently – I rather regretted the change and wished it 'Snowe' again: if not too late – I should like the alteration to be made now throughout the M.S. A <u>cold</u> name she must have – partly – perhaps – on the 'lucus a non lucendo' principle – partly on that of the 'fitness of things' – for she has about her an external coldness.

Charlotte to George Smith; Haworth, 20 November 1852

I send the 3rd Vol. of 'Villette' to-day, having been able to get on with the concluding chapters faster than I anticipated. When you shall have glanced over it – speak, as before, frankly.

I am afraid Mr Williams was a little disheartened by the tranquillity of the 1st & 2nd Vols.: he will scarcely approve the former part of the 3rd, but perhaps the close will suit him better. Writers cannot choose their own mood: with them it is not always high-tide, nor – thank Heaven! – always Storm. But then – the Public must have 'excitement': the best of us can only say: 'Such as I have, give I unto thee' . . . Now that 'Villette' is off my hands – I mean to try to wait the result with calm. Conscience – if she be just – will not reproach me, for I have tried to do my best.

Charlotte to Ellen; Haworth, 22 November 1852

Truly thankful am I to be able to tell you that I finished my long task on Saturday, packed and sent off the parcel to Cornhill. I said my prayers when I had done it. Whether it is well or ill done – I don't know – D.V. I will now try to wait the issue quietly. The book, I think, will not be considered pretentious – nor is it of a character to excite hostility.

Having completed *Villette*, Charlotte now rewarded herself with the long-postponed visit to Ellen at Brookroyd, where she waited in vain for the usual prompt letter of approval from her publishers. Eventually, she could stand the strain no longer.

Charlotte to George Smith; Brookroyd, Birstall, 1 December 1852

I am afraid – as you do not write – that the 3rd Vol. has occasioned some disappointment. It is best, however, to speak plainly about it, if it be so. I would rather at once know the worst than be kept longer in suspense.

Charlotte to George Smith; Brookroyd, Birstall, 6 December 1852

On Sunday morning your letter came and you have thus been spared the visitation of the unannounced and unsummoned apparition of Currer Bell in Cornhill. Inexplicable delays should be avoided when possible, for they are apt to urge those subjected to their harrassment to sudden and impulsive steps.

I must pronounce you right again, in your complaint of the transfer of interest in the 3rd vol – from one set of characters to another. It is not pleasant, and will probably be found as unwelcome to the reader, as it was, in a sense, compulsory upon the writer. The spirit of Romance would have indicated another course, far more flowery and inviting; it would have fashioned a paramount hero, kept faithfully with him and made him supremely 'worshipful' – he should have an idol, and not a mute, unresponding idol – either –: but this would have been unlike Real Life, inconsistent with Truth – at variance with Probability.

Charlotte to Margaret Wooler; Brookroyd, Birstall, 7 December 1852

The money transaction, of course, remains the same – and perhaps is not quite equitable – but when an author finds that his work is cordially approved – he can pardon the rest; indeed my chief regret now lies in the conviction that Papa will be disappointed – he expected me to earn £700 – nor did I – myself – anticipate that a lower sum would be offered; however, 500£ is not to be despised.

Charlotte returned home from her visit to Ellen in a cheerful mood which was soon to be dispelled by a dramatic event. Arthur Bell Nicholls, her father's curate since 1845, unexpectedly proposed marriage to her.

Charlotte to Ellen; Haworth, 15 December 1852

This note – you will see – is from Mr Nicholls.

I know not whether you have ever observed him specially – when staying here – your perception in these matters is generally quick enough – <u>too</u> quick – I have sometimes thought – yet as you never said anything – I restrained my own dim misgivings – which could not claim the sure guide of vision. What Papa has seen or guessed – I will not inquire – though I may conjecture. He has minutely noticed all Mr Nicholls's low spirits – all his threats of expatriation – all his symptoms of impaired health – noticed them with little sympathy and much indirect sarcasm. On Monday evening – Mr N- was here to tea. I vaguely felt – without clearly seeing – as without seeing, I have felt for some time – the meaning of his constant looks – and strange, feverish restraint. After tea – I withdrew to the dining-room as usual. As usual – Mr N- sat with Papa till between eight & nine o'clock. I then heard him open the parlour door as if going. I expected the clash of the front door – He stopped in the passage: he tapped: like lightning it flashed on me what was coming. He entered – he stood before me. What his words were – you can guess, his manner – you can hardly realize – nor can I forget it – Shaking from head to foot, looking deadly pale, speaking low, vehemently yet with difficulty – he made me for the first time feel what it costs a man to declare affection where he doubts response.

The spectacle of one ordinarily so statue-like – thus trembling, stirred, and overcome gave me a kind of strange shock. He spoke of sufferings he had borne for months – of sufferings he could endure no longer – and craved leave for some hope. I could only entreat him to leave me then and promise a reply on the morrow. I asked him if he had spoken to Papa. He said – he dared not – I think I half-led, half put him out of the room. When he was gone I immediately went to Papa – and told him what had taken place. Agitation and Anger disproportionate to the occasion ensued – if I had <u>loved</u> Mr N and had heard such epithets applied to him as were used – it would have transported me past my patience – as it was – my blood boiled with a sense of injustice – but Papa worked himself into a state not to be trifled with – the veins on his temples started up like whip-cord – and his eyes became suddenly blood-shot – I made haste to promise that Mr Nicholls should on the morrow have a distinct refusal.

I wrote yesterday and got this note. There is no need to add to this statement any comment – Papa's vehement antipathy to the bare thought of any one thinking of me as a wife – and Mr Nicholls' distress – both give me pain. Attachment to Mr N- you are aware I never entertained – but the poignant pity inspired by his state on Monday evening – by the hurried revelation of his sufferings for many months – is something galling and irksome. That he cared something for me – and wanted me to care for him – I have long suspected – but I did not know the degree or strength of his feelings.

Charlotte to Ellen; Haworth, 18 December 1852

You ask how Papa demeans himself to Mr N-. I only wish you were here to see Papa in his present mood: you would know something of him. He just treats him with a hardness not to be bent – and a contempt not to be propitiated.

The two have had no interview as yet: all has been done by letter. Papa wrote – I must say – a most cruel note to Mr Nicholls, on Wednesday. In his state of mind and health (for the poor man is horrifying his landlady – Martha's Mother – by entirely rejecting his meals) I felt that the blow must be parried, and I thought it right to accompany the pitiless despatch by a line to the effect that – while Mr N- must never expect me to reciprocate the feeling he had expressed – yet at the same time – I wished to disclaim participation in sentiments calculated to give him pain; and I exhorted him to maintain his courage and spirits. On receiving the two letters, he set off from home. Yesterday came the enclosed brief epistle.

You must understand that a good share of Papa's anger arises from the idea – not altogether groundless – that Mr N. has behaved with disingenuousness in so long concealing his aim – forging that Irish fiction &c. I am afraid also that Papa thinks a little too much about his want of money; he says the match would be a degradation – that I should be throwing myself away – that he expects me, if I marry at all – to do very differently; in short – his manner of viewing the subject – is – on the whole, far from being one in which I can sympathize – My own objections arise from sense of incongruity and uncongeniality in feelings, tastes – principles.

The impossible situation could not continue indefinitely so, in a gesture worthy of one of Charlotte's novels, Mr Nicholls proffered his resignation and applied to become a missionary in Australia. Unable to bear the strain, Charlotte herself fled to London.

Charlotte to Ellen; Haworth, 2 January 1853

I am busy too in my little way – preparing to go to London this week – a matter which necessitates some little application to the needle. I find it is quite necessary that I should go to superintend the press as Mr S[mith] seems quite determined not to let the printing get on till I come. I have actually only recd 3 proof sheets since I was at Brookroyd. Papa wants me to go too – to be out of the way – I suppose – but I am sorry for one other person whom nobody pities but me. Martha is bitter against him: John Brown says <u>he should like to shoot him</u>. They don't understand the nature of his feelings – but I see now what they are. Mr N is one of those who attach themselves to very few whose sensations are close and deep – like an underground stream, running strong but in a narrow channel. He continues restless and ill – he carefully performs the occasional duty – but does not come near the church, procuring a substitute every Sunday.

A few days since he wrote to Papa requesting permission to withdraw his resignation. Papa answered that he should only do so on condition of giving his written promise never again to broach the obnoxious subject either to him or to me. This he has evaded doing, so the matter remains unsettled.

I feel persuaded the termination will be – his departure for Australia. Dear Nell – without loving him – I don't like to think of him, suffering in solitude, and wish him anywhere so that he were happier. He and Papa have never met or spoken yet.

Charlotte to Ellen; 112 Gloucester Terrace, Hyde Park, London,
11 January 1853

All in this house appear to be pretty much as usual and yet I see
some changes – Mrs S[mith] and her daughters look well enough –
but on Mr S- hard work is telling early – both his complexion, his
countenance and the very lines of his features are altered – it is rather
the remembrance of what he was than the fact of what he is which
can warrant the picture I have been accustomed to give of him. One
feels pained to see a physical alteration of this kind – yet I feel glad
and thankful that it is merely physical: as far as I can judge mind and
manners have undergone no deterioration – rather, I think, the
contrary. His Mother's account of the weight of work bearing upon
him is really fearful. In some of his notes to me I half suspected
exaggeration; it was no exaggeration – far otherwise.

Mr T[aylor] is said to be getting on well in India – but there are
complaints of his temper and nerves being rendered dreadfully
excitable by the hot climate; it seems he is bad to live with – I never
catch a pleasant word about him; except that his probity and usefulness
are held in esteem.

Charlotte to Mrs Gaskell; 112 Gloucester Terrace, London,
12 January 1853

I am now in London – as the date above will shew – staying very
quietly at my Publisher's, and correcting proofs &c. Before receiving
yours – I had felt and expressed to Mr Smith – reluctance to come
in the way of 'Ruth'. Not that I think she – (bless her very sweet
face! I have already devoured vol. 1st) would suffer from contact
with 'Villette', we know not but that the damage might be the other
way; but I have ever held comparisons to be odious, and would fain
that neither I nor my friends should be made subjects of the same.
Mr Smith purposes accordingly to defer the publication of my book
till the 24th inst: he says that will give 'Ruth' the start in all the
papers daily and weekly – and also will leave free to her all the
Feb[ruar]y magazines. Should this delay appear to you insufficient
– speak – and it shall be protracted.

I daresay – arrange as we may – we shall not be able wholly to prevent comparisons; it is the nature of some critics to be invidious: but we need not care: we can set them at defiance: they <u>shall</u> not make us foes: they <u>shall</u> not mingle with our mutual feelings one taint of jealousy: there is my hand on that: I know you will give clasp for clasp.

Charlotte to Ellen; 112 Gloucester Gardens, London, 19 January 1853

I still continue to get on very comfortably and quietly in London – in the way I like – seeing rather things than persons –. Being allowed to have my own choice of sights this time – I selected rather the <u>real</u> than the <u>decorative</u> side of Life – I have been over two prisons ancient & modern – Newgate and Pentonville – also the Bank, the Exchange the Foundling Hospital, – and to-day if all be well – I go with Dr Forbes to see Bethlehem Hospital. Mrs S[mith] and her daughters are – I believe – a little amazed at my gloomy tastes, but I take no notice.

Papa – I am glad to say – continues well – I enclose portions of two notes of his which will shew you – better than anything I can say – how he treats a certain subject – one of the notes purports to be written by Flossy!

Patrick, writing as Anne's dog, Flossy, to Charlotte; Haworth, January 1853

Flossy to his much respected and beloved Mistress, Miss Bronte;

My kind Mistress, as having only paws, I cannot write, but, I can dictate and my good Master, has undertaken to set down what I have to say – He well understands, the dog's language, which is not very copious, but is nevertheless, significant and quite sufficient for our purposes, and wants which are not many – I fear that my Master, will not do my simple language justice, but will write too much in his own style, which I consider quite out of character, and wrong – You have condescendingly sent your respects to me, for which I am very grateful, and in token of my gratitude, I struck the ground three times with my tail – But let me tell to you my affairs, just as they stand at present, in my little world, little in your opinion, but great in mine. Being old now, my youthful amusements, have lost their former relish – I no longer enjoy as, formerly, following sheep, and cats, and birds, and I cannot gnaw bones, as I once did – Yet, I am still merry and in good health and spirits – As many things are done before me, which would not be done, if I could speak, (well for us dogs that we cannot speak) so, I see a good deal of human nature, that is hid from those who have the gift of language. I observe these manuoevres, and am permitted to observe many of them, which if I could speak, would never be done before me – I see people cheating one another, and yet appearing to be friends – many are the disagreeable discoveries, which I make, which you could hardly believe if I were to tell them – One thing I have lately seen, which I wish to mention – No one takes me out to walk now, the weather is too cold, or too wet for my master to walk in, and my former travelling companion, has lost all his apparent kindness, scolds me, and looks black upon me – I tell my master all this, by looking grave, and puzzled, holding up one side of my head, and one lip, shewing my teeth there, looking full in his face and whining – Ah! my dear Mistress, trust dogs rather than men – They are very selfish, and when they have the power, (which no wise person will readily give them) very tyrannical – That you should act wisely in regard to men, women, and dogs is the sincere wish, of Yours most

Sincerely – Old Flossy.

Patrick to Charlotte; Haworth, January 1853

You may wish to know, how we have been getting on here especially in respect to <u>Master</u>, and <u>man</u>, On yesterday, I preached twice, but my man, was every way, very queer – He shun'd me, as if I had been a cobra de Capello – turning his head from the quarter, where I was, and hustling away amongst the crowd, to avoid contact – it required no Lavater to see, that his countenance was strongly indicative of mortified pride, and malevolent resentment – People, have begun to notice these things, and various conjectures are afloat – You thought me too severe – but I was not candid enough – His conduct might have been excus'd by the world, in a confirmed rake – or unprincipled army officer, but in a <u>Clergyman</u>, it is justly chargeable, with base design and inconsistency, – I earnestly wish that he had another and better situation – As I can never trust him any more, in things of importance – I wish him no ill – but rather good, and wish that every woman may avoid him forever, unless she should be determined on her own misery – All the produce of the Australian <u>Diggins</u> would not make him and any wife he might have, happy –

★★*Arthur Bell Nicholls to the Secretary of the Society for the Propagation of the Gospel; Haworth, 28 January 1853*

Revd. Sir

I beg to offer myself as a Candidate for Employment as a Missionary in the Australian Colonies. I return 'the papers of Questions' with answers. My present Engagement will be concluded by the end of May next.

I am Revd Sir
Your obt Servt
A:B:Nicholls

★★*The Reverend Sutcliffe Sowden, vicar of Hebden Bridge, to the Secretary of the Society for the Propagation of the Gospel; 31 January 1853*

I have known [Arthur Bell Nicholls] intimately for nearly 8 years, during which he has been a near neighbour. All that time he has fulfilled his duties as Curate in a most exemplary manner; & I have the greatest confidence in stating my confidence, that he will fulfil the duties of a missionary with equal advantage to his people, & credit to himself.

His character and conduct are above all reproach. His abilities are certainly more than average. His piety & zeal are admitted by those who are in his neighbourhood. His temper is firm, but guided by a wise judgement & much discretion. He has tact & good discrimination. During his long Curacy at Haworth he has laboured actively

& diligently, having frequently most of the responsibility of the Parish thro the age of his Incumbent. With the exception of the last 2 months or so, his health has been very good, enabling him to go through much work, & endure much fatigue.

Villette was published in January 1853 to reviews which, though hardly ecstatic, were generally approving. One of them wounded Charlotte deeply, however, because it was written by her friend Harriet Martineau; it led to an angry exchange of letters and, ultimately, to the end of their friendship.

Harriet Martineau, review of Villette, *in the* Daily News, *3 February 1853*

All the female characters, in all their thoughts and lives, are full of one thing, or are regarded by the reader in the light of that one thought – love. It begins with the child of six years old, at the opening – a charming picture – and it closes with it at the last page; and, so dominant is this idea – so incessant is the writer's tendency to describe the need of being loved, that the heroine, who tells her own story, leaves the reader at last under the uncomfortable impression of her having either entertained a double love, or allowed one to supersede another without notification of the transition. It is not thus in real life. There are substantial, heartfelt interests for women of all ages, and under ordinary circumstances, quite apart from love:

Charlotte to Harriet Martineau; Haworth, January/February 1853

I know what love is as I understand it; and if man or woman should be ashamed of feeling such love, then is there nothing right, noble, faithful, truthful, unselfish in this earth, as I comprehend rectitude, nobleness, fidelity, truth, and disinterestedness.

Yours sincerely,
C.B.

To differ from you gives me keen pain.

Review of Villette *in the* Literary Gazette, *5 February 1853*

This book would have made her famous, had she not been so already.
It retrieves all the ground she lost in *Shirley*, and it will engage a
wider circle of admirers than *Jane Eyre*, for it has all the best qualities
of that remarkable book, untarnished, or but slightly so, by its defects
. . . Some traces . . . of the coarseness which occasionally disfigured
Currer Bell's former books still remain; but, viewed as a whole,
there is so obvious an advance in refinement without loss of power,
that it would be invidious to qualify the admiration with which
Villette has inspired us by dwelling upon minor faults.

G. H. Lewes, review of Villette *in the* Leader, *12 February 1853*

Here, at any rate, is an *original book*. Every page, every paragraph, is
sharp with *individuality*. It is Currer Bell speaking to you, not the
Circulating Library reverberating echos. How *she* has looked at life,
with a saddened, yet not vanquished soul; what *she* has thought, and
felt, not what she thinks others will expect her to have thought and
felt; *this* it is we read of here, and this it is which makes her writing
welcome above almost every other writing. It has held us spell-bound.

Charlotte to George Smith; Haworth, 16 February 1853

I should like much to hear what you think of the general tone of
the notices – whether you regard them as reasonably satisfactory.
My Father seems pleased with them, and so am I, as an evidence
that the book is pretty well received.

Review of Villette *in the* Guardian, *23 February 1853*

Mannerism there certainly is about her, and an unpleasant mannerism,
from the somewhat cynical and bitter spirit in which she conceives
her tales. It may be the world has dealt hardly with her; it may be
that in her writings we gather the honest and truthful impressions
of a powerful but ill-used nature; that they are the result of affections
thrown back upon themselves, and harshly denied their proper scope

and objects. But so it is, that, in spite of their ability, they are not pleasant reading, and though their teaching may be necessary, it is too uniformly painful, and too little genial, to be accepted by the generality as unmingled truth . . . Lucy Snowe herself is *Jane Eyre* over again; both are reflections of Currer Bell; and for the reasons above given, though we admire the abilities of these young ladies, we should respectfully decline (ungallant critics that we are) the honour of their intimate acquaintance.

Charlotte to Mrs Gaskell; Haworth, 24 February 1853

I gave Sir James [Kay Shuttleworth] a copy of 'Villette' as an acknowledgement of his friendliness. I believe the gift perplexed him a little; it seemed to imply that of course he would read the book. He took great pains to put into words a neat apology for not giving himself that specially congenial pleasure. I hope some kind-hearted domestic has long ere this 'sided' the volumes out of his reach – thus enabling him to sink into oblivion of their existence.

Charlotte to George Smith; Haworth, 26 February 1853

At a late hour yesterday evening – I had the honour of receiving at Haworth Parsonage a distinguished guest – none other than W. M. Thackeray, Esqre.

Mindful of the rites of hospitality – I hung him in state this morning. He looks superb in his beautiful, tasteful gilded gibbet. For companion he has the Duke of Wellington; (do you remember giving me that picture?) and for contrast and foil – Richmond's portrait of an unworthy individual who – in such society – must be nameless. Thackeray looks away from the latter character with a grand scorn edifying to witness. I wonder if the giver of these gifts will ever see them on the walls where they now hang: it pleases me to fancy that one day he may.

The arrival of Thackeray's portrait was a bright spot in the otherwise increasingly gloomy atmosphere at Haworth. As the date of his departure grew closer, Mr Nicholls' misery became ever more obvious, compounded by the fact that he now regretted his hasty decision to enrol as an Australian missionary.

**★★*Arthur Bell Nicholls to the Secretary of the Society for the Propagation of the Gospel; 26 February 1853*

Since the date of my application, owing to the Solicitations of friends some doubts have occurred to me as to the desirableness of leaving the Country at present – When I have fully made up my mind upon the point I will again communicate with you –

Charlotte to Ellen; Haworth, 4 March 1853

The Bishop has been and is gone. He is certainly a most charming little Bishop – the most benignant little gentleman that ever put on lawn sleeves – yet stately too, and quite competent to check encroachments – His visit passed capitally well – and at its close, as he was going away, he expressed himself thoroughly gratified with all he had seen . . . Mr Nicholls demeaned himself not quite pleasantly – I thought he made no effort to struggle with his dejection but gave way to it in a manner to draw notice; the Bishop was obviously puzzled by it. Mr N also shewed temper once or twice in speaking to Papa. Martha was beginning to tell me of certain 'flaysome' looks also – but I desired not to hear of them. The fact is I shall be most thankful when he is well away – I pity him – but I don't like that dark gloom of his – He dogged me up the lane after the evening service in no pleasant manner – he stopped also in the passage after the Bishop and the other clergy were gone into the room – and it was because I drew away and went upstairs that he gave that look which filled Martha's soul with horror. She – it seems – meantime, was making it her business to watch him from the kitchen door – If Mr N be a good man at bottom – it is a sad thing that Nature has not given him the faculty to put goodness into a more attractive form –

Charlotte to William Smith Williams; Haworth, 23 March 1853

The note you sent this morning from Lady Harriet St Clair is precisely to the same purport as Miss Mulock's request – an application for exact and authentic information respecting the fate of M. Paul Emanuel!! You see how much the ladies think of this little man whom you none of you like. I had a letter the other day announcing that a lady of some note who had always determined that whenever she married, her elect should be the counterpart of Mr Knightley in Miss Austen's 'Emma' – had now changed her mind and vowed that she would either find the duplicate of Professor Emanuel or remain forever single!!!

I have sent Lady Harriette an answer – so worded as to leave the matter pretty much where it was. Since the little puzzle amuses the ladies it would be a pity to spoil their sport by giving them the key

Charlotte to George Smith; Haworth, 26 March 1853

With regard to that momentous point – M. Paul's fate – in case any one in future should request to be enlightened thereon – they may be told that it was designed that every reader should settle the catastrophe for himself, according to the quality of his disposition, the tender or remorseless impulse of his nature – Drowning and Matrimony are the fearful alternatives. The merciful – like Miss Mulock, Mr Williams, Lady Harriet St Clair and Mr Alexander Frazer [*i.e.* George Smith] – will of course choose the former and milder doom – drown him to put him out of pain. The cruel-hearted will on the contrary pitilessly impale him on the second horn of the dilemma – marrying him without ruth or compunction to that – person – that – that – individual – 'Lucy Snowe.'

★★*Arthur Bell Nicholls to the Secretary of the Society for the Propagation of the Gospel; 1 April 1853*

As, owing to the Severity of the weather, the Rheumatic affection, with which I have been troubled during the winter has not abated as rapidly as I expected, I have been induced by my friends to relinquish for the present my intention of going abroad –

Will you therefore convey to your Committee my sincere thanks for their kindness in entertaining my application; & also my hope, that I shall meet with a like consideration, if in the course of a few months I should wish to renew the subject?

Charlotte to Ellen; Haworth, 6 April 1853

You ask about Mr N. I hear he has got a curacy – but do not yet know where – I trust the news is true. He & Papa never speak. He seems to pass a desolate life. He has allowed late circumstances so to act on him as to freeze up his manner and overcast his countenance not only to those immediately concerned but to every one. He sits drearily in his rooms – If Mr Cartman or Mr Grant or any other clergyman calls to see and as they think to cheer him – he scarcely speaks – I find he tells them nothing – seeks no confidant – rebuffs all attempts to penetrate his mind – I own I respect him for this – He still lets Flossy go to his rooms and takes him to walk – He still goes over to see Mr Sowden some times – and poor fellow – that is all. He looks ill and miserable. I think and trust in Heaven he will be better as soon as he fairly gets away from Haworth. I pity him inexpressibly. We never meet nor speak – nor dare I look at him – silent pity is just all I can give him – and as he knows nothing about that – it does not comfort. He is now grown so gloomy and reserved – that nobody seems to like him – his fellow-curates shun trouble in that shape – the lower orders dislike it – Papa has a perfect antipathy to him – and he – I fear – to Papa – Martha hates him – I think he might almost be <u>dying</u> and they would not speak a friendly word to or of him. How much of all this he deserves I can't tell – certainly he never was agreeable or amiable – and is less so now than ever – and alas! I do not know him well enough to be sure that there is truth and true affection – or only rancour and corroding disappointment at the bottom of his chagrin. In this state of things I must be and I am – <u>entirely passive</u>. I may be losing the purest gem – and to me far the most precious – life can give – genuine attachment – or I may be escaping the yoke of a morose temper – In this doubt conscience will not suffer me to take one step in opposition to Papa's will – blended as that will is with the most bitter and unreasonable prejudices. So I just leave the matter where we must leave all important matters.

Charlotte to Ellen; Haworth, 16 May 1853

– yesterday was a strange sort of day at church. It seems as if I were to be punished for my doubts about the nature and truth of poor Mr N–'s regard. Having ventured on Whitsunday to stay the sacrament – I got a lesson not to be repeated. He struggled – faltered – then lost command over himself – stood before my eyes and in the sight of all the communicants white, shaking, voiceless – Papa was not there – thank God! Joseph Redman spoke some words to him – he made a great effort – but could only with difficulty whisper and falter through the service. I suppose he thought; this would be the last time; he goes either this week or the next. I heard the women sobbing round – and I could not quite check my own tears.

What had happened was reported to Papa either by Joseph Redman or John Brown – it excited only anger – and such expressions as 'unmanly driveller.' Compassion or relenting is no more to be looked for than sap from firewood.

I never saw a battle more sternly fought with the feelings than Mr N– fights with his – and when he yields momentarily – you are almost sickened by the sense of strain upon him. However he is to go – and I cannot speak to him or look at him or comfort him a whit – and I must submit. Providence is over all – that is the only consolation

Charlotte to Ellen; Haworth, 19 May 1853

I cannot help feeling a certain satisfaction in finding that the people here are getting up a subscription to offer a testimonial of respect to Mr N– on his leaving the place. Many are expressing both their commiseration and esteem for him. The Churchwardens recently put the question to him plainly. Why was he going? Was it Mr Brontë's fault or his own? His own – he answered. Did he blame Mr Brontë? 'No: he did not: if anybody was wrong it was himself.' Was he willing to go? 'No: it gave him great pain.' Yet he is not always right. I must be just –. He shows a curious mixture of honour and obstinacy; feeling and sullenness. Papa addressed him at the school tea-drinking – with <u>constrained</u> civility, but with <u>civility</u>. He did not reply civilly: he cut short further words. This sort of treatment offered in public is what Papa never will forget or forgive – it inspires him with a silent bitterness not to be expressed. I am afraid both are unchristian in their mutual feelings: Nor do I know which of them is least accessible to reason or least likely to forgive. It is a dismal state of things.

Charlotte to Ellen; Haworth, 27 May 1853

You will want to know about the leave-taking – the whole matter is but a painful subject but I must treat it briefly.

The testimonial was presented in a public meeting: Mr Fawsett and Mr Grant were there – Papa was not very well and I advised him to stay away which he did.

As to the last Sunday – it was a cruel struggle. Mr N ought not to have had to take any duty.

He left Haworth this morning at 6 o'clock. Yesterday evening he called to render into Papa's hands the deeds of the National School – and to say good bye. They were busy cleaning – washing the paint &c. in the dining-room so he did not find me there. I would not go into the parlour to speak to him in Papa's presence. He went out thinking he was not to see me – and indeed till the very last moment – I thought it best not – But perceiving that he stayed long before going out at the gate – and remembering his long grief I took courage

371

and went out trembling and miserable. I found him leaning against the garden-door in a paroxysm of anguish – sobbing as women never sob. Of course I went straight to him. Very few words were interchanged – those few barely articulate: several things I should have liked to ask him were swept entirely from my memory. Poor fellow! But he wanted such hope and such encouragement as I <u>could</u> not give him. Still I trust he must know now than [*sic*] I am not cruelly blind and indifferent to his constancy and grief. For a few weeks he goes to the south of England – afterwards he takes a curacy somewhere in Yorkshire but I don't know where.

Papa has been far from strong lately – I dare not mention Mr N.s name to him – He speaks of him quietly and without opprobrium to others – but to me he is implacable on the matter.

However he is gone – gone – and there's an end of it. I see no chance of hearing a word about him in future – unless some stray shred of intelligence comes through Mr Grant or some other second-hand source. In all this it is not <u>I</u> who am to be pitied at all and of course nobody pities me – they all think in Haworth that I have disdainfully refused him &c. if pity would do Mr N- any good – he ought to have and I believe has it. They may abuse me, if they will, whether they do or not – I can't tell.

Chapter Sixteen

1853—5

Once Mr Nicholls had left Haworth, Charlotte tried hard to distract herself from dwelling on him. Reading a copy of Thackeray's newly published lectures should have been a treat; instead, it provoked bitter memories of Branwell's fate. An attempt to arrange a long-promised visit by Mrs Gaskell was thwarted by Charlotte's own ill-health and even a trip to Scotland with Mary Taylor's brother, Joe, and his family turned into a disaster.

★Charlotte to George Smith; Haworth, May 1853

The 'Lectures' arrived safely; I have read them through twice. They must be studied to be appreciated. I thought well of them when I heard them delivered, but now I see their real power, and it is great . . . I was present at the Fielding lecture: the hour spent in listening to it was a painful hour. That Thackeray was wrong in his way of treating Fielding's character and vices – my conscience told me. After reading that lecture – I trebly feel that he was wrong – dangerously wrong. Had Thackeray owned a son grown or growing up – a son brilliant but reckless – would he of [sic] spoken in that light way of courses that lead to disgrace and the grave?

He speaks of it all as if he theorized; as if he had never been called on in the course of his life to witness the actual consequences of such failings; as if he had never stood by and seen the issue – the final result of it all. I believe if only once the spectacle of a promising life blasted in the outset by wild ways – had passed close under his eyes – he never <u>could</u> have spoken with such levity of what led to its piteous destruction. Had I a brother yet living, – I should tremble to let him read Thackeray's lecture on Fielding; I should hide it away from him. If, in spite of precaution, it fell into his hands, – I should earnestly pray him not to be misled by the voice of the charmer – let him charm never so wisely.

Charlotte to Mrs Gaskell; Haworth, 1 June 1853

When you take leave of the domestic circle and turn your back on Plymouth Grove to come to Haworth, you must do it in the spirit which might sustain you in case you were setting out on a brief trip to the backwoods of America. Leaving behind your husband, children, and civilisation, you must come out to barbarism, loneliness, and liberty. The change will perhaps do good, if not too prolonged.

Patrick to Mrs Gaskell; Haworth, June 1853

I am obliged to act as amanuensis for my Daughter, who is at present, confined for the most part, to her bed, with influenza, and frequent sharp attacks of 'tic-douloureax,' in the head, which have rendered her utterly unable to entertain you as she could wish – and besides this, she is afraid of communicating the complaints by contagion, which would be cause for sad reflection should you have to suffer from your intended kind visit – I can assure you, that your not visiting us, as we wished and expected, will be a great disappointment both to my Daughter and me – From what I have heard my Daughter say respecting you, and from the perusal of your literary works, I shall give you a most hearty welcome, whenever you may come –

Charlotte to Mrs Gaskell; Haworth, 9 July 1853

A thought occurs to me. Do you – who have so many friends, so large a circle of acquaintance – find it easy, when you sit down to write – to isolate yourself from all those ties and their sweet associations – as to be quite your own woman – uninfluenced, unswayed by the consciousness of how your work may affect other minds – what blame, what sympathy it may call forth? Does no luminous cloud ever come between you and the severe Truth – as you know it in your own secret and clear-seeing Soul? In a word, are you never tempted to make your characters more amiable than the life — by the inclination to assimilate your thoughts to the thoughts of those who always <u>feel</u> kindly, but sometimes fail to <u>see</u> justly? Don't answer the question. It is not intended to be answered.

Charlotte to Margaret Wooler; Haworth, 30 August 1853

My late absence was but for a week, when I accompanied Mr & Mrs Joe Taylor and baby on a trip to Scotland. They went with the intention of taking up their quarters at Kirkcudbright or some watering-place on the Solway Frith [*sic*]. We barely reached that locality, and had stayed but one night — when the baby (that rather despotic member of modern households) exhibited some symptoms of indisposition. To my unskilled perception its ailments appeared very slight — nowise interfering with its appetite or spirits, but parental eyes saw the matter in a different light: the air of Scotland was pronounced unpropitious to the child — and consequently we had to retrace our steps. I own I felt some little reluctance to leave 'bonnie Scotland' so soon and so abruptly, but of course I could not say a word, since however strong on my own mind the impression that the ailment in question was very trivial and temporary (an impression confirmed by the issue — as the slight diarrhoea disappeared in a few hours) I could not be absolutely certain that such was the case — and had any evil consequences followed a prolonged stay — I should never have forgiven myself.

Ilkley was the next place thought of. We went there, but I only remained three days — for in the hurry of changing trains at one of the stations — my box was lost and without clothes, I could not stay. I have heard of it since — but have not yet regained it. In all probability it is now lying at Kirkcudbright where it was directed.

Charlotte to Mrs Gaskell; Haworth, September 1853

I was glad to get your little note, glad to hear you were at home again. Not that, practically, it makes much difference to me whether you are in Normandy or Manchester: the shorter distance separates perhaps as effectually as the longer, yet there is a mental comfort in thinking that but thirty miles intervene.

Come to Haworth as soon as you can; the heath is in bloom now; I have waited and watched for its purple signal as the forerunner of your coming. It will not be quite faded before the 16th, but after that it will soon grow sere. Be sure to mention the day and hour of your arrival at Keighley.

At last, in mid-September, Charlotte and Patrick were able to welcome Mrs Gaskell to Haworth Parsonage. She stayed a brief few days but the visit confirmed all her prejudices about Charlotte's background, most particularly those about Patrick, for whom she had a preconceived dislike. It passed off happily enough at the time, but the enduring consequences were only to be seen four years later when Mrs Gaskell published her *Life of Charlotte Brontë*. Her immediate impressions were no less powerful and emotive – and mistaken – as she recorded in an evocative letter written on her return home.

Mrs Gaskell to a friend; September 1853

We turned up a narrow bye lane near the church – past the curate's, the schools and skirting the pestiferous church yard we arrived at the door into the Parsonage yard. In I went, – half-blown back by the wild vehemence of the wind which swept along the narrow gravel walk – round the corner of the house into a small plot of grass, enclosed within a low stone wall, over which the more ambitious grave-stones towered all round. There are two windows on each side the door & steps up to it . . . in at the door into an exquisitely clean passage, to the left into a square parlour looking out on the grass plot, the tall head-stones beyond, the tower end of the church, the village houses & the brown moors.

Miss Brontë gave me the kindest welcome, and the room looked the perfection of warmth, snugness & comfort, crimson predominating in the furniture, w[hi]ch <u>did well</u> with the bleak cold colours without. Every thing in her department has been new within the last few years; and everything, furniture, appointments, &c. is admirable for its consistency. all simple, good, sufficient for every possible reasonable want, & of the most delicate and scrupulous cleanliness. She is so neat herself I got quite ashamed of any touches of untidiness − a chair out of its place, − work left on the table were all of them, I could see, annoyances to her habitual sense of order; not annoyances to her temper in the least − you understand the difference. There was her likeness by Richmond, given to her father by Messrs Smith & Elder, the later print of Thackeray, & a good likeness of the Duke of Wellington, hanging up. My room was above this parlour, and looking on the same view, which was really beautiful in certain lights moon-light especially. Mr Brontë lives almost entirely in the room opposite (right hand side) of the front door: behind his room is the kitchen behind the parlour a store room kind of pantry. Mr Brontë's bedroom is over his sitting room, Miss Brontë's over the kitchen, the servants over the pantry. Where the rest of the household slept when they were all one large family I can't imagine. The wind goes piping & wailing and sobbing round the square unsheltered house in a very strange unearthly way . . . Mr Brontë came in at tea − an honour to me I believe. Before tea we had had a long delicious walk right against the wind on Penistone Moor which stretches directly behind the Parsonage going over the hill in brown & purple sweeps and falling softly down into a little upland valley through which a 'beck' ran; & beyond again was another great waving hill, − and in the dip of that might be seen another yet more distant, & beyond that the said Lancashire came; but the sinuous hills seemed to girdle the world like the great Norse Serpent, & for my part I don't know if they don't stretch up to the North Pole. On the moors we met no one − Here and there in the gloom of the distant hollows she pointed out a dark grey dwelling − to the Scotch firs growing near them often, − & told me such wild tales of the ungovernable families who lived or had lived therein that Wuthering Heights even seemed tame comparatively. Such dare-devil people, − men especially, − & women so stony & cruel in some of their feelings & so passionately fond in others − They are a queer people up there. Small landed proprietors − dwelling on one spot since Q. Eliz. − and lately adding marvellously to their incomes by using the water power of the becks in the woollen manufacture which has sprung up during the last 50 years: – uneducated – unrestrained by public opinion – for their equals in position are as bad as themselves, & the poor, besides being densely ignorant are all dependent on their employers . . . These people build grand houses, & live in the kitchens, own hundreds of thousands of pounds & yet bring up their sons with only just enough learning to qualify them for over-lookers during their father's lifetime & greedy grasping money-hunters after his death . . . In the evening Mr Brontë went to his room & smoked a pipe, – a regular clay – & we sat over the fire & talked – talked of long ago when that very same room was full of children; & how one by one they had dropped off into the church-yard close to the windows. At ½ past 8 we went in to prayers, – soon after nine every one was in bed but we two; – in general there she sits quite alone thinking over the past; for her eye-sight prevents her reading or writing by candlelight, & knitting is but very mechanical, & does not keep the thoughts from wandering. Each day – I was 4 there – was the same in outward arrangement – breakfast at 9, in Mr Brontë's room, – which we left immediately after   What he does with himself through the day I cannot imagine! He is a tall fine looking old man, with silver bristles all over his head; nearly blind; speaking with a strong Scotch accent (he comes from the North of Ireland, raised himself from the ranks of a poor farmer's son, – & was rather intimate with Lord Palmerston at Cambridge, a pleasant soothing recollection now, in his shut-out life. There was not a sign of engraving map writing materials beyond a desk &c. no books but those contained on two hanging shelves between the windows, – his pipes, & a spittoon, if you know what that is)   He was very polite & agreeable to me; paying rather elaborate old-fashioned compliments, but I was sadly afraid of him in my inmost soul; for I caught a glare of his stern eyes over his spectacles at Miss Brontë once or twice which made me know my man; and he talked at her sometimes . . . Moreover to account for my fear – rather an admiring fear after all – of Mr Brontë, please to take into account that though I like the beautiful glittering of bright flashing steel I don't fancy fire-arms at all; and Miss Brontë never remembers her father dressing himself in the morning without putting a loaded pistol in his pocket, just as regularly as he puts on his watch. There was this little deadly pistol sitting down to breakfast with us, kneeling down to prayers at night − to say nothing of a loaded gun hanging up on high ready to pop off on the slightest emergency . . . But all this time I wander from the course of our day, which is the course of her usual days. Breakfast over, the letters come; not many, sometimes for days none at all. About 12 we went out to walk. At 2 we dined about 4 we went out again; at 6 we had tea; by nine every one was in bed but ourselves. Monotonous enough in sound, but not a bit in reality.

Charlotte to Mrs Gaskell; Haworth, 25 September 1853

After you left, the house felt very much as if the shutters had been suddenly closed and the blinds let down. One was sensible during the remainder of the day of a depressing silence, shadow, loss, and want. However, if the going away was sad, the stay was very pleasant and did permanent good. Papa, I am sure, derived real benefit from your visit; he has been better ever since.

Mrs Gaskell had left Haworth determined to further her friend's relationship with Mr Nicholls, and promptly set about plotting how to secure him an income that would make him an acceptable suitor in Patrick's eyes.

Mrs Gaskell to Richard Monckton Milnes; Plymouth Grove, Manchester, 29 October 1853

I felt sure you would keep the story secret, − if my well-meant treachery becomes known to her I shall lose her friendship, which I prize most highly. I have been thinking over little bits of the conversation we had relating to a pension. I do not think she would take it; and I am quite sure that <u>one</u> hundred a year given as acknowledgement of his merits, as a good faithful clergyman would give her ten times the pleasure that <u>two</u> hundred a year would do, if bestowed upon her in her capacity as a writer. I am sure he is a thoroughly good hard-working, self-denying curate . . . Her father's only reason for his violent & virulent opposition is Mr Nicholls's utter want of money, or friends to help him to any professional advancement.

Mr Nicholls' suit received another indirect and equally unexpected boost in November when any lingering hopes Charlotte had cherished about the possibility of one day marrying her publisher, George Smith, were cruelly dashed. Fearing the worst, she could not bring herself to apply directly to him but wrote, instead, to his mother.

★★*Charlotte to Mrs Smith; Haworth, 21 November 1853*

I had not heard from your Son for a long time − and this morning I had a note from him which tho' brief and not explicit seemed indicative of a good deal of uneasiness & disturbance of mind. The cover was edged & sealed with black but he does not say what relative he has lost. As it is not deep mourning I trust no harm has befallen any one very near to him, but I cannot resist writing to you for a word of explanation. What ails him? Do you feel uneasy about him, or do you think he will soon be better? If he is going to take an important step in life − as some of his expressions would seem to imply − is it one likely to conduce to his happiness and welfare?

Mrs Smith to Charlotte; London, c. 22−23 November 1853

I shall answer you[r] kind enquiries about my Son with a great deal of pleasure − he is quite well and very happy − he is thinking of taking a very important step in Life the most important and I think with every prospect of happiness I am very thankful and pleased about it − I am sure he will as soon as it is quite settled enter into all the particulars with you − it is not so yet tho' I have no doubt in my own mind all will be as his best Friends could wish and you will soon hear from him again −

Charlotte could not but feel the implicit reproof in Mrs Smith's letter. Mortified, she reacted by severing all her links with Cornhill − even with the kindly William Smith Williams − and wrote a venomous letter of congratulation to George Smith himself.

Charlotte to William Smith Williams; Haworth, 6 December 1853

My dear Sir

I forwarded last week a box of return books to Cornhill which –
I trust arrived safely. To-day I received the 'Edinburgh Guardian,'
for which I thank you.

Do not trouble yourself to select or send any more books. These
courtesies must cease some day – and I would rather give them up
than wear them out

Believe me
Yours sincerely
C Brontë

Charlotte to George Smith; Haworth, 10 December 1853

My dear Sir

In great happiness, as in great grief – words of sympathy should
be few. Accept my meed of congratulation – and believe me

Sincerely yours
C.Brontë

George Smith's desertion had followed hard on the heels of a quarrel with
Ellen, whose implacable opposition to the very idea of Charlotte marrying
Mr Nicholls had caused a serious breach between the two friends. Char-
lotte's isolation was becoming increasingly marked.

Charlotte to Margaret Wooler; Haworth, 12 December 1853

I wonder how you are spending these long winter evenings. Alone
– probably – like me. The thought often crosses me, as I sit by myself
– how pleasant it would be if you lived within a walking distance,
and I could go to you sometimes, or have you to come and spend
a day and night with me . . . I fear you must be very solitary at
Hornsea. How hard to some people of the world it would seem to
live your life – how utterly impossible to live it with a serene spirit
and an unsoured disposition! It seems wonderful to me – because

you are not like Mrs Ruff – phlegmatic and impenetrable – but received from nature feelings of the very finest edge. Such feelings when they are locked up – sometimes damage the mind and temper. They don't with you. It must be partly principle – partly self-discipline which keeps you as you are.

Charlotte to Mrs Gaskell; Haworth, 27 December 1853

If ever it should befal you to live a very still lonely life (which I believe it never will, for you are too genial to sink to the obscure lot) you will find once and again that the Post shall bring you a letter which you shall receive eagerly, read with keen interest, mark in it facts you wish further elucidated – points of information on which you incline to dwell and ask the further developement – you shall feel in it perhaps a friendly feeling breathed throughout which warms you and makes you grateful to the heart's core; in short you shall find in this letter everything to stimulate to an immediate answer on your part. You put it away, saying in about three days I shall reply. The three days pass; you happen to be a little downcast; it seems to you that you have nothing to say worth saying. It may be very pleasant to you to <u>receive</u> letters, but what can <u>you</u> write worth imparting? You let this impression prevail, and it grows, and for a time masters you.

This predicament is often mine, and I stand thus with regard to your last letter.

One person whose letters had not gone unanswered was Mr Nicholls, with whom Charlotte had reluctantly been drawn into a secret correspondence. Others had been active on his behalf, too, but it was not until Charlotte herself decided that she wanted to get to know him better that matters finally came to a head.

Richard Monckton Milnes to Mrs Gaskell; 30 January 1854

I must tell you that I made Mr Nicholls' acquaintance in Yorkshire. He is a strong-built, somewhat hard-featured man, with a good deal of Celtic sentiment about his manner & voice – quite of the type of the northern Irishman.

He seemed sadly broken in health & spirits & declined two cures, which Dr Hook enabled me to offer him – one in Lancashire of considerable interest, but requiring much energy – another in Scotland, requiring none at all. He gave me the impression of a man whose ardour was burnt out. I was amused at his surprise at the interest I took in him & I carefully avoided any mention of you. He spoke with great respect of Mr Bronte's abilities & character & of her simply & unreservedly.

Mary Taylor to Ellen; New Zealand, 24 February 1854

You talk wonderful nonsense ab[ou]t C Brontë in y[ou]r letter. What do you mean about 'bearing her position so long, & enduring to the end'? & still better – 'bearing our lot whatever it is'. If its C's lot to be married sh[oul]d n't she bear that too? or does your strange morality mean that she sh[oul]d refuse to ameliorate her lot when it lies in her power. How w[oul]d she be inconsistent with herself in marrying? Because she considers her own pleasure? If this is so new for her to do, it is high time she began to make it more common. It is an outrageous exaction to expect her to give up her choice in a matter so important, & I think her to blame in having been hitherto so yielding that her friends can think of making such an impudent demand.

Charlotte to Ellen; Haworth, 11 April 1854

Mr Nicholls came on Monday 3rd – and was here – all last week. Matters have progressed thus since last July. He renewed his visit in Septbr – but then matters so fell out that I saw little of him. He continued to write. The correspondence pressed on my mind I grew very miserable in keeping it from Papa. At last sheer pain made me gather courage to break it – I told all. It was very hard and rough work at the time – but the issue after a few days was that I obtained leave to continue the communication. Mr N– came in Jan[uar]y he was ten days in the neighbourhood. I saw much of him – I had stipulated with Papa for opportunity to become better acquainted – I had it and all I learnt inclined me to esteem and, if not love – at least affection – Still Papa was very – <u>very</u> hostile – bitterly unjust. I told Mr Nicholls the great obstacles that lay in his way. He has persevered – The result of this his last visit is – that Papa's consent is gained – that his respect, I believe is won – for Mr Nicholls has in all things proved himself disinterested and forbearing. He has shewn too that while his feelings are exquisitely keen – he can freely forgive. Certainly I must respect him – nor can I withhold from him more than mere cool respect. In fact, dear Ellen, I am engaged. Mr Nicholls in the course of a few months will return to the curacy of Haworth. I stipulated that I would not leave Papa – and to Papa himself I proposed a plan of residence – which should maintain his seclusion and convenience uninvaded and in a pecuniary sense bring him loss instead of gain [*sic*]. What seemed at one time – impossible – is now arranged – and Papa begins really to take a pleasure in the prospect.

For myself – dear Ellen – while thankful to One who seems to have guided me through much difficulty, much and deep distress and perplexity of mind – I am still very calm – <u>very</u> – inexpectant. What I taste of happiness is of the soberest order. I trust to love my husband – I am grateful for his tender love to me – I believe him to be an affectionate – a conscientious – a high-principled man – and if with all this, I should yield to regrets – that fine talents, congenial tastes and thoughts are not added – it seems to me I should be most presumptuous and thankless.

Providence offers me this destiny. Doubtless then it is the best for me – Nor do I shrink from wishing those dear to me one not less happy . . . I mean to write to Miss Wooler shortly. Good-bye – There is a strange – half-sad feeling in making these announcements – The whole thing is something other than imagination paints it beforehand: cares – fears – come inextricably mixed with hopes.

Charlotte to Margaret Wooler; Haworth, 12 April 1854

It gives me unspeakable content to see that – now my Father has once admitted this new view of the case – he dwells on it complacently. In all arrangements his convenience and seclusion will be scrupulously respected. Mr Nicholls seems deeply to feel the wish to comfort and sustain his declining years. I think from Mr N.'s character – I may depend on this not being a mere transitory impulsive feeling, but rather that it will be accepted steadily as a duty – and discharged tenderly as an office of affection.

The destiny which Providence in His goodness and wisdom seems to offer me will not – I am aware – be generally regarded as brilliant – but I trust I see in it some germs of real happiness. I trust the demands of both feeling and duty will be in some measure reconciled by the step in contemplation. It is Mr N's wish that the marriage should take place this Summer – he urges the month of July – but that seems very soon.

Charlotte to Ellen; Haworth, 15 April 1854

The feeling which had been disappointed in Papa – was <u>ambition</u> – paternal <u>pride</u>. ever a restless feeling – as we all know. Now that this unquiet spirit is exorcised – Justice, which was once quite forgotten – is once more listened to – and affection – I hope – resumes some power.

My hope is that in the end this arrangement will turn out more truly to Papa's advantage – than any other it was in my power to achieve. Mr N- only in his last letter – refers touchingly to his earnest desire to prove his gratitude to Papa by offering support and consolation to his declining age. This will not be mere <u>talk</u> with him – he is no talker – no dealer in professions.

Charlotte to Mrs Gaskell; Haworth, 18 April 1854

I could almost cry sometimes that in this important action in my life I cannot better satisfy papa's perhaps natural pride. My destiny will not be brilliant, certainly, but Mr Nicholls is conscientious, affectionate, pure in heart and life. He offers a most constant and tried attachment – I am very grateful to him. I mean to try and make him happy, and papa too.

Only one person did not receive a letter from Charlotte announcing her forthcoming marriage. George Smith was simply sent a business letter informing him that it had 'become necessary that my Stock in the Funds should be transferred to another name'. When he responded with congratulations and good wishes, Charlotte relented and wrote him her first – and last – friendly letter since his own marriage. Unable to avoid appearing self-defensive about her choice of husband, she nevertheless managed to end her letter with a sting in its tail.

Charlotte to George Smith; Haworth, 25 April 1854

The step in contemplation is no hasty one; on the gentleman's side, at least, it has been meditated for many years, and I hope that in at last acceding to it – I am acting right; it is what I earnestly wish to do. My future husband is a clergyman. He was for eight years my Father's curate. He left because the idea of this marriage was not entertained as he wished. His departure was regarded by the parish as a calamity – for he had devoted himself to his duties with no ordinary diligence. Various circumstances have led my Father to consent to his return, nor can I deny that my own feelings have been much impressed and changed by the nature and strength of the qualities brought out in the course of his long attachment. I fear I must accuse myself of having formerly done him less than justice. However he is to come back now. He has foregone many chances of preferment to return to the obscure village of Haworth. I believe I do right in marrying him. I mean to try to make him a good wife. There has been heavy anxiety – but I begin to hope all will end for the best. My expectations, however, are very subdued – very different – I dare say – to what <u>yours</u> were before you were married . . . In the course of the year that is gone – Cornhill and London have receded a long way from me – the links of communication have waxed very frail and few. It must be so in this world. All things considered – I don't wish it otherwise

It soon became clear that Mr Nicholls would get his own way and the marriage would be celebrated in the summer. Charlotte embarked on a flurry of preparations for the wedding and paid a series of bridal visits to the Nusseys, Taylors and Gaskells. Though her fiancé was included in the invitations, this was something Charlotte wished to do alone.

Charlotte to Mrs Gaskell; Haworth, 26 April 1854

[Mr Gaskell] must be pleased to be satisfied with only receiving my acknowledgments and thanks for his invitation to Mr Nicholls. The fact is I have not transmitted it to its destination – Mr Nicholls left his church but very lately and will have to leave it again soon – on business – and I think while he is there it is as well not to be instrumental in unsettling him. Yet I trust the day will come when he will see both you and Mr Gaskell. I had a little talk with him about my 'latitudinarianism' and his opposite quality. He did not bristle up at all – nor feel stiff and unmanageable – he only groaned a little over something in 'Shirley' touching 'baptismal regeneration and a wash-hand basin.' Yet if he is indulgent to some points in me – I shall have carefully to respect certain reverse points in him. I don't mean to trifle with matters deep-rooted and delicate of conscience and principle. I know that when once married I shall often have to hold my tongue on topics which heretofore have rarely failed to set that unruly member in tolerably facile motion. But I will not be a bigot – My heart will always turn to the good of every sect and class.

Charlotte to Ellen; Haworth, 28 April 1854

Papa – thank God! continues to improve much. He preached twice on Sunday and again on Wednesday and was not tired – his mind and mood are different to what they were – so much more cheerful and quiet. I trust the illusions of Ambition are quite dissipated – and that he really sees it is better to relieve a suffering and faithful heart – to secure in its fidelity a solid good – than unfeelingly to abandon one who is truly attached to his interests as well as mine – and pursue some vain empty Shadow –

As the wedding day drew closer, pre-marital nerves affected both Charlotte and Mr Nicholls.

Charlotte to Ellen; Haworth, 22 May 1854

I had a letter a day or two since announcing that Mr Nicholls comes to-morrow. I feel anxious about him – more anxious on one point than I dare quite express to myself. It seems he has again been suffering sharply from his rheumatic affection. I hear this not from himself but from another quarter – He was ill while I was at Manchester and Brookroyd. He uttered no complaint to me, dropped no hint on the subject. Alas! He was hoping he had got the better of it – and I know how this contradiction of his hopes will sadden him. For unselfish reasons he did so earnestly wish this complaint might not become chronic. I fear – I fear – but however I mean to stand by him now whether in weal or woe. This liability to rheumatic pain was one of the strong arguments used against the marriage. It did not weigh somehow – If he is doomed to suffer – it seems that so much the more will he need care and help. And yet the ultimate possibilities of such a case are appalling. You remember your Aunt Nussey. Well – come what may – God help and strengthen both him and me. I look forward to to-morrow with a mixture of impatience and anxiety. Poor fellow! I want to see with my own eyes how he is.

Charlotte to Ellen; Haworth, 27 May 1854

Mr Nicholls has just left me this morning. Your hopes were not ill-founded. At first I was thoroughly frightened by his look when he came on Monday last – It was wasted and strange, and his whole manner nervous. My worst apprehensions – I thought were in the way of being realized. However – inquiry gradually relieved me. In the first place – he could give his ailment no name. He had not had one touch of rheumatism – that report was quite groundless – He was going to die, however, or something like it, I took heart on hearing this – which may seem paradoxical – but you know – dear Nell – when people are really going to die – they don't come a distance of some fifty miles to tell you so.

Having drawn in the horns of my sympathy – I heard further that he had been to Mr Teale – and was not surprised to receive the additional intelligence that that gentleman informed him that he had no manner of complaint whatever except an over-excited mind – In short I soon discovered that my business was – instead of sympathizing – to rate him soundly. He had wholesome treatment while he was at Haworth – and went away singularly better. Perfectly unreasonable however on some points – as his fallible sex are not ashamed to be – groaning over the prospect of a few more weeks of bachelorhood – as much as if it were an age of banishment or prison. It is probable he will fret himself thin again in the time – but I certainly shall not pity him if he does – there is not a woman in England but would have more sense – more courage – more sustaining hope than to behave so.

Man is indeed an amazing piece of mechanism when you see – so to speak – the full weakness – of what he calls – his strength. There is not a female child above the age of eight but might rebuke him for the spoilt petulance of his wilful nonsense.

Charlotte to Margaret Wooler; Haworth, 16 June 1854

Mr Nicholls enters with true kindness into my wish to have all done quietly, and he has made such arrangements as – I trust – will secure literal privacy. Yourself, E Nussey & Mr Sowden will be the only persons present at the ceremony – Mr & Mrs Grant are asked to the breakfast afterwards. I know you will kindly excuse this brief note – for I am and have been <u>very</u> busy – and must still be busy up to the very day. Give my sincere love to all Mr Carter's family – I hope Mr Carter and Mr Nicholls may meet some day – I believe mutual acquaintance would, in time, bring mutual respect – but one of them at least requires <u>knowing</u> to be <u>appreciated</u> – And I must say that I have not yet found him to lose with closer knowledge – I make no grand discoveries – but I occasionally come on a quiet little nook of character which excites esteem – He is always reliable, truthful, faithful, affectionate; a little unbending perhaps – but still persuadable – and open to kind influence. A man never indeed to be driven – but who may be led.

Charlotte and Arthur Bell Nicholls were married as quietly as Charlotte wished on 29 June 1854, in Haworth church. Patrick did not attend the service, which was performed by Arthur's old friend, the Reverend Sutcliffe Sowden. The bride was given away by her old head-mistress, Miss Wooler, and Ellen acted as bridesmaid. Immediately after the ceremony, the newly-weds left for Ireland, where Charlotte was to be introduced to her husband's family, an experience which proved a pleasant surprise.

Charlotte to Margaret Wooler; Banagher, 10 July 1854

Three of Mr Nicholls' relatives met us in Dublin – his brother and 2 cousins. The Ist (brother) is manager of the Grand Canal from Dublin to Banagher – a sagacious well-informed and courteous man – his cousin is a student of the University and has just gained 3 premiums. The other cousin was a pretty lady-like girl with gentle English manners. They accompanied us last Friday down to Banagher – his Aunt – Mrs Bell's residence, where we now are.

I cannot help feeling singularly interested in all about the place. In this house Mr Nicholls was brought up by his uncle Dr Bell – It is very large and looks externally like a gentleman's country-seat – within most of the rooms are lofty and spacious and some – the drawing-room – dining-room &c. handsomely and commodiously furnished – The passages look desolate and bare – our bed-room, a great room on the ground-floor would have looked gloomy when we were shewn into it but for the turf-fire that was burning in the wide old chimney – The Male members of this family – such as I have seen seem thoroughly educated gentlemen. Mrs Bell is like an English or Scotch matron quiet, kind and well-bred – It seems she was brought up in London.

Both her daughters are strikingly pretty in appearance – and their manners are very amiable and pleasing. I must say I like my new relations. My dear husband too appears in a new light here in his own country. More than once I have had deep pleasure in hearing his praises on all sides. Some of the old servants and followers of the family tell me I am a most fortunate person for that I have got one of the best gentlemen in the country. His Aunt too speaks of him with a mixture of affection and respect most gratifying to hear. I was not well when I came here – fatigue and excitement had nearly knocked me up – and my cough was become very bad – but Mrs

Bell has nursed me both with kindness and skill, and I am greatly better now.

I trust I feel thankful to God for having enabled me to make what seems a right choice – and I pray to be enabled to repay as I ought the affectionate devotion of a truthful, honourable, unboastful man.

Charlotte to Katie Winkworth; Cork, 27 July 1854

Yes – I am married – a month ago this very day I changed my name – the same day we went to Conway – stayed a few days in Wales – then crossed from Holyhead to Dublin – after a short sojourn in the capital – went to the coast – such a wild, iron-bound coast – with such an ocean-view as I had not yet seen – and such battling of waves with rocks as I had never imagined.

My husband is not a poet or a poetical man – and one of my grand doubts before marriage was about 'congenial tastes' and so on. The first morning we went out on to the cliffs and saw the Atlantic coming in all white foam, I did not know whether I should get leave or time to take the matter in my own way. I did not want to talk – but I <u>did</u> want to look and be silent. Having hinted a petition, licence was not refused – covered with a rug to keep off the spray I was allowed to sit where I chose – and he only interrupted me when he thought I crept too near the edge of the cliff. So far he is always good in this way – and this protection which does not interfere or pretend – is I believe a thousand times better than any half sort of pseudo sympathy. I will try with God's help to be as indulgent to him whenever indulgence is needed.

We have been to Killarney – I will not describe it a bit. We saw and went through the Gap of Dunloe. A sudden glimpse of a very grim phantom came on us in the Gap. The guide had warned me to alight from my horse as the path was now very broken and dangerous – I did not feel afraid and declined – we passed the dangerous part – the horse trembled in every limb and slipped once but did not fall – soon after she (it was a mare) started and was unruly for a minute – however I kept my seat – my husband went to her head and led her – suddenly without any apparent cause – she seemed to go mad – reared, plunged – I was thrown on the stones right under her – my husband did not see that I had fallen – he still held her – I saw and felt her kick, plunge, trample round me. I had my thoughts about the moment – its consequences – my husband – my father – When my plight was seen, the struggling creature was let loose – she sprung over me. I was lifted off the stones neither bruised by the fall nor touched by the mare's hoofs. Of course the only feeling left was gratitude for more sakes than my own.

Charlotte to Ellen; Haworth, 9 August 1854

Since I came home I have not had an unemployed moment; my life is changed indeed – to be wanted continually – to be constantly called for and occupied seems so strange: yet it is a marvellously good thing. As yet I don't quite understand how some wives grow so selfish – As far as my experience of matrimony goes – I think it tends to draw you out of, and away from yourself.

Charlotte to Margaret Wooler; Haworth, 22 August 1854

We have had many callers too – from a distance – and latterly some little occupation in the way of preparing for a small village entertainment. Both Mr Nicholls and myself wished much to make some response for the hearty welcome and general good-will shewn by the parishioners on his return; accordingly the Sunday and Day-Scholars and Teachers – the church ringers, singers &c. to the number of 500 were asked to Tea and Supper in the school-room – They seemed to enjoy it much, and it was very pleasant to see their happiness. One of the villagers in proposing my husband's health described him as 'a consistent Christian and a kind gentleman.' I own the words touched me – and I thought – (as I know you would have thought – had you been present) – that to merit and win such a character was better than to earn either Wealth or Fame or Power. I am disposed to echo that high but simple eulogium now. If I can do so with sincerity and conviction seven years – or even a year hence – I shall esteem myself a happy woman.

Charlotte to Margaret Wooler; Haworth, 19 September 1854

You ask what visitors we have had? – A good many amongst the clergy &c. in the neighbourhood, but none of note from a distance. Haworth is – as you say – a very quiet place; it is also difficult of access, and unless under the stimulus of necessity or that of strong curiosity – or finally that of true and tried friendship – few take courage to penetrate to so remote a nook. Besides, now that I am married I do not expect to be an object of much general interest. Ladies who have won some prominence (call it either <u>notoriety</u> or celebrity) in their single life – often fall quite into the background when they change their names; but if true domestic happiness replace Fame – the exchange will indeed be for the better . . . My own life is more occupied than it used to be: I have not so much time for thinking: I am obliged to be more practical, for my dear Arthur is a very practical as well as a very punctual, methodical man. Every Morning he is in the National School by nine o'clock; he gives the children religious instruction till ½ past 10. Almost every afternoon he pays visits amongst the poor parishioners. Of course he often finds a little work for his wife to do, and I hope she is not sorry to help him.

I believe it is not bad for me that his bent should be so wholly towards matters of real life and active usefulness – so little inclined to the literary and contemplative. As to his continued affection and kind attentions – it does not become me to say much of them but as yet they neither change nor diminish.

Charlotte's growing happiness in her marriage was a source of gratitude and wonder to herself. Unfortunately, it made Ellen feel increasingly excluded and she came to resent bitterly what she considered the usurpation of her own intimacy with Charlotte by her friend's husband. She would never forgive him for what she considered his interference in their correspondence and, more particularly, for the extraction of a promise which she would not and did not keep.

Charlotte to Ellen; Haworth, 20 October 1854

Arthur has just been glancing over this note – He thinks I have written too freely . . . Men don't seem to understand making letters a vehicle of communication – they always seem to think us incautious. I'm sure I don't think I have said anything rash – however, you must <u>burn</u> it when read. Arthur says such letters as mine never ought to be kept – they are dangerous as lucifer matches – so be sure to follow a recommendation he has just given 'fire them' – or 'there will be no more' such is his resolve. I can't help laughing – this seems to me so funny. Arthur however says he is quite 'serious' and looks it, I assure you – he is bending over the desk with his eyes full of concern.

Charlotte to Ellen; Haworth, 31 October 1854

Dear Ellen – Arthur complains that you do not distinctly promise to burn my letters as you receive them. He says you must give him a plain pledge to that effect – or he will read every line I write and elect himself censor of our correspondence.

He says women are most rash in letter-writing – they think only of the trustworthiness of their immediate friend – and do not look to contingencies – a letter may fall into any hand. You must give the promise – I believe – at least he says so, with his best regards – or else you will get such notes as he writes to Mr Sowden – plain, brief statements of facts without the adornment of a single flourish – with no comment on the character or peculiarities of any human being – and if a phrase of sensibility or affection steals in – it seems to come on tiptoe – looking ashamed of itself – blushing 'pea-green' as he says – and holding both its shy hands before its face. Write him out his promise on a separate slip of paper, in a <u>legible</u> hand – and send it in your next.

Ellen to Arthur Bell Nicholls; Brookroyd, November 1854

My dear Mr Nicholls,

As you seem to hold in great horror the ardentia verba of feminine epistles, I pledge myself to the destruction of Charlotte's epistles, henceforth, if you pledge yourself to <u>no</u> censorship in the matter communicated.

Yours very truly,
E Nussey

Charlotte to Ellen; Haworth, 7 November 1854

Arthur thanks you for the promise. He was out when I commenced this letter, but he is just come in – on my asking him whether he would give the pledge required in return – he says 'yes we may now write any dangerous stuff we please to each other – it is not "<u>old friends</u>" he mistrusts, but the chances of war – the accidental passing of letters into hands and under eyes for which they were never written.'

All this seems mighty amusing to me: it is a man's mode of viewing correspondence – Men's letters are proverbially uninteresting and uncommunicative – I never quite knew before <u>why</u> they made them so. They may be right in a sense. Strange chances do fall out certainly. As to my own notes I never thought of attaching importance to them, or considering their fate – till Arthur seemed to reflect on both so seriously.

Charlotte to Margaret Wooler; Haworth, 15 November 1854

We are all – indeed – pretty well – and for my own part – it is long since I have known such comparative immunity from headache, sickness and indigestion, as during the last three months.

My life is different to what it used to be. May God make me thankful for it! I have a good, kind, attached husband, and every day makes my own attachment to him stronger.

Charlotte to Ellen; Haworth, 29 November 1854

I intended to have written a line yesterday – but just as I was sitting down for the purpose Arthur called to me to take a walk. We set off not intending to go far – but though wild and cloudy it was fair in the morning – when we had got about half a mile on the moors – Arthur suggested the idea of the waterfall – after the melted snow he said it would be fine. I had often wanted to see it in its winter power – so we walked on. It was fine indeed – a perfect torrent raving over the rocks white and bountiful. It began to rain while we were watching it – and we returned home under a streaming sky – however I enjoyed the walk inexpressibly – and would not have missed the spectacle on any account.

Charlotte to Ellen; Haworth, 26 December 1854

I must make this note short that it may not be overweight. Arthur joins me in sincere good wishes for a happy Christmas & many of them to you and yours. He is well – thank God – and so am I – and he is 'my dear boy' certainly – dearer now than he was six months ago – in three days we shall actually have been married that length of time! Good-bye dear Nell

Yours faithfully
CB Nicholls

Perhaps the greatest irony of Charlotte's life was that, having discovered health and happiness so late, they, and life itself, were about to be snatched from her. At thirty-eight years of age, she became pregnant, something Patrick had feared from the outset of her marriage. The sickness became chronic and her decline was as rapid as it was inexorable.

Charlotte to Ellen; Haworth, 19 January 1855

My health has been really very good ever since my return from Ireland till – about ten days ago, when the stomach seemed quite suddenly to lose its tone – indigestion and continual faint sickness have been my portion ever since. Don't conjecture – dear Nell – for it is too soon yet – though I certainly never before felt as I have done lately. But keep the matter wholly to yourself – for I can come to no decided opinion at present. I am rather mortified to lose my good looks and grow thin as I am doing – just when I thought of going to Brookroyd.

Charlotte to Mrs Joe Taylor; Haworth, 21 January 1855

It is an hourly happiness to me dear Amelia to see how well Arthur and my Father get on together now – there has never been a misunderstanding or wrong word.

Arthur Bell Nicholls to Ellen; Haworth, 29 January 1855

As Charlotte continues unwell I again write a line for her – She has been confined to bed for some days. I have sent for Dr MacTurk today, as I wish to have better advice than Haworth affords – Under these circumstances you will see that it is quite impossible to name any date for our visit to you –

Charlotte sends her love, & says she will write as soon as she is able –

**Patrick to Sir James Kay Shuttleworth; Haworth, 3 February 1855*

Owing to my Dear Daughter's indisposition, she has desired me to answer your kind letter, by return of post – for several days past, she has been confin'd to her bed, where she still lies, oppress'd with nausea, sickness, irritation, & a slow feverish feeling – and a consequent want of appetite and digestion. – her village, surgeon, visits her daily, & we have had a visit from Dr Macturk of Bradford – who, both think her sickness is symptomatic – and that after a few weeks they hope her health, will again return – nevertheless the trying circumstance gives much uneasiness in our little family circle – where till lately, considering our respective ages, we have all been, in good health & spirits –

Arthur Bell Nicholls to Ellen; Haworth, 14 February 1855

It is difficult to write to friends about my wife's illness, as its cause is yet uncertain – at present she is completely prostrated with weakness & sickness & frequent fever – all may turn out well in the end, & I hope it will; if you saw you would perceive that she can maintain no correspondence at present –

Charlotte did manage to scribble a few last brief notes from her sickbed, though capable only of holding a pencil. The spur to her efforts was her desire to testify to the love and loyalty of the man who had waited so long for her and was now about to lose her.

Charlotte to Laetitia Wheelwright, her Brussels schoolfriend; Haworth, 15 February 1855

A few lines of acknowledgment your letter <u>shall</u> have, whether well or ill. At present I am confined to my bed with illness, and have been so for 3 weeks. Up to this period, since my marriage, I have had excellent health – my husband and I live at home with my Father – of course I could not leave <u>him</u>. He is pretty well – better than last summer. No kinder, better husband than mine, it seems to me, can there be in the world. I do not want now for kind companionship in health and the tenderest nursing in sickness.

Charlotte to Ellen; Haworth, 21 February 1855

My dear Ellen

I must write one line out of my weary bed . . . I am not going to talk about my sufferings, it would be useless and painful – I want to give you an assurance which I know will comfort you – and that is that I find in my husband the tenderest nurse, the kindest support – the best earthly comfort that ever woman had. His patience never fails and it is tried by sad days and Broken nights . . . Papa thank God! is better – Our poor old Tabby [Aykroyd] is <u>dead</u> and <u>buried</u>. Give my truest love to Miss Wooler. May God comfort and help you.

CB Nicholls

Charlotte to Mrs Joe Taylor; Haworth, February 1855

Dear Amelia

Let me speak the plain truth – my sufferings are very great – my nights indescribable – sickness with scarce a reprieve – I strain until what I vomit is mixed with blood. Medicine I have quite discontinued – If you <u>can</u> send me anything that will do good – <u>do</u>.

As to my husband – my heart is knit to him – he is so tender, so good, helpful, patient.

Poor Joe! long has he to suffer. May God soon send him, you, all of us health, strength – comfort.

CB Nicholls

Patrick to Ellen; Haworth, 30 March 1855

My Dear Madam,

We are all in great trouble, and Mr Nicholls so much so, that he is not so sufficiently strong, and composed as to be able to write – I therefore devote a few moments, to tell you, that My dear daughter is very ill, and apparently on the verge of the grave – If she could speak, she would no doubt dictate to us whilst answering your kind letter, but we are left to ourselves, to give what answer we can – The Doctors have no hope of her case, and fondly as we a long time, cherished hope, that hope is now gone, and we [have] only to look forward to the solemn event, with prayer to God, that he will give us grace and strength sufficient unto our day –

Arthur Bell Nicholls to Ellen; Haworth, 31 March 1855

Dear Miss Nussey,

Mr Brontè's letter would prepare you for the sad intelligence I have to communicate – Our dear Charlotte is no more – She died last night of Exhaustion. For the last two or three weeks we had become very uneasy about her, but it was not until Sunday Evening that it became apparent that her sojourn with us was likely to be short – We intend to bury her on Wednesday morn[in]g.

Believe me, sincerely yours,
A: B: Nicholls

★★Ellen to George Smith; 1 June 1860

I started to Haworth by the first available train after Mr Brontë's letter (I had begged to go before, but Mr Brontë and Mr Nicholls objected, fearing the excitement of a meeting for poor Charlotte) She had breathed her last some hours before I arrived. Mr Brontë did not appear at first, but he sent me a message requesting me to stay our dear Charlotte's interment which was to take place on the 4th day – I did stay for the interment, & left about an hour after.

Ellen to George Smith; 28 March 1860

. . . her death chamber is in vivid remembrance, I last saw her in death. Her maid Martha brought me a tray full of evergreens & such flowers as she could procure to place on the lifeless form – My first feeling was, no, I cannot cannot do it – next I was grateful to the maid for giving me the tender office – what made the [task] impossible at first was the rushing recollection of the flowers I spread in her honour at her wedding breakfast & how she admired the disposal of the gathering brought by Martha from the village gardens –

Patrick to Mrs Gaskell; Haworth, 5 April 1855

I thank you for your kind sympathy – My Daughter, is indeed, dead, and the solemn truth presses upon her worthy, and affectionate Husband and me, with great, and it may be with unusual weight – But, others, also, have, or shall have their sorrows, and we feel our own the most – The marriage that took place, seem'd to hold forth, long, and bright prospects of happiness, but in the inscrutable providence of God, all our hopes have ended in disappointment, and our joy in mourning – May we resign to the will of the Most

High – After three months of sickness, a tranquil death closed the scene. But our loss we trust is her gain – But why should I trouble you longer with our sorrows. 'The heart knoweth its own bitterness' – and we ought to bear with fortitude our own grievances, and not to bring others – into our sufferings –

Arthur Bell Nicholls to Ellen's friend, Mary Hewitt; Haworth, 11 April 1855

Mr Brontë and myself thank you very sincerely for your sympathy with us in our sad bereavement – our loss is indeed great – the loss of one as good as she was gifted – Altho' she had been ill from the beginning of January, it was only a few days previous to her death that we became alarmed for her safety – On [the] whole she had not much suffering – she spoke little during the last few days, but continued quite conscious – Mr Brontë is pretty well, tho' of course the present trial is a great shock to him –

Charlotte had died of hyperemesis gravidarum, excessive vomiting during pregnancy, just three weeks before her thirty-ninth birthday. Her unborn child died with her. Their mortal remains were buried in the family vault under Haworth church which would be opened only one more time, in June 1861, when Patrick, who had outlived all the rest of his family, finally joined them in the tomb. Arthur Bell Nicholls, who had loved Charlotte for so many years in silence and then lost her after only nine months of marriage, stayed on at the Parsonage as the devoted companion of her father, just as he had promised to do. After Patrick's death, he returned to his native Ireland, where he lived on for a further forty-five years, content to see his wife's literary reputation flourish but preferring obscurity for himself.

There have been many tributes paid to Charlotte Brontë over the passing years, her friend Mrs Gaskell's enduringly popular biography being not the least of them, but the most powerful – moving in its sincerity, eloquent in its brevity and profound in its simplicity – was written just three weeks after her death by her father. There could be no more fitting monument to the woman of genius, the last and greatest of Patrick Brontë's remarkable children, than these words by the patriarch of the family.

Patrick to George Smith; Haworth, 20 April 1855

My Dear Sir,

I thank you for your kind sympathy. Having heard my Dear Daughter speak so much about you and your family, your letter seem'd to be one from an Old Friend. Her Husband's sorrow and mine, is indeed very great – We mourn the loss of one, whose like, we hope not, ever to see again – and as you justly state we do not mourn alone – That you may never experimentally know, sorrow such as ours, and that when trouble does come, you may receive, due aid from Heaven, is the sincere wish and ardent prayer, of

Yours, very respectfully & truly,
P.Brontë

List of Correspondents

Arnold, Matthew: (1822–88), poet, literary critic and educationalist; son of Dr Thomas Arnold, of Rugby School; professor of poetry at Oxford 1857–67 and inspector of schools 1851–83.

Aylott & Jones: a small firm of booksellers, stationers and publishers, specializing in classical and theological works, based in Paternoster Row, London; they published *Poems* by Currer, Ellis and Acton Bell in 1846 but refused the Brontës' novels.

Branwell, Elizabeth ('Aunt Branwell'): (1776–1842), elder sister of Mrs Maria Brontë. She came to Haworth in 1821 to look after the Brontë children after their mother's death and remained there for the rest of her life.

Branwell, Maria: (1783–1821), married Patrick Brontë in 1812, mother of his six children, Maria (d.1825), Elizabeth (d.1825), Charlotte, Branwell, Emily and Anne; died of ovarian cancer at Haworth in 1821.

Brown, John: (d.1855), sexton of Haworth, friend of Branwell Brontë and father of Martha, the Brontë servant; he was appointed Worshipful Master of the Three Graces Lodge in Haworth in 1832 and held that office for fourteen years.

Buckworth, Reverend John: (d.1835), vicar of Dewsbury (1806–35), friend and patron of Patrick Brontë, who was his curate 1809–11.

Colburn, Henry: (d.1855), highly successful, if unscrupulous, publisher of *Colburn's New Monthly Magazine* and much popular circulating library fiction.

Coleridge, Hartley: (1796–1849), eldest son of Samuel Taylor Coleridge, brought up by Robert Southey; a poet, journalist and schoolmaster, he was also a contributor to the Brontës' favourite periodical, *Blackwood's Magazine*.

Dobell, Sydney Thompson: (1824–74), poet and literary critic, author of an appreciative article about the 'Bells' in the *Palladium*, and two dramatic poems, *The Roman* and *Balder*.

Evans, Miss Ann: (d.1857), first official superintendent of the Clergy Daughters' School at Cowan Bridge; left to marry the Reverend James Connor of Melton Mowbray in 1826.

Forster, Mrs Jane: eldest daughter of Dr Arnold of Rugby School, married in 1850 William Edward Forster (1818–86), wool merchant, Quaker sympathizer and, for many years, Liberal MP for Bradford.

Frobisher, John: (fl.1830s–40s), organist at Halifax parish church, pianist and leader of the Halifax Quarterly Choral Society; acquaintance of Branwell Brontë.

Garrs, Sarah: (1806–99), nursemaid, with her sister, Nancy, to the Brontë children at Thornton and Haworth, leaving in 1824. She married William Newsome and in 1843 emigrated to the United States.

Gaskell, Mrs Elizabeth Cleghorn: (1810–65), friend and biographer of Charlotte Brontë, author of *Mary Barton*, *Cranford*, *Ruth*, and *The Life of Charlotte Brontë* (1857).

Gorham, Mary: (1826–1917), Sussex friend of Ellen Nussey, who married the Reverend Thomas Hewitt in 1852; though she never met Charlotte Brontë, they were known to each other through Ellen's letters.

Grundy, Francis: (b.?1822), railway engineer working on the new Yorkshire railway lines during the 1840s; met and became friendly with Branwell Brontë while the latter was a clerk on the Manchester and Leeds Railway at Sowerby Bridge; author of memoirs, *Pictures of the Past* (London, Griffith & Farrar, 1879), which feature Branwell prominently.

Heald, Canon William Margetson: (1803–75), succeeded his father as vicar of Birstall in 1837, friend of Ellen Nussey and, with his father, regarded as the model for Cyril Hall in *Shirley*.

Heger, Constantin: (1809–96), professor at the Athénée Royal in Brussels, where he was principal from 1853–5, and master of literature at his wife's school, the Pensionnat Heger. Charlotte Brontë fell in love with him but her passion was not reciprocated.

Hewitt, Mary: see *Gorham, Mary*

Houghton, Lord: see *Milnes, Richard Monckton*

Lewes, George Henry: (1817–78), novelist, philosopher and literary critic, jointly responsible for *The Leader* with Thornton Leigh Hunt; though married to another woman, from 1854 he lived with Mary Ann Evans (George Eliot), and encouraged her fiction writing.

Leyland, Francis: (1813–94), antiquarian brother of Branwell Brontë's friend, Joseph Bentley Leyland, author of *The Brontë Family with Special Reference to Patrick Branwell Brontë* (1886).

Leyland, Joseph Bentley: (1811–51), Halifax sculptor who exhibited to great acclaim in London, Manchester and Leeds and produced a medallion portrait of Branwell Brontë, with whom he enjoyed a close friendship throughout the 1840s.

Lockhart, John Gibson: (1794–1854), biographer, poet, contributor to *Blackwood's Magazine* and editor of *Quarterly Review*, who married the eldest daughter of Sir Walter Scott; author of *Life of Burns* and *Life of Sir Walter Scott*.

Martineau, Harriet: (1802–76), author of several works popularizing economic subjects, children's books and a novel, *Deerbrook*, which was much admired by Charlotte Brontë, who sought her acquaintance and was her friend until they quarrelled over her review of *Villette*; notorious for her advocacy of mesmerism and atheism.

Milnes, Richard Monckton (Lord Houghton): (1809–85), poet, patron of writers and politician; MP for Yorkshire, created first Baron Houghton in 1863. Friend of Mrs Gaskell.

Nicholls, Reverend Arthur Bell: (1819–1906), curate of Haworth 1845–53 and 1854–61, married Charlotte Brontë in 1854; after her death in 1855 stayed on at Haworth Parsonage to look after her father then, after his death six years later, returned to his native Ireland. His second marriage, in 1864, to his cousin, Mary Bell, was also childless.

Nussey, Ellen: (1817–97), daughter of a Birstall cloth merchant, who became one of Charlotte's closest friends when they met as pupils at Roe Head school. Though intimate with the Brontë family, she knew nothing of their publishing ventures until after the deaths of Branwell and Emily.

Nussey, Reverend Henry: (1812–67), brother of Charlotte Brontë's friend, Ellen, he proposed to Charlotte in 1839; having held curacies at Dewsbury and Burton Agnes in Yorkshire and at Donnington in Sussex, he was vicar of Hathersage in Derbyshire for three years, then retired to the Continent with his wife in an apparently vain search for health.

Rand, Ebenezer: (fl.1840s), first master of the Church Day School opened in Haworth in 1844; his wife, Sarah, was responsible for the girls at the school; they took up similar appointments at the National School at Staley Bridge the following year and eventually moved to Ipswich, but remained in contact with the Brontës.

Redman, Joseph: (d.1862), parish clerk of Haworth and secretary of the Three Graces Lodge.

Ringrose, Amelia: see *Taylor, Mrs Joe*

Robinson, William: (1799–1838), Leeds-based portrait painter, who had studied at the Royal Academy and been a free pupil of Sir Thomas Lawrence; though his work was much admired and widely exhibited, he died in poverty. For at least two years, he tutored Branwell Brontë in the art of portraiture.

Shuttleworth, Sir James Kay: (1804–77), doctor and educationalist, Secretary to the Committee of the Council on Education, created baronet 1849; determined to patronize Charlotte Brontë, he invited her to Gawthorpe Hall, at Padiham, near Burnley, which he had inherited through his wife, Lady Janet, and to his holiday home at Briery Close on Lake Windermere.

Smith, George: (1824–1901), dynamic young head of the firm of Smith, Elder & Co., which his father had founded in 1816; publisher of Charlotte Brontë, William Makepeace Thackeray and John Ruskin and founder of the *Cornhill Magazine*, the *Pall Mall Gazette* and the *Dictionary of National Biography*.

Smith, John Stores: (1828–92), a Manchester manufacturer and author of *Mirabeau* (1848) and *Social Aspects* (1850), both of which he sent to Charlotte Brontë; shortly after visiting her he went to London, lost a small fortune attempting to set up *Leigh Hunt's Journal*, and returned to the cotton trade. He later became wealthy as a manager of Derbyshire mines.

Smith Williams, William: (1800–1875), reader at Smith, Elder & Co., who was the first to recognize Charlotte Brontë's talent and was responsible for her joining the firm; he became her trusted friend and sympathetic confidant.

Southey, Robert: (1774–1843), poet of the Lake School and author of many historical works, including *Life of Nelson* and *History of the Peninsular War*; friend of Wordsworth and Coleridge; Poet Laureate 1813–43.

Sowden, Reverend Sutcliffe: (d.1861), appointed vicar of Hebden Bridge in

1835, friend of both Branwell Brontë, when he was working on the Manchester and Leeds Railway, and Arthur Bell Nicholls; married the latter to Charlotte Brontë in 1855; drowned in the canal at Hebden Bridge and was buried by Arthur Bell Nicholls.

Taylor, James: (1817–74), manager and occasional reader at Smith, Elder & Co., who went to Bombay to take charge of the firm's Indian operation in 1851. Before leaving, he proposed to Charlotte Brontë, suggesting that the marriage be deferred till his return in five years time; Charlotte was unenthusiastic, their correspondence soon ended and she married Arthur Bell Nicholls. By the time he returned, she was dead. He went back to Bombay in 1863, embarking on a journalistic career as editor of several local papers, and died there in 1874.

Taylor, Martha: (1819–42), younger sister of Mary Taylor, friend of Charlotte Brontë and fellow pupil at Roe Head school; she died of cholera at the Château de Koekelberg in Brussels while Charlotte and Emily were at the Pensionnat Heger there.

Taylor, Mary: (1817–93), daughter of a Gomersal cloth-merchant, who became one of Charlotte Brontë's closest friends when they met as pupils at Roe Head school; her letters from Europe prompted Charlotte to go to Brussels. In 1845 she emigrated to New Zealand, not returning to England till after Charlotte's death.

*Taylor, Mrs Joe (*née *Ringrose*): daughter of a Hull merchant, her engagement to George Nussey, Ellen's brother, was broken off when he became insane; in 1850 she married Joe Taylor, Mary's brother, outliving both him (d.1857) and their only daughter (d.1858).

Taylor, Mrs: probably Mary, widow of Stephen Taylor of Stanbury (d.1831), who had been one of the leading Church Trustees at Haworth.

Thackeray, William Makepeace: (1811–63), novelist, satirist and journalist, author of *Vanity Fair, Pendennis* and *Henry Esmond*; separated from his wife on account of her insanity in 1840; admired by Charlotte Brontë, though not uncritically, as the greatest contemporary novelist.

Trobe, Reverend James La: (1802–97), Minister of the Well House Moravian Church at Mirfield 1836–41, during which time he visited Anne Brontë when she was seriously ill at Roe Head; he was appointed a bishop in 1863.

Wheelwright, Laetitia: (1828–1911), eldest of the five daughters of Dr Thomas Wheelwright who had been brought to Brussels to be educated at the Pensionnat Heger; three of her younger sisters were taught music by Emily. Both Brontë sisters visited the Wheelwrights while they lived in Brussels and Charlotte remained on friendly terms with Laetitia afterwards, visiting her in London.

Winkworth, Catherine (Katie): (1827–78), author and translator, friend of Charlotte Brontë, Mrs Gaskell and Harriet Martineau.

Wooler, Margaret: (1792–1885), eldest of the five sisters who ran Roe Head School at Mirfield from 1830, moving to Dewsbury Moor early in 1838. Charlotte, Emily and Anne were all pupils there and Charlotte also taught at the school for some years. After its closure in 1841, and especially after the loss of her sisters, Charlotte became increasingly friendly with Miss Wooler, whom she regarded as a model for spinsterhood.

Wordsworth, William: (1770–1850), one of the Lake Poets, most famous for his *Lyrical Ballads*, *The Prelude*, *Ode: Intimations of Immortality* and the *Lucy* poems; his poems and theories about poetry hugely influenced the Brontës' own work and ideas; Poet Laureate 1843–50.

Index of Proper Names

413

Index of Correspondents

(Page numbers in roman type refer to the writer of the letter, those in italic to the recipient)

et Mademoiselle Charlotte — vous n'êtes plus de
... — je vous ai oubliée "

Eh bien ' Monsieur dites - moi cela franchement .
... moi un choc — n'importe ce sera toujours ...
... que l'incertitude .

Je ne veux pas relire cette lettre — je l'envoie co...
... ai écrite — Pourtant j'ai ... la conscience ...
Il y a des personnes froides et sensées qui diraie...
... "Elle déraisonne " — Pour toute vengeance
... les personnes ... un seul jour des tourment...
... Depuis huit mois — on verrait alors s'e...
... pas de même

On souffre en silence tant qu'on en a la force ...
... force manque on parle ... sans tro...
paroles .

... ...
... ...

Je souhaite à Monsieur le bonheur et la prospéri...